The Band Name Book

For Melbourne, Australia's infamous Fred Negro,

cartoonist, satirist, songwriter, musician and frontman for the bands

The Eggs

The Twits

Shonkytonk

57 Pages of Pink

The Gravybillies

I Spit on Your Gravy

Squirming Gerbil Death

They Might Be Negroes

The Band Who Shot Liberty Valance

The Brady Bunch Lawnmower Massacre

and bands I can't name this early in the book.

Pavlov's Woody • Vampire Weekend • Alien's Cab
Hoodoo Gurus • Dirty Lenin • Oingo Boingo
Big Thumb Bowlers • a-ha • Hindu Garage Sale
Velvet Underground • Fatkid Dodgeball • Yes
Amazed by Lightbulbs • Gin Piston • Frumious
Bandersnatch • Scissor Sisters • Pearl Jam
Deep Banana Blackout • Disgruntled Sherpa Project
Faster Pussycat • Moby Grape • The Beatles

The Band Name Book

Kajagoogoo • Sigue Sigue Sputnik • Pimp the Cat
Hüsker Dü • Led Zeppelin • Hard Broccoli
Romeo Void • Big Thumb Bowlers • Foo Fighters
Full Throttle Aristotle • Fine Young Cannibals
Flaming Lips • Spooky Tooth • Blue Öyster Cult

NOEL HUDSON

The BOSTON
MILLS PRESS

Published by Boston Mills Press, 2008
132 Main Street, Erin, Ontario N0B 1T0
Tel: 519-833-2407 Fax: 519-833-2195

In Canada:
Distributed by Firefly Books Ltd.
66 Leek Crescent
Richmond Hill, Ontario, L4B 1H1

In the United States:
Distributed by Firefly Books (U.S.) Inc.
P.O. Box 1338, Ellicott Station
Buffalo, New York 14205

The publisher gratefully acknowledges for the financial support of our publishing program
the Government of Canada through the Book Publishing Industry Development Program (BPIDP).

All images herein are used in a promotional context
by the generous permission of the bands, poster artists, record companies, etc.
For more specific copyright information, please refer to the Image Credits at the back of this book.

Publisher Cataloging-in-Publication Data (U.S.)

Hudson, Noel
The band name book / Noel Hudson.

[400] p. . col. photos. , cm.
Includes bibliographical references and index.
Summary: How, where when and why the best-named bands got their names,
with notes on band name origins, genres and the best album titles, including names-still-available.

ISBN: 13: 978-1-55046-487-0 (pbk.)

1. Rock groups — Names. 2. Musical groups — Names. 2. Music — Humor. I. Title.
782.42166 dc22 ML3534.H837 2008

Library and Archives Canada Cataloguing in Publication

Hudson, Noel
The band name book / Noel Hudson.

Includes index.
ISBN 978-1-55046-487-0. — ISBN 1-55046-487-6

1. Rock groups. 2. Music — Humor. I. Title.

ML3534.H886 2008   782.42166   C2008-901569-X

Design by Gillian Stead
Additional research by Simon Rogers

Printed in Canada

The Band Name Book

CONTENTS

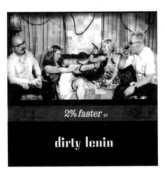

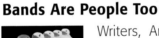

Preface

Every city has at least one alternative weekly entertainment magazine, and somewhere amid the ads for discount computer peripherals and transvestite escort services are the week's live music listings. This weekend, for instance, the Giant Baby is at the El Mocambo, Hooded Fang at Rancho Relaxo, Wordburglar at Lula Lounge, Box Full of Cash is at Gorilla Monsoon, and the Hymen Smashers are at

Sneaky Dee's with Hollywood Swank. Never heard of them? They're big. Well, big-*ish*. They have CDs and MySpace pages and choice gigs in a major city. And they have great band names.

This book is about those bands. While it addresses the name origins of well-known bands, it gives equal time to lesser known bands and shines a spotlight on independents, the tenacious club acts and the day-job holders who strap on guitars and hit local stages on weekends. Of course, rock music has always worked this way, but now, with affordable digital recording technology and personal websites, a local band can develop a global fan-base, and listeners can discover favorite new bands with a couple of mouse clicks. I hope that as you read this book, certain names, facts, trivia and artwork will lead you to check out new bands, no matter what type of music you like.

A percentage of these band names were obviously created to shock and offend those easily shocked and offended. The risqué aspects of rock & roll have been with us since Little Richard donned eyeliner and squealed, since Jerry Lee Lewis married his underage cousin, since Elvis unleashed his pelvis. It's part of the fun. To use the name of a current band, Does It Offend You, Yeah? Well, it's the reason this music exists and thrives.

There are plenty of lists out there with hilarious names for bands whose existence cannot be proven (i.e., 350,000 Crazed and Fully Africanized "Welcome to Disneyworld" Bees). I decided to insist on hearing some music by each artist in this book. As further proof, I thought I'd include some CD covers. Of course, this became addictive: so many bands with cool names and album art; so many great posters. All of the artwork was generously contributed by the bands and artists.

Due to space concerns, a few shorter chapters near the end of the book failed to make the final cut. I would like to apologize to the members of U2, AFI, UB40, INXS, XTC, MC5, 10cc, Blink-182, 54-40 and the many other letter and number bands who were to have appeared in those missing chapters. Likewise, I beg forgiveness of the Kings of Leon and King Crimson, of Queen and Queens of the Stone Age — of all the royalty bands, as well as the philosophers, dragons, elves, dwarves, pixies and giants. And

others. You know who you are; I won't call attention to your absence. (You're in the sequel, I promise.)

Lastly, if you're thinking of starting a band and feel, after reading this book, that all the good names have been taken, please feel free to help yourself to one of the Names Still Available or maybe try your luck with one of the dozen or so online "band name generators." Better yet, do what so many bands have done in the past: Make something up as you step on stage for your first gig.

A Few Things First

You are driving along, bobbing your head to a tune on the car radio. It fades out. The DJ announces, "That was Kajagoogoo with 'Ooh to Be Ah.'" Let's get straight to some of the "Say what?!" bands.

Mott the Hoople

Mott the who? This legendary glam band started out in Hereford, UK, with the lackluster name Silence.

They were anything but lackluster as musicians, however, and a year later, in 1969, with an Island Records contract, they moved to London to work with producer Guy Stevens. Stevens suggested the name change to Mott the Hoople, the title of a novel he had read while doing a short stint in prison for a drug-related offense. The book, by Los Angeles writer Willard Manus, concerns a man who works in a circus freak show. Stevens was enamored with the book's title, reportedly telling his wife that Mott the Hoople would make a great band name "with all its O's and T's." Stevens had previously named Procol Harum after a friend's cat.

Two albums into their career, the Hoops had managed to gather only a cult following, but that cult included David Bowie, who offered them his song "Suffragette City." When the band politely declined, Bowie wrote them "All the Young Dudes" and went on to produce their album of the same name.

The Bowie-backed *All the Young Dudes* yielded the chart hits "Honaloochie Boogie" and "All the Way from Memphis," and sent the band to the head of the glam-band pack. Their 1974 headline tour of the US featured an opening act named Queen.

Ookla the Mok
Buffalo, New York, USA

Ookla the Mok was a weirdly pupil-less man-lion in the animated TV series *Thundarr the Barbarian*, which was produced by the co-creators of *Scooby-Doo* and ran on American television in the early '80s. The show was a futuristic *Conan the Barbarian*. The band considers itself a "filk band," from a typo in "folk band" and referring to a type of music appealing to followers of science fiction and fantasy. Rock the nerds! They are regular musical guests at sci-fi and comic book conventions, and their songs have been featured on Dr. Demento compilations.

Kajagoogoo
Leighton Buzzard, Bedfordshire, UK

Started out as Art Nouveau in '79 but couldn't catch a break. Hired a singer named Christopher Hamill, who made an anagram of his surname and started calling himself Limahl. The boys cultivated teased-on-top '80s hair, and barefoot bassist Nick Beggs coined the name Kajagoogoo (looking for something a baby might say). The rest is a handful of hit singles, split-ups and reunions. Make your own KajaGooGoo Dolls joke.

Hoobastank
Agoura Hills, California, USA

Singer Doug Robb on MTV: "I just want to know, why does it have to mean anything? I love Jamiroquai, but I don't go diving into what it means." Drummer Chris Hesse in a separate interview: "Doug's brother is the vice-president of BMW Motorcycles and lives in Germany. And there is this street out by his house that is called Hooba Street, or something like that, and before Doug could pronounce the name, he called it 'Hoobastank.'" Doug: "It doesn't mean anything."

Jamiroquai
London, UK

A mishmash of the musical term "jam" and the Native American confederacy known as the Iroquois (the latter known for wearing big faux-fur hats and their frequent use of disco synth lines).

Fugazi
Washington, DC, USA

Guitarist-vocalist Ian MacKaye took the band's name from a Vietnam War-time acronym for "Fucked Up, Got Ambushed, Zipped In," from the Mark Baker book *Nam*.

Chumbawamba
Leeds, Yorkshire, UK

Though often pegged as one-hit wonders (1997's poppy "Tubthumping"), Chumbawamba has been around in one form or another since 1982, mostly penning anti-establishment punk anthems. The band regularly admits that the name means nothing at all, but the question still arises in most interviews. Some of the answers band members have supplied: a dream in which men were "chumbas," women were "wambas"; the result of a monkeys-with-typewriters experiment; a chant by African street musicians in Paris; the name of a football mascot.

Oingo Boingo
Los Angeles, California, USA

Richard Elfman (cult film *Forbidden Zone*) founded the musical-theater troupe the Mystical Knights of the Oingo Boingo in 1972. Brother Danny Elfman ("Simpsons Theme," Tim Burton film soundtracks) took over as lead vocalist and helped turn the troupe into a viable new wave band in the '80s. The younger Elfman's work for TV and film increased exponentially over the years, and most of it featured the work of Oingo Boingo guitarist Steve Bartek.

The Vermicious Knid
Brantford, Ontario, Canada

From Roald Dahl's *Charlie and the Great Glass Elevator*. Vermicious knid come from the planet Vermes, and in this sequel to *Charlie and the Chocolate Factory*, they invade the Space Hotel USA. They are also mentioned in *James and the Giant Peach*.

Alex Wise of the San Francisco "funk explosion" band the **SHREEP** came up with the term "shreep" while in boarding school in Massachusetts in the mid-80s. "We used it as a noun ('that guy's a bad shreep', or 'psyched to the shreep') and my college nickname was 'The Shreep.'" Pretty soon, the word had traveled to nearby universities, out into communities and between generations. "When I met with this jewelry designer who went to Brown, to commission her to design an engagement ring for my wife, the woman asked me, 'Is it true you invented the word shreep?' We're all known for something, right? When it came time for a band name, the Shreep was a no-brainer." The Shreep's *Shreepwalkin'* CD was released on Japan's Gianormous Records label.

Scritti Politti Leeds, Yorkshire, UK
The writings of Italian Marxist Antonio Gramsci (1891–1937) were collectively known as *Scritti Politici*. Bandleader Green Gartside altered the spelling to make it sound more like "Tutti Frutti."

The Rezillos Edinburgh, Scotland
Said to have been the name of a nightclub in the first edition of the comic-book version of *The Shadow*.

NAMES
STILL AVAILABLE

More Than One Oop

The Pickwick Rolling Papers

Onomatopoeia Ono

Mott's Sister Hula

Gerfalconian Armrest

The Bountiful Diva Vistas

Gobbledygeekspeaker

Rarely if Everest

Tsk Tsk Daffodil

Self Returning Shopping Carts

When Nothing Happens Moot Matters

Apostles of Muscles

Avarice Knot
Reading, Pennsylvania, USA

An Indian wise man named Padampa Sangye went to Tibet early in the 12th century. In the Tingri area, on the slopes of what is now Mt. Everest, he established a monastery and wrote his *Hundred Verses of Advice*. Coming in at #6 is "Wealth and poverty, like a magic show, just seduce and deceive; Peope of Tingri, do not let the knot of avarice bind you." Don't be greedy. And have a monk accompany you if you go anywhere near the band's violently graphic Freewebs site.

Kula Shaker   London, UK
From the 9th-century Indian emperor and holy man Kulashekhara.

Wang Chung   London, UK
The band once explained their name as the Chinese term for the perfect pitch. The literal translation of *huang chung* is said to be "yellow bell," but also refers to a standard bass pitch in traditional Chinese music.

Mungo Jerry   Staffordshire, UK
In the summertime, when T.S. Eliot is hot…. Mungojerrie is a character from Eliot's *Old Possum's Book of Practical Cats*. I think there was a musical.

The Mooney Suzuki
New York City, New York, USA

The first two singers of the German experimental group Can were American-born Malcolm Mooney and Japan's Kenji "Damo" Suzuki. Guitarist-vocalist Sammy James Jr. is a big Can fan.

Lacuna Coil   Milan, Italy
Previous names: Sleep of Right and Ethereal. Lacuna coil means "empty spiral."

Among the most colorful and interesting Australian bands of the '90s, Melbourne's **the Ergot Derivative** were hailed by critics for both their music and their "travelling freak squad." The band's six main members played not just band-standard guitar, keys, bass and drums, but also violin, viola, cello, mandolin, recorder, harmonica, conga, tabla and even sound samples. Live appearances included dancers, jugglers and light shows. Ergot derivatives are medicinal alkaloids sourced from a black fungus that occurs on rye grain. Though toxic in their primary form, the derivatives are known to facilitate smooth muscle contraction and therefore were once widely used in obstetrics and in the treatment of migraine headaches.

Gonculator
Rochester, New York, USA

The *Hogan's Heroes* episode "Klink vs. the Gonculator" first aired in October 1968. A gonculator is a fictitious piece of machinery or electronics that is touted as doing amazing things or needs to be replaced at huge cost: "I think it may be your gonculator, sir. If so, it could be $2,200."

Lynyrd Skynyrd
Jacksonville, Florida, USA

From Leonard Skinner, the zealously pro-haircut gym teacher at Robert E. Lee High School.

Sleater-Kinney
Seattle, Washington, USA

The band has neither a Sleater nor a Kinney. The name comes from the junction of two roads near Lacey, Washington, where band founders Carrie Brownstein and Corin Tucker had a rehearsal space.

moe.   Utica, New York, USA
Though talented and basically likable, the band issues press notices insisting that their name be lowercased and followed by a period. how. annoying is that? they. are said to have named themselves after the Louis Jordan song "Five Guys Named Moe." five. guys named. moe.

Marillion
Aylesbury, Buckinghamshire, UK

The J.R.R. Tolkien book *Silmarillion* was on the table in the room where the band was meeting to decide on a name. Concerned about copyright issues, they dropped the Sil. Active since 1979, Marillion is considered one of the first mainstream rock bands to have developed an internet fan base.

My Life with the Thrill Kill Kult
Chicago, Illinois, USA

While touring with Ministry as a lighting technician, Frankie Nardiello wrote some songs with bandleader Al Jourgensen. One of those songs was entitled "Thrill Kill Kult." Enamored with the title, Nardiello and friend Marston Daley recorded music for a proposed film, *Hammerhead Housewife and the Thrill Kill Kult*. They two soon adopted the pseudonyms Groovie Mann and Buzz McCoy and began to record college-and-club-friendly tunes as My Life with the Thrill Kill Kult.

The Animals

The Animals

Bow Wow Wow

Shortly after being hired to manage Adam & the Ants, Sex Pistols manager Malcolm McLaren convinced the Ants to leave Adam and form their own group. Fourteen-year-old Anglo-Burmese singer Annabella Lwin successfully auditioned as singer.

"Malcolm came up with the name Bow Wow Wow," Lwin explained in an interview with *Exclusive* magazine. "Apparently it was because we were signing with the record label RCA." RCA Records' symbol has long been based on *His Master's Voice*, Francis Barraud's painting of a terrier, Nipper, listening to a 19th-century gramophone.

The band's biggest hits were "Go Wild in the Country" and their cover of the Strangeloves' "I Want Candy." The band also boasts one of rock's longest album titles with 1981's *See Jungle! See Jungle! Go Join Your Gang, Yeah. City All Over! Go Ape Crazy.*

Scotland Yard investigated the alleged exploitation of a minor for immoral purposes following the creation of an album cover that featured 15-year-old Annabella naked in a recreation of Manet's painting *The Luncheon in the Grass.*

The Fabulous Housepets

The Pet Shop Boys London, UK
The long-running electro-pop duo of Neil Tennant and Chris Lowe. While the two met in an electronics shop in Chelsea, friends of theirs worked in a pet shop in Ealing, and it was suggested that the name Pet Shop Boys sounded like a polite English rap group.

Pet Hate UK
Taking your pet peeve a step farther. They released two albums in the mid-80s and supported Hanoi Rocks on a UK tour.

Be Your Own Pet Nashville, Tennessee, USA
But take yoga classes before sleeping on your own lap. Their music is "fast, loud and totally wired." First EP: *Damn Damn Leash*. Their new CD, *Get Awkward*, is getting standout reviews. "I was nervous because it was our second record," says guitarist Jonas Stein. The guitarist and drummer also play in a band named Turbo Fruits. ■

Dogs

Bubble Puppy
San Antonio, Texas, USA
This popular Texas rock band took their name from "Centrifugal Bumble-puppy," a futuristic children's game in Aldous Huxley's *Brave New World*.

Skinny Puppy
Vancouver, British Columbia, Canada
From *Encyclopedia Gothica*: "The basic idea is that of an abused, neglected animal who doesn't speak much but when he does it is a pain-filled yelp. Early on, the concept for the band was to look at the whole world through the eyes of a dog."

Dogs with Jobs
Toronto, Ontario, Canada
Early '90s thrash-metal with a sense of humor. The band's promo photo shows them looking tough in front of a dog-grooming establishment.

Lousy House Pets
According to guitarist Jimmy St. James, "We were at a jam session, and someone had this 'House Pets' phrase on a drum kit, which I was told was a joke. For whatever reason, I remembered the old Dana Carvey skit 'Chickens Make Lousy House Pets.'

And we had a band name." This rules out a literal interpretation of the word "lousy," which might have explained the trio's shaved heads. The upstate New York group includes St. James, Bip Beck (bass/vocals) and Cletus Head (drums). Check out *Ipso Shitzo: The Best of LHP*.

Cat House Dogs

The five Dogs are based in the Cat House formally known as Toronto. "To be a dog in a cat's house is to be a square peg in a round hole, so to speak," says guitarist Mark Higginbottom, who gave the band their name. Or a furry guardian of a bordello. Their latest CD is entitled *That Was Now*.

that dog.
Los Angeles, California, USA

I like you, that dog., but did you have to lower yourselves to lowercasedness and cut yourselves off from the rest of us with the period? Did you have to pre-moe. moe.? These are well-pedigreed dogs: Anna Waronker is daughter of record exec Lenny Waronker and the sister of drummer-producer Joey Waronker; Petra and Rachel Haden are two of jazz bass legend Charlie Haden's triplet daughters; Tony Maxwell is a frequent collaborator with director Spike Jonze.

Ghost Dog
Mo i Rana, Nordland, Norway

This band and their dog, who appears to be very much alive, come from a town just south of the Arctic Circle. The Jim Jarmusch film *Ghost Dog: Way of the Samurai* was released in 1999.

Bonzo Dog Band London, UK

The Bonzos made use of wind instruments, horns, banjos and vivid imagination in blending music-hall jazz and art-rock. The Beatles were big fans and had them perform their song "Death Cab for Cutie" in the made-for-television film *Magical Mystery Tour*. The name came from combining the name of a 1920s cartoon character, Bonzo the Dog, with the name of the art and cultural movement Dada. The Bonzo Dog Dada Band became the Bonzo Dog Doo-Dah Band and simply the Bonzo Dog Band by their second album, in 1968. A 2006 double live-concert CD, *Wrestle Poodles...and Win!*, saw the band re-adopt their Doo-Dah.

Dogs on Prozac
Rotorua, New Zealand

The Prozac isn't working. EP title: *Songs for the Soon to Be Dead*.

The Laughing Dogs
Penn Valley, California, USA

They deserve to laugh. Solid songwriters with great chops, they backed Davy Jones and Mickey Dolenz on the Monkees' 1977 reunion tour, played their originals at CBGBs and the Bottom Line, released two albums on Columbia, toured with Blondie, Cheap Trick and the Patti Smith Group, and they still continue to perform and release independently.

Three Dog Night
Los Angeles, California, USA

Three vocalists and some ace backing musicians rack up 13 gold albums and 18 *Billboard* Top 40 hits between 1969 and 1977. The name comes from the historic aboriginal practice of bringing the dogs in to sleep with the humans on cold nights. The colder the night, the more dogs required.

Bad Dog No Biscuit
Arizona, USA

Main Bad Dog Steve Di Laudio dedicates his website to his late retriever, Charlie.

Moondog One
Manchester, UK

Includes members of the Smiths, Buffalo 66 and Oasis. Their name is said to have come from a discussion of the Beatles' early names, which included Johnny & the Moondogs.

The Leg Hounds
Sheboygan, Wisconsin, USA

Leg hounds are always happy to see you. Or at least your leg. These frisky guys record on Alien Snatch Records.

17

Dogs D'Amour London, UK
They were the Bordello Boys until the recruitment of LA singer Ned Christie (Robert Stoddard), when they became the slightly more romantic Dogs D'Amour. More romantic than Leg Hounds, presumably, but there was no love lost in the creative mix of Christie and band founder-guitarist Tyla. Christie left before they recorded the first album.

Dogbones Vilnius, Lithuania
They were nominated as favorite band at the 1996 Lithuanian Festival of Worst Groups.

Cold Dog Soup Glasgow, Scotland
Cold Dog Soup is a 1985 novel by American writer Stephen Dobyns. The 1990 film based on the novel enjoyed a cult following.

Dogliveroil UK
Experimental rock. Fellow Catch 23 Recordings artists include English Peasants Ensemble, Evil Robot Ted, and Gimp Nipples.

Dogs Die in Hot Cars Glasgow, Scotland
The name comes from a Royal Society for the Prevention of Cruelty to Animals campaign. EP: *Man Bites Man*, featuring the song "Nobody Teaches Life Anything."

Dogbreath Solleftea, Sweden
New CD: *Taste It!* Dogbreath is "as sharp as barbed wire and as heavy as a steamroller and impossible to defend oneself against," says reviewer Dan Marklund.

TVforDogs London, UK
Their website has a quote by Tom Allalone of Tom Allalone & the 78s: "TVforDogs are really good. They make a big rocking type of noise. There are only 3 of them but it sounds like at least 3 and a 1/2." He's right. To be fair, they have a song entitled "Radio for Cats."

Pitbull Daycare San Antonio, Texas, USA
Latest album: *You, Me and the Devil Make Three*. Video: *You Make Me Feel So Dead*. Fans are known as "Pitbull Puppies."

Peace, Love & Pitbulls Sweden and the Netherlands
It is said that Marilyn Manson has mentioned this band as a source of inspiration. Album title: *Red Sonic Underwear*.

FLUFFY THE PITBULL

GABARDINE SWINE

Fluffy the Pitbull ———
from Calgary, Alberta, Canada, stirs up "Klez-met-tal-lic-al-ter-men-co-folk-a-bil-ly-borscht-punk!" Fluffy warns: "If you like disco, country, easy listening, lounge, 'lite' rock or that schlocky pop stuff usually sung by cute female singers who sound like they have asthma, you won't like my music at all."

The Fabulous Poodles London, UK
The Poodles went nowhere. But after acquiring a new rhythm section and adding Fabulous to their name, things picked up dramatically. The band's first album was produced in 1977 by Who bassist John Entwistle, and the late '70s saw them tour the US with Tom Petty & the Heartbreakers and the Ramones. Frank Zappa is sometimes given credit for making the Poodles the Fabulous Poodles, but this is based on a line in "Mudd Club" off 1981's *You Are What You Is*. The song, about the chic TriBeCa nightclub, mentions "a few of them Fabulous Poodles doin' the Peppermint Twist for real" — at least two years after they'd already turned Fabulous and after releasing their third album, *Think Pink!*, containing the song "Pink City Twist."

The Spaniels Gary, Indiana, USA
The African-American vocal group responsible for the 1954 hit "Goodnight, Sweetheart, Goodnight." A band member's wife is said to have commented that the quintet sounded "like a pack of dogs."

Echo Mutt Silver Spring, Maryland, USA
"Most people get freaked out when I start licking my bass," says bassist John Celia, "but not these guys." 2002 CD: *Virtual Chew Toy*.

Mozart Rottweiler & the Sinister Undertones Mahopac, New York, USA
On Bones Don't Float Records.

Hard Chihuahuas • Los Angeles, California, USA • "Once, in the desert between Inyokern and Las Vegas, the band saw a fire burning off in the distance. The full moon overhead seemed to guide them as they hiked through the rocky scrub terrain toward the orange glow. When they arrived, they were amazed to see a chihuahua and a mountain lion sitting together as the flames lit up the cold sky around them. The chihuahua barked, 'I am small, but nothing scares me. In these parts, one must be strong to survive. I survive because I am a Hard Chihuahua!'"

Bloodhound Gang
Trappe, Pennsylvania, USA
Started out as Bang Chamber 8. The name Bloodhound Gang comes from the title of a segment on the PBS TV series *3-2-1 Contact* that involved kids solving crimes with scientific techniques. Albums: *Use Your Fingers*, *One Fierce Beer Coaster*, *Hooray for Boobies*, *Hefty Fine*.

Poi Dog Pondering
Chicago, Illinois, USA
The original Hawaiian poi dog, brought to the islands by the Polynesians more than 1,000 years ago, is now extinct. This may in part be due to the fact that the native people fattened them up on a vegetarian diet and ate them. Band founder Frank Orrall hails from Hawaii.

Bluedog
Minneapolis, Minnesota, USA
Nominated for Best Blues/Jazz Recording for the 2007 Native American Music Awards. No connection to the "Blue Dog" paintings of Cajun artist George Rodrigue.

The Korgis Bristol, UK
Great songwriters, but it's unclear who to blame for the name. Her Royal Majesty?

See Spot Groove
San Diego, California, USA
Spot embraces his inner Bootsy Collins. The *Dick and Jane* series of beginning-reader books written by Dr. William S. Gray were widely used in American schools from the 1930s to the 1970s. Spot was the dog. Millions of adults have "See Spot. See Spot run!" burned into their brain cells due to Dr. Gray's use of repetitive catch phrases.

Temple of the Dog
Seattle, Washington, USA
Following the death-by-overdose of Mother Love Bone singer Andrew Wood in 1990, Soundgarden's Chris Cornell started writing songs in tribute to his lost friend. To perform them, he enlisted Mother Love Bone's Stone Gossard and Jeff Ament, Soundgarden drummer Matt Cameron, Love Chile guitarist Mike McCready, and Eddie Vedder on background vocals. The band and the album were called Temple of the Dog. Cornell returned to Soundgarden, but he had sowed the seeds for Pearl Jam by bringing Ament, Gossard, McCready, Vedder and Cameron together. In Hinduism, the dog is thought to be a messenger for the angel of death. They are also believed to guard the gates of heaven.

NAMES
STILL AVAILABLE

Bone Pugs-N-Harmony

Mongrel Empire

Nein Mein Kanine!

The Joe Cocker Spaniels

Spoonhounds

Red Bull Mastiffs

Hell to Spay

Lhasa Apso
Shih Tzu
Surfers

The Fabulous
Doberpersons

I Married Mutt

Kennel Club Rejects

Husky Voices of
Siberian Girls

19

Faster Pussycat

Named for director Russ Meyer's cult classic *Faster — Pussycat! Kill! Kill!*, this Hollywood-based glam-metal band had its greatest success in the big-hair-and-sleazy-video days of the late '80s. Former Guns N'Roses guitarist Tracii Guns briefly considered using the name Faster Pussycat for his new project but instead decided to resurrect his previous band name, L.A. Guns. His friend, vocalist Taime Downe, took the name and ran with it.

Faster Pussycat's self-titled first album reached rock radar through a series of videos on MTV and tours with Motörhead and Alice Cooper. Their second album, *Wake Me Up When It's Over*, sold a half-million units. But grunge was on its way, and glam metal was soon knocked from the charts.

After breaking up in the early '90s, the various band members drifted into new projects. Downe took a liking to industrial rock and formed the Newlydeads. But the Faster Pussycat came back, and in 2006 Downe and former lead guitarist Brent Muscat were each fronting bands under the name. Threats and litigation ensued.

In March 2007 Muscat stated in an interview: "I love Taime, but I believe he is caught up in a dark, fake and lonely place...Hollywood has been dead for a few years now...I'm so glad I got away from there and moved to Las Vegas."

Cats

The Meow Meows
Brighton and Hove, UK

Happy ska'n'rollers: "We formed back in summer 2005, mainly as an excuse to drink on a weeknight." The Japanese interactive adult anime SIM game *Let's Meow Meow* was released to the English-speaking world in 2004. It involves a young man named Ibuki and group of "animal-girls" in 18+ adventures.

Hurts to Purr Austin, Texas, USA

It may hurt to purr, but Liz Pappademas's vocals sound just fine. The band stayed together for just one CD. I'm not saying they necessarily indicate internal conflict, but song titles include "I Didn't Mean It," "What's Wrong," "The Salesman's Wife" and "What Did You Fill Me Up With?"

Sex Kittens Yorkshire, UK

All boy kittens. Glam-rock from the late '80s with Rich (vocals), Heathy (guitar), Nik O'Teenage (guitar), Timbo Tornado (bass) and Pete Pout (drums). The term "sex kitten" was first used to describe French actress Brigitte Bardot as a result of her performance in the 1957 film *And God Created Woman*.

Kitten with a Whip
San Diego, California, USA

The name is the title of a 1959 pulp novel by Wade Miller (the writing team of Robert Wade and William Miller). A 1964 film version featured Ann-Margret in the lead role of Jody the juvenile delinquent. The tagline: "She's out for kicks…and every inch of her spells excitement!"

Loudmouthkitten
Miami, Florida, USA

Song: "Suburban White in a White Suburban."

Chainsaw Kittens
Norman, Oklahoma, USA

A post-punk name referring to the sound of their guitars and band members' young ages when they formed in 1989. They have toured with the Smashing Pumpkins. Singer Tyson Meade also performed the in psychedelic band Defenestration and in Dali Does Windows in the mid-80s.

Cat Power & the Memphis Rhythm Band Miami, Florida, USA
Now working as a solo artist, Cat Power (born Chan Marshall) is the daughter of blues pianist Charlie Marshall.

Lead singer Drama: "**Switchblade Kittens** was a perfect name 'cause I wanted a feminist, we-are-all-grrls-in-this-together name, but we are by no means woose grrls. I liked the fact that Switchblade brings to mind toughness and Kitten is a slur for female, so people would know we are tough grrls with a soft side." The Los Angeles quartet is currently promoting their second CD, *The Weird Sisters*.

FOUR HAPPINESS

CATSPLASH

"You know my cat has nothing on you, but I do." Well-written melodic rock from Chicago musicians John Luckhaupt (guitar, vocals), Clarissa Novales (keyboards, samples, vocals), Bill Aldridge (bass) and Tim Tully (drums).

Stray Cats
Long Island, New York, USA

Lead singer-guitarist Brian Setzer got together with drummer Slim Jim Phantom (James Macdonnell) and bassist Lee Rocker (Leon Drucker) in 1979 after Setzer's previous band, the Bloodless Pharaohs, dissolved. Their distinctly punkish, back-alley rockabilly sound, produced on record by Dave Edmunds of Rockpile, caught the ear of radio listeners and led to four Top 10 hits. The Stray Cats officially broke up in 1984 but have regrouped for numerous tours and recordings.

Kick the Cat   USA and UK

To release your frustration upon the helpless. Strange choice for a band name, but at least two exist. The Chicago, Illinois, band Kick the Cat plays jazz-rock fusion, while the Bristol, UK, Kick the Cat plays weddings and other events as a Blues Brothers Revue tribute band.

Stiff Dead Cat
Forestville, California, USA

Question from band's home page "How many Stiff Dead Cats does it take to stuff a sausage?" They claim to have been banned from the Sonoma Country Folk Society.

Cats Don't Have Souls
Albany, New York, USA

Though they may not possess souls, this band errs on the side of giving them a good life, with links to an animal rights page. In related news, Sega Japan appears to have created a lifelike robotic cat.

PIMP THE CAT

"The band name really came from our song title 'Pimp The Cat,'" says founder-drummer Mark Greenberg. "My favorite anecdote though is about our album *People Makes Crazy* on the Japanese label Keni International. Kenny-san has been an active promoter in the Japanese jam band scene. He wanted to bring our CD to Japan to see if there was interest in creating a tour. His response was 'I played your Pimp CD for my office when I go home. When people listens to your CD, people makes crazy! We have loved that title ever since.'" The New York-based band's members have played with the Allman Brothers, Dave Matthews Band, Norah Jones, Charlie Hunter, Joe Morello, Josh Stone, the Doobie Brothers and Bob Weir & RatDog.

NAMES
STILL AVAILABLE

Coffee Cat Killers

Sylvester's
Speech Therapist

Tailchopping
Manxwhackers

Fangji Cat Meatballs

Anarchy & Mehitabel

The Catnip Nipples

Mr. Bigglesworth
in Boots

Cheshire Cat
Dental School

The Cat Came Black

Scratching Post
Allstars

Notorious Big'n'Frisky

Schrödinger's Catnap

Curiosity Killed the Cat
London, UK

Their debut album entered the UK charts at #1. Andy Warhol took part in their video for "Misfit." The expression "care'll kill a cat" appeared in Ben Jonson's 1598 play *Every Man in His Humour*. The expression appears to have transformed by 1909, according to O. Henry's *Schools and Schools*: "Curiosity can do more things than kill a cat."

The Deadcats
Vancouver, British Columbia, Canada

Their *Bad Pussy* CD cover features burlesque dancer Babette La Fave with pasties.

Radioactive Cats
Burbank, California, USA

Seventies-style retro metal from the early '90s (must have been the radioactivity).

Ten Gallon Cats
San Francisco, California, USA

Formed in 1995 with Telecaster ace Jim Campilongo as frontman. Songs include "Bought Some Swampland in Florida," "Hamster Wheel" and "Mozart Woulda Played a Tele." A Bernard "Hap" Kliban cartoon depicted a "ten gallon cat." As for the ten-gallon *hat*, it is probably a linguistic mixup. *Galón* is the Spanish word for braid; therefore, ten-braided hatband. The largest cowboy hat would hold less than four gallons.

Cats on XTC
West Palm Beach, Florida, USA

"Psychedelic goth." But that goes without saying.

The current **Hudson & the Hoo Doo Cats** lineup features Austin, Texas, native Hudson Harkins on drums and vocals, John Logan on guitar and Mike Graham on "slap bass." Since 1995 the band has called St. Louis, Missouri, home, but 1994's *It's HooDoo Time* was recorded in Austin and includes contributions from the legendary Johnnie Johnson and W.C. Handy award-winner W.C. Clark.

Cathouse   Italy

They appear to have a robust appreciation of tattoos, fetishism and porn. Hey, it's rock-and-roll from an Italian Cathouse.

Cat Butt
Seattle, Washington, USA

Late '80s grunge rock. Album: *Journey to the Center of Cat Butt*.

Cattywompus
Dogtown, California, USA

They are now based in Austin, Texas. It is unclear whether they traveled in a cattywompus (crooked, not straight) manner to get there. CD: *Gospel Hymns and Original Sins*.

Birchville Cat Motel
Lower Hutt, New Zealand

From an interview with *Perfect Sound Forever* online: "Birchville is a little semi-rural suburb way the hell out the sticks in Wellington. One of those crazy little *Edward Scissorhands* suburbs…about three quarters of an hour north of the city on the main road, you'll come to an AA sign that says BIRCHVILLE and underneath it there's another sign that says CAT MOTEL. I drove past it one day and it kinda stuck." Album: *Birds Call Home Their Dead*.

From Dez Presley and Miss Meow:

Our band name, the **SophistiCats & the SophistiKittens**, is a reaction to what we felt was lacking in the local music scene. We wanted to create something new and exciting that recalled music that was overlooked or forgotten. More specifically, we are an anti-jam band. All of our songs are less than three minutes long. We believe that our audience deserves to be entertained visually — cool threads and go-go dancers. And sonically — cool tunes, obscure '50s-'60s instrumentals and originals, played with vintage gear. Me-Yow, baby!"

On Maggie's Farm

Goat to Sheep

Billy Goat

Kansas City, Missouri, USA

Like a billy goat, frontman Mike Dillon was a tad randy and out of control in his younger days — and occasionally prone to performing naked and sticking his boy parts in foodstuffs.

Shower with Goats

Charlotte, North Carolina, USA

"Raw East Coast Pop Punk Since 1994." Actually, frontman Steve Neurotic called it quits in 2000. Tired of showering with goats, he turned to pinup and fetish photography, including a three-year stint as an official photographer for the infamous Suicide Girls website. But Neurotic is back, with a new crew and a planned SWG release for 2008.

Lubricated Goat

Perth-Sydney, Australia

Similarly, the punkish Lubricated Goat experienced widespread attention after performing a lip-synched version of their 1988 single "In the Raw" nude on national television. Doesn't the name Lubricated Goat seem like a public decency warning?

SuperHeavyGoatAss

Austin, Texas, USA

They made *The Onion* A.V. Club's Worst Band Names of 2007 list. There's stuff on the band's website about it being the perfect name for what they do. Briefly, Super = extreme, Heavy = loud, Goat = Satanic symbol, Ass = beast of burden. They're not bad. Or they are bad. You know what I mean.

Ram Jam

Woah, Black Betty (bam-ba-lam)!

Former Lemon Pipers guitarist Bill Bartlett rearranged and electrified Leadbelly's minute-long interpretation of the traditional work song "Black Betty" in 1976 while in a band called Starstruck, then released it in Cincinnati on the band's independent label. It was a solid local success and was soon picked up and rereleased by a New York record company. Though it was originally an African-American "field song" with vague lyrics, it was considered by many listeners to demean black women, particularly when sung by a white rock-and-roll singer. But Bartlett's hard-driving version of the song received huge airplay and made it into the Top 10 in Australia and the UK, as well as hitting #18 in the US.

Three jaded decades later, the band name Ram Jam sounds slightly nonsensical, if not downright icky, but it was the band name that the record was released under and the title of the album featuring the "Black Betty" single. The *Ram Jam* LP made it into the *Billboard* Top 40, but the band's subsequent album, *Portrait of the Artist as a Young Ram* (a pun on Irish writer James Joyce's classic *Portrait of the Artist as a Young Man*), failed to achieve liftoff, and to this day Ram Jam remain known for their lone chart hit.

The Mountain Goats

Durham, North Carolina, USA

Not, strictly speaking, a farm-animal band, but goats are goats. These goats are from Durham, North Carolina, and their name comes from the Screamin' Jay Hawkins song "Big Yellow Coat." Central creative force John Darnielle, bassist Peter Hughes and a coterie of contributing musicians produce songs with haunting melodies and intricately imagined characters. Darnielle: "The sexual tension between characters in your average Mountain Goats song could split the atom if the power could be harnessed, but it can't, so forget it.... Go forth and sin no more."

Theatre of Sheep
Portland, Oregon, USA

I think it went like this: The Inputs became the Briefcases, which in 1980 became Theatre of Sheep. Sheep Street is just around the corner from the Royal Shakespeare Theatre in Stratford-on-Avon.

Neglected Sheep
Charlotte, North Carolina, USA

"Neglected Sheep is currently writing, rehearsing, and preparing for the next album and tour. Keep an eye out on the East Coast and the Midwest for Neglected Sheep." How to recognize a neglected sheep...

Sheep on Drugs   London, UK

"Formed in response to the so-called 'Second Summer Of Love' by Duncan X and Lee Fraser, the splendidly named Sheep On Drugs set out to simultaneously mock and revel in the excesses of pop culture. Blending a mixture of sleazy rock, hard techno and punk nihilism into their own peculiar cabaret act of a rock'n'roll band, they set out on tour with buckets of blood, syringes and a pulpit from which Duncan could rant at Punter (as they termed the audience), who lapped it up with a knowing postmodern acceptance of their own commodification." Their name abbreviated: SOD.

Marble Sheep   Japan

Marble Sheep is an old-school arcade-style PC game. Guitarist-producer Ken Matsutani started Marble Sheep in 1987. The band has long had a strong following in Japan and began to tour overseas in 2002. Their live shows feature two drummers and a female bass player who often dresses as the sheep-girl mascot "Marby."

A SHEEP AT THE WHEEL *Dreams & Debris*

VANCOUVER, BRITISH COLUMBIA'S **A Sheep at the Wheel** have opened for acts such as Fingereleven and Wide Mouth Mason. Two tracks from their 2005 CD, *Blend*, were featured in independent film soundtracks, and their 2008 CD, *Dreams & Debris*, has gleaned good reviews. On their name: "A Sheep at the Wheel is about the illusion of control. Be it God, the media that shapes our ideas of God, the corporations that own the media, or the individual consumers/shareholders that direct the corporations; our desires, our morality, and our decisions are being dictated by forces beyond our control. We think we're in charge of our lives, but we're just sheep being led (hopefully not to the slaughter). Also we just like puns."

The Odd Lamb
New York City, New York, USA

Jonathan Atchley is the Odd Lamb: "I, Jonathan, (in my home studio) write, record, produce, layer, mix, manipulate, cut and paste, sing, tweak, play etc. etc. all the music just 'cause I don't really know anyone who shares my visions at all...."

Anger of the Lamb
Paterson, New Jersey, USA

The lamb is not happy with the world, but we will like its music if we are "amongst the sheep that will no longer follow the shepherd of content." ▪

Chickens, Ducks, Geese

Five Ton Chicken
Austin, Texas, USA
It's big. Maybe because of its horn section. The average chicken weighs 5 to 7 lbs. (2.3-3.2 kg).

Ten Ton Chicken
Berkeley, California, USA
Twice as big as a Five Ton Chicken. From an article in the UCLA *Daily Bruin*: "A friend of the band's used to casually produce a fake magazine, which featured, among other elements of artifice, reviews of fake bands. One was named Ten Ton Chicken, and, as ridiculous as it sounded, the name seemed to suit the vibe they were going for."

THE RADIOACTIVE CHICKEN HEADS report, "We were forced to be named the Radioactive Chicken Heads because of new government regulations which require all radioactive farm products to be labeled clearly." The Los Angeles group is comprised of Carrot Topp (vocals), Bird Brain and Cherry Tomato (guitars), Pastafarian (bass), Frankenchicken (keyboards), Bonehead (trumpet), El Pollo Diablo (percussion) and Puke Boy (drums). *Poultry in Motion* is their 2005 CD.

Big Fat Hen
Panama City, Panama
Changed their name to Polyphase in 2003. Big Fat Hen was formed in 1997. Song titles: "God's Beer" and "Natural Things That Burn." From the counting rhyme: "...7, 8, lay them straight... 9, 10, a big fat hen. Let's get up and count again!"

Chicken Head
Köln, Germany
They sing the blues in both German and English. Old-school amplifier knobs, round but with beak-like directional pointers, are called chicken-head knobs.

Chicken Head Turbo
Indianapolis, Indiana, USA
Their 2007 CD: *Your Darkest Wet Dream*. The term "chicken head" is often used to depict . . . based on the bobbing action of a chicken's head.

Bump of Chicken
Sakura City, Japan
Bumpin' J-pop. Band members met in kindergarten. A lot of their music has been used in Japanese video game soundtracks.

Chicken Legs Weaver
Sheffield, UK
Chicken Legs Weaver is named for its apparently irregularly limbed frontman, slide guitarist Andy Weaver.

Scary Chicken
Buffalo, New York, USA
Songs: "Is That Your Beer?" and "If I Showered."

Atomic Rooster

This noteworthy UK band was formed in 1969 by musicians from the *Crazy World of Arthur Brown* recording sessions. The initial lineup consisted of Carl Palmer (drums) and Vincent Crane (keyboards) with bassist Nick Graham (also vocals, flute). They were joined by guitarist John Du Cann (of Andromeda), Paul Hammond (replacing Palmer) and vocalist Peter French.

A fan site posting offers this information: "The name of the band [was] taken from a member of the US band Rhinoceros, who whilst undertaking a 'spiritual quest,' emerged with a personae which he named as the Atomic Rooster, a name which obviously struck a chord with Carl and Vincent. Interestingly enough, 1969 was the Year of the Rooster in the Chinese calendar." Rhinoceros's 1969 album is entitled *Satin Chickens*.

Albums: *Atomic Rooster* (1970), *Death Walks Beside You* (1970), *In Hearing of Atomic Rooster* (1971), *Made in England* (1972) and *Nice 'n' Greasy* (1973). The band's biggest hits were 1971's "Tomorrow Night," which hit #11 on the UK charts, and "The Devil's Answer," which went all the way to #4.

Band members went on to play with Emerson, Lake & Palmer, Hard Stuff, Cactus and Dexy's Midnight Runners. Crane committed suicide in 1989, and Hammond overdosed in 1992.

25

NAMES
STILL AVAILABLE

Red Cöckerël Cult

Cock It & Pullet

The Broody Roosters

Junglefowl 5

Henpecked
Chicken Sexers

Choke on My Yolk

Free-Range
Party Peckers

Kentucky Fried
My Family

Rubber Chicken
Rubbers

The Legend
of Al Capon

Ducks Limited

Goose Step Mothers

The **KUNG PAO CHICKENS** aren't a rock band, but I liked their name. They play hot gypsy jazz in the Portland area, including no-cover Monday nights at the Laurelthirst Pub. *Live at the Roost* is their 2007 CD. Kung pao chicken is a classic Chinese dish from the Sichuan province and is named for a title held by Shandong governor Ding Baozhen, Gong Bao ("palatial guardian").

Blood Sledge Electric Death Chickens

Howell, Michigan, USA

A late 1990s Detroit-area parody punk-rock band. Guitarist, drummer and hair stylist Tim Jack is also a visual artist.

Swamp Chicken

Utrecht, Netherlands

Did American musician Erik Kearns buy swampland in Europe?

Bald Knob Chicken Snatchers

Frederick, Maryland, USA

Combine ""bald knob" with the expression "choke the chicken" and you get the, uh, gist. From a Pitchforkmedia.com article: "Fonotone [Records]contributors were encouraged to operate under regional names (chances are [studio head Joe] Bussard made most up on the spot), and the post-adolescent, backwoods humor of titles like the Tennessee Mess Arounders, Gabriel's Holy Testifiers, the Mash Mountain Boys, and the Bald Knob Chicken Snatchers is hardly lost here." Their 1964 title "Sugar in My Gourd" is a reference to a post-coital condition.

Chicken Poodle Soup

Minneapolis, Minnesota, USA

Sometimes bill themselves as "The Last Living Ska Band Ever, Ever."

Norman, Oklahoma's **AMAZING RHYTHM CHICKENS** assembled as an ad hoc band in 1973 to celebrate vocalist-harp player Greg Mohr's 25th birthday. They stayed together for 30 years. Neil Kingsley (guitar, keys, vocals): "The Rhythm Chicken name came from a sarcastic remark made by one of our friends when our drummer kept screwing up the rhythm during rehearsal. The Amazing Rhythm Aces and the Fabulous Thunderbirds were both popular at the time. We sometimes used Amazing and sometimes used Fabulous, but Amazing won out in the long run."

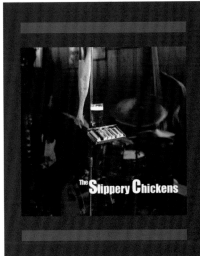

The Slippery Chickens cultivate rockabilly and New Orleans-style blues in New York City. Their most recent CD is entitled *We Ain't Scared...We're Just Chicken*, which vocalist-harp player Jerry Scaringe says was "recorded live in the studio (my girlfriend's apartment)...what I mean by recorded live is that there are no overdubs. Every plinkety plink of the guitar, every thumpety thump of the bass, every wee haw of the harmonica, every bang boom bam of the drums and every yodalady croakety croak of the vocals were recorded at the same moment in time."

Mary Carves the Chicken
Simi Valley, California, USA

From their MySpace bio: "Mary Carves the Chicken takes its audiences through a maze of New Orleans funk and soul, pounding rock and roll, classic country, amazing blues, cow punk, rockabilly, blistering guitar duels, far-fetched medleys, and spacey, often driving jams that go on as long as they feel good." Then Mary carves the chicken.

Rooster Cruiser
Los Angeles, California, USA

This, uh, "ska-metal" band has a fan club called the Rooster Boosters.

Rooster
London, UK

The band settled on the name Rooster when vocalist Nick Atkinson came home £250 richer from his bet on a horse named Rooster Booster. The quartet is said to have been the first band to broadcast a concert live to mobile phones, on November 2, 2004.

Jungle Rooster
San Francisco, California, USA

Slogan: "Jungle Rooster puts the 'hard' in rock." "Jungle rooster" is a slang expression for a prankish college girl with no domestic skills. Which makes it a weird name for an aging male band.

Big Metal Rooster
Lawrence, Kansas, USA

The five-man jam band takes their name from "a quirky housewarming gift."

Cock Sparrer   London, UK

Meant to be Cocksparrow, the familiar male sparrow. "It's an old East End greeting, as in, 'Hello, me ol' cock-sparrer!' We changed [our name] from Cocksparrow to Cocksparrer because people weren't pronouncing it right. It sounded too posh, like you had a plum in your mouth when people said Cocksparrow. For one gig with the Small Faces at the Roundhouse, we changed our name to the Blades, but it wasn't us."

The Ducks
Santa Cruz, California, USA

For seven weeks in the summer of 1977, Neil Young joined singer Jeff Blackburn, bassist Bob Mosley (formerly of Moby Grape) and drummer Johnny Craviotta to form a $3-cover bar band. The band started a city-wide duck craze that summer, with people buying up duck calls to blow at gigs. Due to Young's touring arrangement with Crazy Horse, the Ducks could only perform in Santa Cruz, which they did 22 times before disbanding.

Busty Duck   Brussels, Belgium

Members of the Fucking Ashtrays, Piggy Pooh and Mouse's Blood get together and do the Busty Duck.

Dick Duck & the Dorks
Toronto, Ontario, Canada

The house band at the Edge, a punk-band hotspot in the late 1970s and early '80s. Lead singer Paul Ekness also fronted the Wads and the Gunslingers.

The Roosters is a perennially popular name, and not just for cock rock: Moorehead, Minnesota (Americana); Nacogdoches, Texas (Americana); Columbia, Missouri (grunge); Glendale, California (Celtic punk); Hillsdale, New Jersey (hardcore); West Midlands, UK (blues); Cranleigh, UK (punk); Warsaw, Poland (pop-punk); Denmark (classic southern rock).

Ducks Deluxe London, UK

Ducks Deluxe lasted from 1972 until '75 when Martin Belmont (guitar), Sean "Godfather of Boogie" Tyla (vocals), Nick Garvey (vocals, guitar), Ken Whaley (bass) and Tim Roper (drums) went on to form more successful bands, including the Rumour, the Tyla Gang and the Motors. Belmont and Tyla reformed the band in 2007 for Ducks' 35th anniversary.

Ducky Boys
Boston, Massachusetts, USA

The band's name is the name of an Irish street gang in the 1979 film *The Wanderers*.

The Fabulous Minnesota Barking Ducks
Minneapolis, Minnesota, USA

Band slogan: "Nothin' beats fun for havin' a good time."

Oakland, California-based punk accordionist **Duckmandu** (Aaron Seeman) plays the first Dead Kennedys album in its entirety, note-for-note. "His repertoire also includes, but is not limited to, '70s rock, Broadway show tunes, klezmer, classical, country, Sousa marches, punk rock, and even a polka or two." Seeman is a founding member of the San Francisco Punk Rock Orchestra and plays accordian in the gypsy folk-fusion band Fishtank Ensemble.

Galapagos Duck
Sydney, Australia

Darwinian album titles include *Voyage of the Beagle* (1983) and *Endangered Species* (1985). From band website: "The inspiration [for our name] came from Spike Milligan and was somehow derived from one of his comedy sketches involving the auctioning of a 'giant Galapagos turtle upon wheels with clockwork revolving eyes.'" Milligan became a friend of the band and wrote the words to one of their songs.

Goose
Kortrijk, Belgium

The Belgian Goose performs "electro dance-club rock" and their songs have been used for. Coca Cola and Heineken ads in Europe.

Pigs

Abattoir Pigs
Kettering, Northamptonshire, UK

Debut death-metal EP: *Putting the Laughter in Slaughter*

Blodwyn Pig Luton, UK

Formed by Mick Abrahams (guitar, vocals) after he left Jethro Tull: "[We were] dubbed Blodwyn Pig by a stoned hippy friend just back from the Buddhist trail."

The Groove Hogs
Branch, Wisconsin, USA

Ten-piece blues band with horns. Song: "Ingrown Tonation."

Groove Pigs
San Francisco, California, USA

The Pigs claim to have sent a demo tape wrapped in bacon to *BAM magazine*. Members also played in the Himalayans, which also included Counting Crows singer Adam Duritz.

Die Kapitalist Pig
Portland, Oregon, USA

MySpace page requests: "Do Not Buy Our Record. Please Download It For Free." Debut CD: *Killyourselfishness*.

Fetal Pigs in Brine
Santa Cruz, California, USA

Surf-punk sounds for the Biology 101 dissection lab.

HONEY PIG features the harmonies of Debi Derryberry, Laura Milby and Melissa Sills. The Los Angeles-based trio began performing to enthusiastic audiences at clubs and coffee houses in 1998. *Exactly As They Are* is their 2001 CD.

Oink! is the first album by **THE PIGS** on musician-producer Geoff Westen's Disturbing Music label. Many years ago, Westen's graphics company, Oz Studios, was asked to come up with concepts for a Rolling Stones tour: "One of the concepts was the image of the group 'pigging out' — their M.O. in those days. Thus was born the 'Tour of the Pigs' concept. We came up with some wicked ideas on how to apply a Pigs theme to everything from their logo to their merch and their airplane. I stated at the time that if the Stones didn't use the Pigs idea, someday I would."

Female Chauvinist Pigs
San Pedro, California, USA
An all-female band formed in August 1997, "they have blazed a trail and brutalized men in the South Bay punk scene with hundreds of fast-paced shows."

Billy Bacon & the
Forbidden Pigs Austin, Texas, USA
Billy Bacon (bass, vocals) chose the band's weirdly vague name Forbidden Pigs for a reason: "It wouldn't put us in any genre. I could do an all Tex-Mex record and the next record could be all blues or all pop."

Pigbag
Cheltenham, UK
Founder Chris Hamlin's scruffy cloth bag depicted a warthog. Their 1983 single "Papa's Got a Brand New Pigbag" was a hit on UK indie charts.

Pigface
Chicago, Illinois, USA
Formed in 1990 by Martin Atkins (Public Image Limited, Nine Inch Nails, Killing Joke) and William Rieflin (Revolting Cocks, R.E.M., KMFDM), both with Ministry. Pigface is also a common name for a genus of ground-creeping plants.

Pearls Before Swine
Melbourne, Florida, USA
This psychedelic-folk band (1964–74) took their name from the Bible passage "Give not that which is holy unto dogs, neither cast your pearls before swine…." Lyricist Bernie Taupin is said to have acknowledged Pearls Before Swine singer Tom Rapp's song "Rocket Man" as an inspiration for the Elton John/Bernie Taupin song by the same name. (Both were based on Ray Bradbury's short story "The Rocket Man.")

Pig Farm on the Moon
Caracas, Venezuela
From the *Orbital* album liner notes: "There's a huge farm on the moon, where pigs live peacefully, sheltered under the beautiful image of The Blue Sphere. Once they were speechless…." Progressive rock that talks to swine.

Pigs Might Fly
Budapest, Hungary
An expression of unlikelihood. Like this band playing Starbucks.

Big Pig
Australian drummer Oleh Witer and singer Nick Disbray met in London in 1985, then returned to Melbourne to recruit the five additional members of the new-wave synth-pop band Big Pig. The band's debut album, *BONK*, went platinum in Australian, with three hit singles: "Hungry Town," "Big Hotel" and "Breakaway." The latter hit #60 in the US and was used in the soundtrack for the 1989 comedy *Bill and Ted's Excellent Adventure*. Other songs were used in the movie *Young Einstein*, the US television series *Miami Vice* and the BBC *Rough Guides* series.

Little remembered today, Big Pig was genuinely unique at the time (and today), with its absence of guitars and its saturation of drums and percussion, both live and synthesized. Most of band sang, banged on something and wore blacksmith-style leather aprons. Lead vocalist Sherine Abeyratne kicked the band into persona overdrive. She was a fiery, diminutive singer with seemingly boundless energy. In addition to her contribution to Big Pig, she joined her twin sister Zan as a background vocalist for bands such as INXS and U2.

Big Pig disbanded soon after the release of their second album, *You Lucky People*, in 1991.

NAMES
STILL AVAILABLE

Pork Asylum

Pig Iron & Swine

The Truffle Snouts

Boar War

Perry Feral's
Pig Addiction

Three Little

Death Cab
for Babe

The Bacon Sisters

Applemouth

Hugo Boss Hog

Spider Pig's
Web

Slophappy
Pork Pappies

Baltimore songwriter Liz Dowling was born in her family's 3 Pigs Café in Dadeville, Alabama, during a lunchtime rush. "Momma was heaved up on the table next to the chopped-pork vat by two catch-women who were working as cooks, and there I was delivered." She named her group **RADIANT PIG**, "delving into the spiritual nature of pigs, and Wilbur from *Charlotte's Web*, in particular." *Daily Grace* was released in 2002. The most recent incarnation of her band is Lurch & Holler.

Pig Farmers of the Apocalypse
Fort Wayne, Indiana, USA
"As you know, it has been some centuries since human kind obliterated themselves…But now that the chemical levels have returned to normal and the prophesy of the ancient sisterhood, that 'All Men Are Pigs,' has finally been fulfilled…."

The Porktrashers
Toronto, Ontario, Canada
Started on the porch of drummer Mark Adilman's place behind a pork slaughterhouse in downtown Toronto.

The Pork Dukes   London, UK
"Formed in 1976, the Pork Dukes were ruder than the Sex Pistols…."

Horses

Venus DeMars
& All the Pretty Horses
Minneapolis, Minnesota, USA
Led by transgendered performance artist S. Grandell (Venus DeMars). According to DeMars, "In the Voudoun [voodoo] tradition, one of the world's most danceable religions, a 'horse' is a person one of the gods chooses to ride; a form of benign possession that can explode gender boundaries." *All the Pretty Horses* is the title of Cormac McCarthy's 1992 novel.

Sparklehorse
North Carolina/Virginia, USA
Surreal folk-rock. The name appears to suggest motorcycles as iron horses.

Spook the Horse
Seattle, Washington, USA
Winners of the 2006 Red Hook Brewery's Emerging Artist Award.

Hollow Horse
Glasgow, Scotland, UK
The Trojans did it first, but *Diary of a Hollow Horse* was the name of the 1989 album by the Liverpool band China Crisis. Hollow Horse's 2008 *Escaping from a Submarine* features guest musician Brian McNeil, who played keyboards with China Crisis. According to the *Little Illiad*, the Trojan Horse contained 3,000 troops in its belly, 2 spies in its mouth and 3 dancing fairies in its testicles.

Dark Horse
St. Paul, Minnesota, USA
This metal band has been featured in two documentaries, *The Atlas Moth* and *Driver 23*, the former getting its title from subject of bass player Sean Cassidy who died in 2004 and was raising atlas moths.

TECHNOLOGY VERSUS HORSE brings the post-punk funk from Bowling Green, Kentucky, in Zappa-esque time signatures. Their name comes from the 2002 film *Adaptation*, in which Nicholas Cage plays twin brothers: an accomplished-but-troubled scriptwriter and a cocky, would-be scriptwriter. There is a scene in which the would-be writer tells his more insecure brother about a chase scene he has in mind that would involve a motorcycle and a horse, "like technology versus horse" (in fact, mocking the film *True Lies*, in which Arnold, on horseback, chases a bad guy on a motorcycle).

Last Charge of the Light Horse
Coram, New York, USA

Singer songwriter Jean-Paul Vest: "The name came from a few things. I was born in the Chinese year of the horse, and I grew up riding horses. Also I'm a big fan of George Harrison, and his record label was Dark Horse, so Light Horse seemed like a natural counterpoint. And then that got me thinking about *The Charge of the Light Brigade*, and about Peter Weir's movie *Gallipoli*, which is one of my all-time favorites. Finally, I wanted the name to reflect our roots in some older musical traditions, and the attitude that we don't want to hold anything back, because who knows if we'll get another chance to do this."

Pale Horse
Gloucester City, New Jersey, USA

Book of Revelation 6:8: "And I looked, and behold a pale horse: and his name that sat on him was Death, and Hell followed with him." Early 1990s, reformed in 2005 — name chosen because it reflected guitarist Jerry's sense of his own musical development from earlier efforts in Thanatopsis and Hostility (whatever that means). This doom-death-thrash-metal band supposedly signed with a Christian label in Florida.

Kicking a Dead Horse
Rangeley, Maine, USA

Trying to evoke change in the unchangeable. "During one rather spirited rehearsal Augie managed to put the bass drum beater through the bass drum head! Someone made the comment about kicking a dead horse, and someone else said something about it being like the music business! Hey, great name for a band."

Crazy Horse
Laurel Canyon, California, USA

Best known as Neil Young's backup band, these guys started in 1962 as doo-wop crew Danny & the Memories, became the rockier Rockets in '66 and then Crazy Horse in '69 for album *Everybody Knows This Is Nowhere*. Filmmaker Jim Jarmusch followed the band's world tour in the documentary *Year of the Horse*. On a historical note, Oglala Lakota chief Crazy Horse fought in vain to stem the westward expansion of European settlement. His childhood nickname was Curly.

Crack Horse   Wales, UK
Crack horse sounds like crack whores.

Band of Horses

Founders Ben Bridwell (vocals, guitar) and Mat Brooke (guitar) played together for ten years in Seattle's Carissa's Weird before forming Horses in 2004, which soon after became Band of Horses. Brooke left to focus on his other band, Grand Archives, in 2006, and the band (with Creighton Barrett on drums and Rob Hampton on bass) relocated to Bridwell's home state, South Carolina.

In a Pitchforkmedia.com interview, Bridwell had this to say about the band's name: "I always give the stock answer about why we named ourselves Band of Horses. And I always talk about the Don Johnson thing, about how he had a band called Horses in the '60s, so the label advised us that it might confuse the marketplace. We were called Horses because of that song by Palace on *Lost Blues* ['Horses']. When I was homeless in Seattle, sleeping on this Masonic temple's side door, like delivery door, I would sleep there. And I used to get kinda nervous at night, thinking someone would come rob me. And I would always listen to that song. It would zen me out. So that's why I named the band Horses."

Chicago's **TECHNICOLOUR STALLION** describes themselves as "like a power trio, but with two extra dudes." In reviewing their recent CD, Spacepony, *Farmhouse Magazine* noted that the music "harkens back to the origins of indie rock, when bands were willing to take risks...their whimsical, self-aware lyrics provide a nice counter-weight to the music's sense of grandeur." The saturated color levels of the innovative Technicolor process brought new life to the American motion picture industry beginning with 1920s classics such as *The Ten Commandments, Ben-Hur* and *The Black Pirate*.

Dead Horse
Houston, Texas, USA
The horse that is kicked or flogged in futility.

The Golden Palominos
New York City, New York, USA
Headed by drummer-composer Anton Fier. Players involved in the seven recordings include Bill Laswell, Arto Lindsay, John Zorn, Fred Frith, John Lydon, Michael Stipe, Richard Thompson, T-Bone Burnett and Matthew Sweet. Pretty golden.

The Ass Ponys
Cincinnati, Ohio, USA
From band bio: "Dan had [it] written on the end of an old possible-band-names list. We figured we'd change it later and never have." Vocalist-guitarist Chuck Cleaver's new band is called Wussy.

Pony Up!
Montreal, Quebec, Canada
A variation on the term "ante up" or "fork over." All-girl band. Song: "Marlon Brando's Laundromat"

Dragmules
New York City, New York, USA
Mules toiling for the Man, man. Dragging plows. Dragging for mussels.

Snowpony London, UK
A snowpony is an otherwise functioning professional who routinely disappears to score or snort cocaine. Also a supergroup comprised of vocalist-keyboardist Katherine Gifford (Stereolab), bass player Debbie Googe (My Bloody Valentine) and drummer Max Corradi (Quickpace), later joined by guitarist Debbie Smith (Echobelly, Curve), with Kevin Bass replacing Corradi.

Gov't Mule
Asheville, North Carolina, USA
Following the Civil War, the US government awarded freed African-American slaves 40 acres of land and a mule to drag a plow. This Allman Brothers side project formed as a power trio with Warren Haynes on guitar, Matt Abts on drums and Allen Woody on bass. Woody was found dead in 2000. The unreleased cause of death remains a point of fan speculation. Warren Haynes says of the name Gov't Mule, "Jaimoe, who is one of the drummers for the Allman Brothers, kinda dubbed us Gov't Mule, and it just stuck. We thought it applied to us and liked all of the different meanings that it took on and the fact that everybody had a different idea of what it meant, so we kinda stuck with it."

Cows

The Cows

Minneapolis, Minnesota, USA

Anything but pastoral. From interview in *Exclaim* magazine: Q: What do you expect people to take home from a Cows show? A: Tinnitus! Albums include *Cunning Stunts* and *Sorry in Pig Minor*.

The Cowsills

Newport, Rhode Island, USA

Cowsills are ledges on cows upon which to display potted geraniums. No? Then they are a late '60s bubblegum-pop family band. Navy recruiter dad Bud Cowsill reportedly kicked son Billy out of the band in 1971 for smoking marijuana.

Down Cows

San Francisco, California, USA

The Down Cows debut EP bears the title *Moo. Thud.* Cowtipping is predicated on the false assumptions that cows sleep standing up and that a cow's legs will remain stiff during the act of tipping. Drunken engineering students should stick to dismantling large inanimate objects and reassembling them elsewhere.

The Cow Trippers

Portland, Oregon, USA

Self-description: "Sounds and sounds and sounds of ton." There is no proof that the Cow Trippers have indulged in cowtipping — that is, pushing over standing cows for entertainment.

Two Cow Garage

Columbus, Ohio, USA

Like many band names, this one was suggested by a friend as a joke, was used for the gig and stuck.

Holy Cow

South Dartmouth, Massachusetts, USA

Self-description: "Electric drones, glass crashing, pounding drums and the human groan of pain and agony..." Yikes. The cow is considered sacred in Hinduism and Zoroastrianism.

Congress of the Cow

San Diego, California, USA

The name comes from the *Kama Sutra*: "The congress of a cow: The woman takes a hands-and-knees position while the man mounts her from behind."

The Herd

Formed in London in 1965, the quintet the Herd underwent several lineup changes in its first two years. In 1967 the band's record company, Parlophone, designated the band's sometime fill-in guitarist, Peter Frampton, as frontman. (Frampton's previous band, the Preachers, had been managed by Bill Wyman of the Rolling Stones.)

Though the Herd had aspirations as a serious band, the label's marketing department saw teen-idol-handsome Frampton as a fan-magazine natural. In fact, Frampton was voted "The Face of 1968" by *Rave* magazine readers, following the chart success of the single "I Don't Want Our Loving to Die."

Frampton soon tired of the teen scene and left the Herd in 1969 to form Humble Pie with equally disgruntled Small Faces singer-guitarist Steve Marriott. The remaining members of the Herd soldiered on briefly without Frampton, but the public lost interest and followed their golden boy to his new, edgier band. Humble Pie's debut single, "Natural Born Bugie," hit #4 on the UK Singles chart, and the subsequent album is said to have been the first record referred to as "heavy metal," by *Rolling Stone* reviewer Mike Saunders. (Saunders went on to front his Angry Samoans, which coincidentally included Gregg Turner, now of Blood Drained Cows.)

Reincarnation is the first EP from Japan's **USED COWS**, featuring Ritchie (vocals), Naoki (bass), Hikoichi (guitar), Ruri (violin) and Ken (drums). This 2006 EP was mastered by Tom Baker, who has mastered such artists as the Beastie Boys, Nine Inch Nails, P.O.D., Papa Roach and Stone Temple Pilots. The track "Insomnia" is the end theme for the PS2 game *Shinbido: Way of the Ninja*.

33

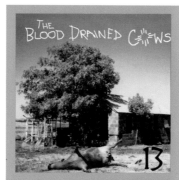

BLOOD DRAINED COWS leader, ex-Angry Samoan, alien-abduction theorist and university math professor Gregg Turner explains: "There was an article in the Santa Fe *New Mexican* about how a veterinarian had examined what appeared to be the bloated but bone-dry viscera of cow entrails high up in the New Mexico desert above Santa Fe. When the vet was asked what was the most shocking aspect of the 'cow mountain mutilations,' he took issue that this, in fact, was a mutilation at all: 'It was just one damn blood-drained cow.' I was impressed and mentioned the story to my friend Sandy Pearlman, former producer and manager of Blue Öyster Cult, lately on faculty at McGill University. His response was, 'Well, it happens.'" THE BLOOD DRAINED COWS' new CD, *13*, is perfect music to track aliens by.

20 Bulls Each Dublin, Ireland
"There was a [newspaper] piece about the Spanish running of the bulls, where they just unleash a herd of cattle on the town and people run like hell. One of the sentences was '20 Bulls Each,' so that would do for a while. But it just stuck. It was either that or 'Spoon Included' from a yogurt ad."

Mechanical Bull
Woodstock, New York, USA
Song: "My Baby's Just a 6 Pack Away."

Bullistic
Richmond, Virginia, USA
Self-description: "Blue-collar beer metal."

Boolfight Paris, France
Not just an intentional misspelling. Modern computer science is based on the work of British mathematician George Boole. Boolean Algebra. "In this environment, the only elements that exist are 'true' or 'false', i.e., in computer language, 0 or 1...However, our reality simply cannot be summarized with a mere sequence of numbers, zeroes and ones. In that respect, the meaning of 'Boolfight' can be described as an allegory about the modern human condition. That is: the conflict of human nature (being alive, rather complex and able to adapt) versus the growing alliance of community and digitalism, and their joint effort in over-simplification, abstraction and rigidity."

Cattlehead
Lafayette, Louisiana, USA
"Back in 7th grade, Ryan [guitar, vocals] used to make fun of a guy by the name of Huy Nguyen (all in good fun, no harm intended!). Huy didn't appreciate the butchering of his name, so he started calling Ryan Cazares 'Ryan Cattlehead.' It caught on and has never left."

Cattle Decapitation
San Diego, California, USA
There is something deeply unsettling about the listing "Upcoming Cattle Decapitation Shows." These guys are the real gore-grind deal. Albums with titles such as *Karma Bloody Karma*, *Humanure*, *Homovore* and *Human Jerky* present the band's controversial pro-vegetarian/anti-human position.

The Birds

Birdsongs of the Mesozoic
Boston, Massachusetts, USA

Roger Miller (piano) and Erik Lindgren (synthesizers) from defunct Moving Parts collaborated with tape artist Michael Swope (who played with Miller in Mission to Burma) for one show, but they decided to continue. The band's name, chosen by Miller, is a reference to a *Birdsongs of America* album that Swope sampled during the sessions and to theories about the dinosaur ancestry of birds.

A Flock of Seagulls Liverpool, UK
The band with the signature hair took their name from a line in the Stranglers' song "Toiler on the Sea." Mike Score (vocals, keys) was a hairdresser.

Damn Seagulls Helsinki, Finland
Album *Soul Politics* reached top of the charts in Finland. Seagulls are a huge problem in Helsinki's Market Square. Oral contraceptives hidden in food have been considered, but seagulls live to be more than 30 years old, so it would take a while. Damn seagulls.

Seagull Screaming
Kiss Her Kiss Her
Tokyo, Japan

From the title of a track on XTC's 1984 album, *The Big Express*.

An Albatross
Wilkes-Barre, Pennsylvania, USA

Debut album: *Eat Lightning, Shit Thunder*, featuring the track "Uncle Funky Pants."

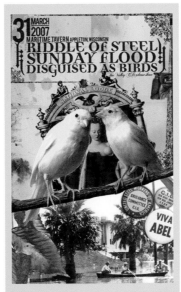

Disguised as Birds
Milwaukee, Wisconsin, USA

Kevin DeMars, Kristopher Endicott, Tony Ciske and Chris Chuzles rock out on 2008's *Seeds*. The name comes from the Czeslaw Milosz poem "Dedication": *They used to pour millet on graves or poppy seeds / To feed the dead who would come disguised as birds.* Also from the title of an Alfredo Castaneda painting, *Dialogue of Two Poets Disguised as Birds*.

Raven Newcastle, UK
Opened for punk bands the Stranglers and the Motors in the late 1970s, carried on as a metal band until 2001, reformed in 2006. Toured with Metallica and Anthrax.

The Byrds

In 1964 the Los Angeles duo of Gene Clark and Roger McGuinn was joined by David Crosby, and soon after by Chris Hillman and Michael Clarke. The group briefly called themselves the Jet Set, then released a single as the Beefeaters before signing to Columbia Records and changing their name to the Byrds. They were looking for a name that suggested flight and freedom. The spelling was altered to avoid the British slang term for girls. (The band didn't want to be thought of as "the Girls" in the event they were to tour the UK.) Birdsies was rejected, as was Burds. Roger McGuinn is said to have come up with the spelling Byrds.

The Byrds' harmonies combined with the sound of McGuinn's 12-string Rickenbacker guitar to create a fresh sound in folk-rock, and the band had major success with their covers of "Mr. Tambourine Man" (Dylan) and "Turn, Turn, Turn" (traditional, Seeger arrangement).

By late 1965, the Byrds had begun to experiment with more psychedelic sounds and themes, notably the single "Eight Miles High." Their disillusionment with mid-60s manufactured pop led to "So You Want to Be a Rock'n'Roll Star."

Certainly Crosby wanted to be more of a star, and his need to be the focus of the attention at live performances in 1967 (including long political rants and pro-LSD statements) led to his "firing" by fellow band members. Ironically, Crosby then began performing as an equal partner in Crosby, Stills & Nash.

Counting Crows
San Francisco, California, USA

Took their name from a divination rhyme heard by singer Adam Duritz in the 1989 film *Signs of Life*. This rhyme is used at the end of their song "A Murder of One": *One crow for sorrow / Two crows for joy / Three crows for a girl / Four crows for a boy / Five crows for silver / Six crows for gold / Seven crows for a secret never to be told.*

The Housemartins   Hull, UK
Vocalist Paul Heaton started the band in 1983 with Stan Cullimore (guitar), Ted Key (bass) and Chris Lang (drums). From their fan site: "The name had been Paul's idea, inspired by his favorite writer, Peter Tinniswood. Birds are often used in his books as metaphors for the seasons and events. Tinniswood once described himself as 'a serious writer who has a gloomily optimistic view of life,' and this seems to echo Paul's approach to songwriting." Norman Cook (aka Fatboy Slim) replaced Key, and a shuffle of drummers ended with the hiring of Dave Hemingway. When the Housemartins split in '88, Hemingway, Heaton and roadie Sean Welch formed the Beautiful South.

The Black Crowes
Atlanta, Georgia, USA

Began as Mr. Crowe's Garden, possibly after the children's story "Mr. Crow's Garden" from *The Hollow Tree Snowed-In Book* by Albert Bigelow Paine (1910). Signed to Def American, who wanted a name change. Already known as "the Crowes," so they picked a nice color.

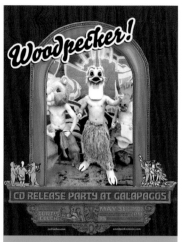

Brooklyn's decidedly un-Brooklyny, bluegrassy **WOODPECKER!** is "your favorite ivory-billed, red-bellied, sap-sucking string band. We feature four musicians and vocalists who play the guitar, mandolin, banjo and cello." In fact, they play them well and their lyrics are often quite clever. Album: *F-Hole*.

Black Canary
Columbus, Ohio, USA

The Black Canary is a DC Comics heroine with martial-arts skills and a "Canary cry" that can shatter objects and render villains helpless. Canaries were once released into coal mines to detect methane and carbon monoxide gases.

The Pigeon Detectives   Leeds, UK
Drummer Jimmi Naylor: "I never liked the name at first. But it's stuck, and it's probably got us more attention having a silly name. It came from an Australian guy who we met at the Leeds Festival. We were just discussing band names, and he came up with the Pigeon Detectives. It became an in-joke for the rest of the festival."

The Mutton Birds
Auckland, New Zealand

Better known outside NZ as the sooty shearwater, the muttonbird coos and croaks loudly while on its breeding grounds. The Maori collect fledglings from their burrows, pluck them and preserve them in salt for later consumption. Members of the Mutton Birds came from Dribbling Darts, Six Volts, Sneaky Feelings and Blam Blam Blam. A big band in New Zealand through the '90s.

The Mynah Birds
Toronto, Ontario, Canada

Notorious funkateer Rick James came to Toronto in 1964, having deserted the US Navy. He was playing in a cover band called the Sailorboys when Colin Kerr, owner of the Mynah Bird nightclub, saw potential and offered to manage the band. Kerr renamed them the Mynah Birds and had members dress in their namesake bird's colors. The story goes that the band fired Kerr when he requested they shave their heads and don feathered mynah costumes. Bruce Palmer left the Sparrows (who became Steppenwolf) to join the Mynah Birds. The band was signed to Motown in '66 and added Neil Young as guitarist. Palmer and Young went on to form Buffalo Springfield. A '67 incarnation included young Bruce Cockburn on guitar.

The Eagles
Los Angeles, California, USA

Originally formed as backing band for Linda Ronstadt in 1971. The name was chosen allegedly as a nod to the Byrds. Inducted into the Rock and Roll Hall of Fame in 1998.

Eagles of Death Metal

Palm Desert, California, USA

Side project for Josh Homme (Queens of the Stone Age). The band envisioned a cross between the Eagles and death metal. Self-description: "bluegrass slide guitar mixed with stripper drum beats and Canned Heat vocals."

The Flamingo Massacres

Nürnberg, Bayern, Germany

Irvine Welsh's 1995 novel *Marabou Stork Nightmares* has a chapter called "The Flamingo Massacres." All-female band (song: "No Sperm Zone") with two bass players (Lari and Eve) and drummer (Micha). Eve and Lari have since formed the band the Sighs of Sissified Resistance.

Killer Flamingos

Dearborn, Michigan, USA

Two songs by the band featured in the Anna Nicole Smith movie *Illegal Aliens*. The Killer Flamingos had nothing to do with Ms Smith's accidental overdose in February 2007.

The Cranes Portsmouth, UK

Industrial gothic, ambient pop. Named for the mechanical loading cranes along Portsmouth's docks.

The Hummingbirds

Sydney, Australia

Formed in 1986 from Bug Eyed Monsters, disbanded in 1993, members went on to form Fragile, Growl, RatCat and Sneeze.

THE SUICIDAL BIRDS • Friesland, Netherlands

Guitarist-vocalist Jessie and bassist-vocalist Chay, the Suicidal Birds, have been tearing up European stages since the release of their 2005 debut album *Z-List*. Their reputation as an A-list live band led to two invitations to support Dinosaur Jr. in Holland and Belgium.

Suicidal birds? In a century-long annual ritual that commences at the end of each monsoon season, thousands of birds, from 44 migratory species, crash to the ground along a narrow ridge in Jatinga, Assam, India, between the hours of 7 and 10 pm.

NAMES
STILL AVAILABLE

New World
Vultures

Wingclipper
Hooligans

The Mime Owls

That Petrel Emotion

Peruvian
Booby Snatchers

Counting Snipes

The Apathetic
Frigatebirds

No Egrets

Porno for Penguins

Tippi Hedron's
Seagull Friends

The Sad Larks

We Are the Word

Penguins with Shotguns
Kenosha, Wisconsin, USA

"We wanted something that expressed our fun nature...and love of playing, plus a name that if you saw [it] once would be easy to remember. Penguins with Shotguns was the end result." In its Fall '07 issue, *The Onion* named Penguins with Shotguns "one of the worst band names ever."

The Pistol Whippin' Party Penguins
Minneapolis, Minnesota, USA

The Onion chose to treat all penguin bands equally in 2007, adding this one to its Worst Band Names of 2007 list.

Lust Penguins
Philadelphia, Pennsylvania, USA

From a Rockbandlounge.com interview: "Being the last to be picked in gym class can leave the deep, lasting scars that later become some of the most angst-ridden lyrics of our time." One notable storyline in Berke Breathed's *Bloom County* comic strip had Opus the Penguin scorned for his "penguin lust."

Radio Birdman   Sydney, Australia
The name comes from an Iggy and the Stooges lyric from the song "1970." "Radio burnin' up above" was misheard as "radio birdman up above." Couldn't find a venue, so took over their own pub and promoted likeminded bands until Hell's Angels violence caused them to shut down. Radio Birdman is seen as the band that started the Sydney punk scene and they were inducted into the Australian Recording Industry Association Hall of Fame in July 2007.

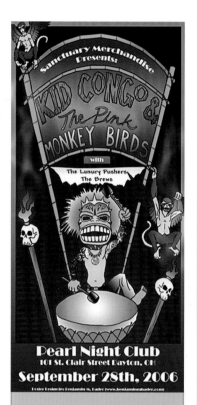

Washington, DC-based Kid Congo Powers (ex-Cramps, Gun Club, Nick Cave & the Bad Seeds, Angels of Light) is an underground guitar legend. *Philosophy & Underwear* is his first album as bandleader. **KID CONGO & THE PINK MONKEY BIRDS** features Congo on guitar and vocals, Kiki Solis on bass and Danny Hole on drums.

Wings   UK
Post-Beatles Paul McCartney named his new band Wings as a result of praying during birthing complications involving wife Linda and daughter Stella. The image of angel wings appeared to him.

Geezerbird
Croydon, Surrey, UK

British slang for a woman who enjoys male activities (a tomboy). They play Heart-like female-fronted glam-rock.

Raised by Swans
London, Ontario, Canada

The band has three songs on the soundtrack of director Atom Egoyan's film *Adoration*.

Zwan
Chicago, Illinois, USA

Post-Smashing Pumpkins Billy Corgan band. The Dutch word for swan is *zwaan*. Netherlands-based Zwanenberg Food Group produces t Zwan brand of luncheon meats and sausages, available in 74 countries.

The Wildbirds
Fox Valley, Wisconsin, USA

Started in 2000 as Number One Fan, became the Wildbirds in 2006. The band lives on their tour bus, which runs on bio-diesel.

The Yardbirds
London, UK

American slang for hobos who hung around railyards waiting for the next train; also a convict confined to the prison yard. Singer Keith Relf wrote a list of names, and band members chose Yardbirds, because of its hobos connotation and as a homage to saxophonist Charlie "Yardbird" Parker. The band's guitar alumni includes Jimmy Page, Eric Clapton and Jeff Beck. The Yardbirds were inducted into the Rock and Roll Hall of Fame in 1992.

Got Aqualung?

Aquatic Creatures

Country Joe & the Fish
California, USA

Joseph Stalin was referred to as "Country Joe" in the 1940s, while "the fish" refers to Mao Zedong's statement that the true revolutionary must "swim among the people as a fish." "Country Joe" MacDonald (vocals) and Barry "The Fish" Melton (guitar) started as a duo. Best known for their Vietnam protest song "I Feel Like I'm Fixin' to Die Rag," played at the original Woodstock concert.

LA Weekly: "For those in need of having their dervish whirled, the Bay Area's **Fishtank Ensemble** are the rompin', stompin' leaders of cross-pollinated Gypsy music." Members of the Ensemble met in 2005 at an Oakland performance space called the Fishtank. They recorded their debut album, *Super Raoul*, just three weeks later. ("Raoul" is Gypsy slang for "cool.") Their recent album is *Samurai Over Serbia*.

Col. Bruce Hampton & the Aquarium Rescue Unit
Atlanta, Georgia, USA

The band has toured with Phish, and members have played in side projects Frogwings and Leftover Salmon. Obviously, this is a band best kept moist. Features guitar hero Jimmy Herring.

Citizen Fish Bath, UK

Evolved from the Subhumans, who reformed in 1998, and band members now play in both groups. Lyrics often focus on vegetarianism, anti-consumerism and radical activism. Name: "Pete the Roadie made it up. It sounded good, so we kept it."

Phish Burlington, Vermont, USA

Known for their live performances and devoted fan base, Phishheads. For their first gig, they went by the name Blackwood Convention, a contract bridge term. (Quick, Mom, gimme a band name!) As often happens, the band had a gig but no name. Drummer Jon Fishman's nickname, "Fish," came in handy, later getting a more creative spelling.

Fishbone
Los Angeles, California, USA

Funk-metal from the band with the highly recognizable circular bony fish logo. They've recorded and toured with the Red Hot Chili Peppers, the Beastie Boys and Outkast. They've appeared in several films, including the blaxsploitation spoof *I'm Gonna Git You Sucka*. Latest album: *Still Stuck in Your Throat*.

Blue Öyster Cult

Long Island, New York's famous Blue Öyster Cult has been playing their melodic form of metal since in 1967. Early names included Soft White Underbelly and Santos Sisters. The name Blue Öyster Cult comes from a poem written by manager Sandy Pearlman in the 1960s. (Pearlman had also come up with the name Soft White Underbelly, a phrase used by Winston Churchill to describe the strategic opening presented by Italy during World War II.) In Pearlman's poetry, the Blue Öyster Cult were aliens who were sent to secretly shape Earth's history. The umlaut was added to Öyster by former keyboardist-guitarist Allen Lanier. (Umlauts are a traditional metal-band badge of honor.)

Blue Öyster Cult was the subject of a *Saturday Night Live* comedy sketch by Christopher Walken and Will Farrell in 2000, when attention was focused on the use of a percussive cowbell in the band's most famous song, "(Don't Fear) the Reaper." The sketch generated the pop-culture catch-phrase "More cowbell!" To show that they can take a joke, the band has responded by having a roadie play a cowbell on stage during performances of the 1976 hit.

Babel Fish Oslo, Norway
The yellow leech-like language translation creature in *The Hitchhiker's Guide to the Galaxy*.

Hootie & the Blowfish
Columbia, South Carolina, USA
The band's name comes from two of singer Darius Rucker's college choir friends, neither of them a band member. One had a round, owlish face and was nicknamed Hootie. The other had puffy cheeks and so was called the Blowfish. Rucker is often thought of as Hootie and the band, the Blowfish. Neither is either.

Rumblefish
Wellington, New Zealand; Istanbul, Turkey; Amsterdam, Netherlands; Hagatna, Guam; Cambridge, Ontario, Canada; Bellville, Illinois, USA; Neuss, Nordrhein-Westfalen, Germany; Korea; etc. *Rumble Fish* is the title of a popular young adult novel by S.E. Hinton.

Hot Tuna
Washington, DC, USA
A spin-off from Jefferson Airplane, formed by bassist Jack Casady and guitarist Jorma Kaukonen. The name Hot Tuna came when someone Kaukonen knew called out, "Hot tuna!" in response to this line in Blind Boy Fuller song "Keep on Truckin'": "What's that smell like fish, oh baby?"

Red Snapper Hammersmith, UK
This experimental-funk trio has toured with Prodigy and the Foo Fighters. A same-named jam band in Springfield, Missouri, got their name from the specials board at the Thai restaurant where they play their weekly gig: "Red Snapper Tonight."

Hamilton, New Zealand's **mOoFiSh** plays "adult alternative modern rock dark eclectic rock acoustic ambient dance and insane folk." Singer-songwriter Rhonda Johnson adds, "The name originated from my nick fish...and we manage a dairy farm, so there's the moo."

Vicious Fishes
Toronto, Ontario, Canada
It just sounds cool.

Kilgore Trout
Seattle, Washington (electric jazz); Jersey City, New Jersey (punk); Silverthorne, Colorado (jam-funk); Midland City, Ohio (garage); Cranston, Rhode Island (ambient); Bochum, Germany (goth-punk).
The science-fiction writer Kilgore Trout is a recurring character in Kurt Vonnegut's novels. Vonnegut has said the character is based on Theodore Sturgeon, a man whom he befriended in Truro, Massachusetts, in the 1950s.

The Northern Pikes
Saskatoon, Saskatchewan, Canada
Northern pikes are among the largest freshwater fish. Members assembled from prairie rock bands the Idols, Doris Daye and 17 Envelope. Songs: "She Ain't Pretty," "Things I Do for Money."

Great White
Los Angeles, California, USA
The great white shark is the largest known predatory fish. The band released *Once Bitten…* in '87, followed by *…Twice Shy* in 1989. In 2003 Great White was playing in a Rhode Island club when their pyrotechnic devices started a fire that killed 100 people, including band guitarist Ty Longley, and injured another 200.

Swimming with Sharks
Coffs Harbour, South Wales, Australia Screamo death-metal to be digested by.

We Versus the Shark
Athens, Georgia, USA
In the water or blindfolded in a WWE cage match in Vegas?

Things Found in Sharks
Ipswich, UK
ReverbNation.com: "Bursting forth from the slurry pool of mediocrity that 'indie music' has become, Things Found In Sharks are here to reaffirm your faith in melodies and riffs. Fuzzed out Fender Jaguars and rhythms with the punch of Ali combine to create an explosion of sonic intensity. They are a band you will grow to love more than the essential organs in your body." Some things that have been found in sharks: an unopened bottle of wine, a human skull, a suit of armor, a torpedo, a bundle of magazines.

Beer for Dolphins
San Diego, California, USA
From a bass-player chat room: "The Beer for Dolphins name comes from a song on Guitarist Mike Keneally's second solo album, *Boil That Dust Speck*."

12.09.03

felix Street

ultradolphins

hercules hercules (7:00) eat the evidence

Ultra Dolphins swim in Richmond, Virginia. They don't have much to say about themselves, and with only a couple of releases, they haven't racked up a lot of press, but they tour hard and are developing a solid fan base in the US and UK. PunkNews.org: "Ultra Dolphins play the type of spasmodic post-hardcore that puts you in situations you should feel uncomfortable in, but somehow, you sort of enjoy."

Squid Vicious   Austin, Texas, USA

A pun on Sid Vicious. Song: "Squid Nachos." Contributed the track "Spy School Graduation Theme" to a Shadowy Men on a Shadowy Planet tribute album.

New Squids on the Dock

Park Ridge, Illinois, USA

New Kids on the Block get the cephalopod treatment. Formed in 2006 as Cap'n Crunch & the Cereal Killers. Winners of $500 top prize at Bobbapalooza battle of the bands at South Park Church.

Close Lobsters   Paisley, Scotland

"According to legend, the band's name was derived from their inability to decide between two prospective names: the Close and the Lobsters."

Chocolate Starfish

Melbourne, Australia

Another name for the, uh, mahogany knot, uh, rusty sheriff's badge….

The Crabs

Great Yarmouth, East Anglia, UK

Formed in 1974, recorded a single as the Fulham Furies, dedicated to Fulham Football Club. Band's slogan: "Catch the Crabs." Some members of the band joined the backup band for Max Splodge after his hit, "Two Pints of Lager and a Packet of Crisps."

Inflatable Boy Clams

San Francisco, California, USA

Post-punk performance art. Members also played in the Pink Section and Naked City. Their song "I'm Sorry" involves two roommates doing increasingly worse things to each other and then apologizing.

Ozric Tentacles   Somerset, UK

Legend has it that in 1984 the musicians who would become Ozric Tentacles met at Stonehenge Free Festival and had a stoned conversation about names for breakfast cereals. Someone suggested Ozric Tentacles, and thus was born one of the most enduring bands of the British festival scene.

The Ominous Seapods

Plattsburgh, New York, USA

If you're influenced by Ozric Tentacles and Phish, what can you call yourself?

Sh! The Octopus

Detroit, Michigan, USA

Sh! The Octopus is an obscure 1937 film involving strangers trapped in a deserted lighthouse, where they are terrorized by a killer octopus and a criminal named after the title creature. Randy Bishop began performing as Sh! The Octopus in July 2003. Guitarist Andy Stachowiak joined in 2005, followed by drummer Joel Pearson, bassist Chris Sesta and vocalist-pianist Christine Baxter.

NAMES
STILL AVAILABLE

Thrill Krill Cult

Sea Slug Run

Beluga Supremacists

Smells Like Fish

The Shark Cards

Manateezer Grind

The Cod Botherers

Flipper's Briny Secret

Lobster College

The Muskelloungers

Giant Clams of the Bikini Atoll

Humble Octopi

The Spider to the Fly

Lime Spiders

Sydney, Australia's Lime Spiders were once described in *Rolling Stone* as "the Sex Pistols on acid." They were heavily influenced by '60s psychedelic rock but brought a post-punk energy as well.

Starting in 1979, the band played two years of pub gigs before entering a 3-week battle of the bands competition with 63 other Sydney-area bands. They won and received a recording contract as first-place prize. (Radio Birdman won 6 years earlier.) Their Australian chart hits include "Slave Girl" and "Weirdo Libido." The Goo Goo Dolls included a cover of the Lime Spiders' "Slave Girl" on their set list for their 1995 *A Boy Named Goo* tour.

The band's name is based on the non-alcoholic Australian cocktail Lime Spider, a combination of vanilla ice cream and lime soda (or lime syrup and lemonade) served in a highball glass.

The Lime Spiders have toured with the Black Crowes, Hoodoo Gurus and Public Image Ltd, among many others. They have disbanded and regrouped numerous times, most recently in 2007.

Spiders, Ticks, Scorpions

Arachnid Marsa, Malta
Death-metal band formed in 1996, its name inspired by the 1990 film *Arachnophobia*. Songs about psychokillers and modern society.

Spider
New York City, New York, USA
Their "New Romance (It's a Mystery)" hit #39 in the US in 1980. Drummer Anton Fig joined Paul Shaffer's band on *Late Night with David Letterman*.

The Amazing Spider Band
Winnipeg, Manitoba, Canada
"Music inspired by the '60s *Spiderman* animated series." They reinterpret the *Spiderman* theme and other songs based on the characters from the Marvel comics series.

The Pink Spiders
Nashville, Tennessee, USA
Power-pop trio formed in 1993. Their "Little Razorblade" has been featured on the TV show *The Hills*. In a Beartrappods.com interview, bassist Jon Decious said, "I guess we made a list of names and that was the one that stood out the most. Also, 'the Pink Spiders' is another term for 'the Assholes.'"

Spidersuit
Los Angeles, California, USA
The question, of course, is *which* spider suit: the usual "good" red-and-black suit or the creeping, evil-alien, black spider suit.

Black Circus Tarantula Rome, Italy
Debut album *UFO HiFi*.
Song: "Chest Brain."

Black Widow Leicester, UK
A turn-of-the-70s band that emerged out of Pesky Gee! More famous for their occult interests than the actual music. The band's stage show centered on the female demon Astaroth. Their 1970 Isle of Wight concert featured the mock sacrifice of a nude woman. Guitarist-vocalist Jim Gannon went on to play with Alice Cooper.

THE YUCCA SPIDERS, from Quedlinburg, Germany. Guitarist-vocalist Val Herdam: "When we first started the band in 1993, we called ourselves Grampa's Toombstones, which was a reference to Grampa Munster. The new name, the Yucca Spiders, seemed cool. It has an urban legend vibe to it. It sounds like a dangerous animal or maybe a South American sports team." *Outsider... Toprider* is the Yucca Spiders' 1999 debut album. Their vinyl-only LP *Zodiac* was released in 2003, and a new, untitled album is now in the can.

THE TICKS are Emma Levy on bass, Sue LaVallee on guitar, Julia Randall on drums, and all three on vocals. This all-female garage-pop trio from Hyannis, Massachusetts, began in 1999. They are often compared to the B-52s for their shared sense of fun, irony and their party-power vocals. "We have songs about the obvious girl-band crap, like boys we love or hate and bad days and stuff, but we also write about kicking each other out of the band and jellyfish and Nancy Drew." Albums: *So Young, So Bad* and *Pick Me!* Songs: "Mental Ethical Breakdown" and "Ginkgo Biloba."

Tarantula   Portugal

Created by the Barros brothers, guitarist Paul and drummer Luís, in 1981. They established a school for rock and metal music in 1990, "teaching young talents how to rock the block properly."

The Tarantula Waltz
Stockholm, Sweden

These Swedes now live in Glasgow. The Italian dance known as the tarantella ("tarantula") is not a waltz, but it is one of the most widely known dances in Italy, with each region having its own variation. One permutation emulates the disjointed agitation of a tarantula-bite victim.

The Twistin' Tarantulas
Detroit, Michigan, USA

Fronted by "Pistol" Pete Midtgard on bass and vocals. Albums: *Attack of the …* [Twistin' Tarantulas], *Welcome to Our Underworld* and *El Destroyo*.

The Soul Mites
Columbia, South Carolina, USA

Pun on soul mates. Members of this funk-rock fusion band met while attending the University of South Carolina in the early '90s. They have performed with George Clinton, Hootie & the Blowfish and Our Lady Peace.

Mitebites   Canberra, Australia

Australian grunge trio with the song "Bite Me." Mites are believed to have existed for about 400 million years. One tropical species is among the strongest animals in the world, known to lift 1,182 times its own weight.

Scorpions   Hanover, Germany

When rhythm guitarist Rudolf Schenker started the hard-rocking Scorpions in 1965, they had a beat band sound. But in 1969, with younger brother Michael Schenker on lead guitar and Klaus Meine on vocals, they soon established their metal edge. Rudolf has said that he wanted a name that sounded deadly and chose Scorpions for their deadly sting. Their biggest hit was the single "Rock You Like a Hurricane." Scorpions were one of the first rock bands to play in the Soviet Union.

Scorpion Wind   USA/UK

Basically a collaboration between Death in June's Douglas P. and industrial music guy Boyd Rice. A solpugid, a non-venomous relative of spiders and scorpions, is often called a wind scorpion.

NAMES
STILL AVAILABLE

With All My Mites

Wolfspidermother

The Spinnerets

Banana Spiders
in Pajamas

Black Widow
Pension Plan

World Wide Web

Big Bag of Ticks

Lyme Lords

Scorpion Corpse

The Blacklight
Scorpions

Daddy Longlegs
& the Hip Replacements

Fly Spiders

43

Adam & the Ants

Stuart Goddard (Adam Ant) started with Bazooka Joe (named for the bubblegum brand). They *headlined* the first Sex Pistols show in 1975, but inspired by the Sex Pistols' performance and London's punk craze, Goddard quit Bazooka Joe to form a new, edgier band. Rehearsing as the B-Sides, sans drummer, the group went nowhere. Meanwhile, Goddard made his way into the city's punk scene.

He formed the Ants in 1977. On the name: "I wasn't shaped like David Bowie or Alice Cooper, who were my heroes. I wasn't skinny. I was more muscular. I felt more like a Renaissance painting of Adam in the Garden of Eden. 'The Ants' was from the Beatles, of course. 'Adam and the Ants' seemed to roll off the tongue well."

A number of lineup changes led to 1980's *Kings of the Wild Frontier* album, which went to #1 in the UK, with the single "Antmusic" hitting #2. The subsequent album, *Prince Charming*, delivered two #1 singles. In 1982 the band won a Grammy award for Best New Artist, and Adam broke up the group to pursue a solo career.

Ants & Termites

AntHill Mob
Stourbridge, UK and Collingswood, New Jersey, USA

The Perils of Penelope Pitstop was a Hanna-Barbera animated TV show that aired from 1969 to 1971. Among the characters in that show were the Ant Hill Mob, seven diminutive gangsters with exaggerated personality traits akin to the Seven Dwarfs. An ant hill discovered in Northumberland, UK, measures over 5 feet 6 inches (168 cm) tall and houses more than 500,000 ants.

Red Ant Army
Vancouver, British Columbia, Canada

A "progressive-metal" band also known as R.A.A. Red ants don't like peppermint. Their fans probably know this; as do their enemies.

Ants Have Voices
Santa Fe, New Mexico, USA

Self-described as "Modern Alternative (Proletariat) Rock." Daniel Trujillo (guitar, vocals) appears to be going for the lowly ant as common man thing. Meanwhile, Dr. Robert Hickling of Ole Miss University posts a fine collection of black fire ant stridulation sounds.

Amazon Ant
Everett, Washington, USA

Self-description: "Paranormal Rock." Album: *Out of the Hole* (2005). Some species of Amazonian ants can't care for their young due to the shape of their mandibles, thus they raid the colonies of similar species and bring back pupae that are raised to perform this duty. Without the "slaves," they wouldn't exist.

International Band of the Year at the 2006 Southern California Music Awards, **ANTHILL** is an alternative power-pop band from Port Coquitlam, British Columbia, Canada. Centered around lead vocalist Mark Osachoff, the band also features Brian Minato (bass), Graham Tuson (keyboards, piano, vocals), JJ Blood (guitar) and Brock Pytel (drums), all of whom contribute to the songwriting process.

Eden Ants

Toronto, Ontario, Canada

Vocalist Adymm Ender from a PeonCulture.com interview: "The band name is inspired by Salvador Dali's works and attempts to embody the concept of a tense dichotomy where extremes are impossible." Ants appear frequently in Dali's work, usually symbolizing decay or simply serving to make inorganic matter appear organic. Eden Ants was founded in 2000 by the Montreal-born Ender brothers. Joining Adymm is guitarist Rob Ender, drummer Ryan MacMaster, bassist Joe False and a guitarist known simply as Wolfgang.

The Fire Ants

Seattle, Washington, USA

This was drummer Chad Channing's band after he left Nirvana and was replaced by Dave Grohl. Vocals and guitar were provided by brothers Kevin and Brian Wood, whose brother Andy Wood was a major figure in the pre-Nirvana Seattle rock scene. Members went on to form the Methodists, East of the Equator, Redband, Devilhead, Regan Hagar and Before Cars. A fire ant will bite then sting. When one stings, they all sting.

Piss Ant

Los Angeles, California, USA

Sexploitation rock. Known for their publicity stunts, falsified background stories, and firing each other on stage. Song: "Your Best Sucks." In the US, a piss ant (or pissant) is a tiny ant that infests homes. The diminutive insult stems from this: "You little piss ant!" The original piss ant was a larger European wood ant responsible for a urine-like odor when its formic acid mixed with its pine nesting material.

Bristol, UK-based **Termites** introduce themselves: "Sam plays the piano and the guitar and sings some things. He likes cheese, salami and shoes. Ali plays guitar, bass, occasional drums and sings the leftovers. Alfonse Mucha is one of his heroes. Stevie plays lead drums, and dabbles with the melodica and musical saw. The boy Joe beats the bass and yells along."

Atomic Ants   Trento, Italy

A funk-metal band formed in 2001. Debut album: *Keep Cool and Dry* (2006). The 1954 horror film *Them!* features giant radioactive ants created by nuclear testing in the American desert and bent on destroying humankind. (In one scene, Leonard Nimoy can be seen taking vital communication from an IBM machine.)

The Termites

Kilmarnock, Scotland

Heyday in the late 1980s but reformed in 2005. The Termites play psychobilly and cowpunk, with themes of violence and speed. Recent album: *Kicked in the Teeth*.

NAMES
STILL AVAILABLE

Antarctic Ants

The Outstanding
War Ants

Drone Bone

Outsourced Workers

Mute Ant Glee Club

Future Ant Farmers
of America

MiscreAnts

Subterranean Homesick
Blue Ants

Termite
Queen for a Day

Mound Pounders

The Cellulose Bistro

This Isn't Rice

The Beatles

John Lennon's first skiffle group was called the Blackjacks, at least until they discovered a more established group with the same name, at which point they became the Quarry Men, named for the Quarry Bank area where the boys lived and Quarry Bank High School.

The group went through several name changes. They were Johnny and the Moondogs for a talent show and handful of gigs. John had been thinking how much he liked "the Crickets," the name of Buddy Holly's band, which led to a discussion of beetles, the intentional misspelling the Beatals, advice leading to Long John & the Silver Beetles, abbreviation as the Silver Beetles, a return to Hamburg as the Silver Beetles, and a final polish to the Beatles.

In the second revised edition of his Beatles biography, Hunter Davies suggests that Beatles' press man Derek Taylor told him the name was inspired by scenes in the film *The Wild One* in which there is a rival bike gang known as the Beetles.

Everyone agrees that no matter who suggested Beetles, John said, yeah, we'll spell it Beatles. We're a beat group.

Beatles & Bugs

The Dead Beetles
Portland, Oregon, USA
A weird name, given the Beatles mortality rate. "Building a More Spacious Pigeon Hole, Keeping Pop Weird." With four-part vocal harmonies, electric and acoustic guitars, bass, cello, flutes and clarinets, drums and percussion.

Beetlefly
Baden-Württemberg, Germany
Songwriting duo Florian König and Lorenz Blankenhorn. Their friend Benni Hägele suggested the name.

Bedbugs
Eskilstuna, Sweden
The common bedbug feeds on the flesh of humans. In this hardcore punk trio Lothar, Dominator and Voyager O.D. are all credited with contributing screams. Songs: "Stick the Pole Through My Heart" and "Oyster Moist."

The Buggles
London, UK
A turn-of-the-80s studio project for Trevor Horn and Geoff Downes, with shared songwriting credit for Bruce Wooley, who co-wrote the band's biggest hit, "Video Killed the Radio Star." Horn says he chose Buggles because "it was the most disgusting name I could think of at that time." But the CD booklet for the remastered *The Age of Plastic* says the name it arose from a pun on Beatles, a private joke between Horn and Downes. Wooley went on to form Camera Club with Thomas Dolby, while Horn and Downes joined Yes temporarily to replace Rick Wakeman and Jon Anderson.

Groove-based Seattle jazz-funk. **Critters Buggin** began in 1993 as a trio, with Matt Chamberlain, Skerik and Brad Houser. John Bush contributed loops and percussion. Bush, Chamberlain and Houser were veterans of Edie Brickell & the New Bohemians. Pearl Jam's Stone Gossard produced their first album for his Loosegroove label. Mike Dillon joined in 1998. Seven albums, as well as a DVD entitled *Get the Clackervalve and the Old Clobberd Biscuits Out and Smack the Grand Ham Clapper's Mother.*

BugGiRL
Wollongong Rock City, Australia
Hard-rocking brother-sister duo with Amber (aka BugGiRL) on guitars and vocals and Clinno (aka Mallets of Mayhem) on drums and backing vocals.

Bughole Limburg, Hesse, Germany
Bughole is a term for an air-bubble cavity in poured concrete. Thrash-metal guys with subtle sentiments. EP: *Fucked Up*. Album: *Fight Me.*

Bughead Orlando, Florida, USA
The term *buggin'* or *bug out* means to be tripping or freaking out. A *bughead* is a large, nicely rolled joint. Bughead plays "drunken reggae for the discriminating alcoholic."

Bug Guts
Laytonville, California, USA
Windshield-washing music. Themes of farms, vegetarianism and animal rights. Songs: "Cattle Battle," "Hope's the Dope," "Magic Garbage Ride."

Bugdust Melbourne, Australia
Alternative metal band formed in 2002. Debut album *Welcome to the City of Snakes* was recorded with producer Neil Kernon (Sex Pistols, Queen, Cannibal Corpse, Judas Priest).

The Ugly Bug Band
Toronto, Ontario, Canada
According to bassist and lead vocalist Michael Kaler, the name came from Daniel Pinkwater. "He's written a whole bunch of children's and young adults' novels, and he mentions a band called the Ugly Bug Band in two of them. He's one of my favorite authors in the world, and I haven't dared ask him for permission to use the name because it would be far too crushing if he said no. His best books are probably *The Snarkout Boys and the Avocado of Doom*, *Lizard Music*, and *Borgel*.

Bugga Cornwall, UK
Glam-punk. "Brought together by the winds of fate, a love of all things pink and a habit of wearing women's clothes out on the piss." Debut EP: *Cool as Fuck* (2006). They bill themselves as the second-best boy band in the UK (after Take That).

The **Bug Nasties**' debut CD asks, *Which Way Ya Wanna Go?* This Seattle quartet is "heavy on '60s soul and UK Mod sounds. We want to see the people dance like they've never been hit!" The current lineup features Brother James Burdyshaw (Sinister Six) on vocals, guitar and harp; Scott LaRose (Aerobic Death) on bass; Vic "The Stick" Hart (ex-Boss Martians) on drums; and Tom "Peerless" Price (Gas Huffer) on Farfisa organ.

The Lightning Bug Situation
San Francisco, California, USA
Songs: "The Unhappy Robot Version of Me vs. Coldplay" and "Enzo Garcia and His Mind Control Device."

Weevil Knievel Chichester, UK
Pun on the name Evil Knievel, legendary motorcycle daredevil. Debut album: *This is Where the Chorus Goes.*

Dämnweevil
Oakland, California, USA
They claim to play trash-sludge-metal. So sludgy and metallic, they require two sets of umlauts in their name. Debut album: *Human Auditory Torture Experiment.*

NAMES
STILL AVAILABLE

Bughuggers

Assassin Bug
Take Out

The Crunchback
of Norma's Drain

Boll Weevil Bowlers

The Whirligig Beetles

Mandible Mandingo

David &
the Goliath Beetles

Grotto of the
Bug Nymphs

Wing Shield
vs Windshield

The Faux Scarab Four

Flicks Me Off

Thugbug

The Bees/
A Band of Bees

The retro-soul Isle of Wight band the Bees started as a duo, but currently records and performs as a six-piece, with most members being multi-instrumentalists. Their first album, *Sunshine Hit Me* (2002), was recorded in band founder Paul Butler's home studio, a shed at the back of his garden.

In the US, they're known as A Band of Bees, owing to a rights conflict over their name. Butler, in the *Sydney Morning Herald*: "Oh, god, the Band of Bees. That's crazy, innit? It's just in America. Only in America. There was a band [also called the Bees] that didn't have a record deal and didn't have an album out, but [who] threatened to sue us. We'd already had an album out, had got a major deal, but, no, they're the Bees. They registered the name in America, so, now [we're] the Band of Bees."

Their cover of the Brazilian song "A Minha Menina" has been used in four advertisements to date and has generated a lot of interest in the band. Their most recent album is 2007's *Octopus*.

Bees, Wasps and Hornets

The Beekeepers
Derby, UK
Mid-90s punk-pop band on Beggars Banquet label. One full-length album, *Third Party, Fear and Theft*. Songs: "Do You Behave Like That at Home?" and "I Only Want to See You Suffer."

The Beekeeper Summit
Belfast, UK
Self-description: "[Sounds like] you're in fourth place in a school race and you realize you haven't got it in the tank to make a medal, and you may as well not have bothered competing." EPs: *On Viper Point* (2003) and *Sea and Sadness* (2007).

National Beekeepers Society
Madison, Wisconsin, USA
Song: "Slackerevolution." They've drawn comparisons with Pavement.

Space Bee Lima, Peru
Peruvian space rock. Debut album: *Live in Space*. Band history: "Space Bee was born out of a dynamic evolution of the species, caused by the continuous mutations, as painful as vital and necessary to explain, by natural selection, its hybrid result." Song: "Where the Sunshine Goes."

Beecake Glasgow, Scotland
Beecake lead singer-guitarist Billy Boyd played Peregrin "Pippin" Took in the *Lord of the Rings* trilogy films. The natural inclination is to assume the F was dropped from Beefcake to create Beecake, but "the inspiration for the final name came from friend Dominic Monaghan [he played "Merry"] who sent Billy an MMS [mobile phone message] of a cake with bees on it during a trip in Spain." Debut EP: *Just B*.

Jaymz Bee
& the Royal Jelly Orchestra
Toronto, Ontario, Canada
Tongue-in-cheek lounge-jazz interpretations of classic Canadian songs by Bryan Adams, Rush, Crash Test Dummies, Alannis Morissette and others. Albums: *ClintEastWoodyAllenAlda* and *Seriously Happy*.

Hive Smasher Massachusetts, USA
"Hive Smasher is being called one of the most aggressive metal bands in Massachusetts."

Honey Bee
Szeged-Budapest, Hungary
Female-fronted electro-pop with a "My Honey Is Makin' Money" t-shirt.

Boobalah

The NYC band **Bee Zoo** released their album *Boobalah* in 1998. Singer-songwriter Rob Kudybah: "One of my ex-girlfriends is French, and her mom used to always end a phone call, or even in person, by saying, 'bisou, bisou,' which means 'kiss, kiss,' so I thought to myself, that would be a cool band name: the Bee Zoo." Kudyba has also played in Exit 8, Area 44, Great Jones, Ivanhoe and Arthur Kill.

Life by Misadventure is the recent album from London's **Bee Stings.** "Recorded over two years in three studios and featuring 14 musicians...." From the band's bio: "If a track requires a brass quartet, a vintage '70s synthesizer or a veterinary surgeon, then that's what [it] will get." They won a reader's poll and Single of the Month on SubbaCulture.com.

The Honeycombs
London, UK

This mid-60s beat band started as the Sheratons, but founder Martin Murray had worked in a hair salon where [drummer] Honey Lantree was his assistant, so they decided to combine Honey and Combs.

Honeytrap Coventry, UK
Exuberantly giddy violin-and-guitar-fronted quartet. Debut album: *Follies in Great Cities* (2008). Songs: "Mussolini's Son," "Great Firewall of China" and "Let's Do Naked Dancing."

Runt Hörnet Barrow, UK
Previously part of 12 ft. Machete. Has an umlaut, so you know it's heavy. Bassist plays the "monobass": "I made it! It's a big lump of metal pipe with one string, no frets and a pickup!"

Hornet Leg
Portland, Oregon, USA

"[Singer-guitarist] Chris Sutton's nickname is Hornet Leg, but that's probably only because 'that guy in all those fucking bands' doesn't have much ring to it." The nickname appears to have something to do with the funny way that he walks.

Green Hornet
Groningen, Netherlands

The Green Hornet was a superhero on an American radio series broadcast in the 1930s. In a 1960s TV series, the role of his sidekick, Kato, was played by martial artist Bruce Lee. The Dutch Green Hornet is a dance-punk trio formed in 1992.

W.A.S.P.
Los Angeles, California, USA

There's a story that a band member saw a wasp, decided to use it as a name, then made it an acronym so it would stand out more. The band and its fans have generated many explanations as to what the acronym stands for: "We Are Satan's People," "We Are Sexual Perverts," "We Ain't Sure Pal," and so on. Famous for their live shows, in which half-naked models are tied to a torture rack and raw meat is hurled at the audience.

Yellowjackets
Southern California, USA

Keyboardist Russell Ferrante: "We were still the Robben Ford Band... Jimmy [Haslip, bass] brought in a sheet full of possible names, most just awful. The one that popped out was Yellowjackets, as it seemed to [denote] something lively, energetic, and something with a 'sting.'"

NAMES
STILL AVAILABLE

A Bee

Hornet Coleman

Yellowjacket Whiteshoes

Beestung Hips

Wasp (Not Wasp)

Tasmanian Crop Pollination Association

Honey Hands

The Tonedeaf Stingers

Cuckoo Wasps

The Hivewreckers

Dub Daubers

Buzz Ted

Crickets, Grasshoppers, Locusts, Cicadas, Roaches

Buddy Holly & the Crickets

There's the legend about the sound of a cricket being heard on tape during playback in the Texas studio where Buddy Holly & the Crickets were recording, but the prevailing story is that the band chose their name from an encyclopedia. Inspired by the name the Spiders (one of Buddy's favorite bands), they flipped through Insects and considered the Grasshoppers and the Beetles but chose the Crickets because they liked the idea of a bug making music by rubbing its legs together.

They had to choose a name in order to record "That'll Be the Day" because Buddy had a contract with another record company, Decca, but they figured Decca might not notice if they used a group name instead of Buddy Holly's name. "That'll Be the Day" took its title from a phrase that John Wayne's character said repeatedly in the 1956 film *The Searchers*. While they were recording "I'm Gonna Love You Too," a cricket did get into the recording studio, and they left the sound on the end of the track.

Cricket Culture
Sacramento, California, USA
From their CDBaby site: "Cricket Culture is a myth that writes itself, a tale that keeps growing…it's an idea devoid of fact, freeform lines that can't draw a box, not static but ecstatic, not mass-produced, but produced for the masses…it's a war of the worlds, it's peace on earth, a madness which begat genius, it's one hand clapping, two bodies slapping, sporadic, erratic…it burns your skin, soothes your inner id, a precise delirium, the universe screaming out!"

The Mooncrickets
Chicago, Illinois, USA
Members come from Chicago-area bands Bourbon Decay, Groovestation, peatmoss, the Falling Wallendas and the Turnstyles. If a cricket chirped on the moon and there was no air there, would it make a sound? Interesting name choice: Moon cricket is a derogatory term for a person of African descent, specifically a neighbor who is noisy after dark.

Deep Cricket Night
Chicago, Illinois, USA
Two percussionists, cello, guitar and mandolin or banjo doing "melodic noir" and "creepy country." Album: *Honeymoon Tattoo*.

Grasshopper Takeover
Omaha, Nebraska, USA
GTO for short. Singer-guitarist Curtis Grubb had a near-fatal accident while hunting pheasant on the Nebraska plains: "I just lay there with this insane ringing in my ears, afraid to open my eyes, thinking I would just see whiteness. When I finally opened my eyes, the entire sky was filled with a swarming, amorphous blackness, and then I lost consciousness. The only thing I remember thinking was that grasshoppers had taken over."

Halo of Locusts
Richmond, Virginia, USA
Sounds like: "Zombie sex…." Not sure how they know, but I suspect they're right.

NEW YORK CITY • The **Grasshoppers** play a melodic retro (in a good way) style of rock, with strong arrangements and harmony vocals. Guitarist-vocalist Marco Joachim: "The name for The Grasshoppers was obviously because we were into the Beatles, but also because we were younger and into smoking some funny cigarettes and thought the double meaning of grass (*grass*hopper) would make a good name."

Members of San Diego's **the Locust** perform in form-fitting, full-body locust uniforms, complete with masks, and prefer to play lined up evenly on the stage (i.e. bass and drums don't hang back). The sound is massive and the lyrics are scathing attacks on mainstream politics and culture. Singer Justin Pearson has said, "I wanted to change the way people perceive music, or maybe just destroy it in general." Their 2007 album is *New Erections*.

Locust Furnace
Eureka, California, USA
Death-metal-grindcore. Song: "Recycled in Vomit." "Locust Furnace" is a song by Birmingham industrial-metal band Godflesh, from their 1989 *Streetcleaner*.

Locust on the Saddle
Budapest, Hungary
A little-known Hungarian western. Debut EP *Tourette Escapism*, followed by 2008's *AlphaMantis*.

Locust Resin   Crawley, UK
Self-description: "Sludge-fueled metalcore."

Cockroach Candies
Dinslaken, Germany
Album: *Blackout Generation*. Song: "Halloween Porn Queen." Members went on to form the Unkrauts and Silent Meow.

Papa Roach
Vacaville, California, USA
Contrary to the belief of many, Papa Roach is not (primarily) a drug reference: pop a roach. The band's name comes from vocalist Jacoby Shaddix's step-grandfather, Howard William Roatch, whose nickname was Papa Roach.

Sonic Roach Destruction Unit
Columbus, Ohio, USA
Vocalist Dave LaRosa: "Me and this guy I used to work with used to spend our breaks walking around and coming up with cool band names. There are so many bands with really lame names. We hit upon Sonic Roach Destruction Unit and we both went into hysterics." Songs: "Stockroom of Limited Insight" and "Exploding Porno Man."

The Cicadas
Nashville, Tennessee, USA
A side project of acclaimed singer-songwriter Rodney Crowell, with frequent collaborators Vince Santoro, Michael Rhodes and Steuart Smith. There are about 2,500 species of cicada worldwide. They are big, noisy, harmless to humans and a food source in parts of Asia, Africa and Latin America.

Cicada Omega
Portland, Oregon, USA
"A transcendental junkyard blues experiment" fronted by Rev. B.D. Winfield, with a band that plays the "suitcase bass" and "kitchenware percussion." Band members originate from Kentucky, and Rev. Winfield describes their sound as "an otherworldly blend of pounding rhythm, southern evangelism and electrified junk."

NAMES
STILL AVAILABLE

Famine Force

Omega

Jiminy Locust

18 Knees
on a Roach

Katydiddlers

The Legendary
Spittlebugs

Peckish Plague Papas

Övipositor!

Luck Less Crickets

Bug Eyed
Thorax Thumpers

Dog Day Cicadas

Will Chirp for Sex

Cricket Beer

Wild, Wild Mammals

Rabbits & Hares

Crusader Rabbit Stealth Band

After Jerry Garcia's death in 1995, fellow members of the Grateful Dead decided to disband, but Phil Lesh, Bob Weir and Mickey Hart soon created solo and group projects as outlets for their music. The remaining Dead most notably performed and toured as the Other Ones, but also appeared as the Crusader Rabbit Stealth Band. Concerts were usually surprise club gigs. Crusader Rabbit was the animated hero of a low-budget B & W TV series in 1950–51, often seen battling his main nemesis, Dudley Nightshade. The program was a collaboration between Jay Ward and cartoonist Alex Anderson. The two went on to found Television Arts Productions, and Ward produced *The Rocky and Bullwinkle Show* based on characters by Anderson. A series of 260 color episodes of *Crusader Rabbit* were made in 1957 and ran sporadically in syndication until the early '70s.

Rabbit   Newcastle, Australia
Rabbit's lead singer was replaced by AC/DC's first lead singer, Dave Evans, in 1974. European rabbits were brought to Australia in 1788 and reached plague numbers by 1890. Australia still battles its rabbit population.

Rabbit Fighter   Missouri, USA
"Rabbit Fighter" is the title of a song on the 1972 T. Rex album *The Slider*.

Year of the Rabbit
Los Angeles, California, USA
People born in the Chinese Year of the Rabbit are thought to be articulate, talented and ambitious.

Welsh Rabbit   Oregon, USA
Welsh Rarebit (or Rabbit) is a meal of grated sharp cheese mixed with beer, butter and mustard, then grilled atop slices of toast.

The Trojan Rabbit
Cincinnati, Ohio, USA
Substitute a huge wooden rabbit in the Trojan Horse myth.

Square Rabbit
New York City, New York , USA.
Not a very rock & roll name. A *square rabbit* is an early nineteenth-century architectural term for a type of flat, narrow molding.

Rabbits with Glasses
Orlando, Florida, USA
Rabbits love carrots; carrot consumption is said to contribute to good eyesight.

Rabbit in Your Headlights
Nizhny Novgorod, Russia
Run, rabbit, run. It's dissonant, low-fi grunge nouveau.

Rabbits Against Magic
New York City, New York, USA.
No more top hats.

Rabbit Pudding
Auckland, New Zealand
The New Zealand White's most common meat uses are as "rabbit roast, rabbit paté, rabbit pudding, rabbit pie, boiled rabbit, curried rabbit and fried rabbit."

Underground Mutton is the 2007 CD from Australian blues band **Jack Rabbit & the Pubic Hares**. "We first tried to register the name as a business in 1979, but they took offence to 'pubic,' so we had to settle for Jack Rabbit & the *Public* Hares and sign a declaration agreeing not to perform without the L. Of course, that lasted till we got out the door." "Underground mutton" was the term used for rabbit meat during the Depression.

Rabbits on Trampolines
Philadelphia–New York, USA
They jump. They jump higher.

Rabbitfoot
Boston, Massachusetts, USA
Good luck.

Rabbit Punch
Beach City, Ohio, and Provo, Utah
A rabbit punch is a hard blow to the back of the head or neck, the method often employed to kill livestock rabbits.

The Black Rabbits Kansas, USA
Their album *Let It Breed* references the copulative frequency of rabbits as well as the Rolling Stones' 1969 album, *Let It Bleed*.

Dead Rabbit
London, UK; Berlin and Königswinter, Germany; Helsinki, Finland; California, Alabama, upstate New York, USA
A great many rabbits died in the days before over-the-counter early pregnancy tests. Around 1927 a couple of scientists discovered that if you inject the urine of a pregnant woman into a female mouse, the levels of human chorionic gonadotropin caused its ovaries to hemorrhage. Of course, they had to cut open the mouse to see the ovaries. By the late 1940s rabbits were often used instead of mice (bigger, easier-to-examine ovaries?), and the term "rabbit test" became synonymous with "pregnancy test." The phrase "the rabbit died" came to mean "I'm pregnant." In fact the rabbit rarely survived either way, as it was deemed much more efficient to examine a dead rabbit than to perform the surgery, examine the ovaries, then stitch the animal back up again.

The Paper Rabbit Band
Puebla, Mexico An origami pattern.

New York City-based **WHITE RABBITS** were nominated for Best New Artist at the 2008 Plug Independent Music Awards. Their excellent new album is *Fort Nightly*. The white rabbit in Lewis Carroll's *Alice in Wonderland* is responsible for leading Alice down the rabbit hole and thus to her adventures in Wonderland. There is a long-held British superstition that on the first day of each month it is lucky to say "white rabbits" three times before speaking any other words.

Sonic Death Rabbit
Los Angeles, California, USA
They acknowledge the influence of "Emma and Georgie (Cristina's bunnies)" and admit to sounding like "a metalhead swallowing a Gameboy."

Rabbit Junk Seattle, Oregon, USA
Rabbits seemingly live to breed. Junk is slang for male genitalia. Rabbit Junk plays something called "hardclash." But they also sell hoodies.

Football Rabbit
Providence, Rhode Island, USA
On Animal Disguise Recordings. Rabbit could have picked a safer disguise.

Dr. Kasper's Rabbit Show Israel
This '90s Israeli rock band had no Dr. Kasper but gave wild performances while wearing make-up and costumes. Guitarist Oren Brazilay would strip to his skivvies, on which was sewn a rabbit.

NAMES
STILL AVAILABLE

Rabbits Dig
Burroughs

They Might Be
Flemish Giants

Hefner's Last Bunny

White Hares
Can't Jump

Herr March Häre

Rabbit-Proof Fez

Long Hare
Freaky People

My Foot in Your Pocket

The Degeneratizer
Bunnies

Hare M
(w/ Timbaland)

Genus Lepus

Immodest Rabbit

Echo and the Bunnymen

LIVERPOOL, UK

A post-punk quartet, Echo & the Bunnymen claim to have chosen their name so that they would never take themselves too seriously. Will Sergeant explained in an interview for the book *Liverpool Explodes!*: "We had this mate [Smelly Elly] who kept suggesting all these names like The Daz Men or Glisserol and the Fan Extractors. Echo and the Bunnymen was one of them. I thought it was just as stupid as the rest." Several sources suggest that the band bestowed the name "Echo" on the drum machine they employed before the arrival of real drummer Pete de Freitas, but the band publicly denied this rumour.

Singer Ian McCulloch is said to have proclaimed the Bunnymen the best group in the world in the mid-1980s, "better than the Mona Lisa... bigger than Henry V." Perhaps not, but at least seven of their albums landed in the UK Top 40 in the '80s and '90s, and a reformed, reconfigured version of the Bunnymen continues to record and perform in 2008.

Harelip Suffield, Connecticut, USA
The physical condition of the mouth known as cleft lip is said to resemble a hare's lip. The Chinese word for cleft lip is *tuchun*, "harelip."

Hare-Brained Unit Tokyo, Japan
Harebrained: foolish, flighty, with no more sense than a hare.

Harevolution Akron, Ohio, USA
Genre note: "black metal, death metal, jazz."

Bunnyranch Coimbra, Portugal
Moonlite BunnyRanch is a famous licensed house of prostitution near Carson City, Nevada.

Bunny Gone Bad
Jämtlands län, Sweden
Cute, fuzzy mammals turn to the dark side.

ULTRABUNNY • Danbury, Connecticut, USA When ideological differences led BunnyBrains to split up into two different bands called, respectively, BunnyBrains and BunnyBrains, fans became confused. Thus one BunnyBrains (the one featuring Bobby Bunny, Malcolm Tent, Pete Beest and "provacatrix" Cheryl) morphed happily into Ultrabunny. The name is a tribute to the band's favorite 1960s Japanese TV hero, Ultraman, as well as "our superlative universal bunnyness."

Bunny Wabbit
Indianapolis, Indiana, USA
Cartoon character Elmer Fudd's pronunciation of "bunny rabbit." The band's album *Straight Outta Briar Patch* combines the 19th-century Br'er Rabbit tale "The Briar Patch" with the landmark 1988 N.W.A. rap album *Straight Outta Compton*.

Bunnyslipper Hallands län, Sweden
Young band members wear pink bunny slippers.

Bunny Hop Samurai
Los Angeles, California, USA
The Bunny Hop dance craze is said to have been created at Balboa High School in San Francisco in 1952. Ray Anthony's big band recorded a tune called "Bunny Hop" as a 45 rpm single with "Hokey Pokey" on the flip side. Given the whole sword and kimono thing, it would be very difficult for a samurai to do the Bunny Hop.

Chubby Bunny
Salinas, California, USA
The game Chubby Bunny involves stuffing one's mouth with marshmallows until there is no more room, then reciting the phrase "chubby bunny." The winner is the person who can hold the most marshmallows without choking or swallowing.

Fluffy Bunny Smackdown
Studio City, California, USA
Cover band, except perhaps for their "Shake Your Bunny Maker." "Fluffy bunny" is a derogatory term applied to someone who claims to follow Wicca beliefs but is largely ignorant of this nature-based religion (known widely as witchcraft). It is also a term used by young males to denote "cute, sexy, chunky girls" they might be interested in.

Ether Bunny Omaha, Nebraska, USA and Toronto, Ontario, Canada
Ah, the ethereal Easter Bunny. Nice lispy pun. The name of an indie folk duo from Omaha and a side-project for Daniel Vahnke of Toronto's Vampire Rodents.

The Rough Bunnies Sweden
Bunnies are not rough. However, Swedish cousins Frida and Anna note that "sometimes life is too much to swallow, then it is fantastic to write a song about it." Their CD *The Flame* is a collaboration between the Rough Bunnies, "a boy called AOMBG and a girl called Lesbo Pig."

Bunny vs. Kitty
Mansfield, Massachusetts, USA
A delightful name for a thrash-metal electro-grindcore band.

Space Bunny
Sherman Oaks, California, USA
Like ski bunny only from outer space. Spacy indie girl pop including the rabbit-happy song "Quickie."

Jungle Bunnys
New Orleans, Louisiana, USA
Their MySpace page is wallpapered with jackalopes (antelope-horned rabbits), with the repeating quote, "There's little more demeaning than getting your butt kicked by a bunch of bunnies." "Jungle bunny" is a racial slur directed at a person of African descent. It's also the title of a filler instrumental tune off Who bassist John Entwistle's 1975 solo album, *Mad Dog*.

BunnySUICIDE
Leipzig, Sachsen, Germany
More true to its name, BunnySUICIDE offers electro-pop death metal with a military-drum twist.

BunnyBrains
Danbury, Connecticut, USA

Bobby Bunny: "Elisa Flynn and I were looking to start a new band to break away from our then current project, Invaders From Sears. We wanted to form the ultimate, shamelessly worst band on earth and … we were driving down this backwoods road and this rabbit stopped in front of us and just stood there. I said, 'Why do rabbits always just stand there waiting to get run over and won't move or anything?' And she said, 'Because they only have little bunny brains.' I immediately knew this was the perfect name for a band that was cute, yet pathetically stupid, and yet fraught with danger."

Chocolate Bunnies from Hell
Winnipeg, Manitoba, Canada
The melting point of chocolate is slightly below body temperature. If you go with the old fire-and-brimstone thing, then Hell is unimaginably hot but can't be hotter than 832 degrees Fahrenheit, the point at which brimstone vaporizes. Let me suggest a new saying: "You don't stand a chocolate bunny's chance in Hell."

Killer Bunny
Iceland
The Killer Rabbit of Caerbannog appears in the film *Monty Python and the Holy Grail* and the theatrical musical *Spamalot*. *Killer Bunnies and the Quest for the Magic Carrot* is a popular board game.

Arctic Monkeys

"It's just a name. Jamie, the guitarist, came up with it at school before we were in a band. He just always wanted to be in a band called Arctic Monkeys. [English fans just] chant 'Monkeys' at shows. In Canada last night they were chanting 'Arctic!'"

This Sheffield, UK, band was among the first to become successful as through its fans' internet response to its music. The group achieved chart success right from the start, with their first single, "I Bet You Look Good on the Dancefloor," climbing to #1 on the UK Singles chart. Their debut album, *Whatever People Say I Am, That's What I'm Not*, was the fastest-selling debut album in British music history, with the band going on to win the 2006 Mercury Prize, 2007 Brit Awards for Best British Album and Best British Band, and the praise of rock critics on both sides of the Atlantic.

The band's second album, 2007's *Favourite Worst Nightmare*, sold a quarter million copies in its debut week, and the group again picked up Brit Awards for Best British Album and Best British Group.

Monkeys • Primates and Rhyme Apes

The Monkees
Los Angeles, California, USA
Created in 1965 by producers for an NBC television series. The name echoed other '60s band names involving animals and minor misspellings, but also reflected the band's mischievous onscreen antics.

Java Monkey   Atlanta, Georgia, USA
Coffee + monkey. Usually not a good idea, but this band is comprised of session and touring musicians who have played with .38 Special, Ted Nugent, Jackson Browne, Dr. Hook, Derek Trucks, Joan Baez, Meatloaf and others.

Hung Monkey   Lancaster, UK
Don't stare.

Blow Monkeys   UK
The lead singer spent his adolescence in Australia. "Blow monkeys" is a derisive term for Aboriginal didgeridoo players.

Brass Monkey   UK
This 1980s folk group's name comes from an expression meaning "something so solid that it can only be affected by extremes." As in, "It's cold enough to freeze the balls off a brass monkey."

Monkey Puzzle
At least two of them, NZ and UK
The monkey puzzle tree is native to Chile but has been cultivated worldwide. Because the tree grows to heights of 130 ft/40 m, it would "puzzle a monkey as to how to climb it."

Monkey Swallows the Universe
Sheffield, UK
Monkeys are big in Sheffield.
(See Arctic Monkeys, left.)

Monkey Steals the Peach   USA
In martial arts, a hard upthrust groin slap to your opponent. Iron Hand followers clench the hand and rip away.

Sprung Monkey
San Diego, California, USA
Released from captivity and now in films on Van's Warped Tour, Conan O'Brien, 6 Australian tours, etc.

Monkey Finger   Bath, UK
"The Monkey's Finger" is a well-known science-fiction story by Isaac Asimov.

Monkey Hole   Valencia, Spain
Self-description: "Psychophonies from a violent party."

Monkey Gone Mad
Schenectady, New York, USA
Schenectady is not a natural environment for monkeys.

The 2006 CD *Monkey Picked Tea* from Scottish duo **Monkeyfrog**. After hours of playing pick-a-name with guitarist Grant Ritchie, musician-producer Marc Twynholm took a break to phone a friend. During the call, he mentioned both monkeys and frogs. Monkeyfrog? "I can see it in shiny metal on a black sleeve!" said Ritchie.

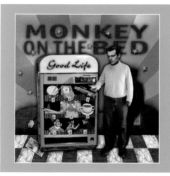

Monkey on the Bed

(1997–2001) was an original blues-rock band from Austin, Texas. Their *Good Life* CD is still available. Their name comes from the lyrics to a children's song: "One little monkey jumping on the bed / One fell off and bumped his head / Mama called the doctor and the doctor said / 'No more monkeys jumping on the bed!'"

Monkey Gun   Manchester, UK
A physics thing: A ball shot from a gun hits a falling target, demonstrating that gravity acts on both objects equally, independent of their initial states of motion. Originally hypothesized as, "If you shoot a falling monkey with a blowgun…."

Monkeys with Guns
British Columbia, Canada
More monkeys, more guns. Album: *Evolver*.

Monkey Jacket
Royal Oak, Michigan, USA
A tight-fitting, waist-length jacket worn by naval officers at formal mess dinners.

Blind Monkey Band
California, USA   See no evil.

Hot Monkey Love
New York City, USA
Best album title: *Speakin' Evil*

Monkey in a Lab Coat
Hopatcong, New Jersey, USA
What the Smartest Monkeys did after moving to New Jersey.

The Smartest Monkeys
Tennessee, USA   The "Scopes Monkey Trial," pitting Creation theory against Evolution theory, took place in Tennessee in 1925.

3 Legged Monkey   Oklahoma, USA
Competition for Hung Monkey.

Strobe Monkey   Japan
Self-description: "Superb latino/ techno tracks … produced by Blip Pilot."

Monkey Paw   Chicago, USA
In voodoo, a monkey paw can bring good luck. Best album title: *Hating You Is So Easy*

Monkeynut   Ohio, USA
Anacardium humile, a relative of the cashew. Also used as another name for peanut.

My Monkey   California, USA
Beatles song off the *The Beatles* white album: "Everybody's Got Something to Hide Except for Me and My Monkey."

Rainbow Butt Monkeys
Burlington, Ontario, Canada
Hey, who can remember the name "mandrill"? (Maybe the guys from the band Mandrill.) The Rainbow Butt Monkeys recorded one album, *Letter from Chutney*, before changing their name to Finger Eleven. See the "Body Parts" section for more on Finger Eleven.

Poptart Monkeys   Pennsylvania, USA
A Pop-Tart is a rectangular toaster pastry made by the Kellogg Company. You know what a monkey is.

THE WHEATMONKEYS

Since the release of their debut CD Danger in 2002, Saskatoon's Wheatmonkeys have toured relentlessly and appeared at such national industry showcases as Prairie Music Week, Canadian Music Week and the Western Canadian Music Awards. Darin Phieffer of Goldfinger plays drums on their new CD, Hotter Than a Pistol, which was mixed by engineer Mike Fraser (Hedley, GOB, Aerosmith, AC/DC, the Cult).

Monkeyshyne
Dallas, Texas, USA
Monkeyshyne is an acoustic-driven rock band with layered harmonies from two lead singers, crafted melodies and vintage rock sounds. "We are not mad at our parents, so we are not your average rock band."

Monkey Trouble
Valleyfield, Quebec, Canada
A popular old-school arcade game. Also, a 1994 film involving a monkey who picks pockets.

Ape Fight
Jersey City, New Jersey, USA
Ape fights aren't pretty, but these six guys do OK. The music is good and they have somehow convinced hot young women to post racy pics of themselves in Ape Fight panties on their band website.

The Apemen
Tilburg and Rotterdam, Netherlands
Surfer apes. First album: *Are You Being Surfed?*

Apeiron   Italy
Apeing '70s and '80s heavy metal bands.

Mandrill
Brooklyn, New York, USA
Formed by three Panamanian-American brothers, '70s funk monsters who took their name from the West African ape because of its "distinctive face and family-oriented social organization."

Baboon Torture Division
Vancouver, British Columbia, Canada
Kyle Ryan of *The Onion* A.V. Club ranks theirs among the Worst Band Names of 2007.

Orang-Utan
London, UK
Their singer is said to have had only one lung, but he used it to make us pronouce orangutan properly. Self-titled LP, 1970.

Gorilla Biscuits
New York City, New York, USA
Quaaludes aka ape shit aka gorilla biscuits.

Gorillaz   Essex, UK
Four animated characters invented by Damon Albarn of Blur and *Tank Girl* comic co-creator Jamie Hewlett. In the *Guinness Book of Records* as Most Successful Virtual Band.

Simian Mobile Disco   Bristol, UK
Following the demise of the electro-rock group Simian, members James Ford and James Anthony Shaw decided to issue their own creations and remixes as Simian Mobile Disco.

Mebane, North Carolina's funkified jam band **Ape Foot Groove** was originally based in Syracuse, New York, and called Funk Ugly. A change of lineup, name and location brought nightclub gigs up and down the east coast, including CBGBs in NYC. Their critically acclaimed third CD, Hung Like a Monkey, was released in 1997.

The Safari So Far

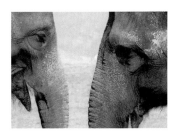

Aardvarks
Bonn, Germany

What better name under which to play metal? Started in 1992 by brothers Guido and Andreas Meyer de Voltaire. Guido also plays in Mistica, Bierbaron, the Reverend, Aach un Kraach and previously fronted Bethlehem, Disco Guido and Augury.

Groovy Aardvark
Montreal, Quebec, Canada

Started by high-school friends as the Schizophrenic Muff Divers but changed name to become a serious band. Guitarist Denis Lepage joined the band after a tour of duty in B.A.R.F. and Guano.

Crazy Elephant
New York City, New York, USA

A 1968-70 one-hit wonder band with transatlantic hit "Gimme Gimme Good Lovin'," produced by Jerry Kasenetz and Jeff Katz for Super K Productions, which also produced singles for Bo Diddley, Ohio Express and the 1910 Fruitgum Company. Elephants are not known to go crazy in the wild, but there are recorded instances of elephant madness in captivity.

Baby Elephant
New York City, New York, USA

The trio of Prince Paul, Bernie Worrell (Talking Heads, P-Funk), and Newkirk. In other words, this is the real funk. Guest collaborators on their 2007 debut album *Turn My Teeth Up* include George Clinton, Nona Hendryx, Yellowman and David Byrne.

Thee Michelle Gun Elephant
Japan

Their name is often abbreviated to TMGE. It originated when a friend mispronounced the title on a cassette tape, the Damned's album *Machine Gun Etiquette*. Select albums: *Maximum! Maximum!! Maximum!!!* (1993), *Chicken Zombies* (1997), *Casanova Snake* (2000).

Rhino Bucket
Van Nuys, California, USA

According to Rockdetector.com, this stadium band combined other suggestions, Rhino Chaser and Bucket of Lard, to achieve Rhino Bucket. Not Lard Chaser?! Their song "Ride with Yourself" was featured on the *Wayne's World* soundtrack.

Winnipeg's **Dust Rhinos** got together in 1992 and mix traditional Celtic material with originals such as the "Jedi Drinking Test" and "Got Guiness." The fifth full-length CD for this Canadian prairie band is entitled *Up Your Kilt*. UrbanDictionary.com defines "dust rhino" as an accumulation of dust or crud of significantly larger proportions than a dust bunny.

Elephants Memory

They were known as the Plastic Ono Elephants Memory Band in 1972 when they backed John Lennon on his *Some Time in New York* album and in 1973 for Yoko Ono's *Approximately Infinite Universe*, but the band was formed in New York in 1967 by drummer Rick Frank and saxophonist-clarinetist Stan Bronstein, who reportedly met on the New York City strip-joint circuit, and briefly included singer Carly Simon.

In 1969 the band had a minor hit with the song "Mongoose," a retelling of the age-old mongoose vs cobra fable. The songs "Jungle Gym at the Zoo" and "Old Man Willow" were featured on the soundtrack for the 1969 film *Midnight Cowboy*. They also have the distinction of having played one night for a chapter of the Hell's Angels with Jerry Garcia and Bo Diddley sharing the bill.

Elephants Memory gained further notoriety with their wild live shows, their giant inflatable sets, and for their self-titled album cover featuring the band naked but body-painted in vivid colors in front of an elephant.

NAMES
STILL AVAILABLE

Oscar Wildebeest

As Disgraceful
as a Gazelle

Rhymes with Oryx

Polychromatic Zebra

Warthog Debutantes

A Chevrolet of Impala

The Passport Sloths

Catwalk Giraffe Envy

The Saltwater Camels

The Wallaby Hives

Clash Bandicoot
& the Fuchsia Knickers

Tasmanian Devil
Worshippers

THE WOMBATS

"We fiddled ourselves a gig in a place called Hannah's Bar in Liverpool," recalls guitarist Matthew Murphy, "and we didn't really have a name. Me and Dan [drummer Dan Haggis] went through a period of calling each other Wombo." Haggis: "Basically Wombo the Wombat was a fictional kind of character in our daily talk." Murphy: "We used to call each other 'stupid wombats' as well. And then we needed a name for this first gig, so Dan was like, 'Just call us **THE WOMBATS.'"** Third member, bassist Tord Øverland-Knudsen, is originally from Norway. Songs: "Let's Dance to Joy Division" and "Backfire at the Disco."

Hungry Hungry Hippos
Berkley, California, USA
Named after the popular Hasbro board game introduced in 1978 and recommended for children aged 3–6. The indie-rock Hippos offer the song "Samurai Kickass Poseur Puppy"; the Saint Clair Shores, Michigan, emo-math-rock Hippos give us "Jude Law and a Semester Abroad" and "Hey Is That a Ninja Up There"; and the Southampton, UK, Hippos somehow combine grindcore and comedy.

Turbopotamos Lima, Peru
A ska-billy band formed in 2000. Band members met in university and bonded over their obsession with the Pixies.

Jolly Llamas
Kitchener, Ontario, Canada
Dalai Lama becomes Jolly Llama. Formed in 1998, fusing of two-tone and pub-rock sounds. Songs: "Ruder Than You," "Toast Coloured Girl," "Jenna's Vegan Docs."

Zebrahead
La Habra, California, USA
Named for the 1992 film *Zebrahead*, an interracial love story set in a Detroit high school. Formed in 1996 over shared interests in Fugazi and rap music. Their song "Playmate of the Year" was featured on soundtrack for *Dude Where's My Car?*

Platypus
Katy, Texas, USA
Keyboardist John Serinian: "The name Platypus happened when we were at [drummer] Rod Morgenstein's house, and we were working on a song...We had a clavinet...and listening to a tape, I remarked that it reminded me of a platypus. And everyone said we should name the band Platypus." Albums: *When Pus Comes to Shove* (1998) and *Ice Cycles* (2000). Three of the four members went on to form the Jelly Jam in 2000. Well-known singer-guitarist Ty Tabor also plays in King's X.

Wild Cats & Dogs

Foxy Leppards
Norway

Glam-metal five-piece all-girl joke band. Very fashion oriented. Foxy!

Atomic Leopards
Barcelona, Spain

Rockabilly leopards. Songs: "Your Mini Skirt Real Tight," "16 Chicks," "Princess of Rock from Outer Space."

Lions
Austin, Texas, USA

Approachable Lions. Nominated for the 2008 *High Times* Magazine Doobie Awards.

Tolsby, Finland's Pepe Trouble and Kido Retro formed **Tigerbömbs** in 2001. They've released three albums: *Loves You* (2004), *Crazy Kids Never Learn* (2006) and *Things That Go Boom* (2007), as well as some recordings with friends from the Mopeds. Live, they are joined by Sepe Ace, Alain Maynenkey and Michael Klight. Please use analgesic Tiger Balm after being tossed by an exploding Tigerbömb.

Pedro the Lion
Seattle, Washington USA

David Bazan with a rotating cast of musicians. The name is something Bazan was going to call a character in a children's book he was thinking about writing. Bazan also is or has been involved with the Undertow Orchestra, Headphones, Starflyer 59, the Soft Drugs and Seldom.

The Tigers
Kyoto, Japan

They were the Funnies, then changed their name to the Tigers to play Ventures-style pop. Had a hit in 1968 with "Zin Zin Ban Ban."

Glass Tiger
Newmarket, Ontario, Canada

Started out as Toyko, but a name and image change resulted from signing a major record deal. Bryan Adams sings backing vocals on hit "Don't Forget Me (When I'm Gone)"; Rod Stewart guests on "My Town."

Pride Tiger Vancouver, British Columbia, Canada

Bassist Mike Payette: "I was hanging out at a Three Inches of Blood video shoot…and I was just doodling and I kept writing 'Pride the Tiger' and 'Pride Tiger,' because we used to listen to Dio. We were like big into Dio and their videos for a little while. On the 'Holy Divers' song he sings 'ride the tiger,' and we were drinking pride pops at the time, which are like apple cider. It's just like Okanagan apple cider. It gets you goofed, though. And yeah, I was like, 'Pride Tiger!'"

Def Leppard

This hard-rock hair band started in Sheffield in 1977 as Atomic Mass. The name Deaf Leopard came from a drawing singer Joe Elliott did in his school days that depicted an imaginary band, but original drummer Tony Kenning suggested they change the name to a less punk spelling, and as indirect homage to Led Zeppelin. (Drummer Rick Allen replaced Kenning in '78.)

The band sold over 65 million albums worldwide in the 1980s. Hits such as "Pour Your Sugar on Me," "Armageddon It" and "Love Bites" have become rock classics and movie soundtrack gold. After 30 years, 15 albums, 46 singles and 41 music videos, Def Leppard maintains its fan base. Their 2008 release *Songs from the Sparkle Lounge*, their 11th studio album, debuted at #5 on *Billboard*'s Top 200 Albums chart and at #1 on the Rock Album and Hard Rock Album charts.

THE MIGHTY ROARS formed in Berlin and now live in Wales, though frontwoman Lara Granqvist is originally from Stockholm. The trio is tight and aggressive, with Granqvist on bass, David Pringuer on drums, Martin Pilkington on guitar and everyone contributing vocals. Granqvist: "The name came from me. We all sing pretty much all of the time and, as we are so loud, we kind of look like animals roaring when singing."

Fond of Tigers Vancouver, British Columbia, Canada
Song: "The Suburbs are for Lovebirds."

Tigers Can Bite You
Los Angeles, California, USA
Formed in 2006 by guitarist Dave Woody. Also known as TCBY, the same initials as the yogurt chain. TCBY (The Country's Best Yogurt) company started in Little Rock, Arkansas in 1981.

Tygers of Pan Tang
Whitley Bay, UK
The band is named after a breed of monsters in the Michael Moorcock novel *Stormbringer*.

Tiger! Shit! Tiger! Tiger!
Umbertide, Perugia, Italy
Trio featuring Tiger G (bass), Tiger D (guitar) and Tiger N (drums). Album: *Be Yr Own Shit* (2008). Song: "Solving Algebra Equations While on Percocet."

The Cougars
Chicago, Illinois, USA
Several former members of Hot Stove Jimmy. Songs: "There's No High in Team," "We Blog the Hardest."

Black Cougar Shock Unit
Atlanta, Georgia, USA
Christian hardcore. Song: "I'm Not Drunk, I Hate You." Is that in the Bible?

Jaguar Bristol, UK
Formed in 1979, in a Leppard-like vein, with singer Paul Merril recruited from former bands Hellraizer and Stormtrooper. Reformed in 1998 to capitalize on metal nostalgia in Japan and Europe.

Jaguar Love
Portland, Oregon, USA
Formed in 2007 by members of the Blood Brothers and Pretty Girls Make Graves. "I wanted something with love in it because I like the energy and the positivity of it, and Johnny really wanted to use jaguar in the name. After about a week and a half of obsessing over a few different names, the three of us decided on Jaguar Love."

Mink Jaguar Sydney, Australia
Song: "Millionaires are Getting Younger." Wishful thinking.

Tav Falco's Panther Burns
Memphis, Tennessee, USA
Sometimes shortened to the Panther Burns. The name comes from the Panther Burn plantation south of Greenville, Mississippi. The town's name is a reference to the wildcat whose "raids and nocturnal shrieks had so disturbed area residents in the 19th century that they set a canebrake on fire to keep it at bay after all attempts to trap or kill it had failed." The story appealed to band members.

Luxurious Panthers
Houston, Texas, USA
Psychobilly surf music. The LPs played at a bar called Catbirds every Friday night in the late '90s. Songs: "Japanese Rockabilly Kat in Outer Space" and "Pomade and Hand Grenades."

Well connected in the NY art scene, Brooklyn's **Japanther** teamed up with Aquadoom, a synchronized swimming group, in 2006 to play the *Dangerous When Wet* event at New York University's Palladium Pool. In their own words: "From basements to museums, rest assured, the kids have a good time when Japanther plays." *Skuffed Up My Huffy* is their 5th full-length album.

Cheetah Melbourne, Australia
The band lasted from 1977 to 1982 and was fronted by vocalist sisters Chrissie and Lyndsay Hammond, who started as session singers singing for bands such as Jo Jo Zep and Flash in the Pan. Lyndsay: "Chrissie chose the name because it sounded right and we wanted something with a feline image."

The King Cheetah
Los Angeles, California, USA
Trio of hardcore British rockers living in LA. Toured with Morrissey in 2002. From their site: "The King Cheetah symbolizes purity, grace and action"

Screamin' Cheetah Wheelies
Nashville, Tennessee, USA
From a 1995 RockCircusTV.com interview (vocalist Mike Farris): "There was

a [*Far Side*] cartoon of these cheetahs on the flats, and there was a couple of them up above, looking down on these cheetahs in the flats. The cheetahs in the flats were up on their back legs and they were spinning out. They were heading down this route and they were doing wheelies. I thought, damn, that would be a pretty cool name." *What was the name going to be before you saw the comic?* Mike: "Big Fuckin' Beltbuckle."

Hyenas
Guarulhos, Brazil (ska/punk); Newcastle, Australia (retro punk); London, UK (gutter punk); Sheffield, UK (hardcore punk); Campbell, Ohio (techno/ rap); Portland, Oregon (progressive ghettotech); South Lake Tahoe, California (rock).

63

Peanut Butter Wolf is a one-man jam from Los Angeles. He adopted the name Peanut Butter Wolf in the late '80s when he realized that a girlfriend's youngest brother feared the "peanut butter wolf monster." In the early '90s he recorded and performed with close friend Charizma, sharing stages with House of Pain, Nas and others. (Charizma lost his life in 1993.) After time away, Peanut Butter Wolf returned to produce, found Stones Throw Records, record and tour the US, Canada, Japan and Europe.

Wolfmother Sydney, Australia
One of the characters in Tim Robbins' novel *Skinny Legs and All* is called Wolfmother, though the band often makes up stories about being raised in the forest or epic dreams in which they are being chased by giant lizards through the snow…fireballs…being surrounded by telepathic wolves, including the wolfmother on her throne. The usual rock images.

AIDS Wolf
Montreal, Quebec, Canada
The name "AIDS Wolf" comes from an urban legend wherein wolves carry AIDS and pass it to house pets who then pass it on to people. Band member Chloe Lum: "It's also a message that we as humans must take care for our animal siblings as their health is a barometer of our own survival."

Wolf Parade
Montreal, Quebec, Canada
From a PitchforkMedia.com interview with guitarist Dan Boeckner: "[The name story is] really thoroughly stupid and not very interesting, but my old band played with this band called Mice Parade from San Diego. They're like Isotope, with funny instruments. We were playing a show with them in Victoria and they were pretty standoffish right from the get go. They spent hours and hours checking all these random instruments, like Chinese harp, and it was just really frustrating. They weren't very nice, so we went outside and changed the marquee out front. We found this enormous airbrush painting of a wolf that we hung up behind them when they were playing, and changed the name to Atlas Strategic and Spirit of Wolf Parade. And then when we were thinking up a name for this band, that's what came up, because we couldn't think of anything else. I had no idea there were so many wolf-themed bands!"

Fox Trotsky
Atlanta, Georgia, USA
Foxes trot. Foxes helped lead the October Revolution. Happy-to-be-angry punk-rock. I'm kinda liking "The Drunk and the Restless." They split a CD with fellow Atlantans Die Benny.

Jackyl Kennesaw, Georgia, USA
During their song "The Lumberjack," singer Jesse James Dupree takes a chainsaw solo, then slices up a wooden stool and tosses it into the audience.

Coyote Bones
Omaha, Nebraska, USA
Formed in 2006 by Mark Matysiuk (Jet By Day) and Mason Brown (Tilly & the Wall), with local players from Bright Eyes, Test Icicles and Son Ambulance. Matysiak: "So one night we were ice fishing in the Arctic Sea, and this ghost wolverine comes up to me and tries to serve me breakfast. Then I woke up from that dream and decided to name the band Coyote Bones."

Seattle's **FLEET FOXES** are unlike anything else happening in pop music at the moment. "We're a group of five from Seattle that sing for the fun of it and are into all kinds of music. We'd call this stuff baroque harmonic pop jams. Our names are Skye, Robin, Joshua, Casey, and Christian. We'll make some mistakes along the way, but we hope you enjoy our little family business." They cite as influences "baroque pop, music from fantasy movies, Motown, block harmonies, hymns, a couple moments approaching shaggy rock stuff, but mostly rather tempered and restrained. Not much of a rock band."

Plains & Woodland Creatures

Bear vs Shark
Highland, Michigan, USA

On their name: "We just thought it was super badass and sounded interesting." Spin-off bands: Cannons, Wildcatting, Champions of History.

If Bears Were Bees
Seattle, Washington, USA

Chronicles songwriter Timothy Justin's sadder moments: his breakup, friends leaving for university, sale of family home, and morbid fascination with death and disappointments. Another *Winnie the Pooh* reference: "It's a very funny thought, that if bears were bees, they'd build their nests at the bottom of trees."

Minus the Bear
Seattle, Washington, USA

Experimental math rock started in 2001. The name Minus the Bear comes from an inside joke among the band members, referring to the '80s TV show *B.J. and the Bear*. (Feel free to call them B.J.) Band members have also played in Kill Sadie, These Arms Are Snakes, Botch, and Sharks Keep Moving.

Edward Bear
Toronto, Ontario, Canada

Began life as the Edward Bear Review, named for Winnie the Pooh's proper name. Quentin Tarantino is said to be a fan of their music.

The Art Bears

Formed by Fred Frith (guitar, bass, violin, keyboards), Chris Cutler (percussion, text) and Dagmar Kraus (vocals) following their departure from the band Henry Cow in 1978. (Avant-garde rockers Henry Cow are said to have derived their name from composer Henry Cowell.)

The Brixton, UK-based Art Bears took their name from a sentence in Jane Ellen Harrison's 1913 book, *Ancient Art and Ritual*: "Even to-day, when individualism is rampant, art bears traces of its collective, social origin." According to Cutler, the words were deliberately removed from their original context quote. "[The name] just sounds intriguing, has an animal in it, plays with ambiguity and is mildly ridiculous."

The Art Bears experimented with drones and dissonance, angularity and extreme dynamics, and were embraced by many followers of progressive music.

Cutler and Kraus went on to form the News From Babel ensemble. All three Art Bears assembled again in 1983 to collaborate on the Berlin Jazz Festival Project "Duck and Cover."

ROCK THE CABIN!

GaNgLy MoOsE

FAIRBANKS, ALASKA
www.ganglymoose.com

www.ganglymoose.com

GaNgLy MoOsE bills itself as "Alaska's funkiest band." Drummer Kliff Hopson: "Back in 1994, two friends in Fairbanks were sitting around watching TV and considering what to call their new band. The opening scene to *Northern Exposure* came on the screen — the scene with a rather scrawny moose wandering the early morning streets of an alleged Alaskan town. One of the friends commented, 'That's a gangly moose.' It only took a few moments for the words to actually sink into their collective consciousness, at which point the band GaNgLy MoOsE was born."

"St. Louis quartet **Vampire Mooose** may well be the meanest musical beast you ever encounter. It certainly will be one of the most unique. Fusing death-metal brutality and raw hardcore intensity with abstract, progressive arrangements and jazz-like instrumental dexterity, Mooose sounds something like the progeny of an insane cross-breeding of Meshuggah, Dillinger Escape Plan and Obituary — only weirder and more vicious."

Moose
London, UK

Sometimes credited with being the first shoegazer band, heads hung, reading lyrics taped to the floor during live shows. Named for guitarist K.J. "Moose" McKillop's nickname. Members have played in Stereolab and Modern English.

Three Blind Moose
Northampton, Massachusetts, USA

Together since 1988. Song: "Alien Whale Probe."

Moose & Squirrel
Australia, California, Michigan, Connecticut

The original Moose and Squirrel, of course, are Rocky and Bullwinkle, characters from the 1960s cartoon.

Unprovoked Moose Attack
Baltimore, Maryland, USA

Late '90s pop band with horns. Moose horns. When the band dissolved in 2002, they released a mock story about dying in a plane crash. When they decided to reform in 2008, they wrote another story, about their miraculous escape from the plane crash. Members have also played in Expensive Hobby, the Slow Learners, the Beltways and 3 Tequila Dance.

Moose Convention
New York City, New York, USA

The Loyal Order of Moose is a charitable fraternal organization started in 1888, with a mandate to care for seniors and children in need. It holds frequent "Moose conventions." This Moose Convention is known for its experimental jazz-funk jams.

Cousins of the Moose
Toronto, Ontario, Canada

You don't have to travel far north of Toronto before chancing a moose encounter. These guys are hockey-happy hosers from the Great White North. Guitarist-mandolin player Paul "Pappy" Morris used to play in the punk band M.S.I. (which stood for More Stupid Initials).

Caribou   Dundas, Ontario, Canada
Caribou Daniel Snaith is said to have chosen the name while on an acid trip with friends in the Canadian wilderness. Started recording as Manitoba, but changed the name after threat of lawsuit from "Handsome Dick" Manitoba, lead singer of the Dictators.

Grant Lee Buffalo
Los Angeles, California, USA

Fronted by guitarist-vocalist Grant-Lee Philips.

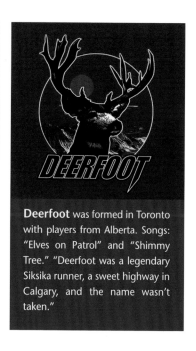

Deerfoot was formed in Toronto with players from Alberta. Songs: "Elves on Patrol" and "Shimmy Tree." "Deerfoot was a legendary Siksika runner, a sweet highway in Calgary, and the name wasn't taken."

Buffalo Springfield
Los Angeles, California, USA

The band took their name from the side of a steamroller: "Made by the Buffalo-Springfield Roller Company." It was an assemblage of out-of-work out-of-towners. Stephen Stills had failed his audition for the Monkees. Neil Young and Brian Palmer had moved out to LA to hook up with Stills after Rick James was arrested and their Toronto band, the Mynah Birds, collapsed. Young had met Stills at a folk club in Thunder Bay, Ontario. When Palmer was arrested for marijuana possession in 1967 and deported back to Canada, he was replaced by Jim Messina.

Deerhoof
San Francisco, California, USA

Experimental post-rock duo of Rob Fisk (guitar-bass) and Greg Saunier (drums). They have toured with the Flaming Lips and Radiohead.

Deer in the Headlights
Austin, Texas, USA
"Folkadelic" side-project for musicians who have played with the People, Oedipus & the Mothers, Spirit, the Supernatural Family Band, Jo Jo Gunne, Firefall, Heart, Stevie Nicks and Dan Fogelberg.

Beaver Amsterdam, Netherlands
Stoner rock. Also known as 13eaver. Rhythm section released a CD with Queens of the Stone Age in 1998. Members also connected to the bands Goatsnake, Earthlings?, God, No Pigs, and Kyuss.

Badger Milk Helsinki, Finland
Pop-punk trio with albums *Chicken Party* and *I Wanna See Your Boobies*. From a FinPop.net interview: "…all the 'good' names were already taken. [The] name comes from the movie called *Animal*. There, that guy buys Badger Milk from TV. Pretty crappy movie, but so were we!"

Icelandic Traffic Badgers
Wolverhampton, UK
"The name came from our drummer — the maddest, coolest, craziest dude I know. According to 'the Don,' whilst parachuting into Reykjavik through Icelandic airwaves during one vacation, [he] witnessed a TV program on which they discussed the plight of the mighty badgers on Icelandic roads! Because of badgers being nocturnal animals and the little amount of daylight in Iceland during certain times of the year, the badgers were getting squished on the roadside. So our Don decided to help the Icelandic traffic badger warden for a while on a voluntary basis, until one day he journeyed home and became drummer in the band, and told us the story of the Icelandic traffic badgers!"

Screeching Weasel
Chicago, Illinois, USA
The band started as All-Night Garage Sale but changed their name to Screeching Weasel, a variation on Screaming Otter, a name suggested by a friend in reference to a T-shirt bearing the message "I've Got a Screaming Otter in My Pants!" Both frontmen, Ben Weasel (vocals) and John Jughead (guitar), have written semi-fictional books about life in a punk band.

Sun Dried Opossum
Waynesboro, Virginia, USA
From the Shenandoah Valley, at the foot of Virginia's Blue Ridge Mountains, where they's possum aplenty.

Squirrel Bait
Louisville, Kentucky, USA
The term *squirrel bait* denotes a person who is "nuts." Metal-flavored math rock hardcore. Started as a high-school band in 1983. Disbanded in '88, but almost everyone from the original band continue to perform music in other groups: Palace Music, Tortoise, Evergreen, Big Wheel, Bitch Magnet, Lemonheads and The For Carnation.

Squirrel Nut Zippers
Chapel Hill, North Carolina, USA
Squirrel Nut Zippers are a peanut-and-caramel candy that dates back to the mid-1920s.

Killer Squirrel
Mill Creek, Washington, USA
A one-man punk band, Killer Squirrel also goes by the name Adam Chaos. The name relates to a dead squirrel that he almost tripped over while walking to school. Songs: "Jesus Loves You (He Wants Me Dead)" and "My Fortune Cookie Lied."

NAMES
STILL AVAILABLE

The Socialist Minks

Beavers with Lego®

Lusty Badger

Titmouse Legmouse

Bear vs Hummer

The Pocket Voles

Deerlobe

Hootie & the Woodchuck

Fox Detector

Wapiti Wapiti

The Creamy Wolverines

Greater Metropolitan Bison

The Dead Sea Squirrels
Falmouth, UK
From Dead Sea Scrolls. Musicians from bands Small Wonder, Delaware and others form a rootsy collective behind the songs of John Greene. Greene was the lighting designer for Boz Scaggs in the '70s (also on Wings, Santana and the Grateful Dead crews) and played bass in such bands as British Intelligence, Breaking Strings, and the Dubious Brothers.

Ratt
San Diego, California, USA
They began in 1976 as Mickey Ratt (a bad-ass Mickey Mouse), but later shortened the name. Ratt was one of the most popular hair-metal bands of the '80s. Their first four records all went platinum.

Rats of Unusual Size
Flint, Michigan, USA
The William Golding book *The Princess Bride* (and the film of the same name) features "rodents of unusual size" as one of the hazards in the Fire Swamp.

Boomtown Rats
Dún Laoghaire, Ireland
Started as the Nightlife Thugs. Boomtown Rats is the name of a gang in Woody Guthrie's autobiography, *Bound for Glory*. They were the first Irish band to score #1 UK hits with songs "Rat Trap" (1978) and "I Don't Like Mondays" (1979), the latter written in response to the case of 16-year-old Brenda Ann Spencer opening fire on a California elementary school, claiming she didn't like Mondays.

Adelaide, Australia's **Exploding White Mice** got their name from the scene in the 1979 film *Rock 'N' Roll High School* in which a laboratory mouse spontaneously explodes when exposed to the music of the Ramones, the band's foremost influence. Members came from other Adelaide bands, such as Zippy & the Coneheads, Crunch Pets, the Deviants and Screaming Believers. The band opened for the Ramones on their 1989 tour of Australia.

The Good Rats
Long Island, New York, USA
Started as the U-Men in 1964. Record company wanted a new name. Their booking agent chose the name, inspired by an album cover featuring a big white rat. Still play their annual "Ratstock" summer festival on Long Island. Select album titles: *From Rats to Riches* (1978), *Ratcity in Blue* (1976), *Rats, the Way You Like 'em* (1979).

Spastic Rats
Annapolis, Maryland, USA
Mid-80s attic band. Released one 7" EP, *Rodentia*. Drummer went on to play in the Hated.

The Field Mice
South London, UK
Immensely popular in France. Founder singer-guitarist Bob Wratten went on to start Northern Picture Library, then Trembling Blue Stars.

Mice Parade
New York City, New York, USA
Mice Parade is an anagram for Adam Pierce, percussionist and founder.

Modest Mouse
Issaquah, Washington, USA
From Virginia Woolf's short story "The Mark on the Wall": "I wish I could hit upon a pleasant track of thought, a track indirectly reflecting credit upon myself, for those are the pleasantest thoughts, and very frequent even in the minds of modest, mouse-colored people." Albums include *Good News for People Who Love Bad News* (2004), *We Were Dead Before the Ship Even Sank* (2007).

Afraid of Mice
Liverpool, UK New-wave dance-pop. The next band Phil Franz-Jones formed after the Next. He went on to form Lumberjack Ballet, Two's a Crowd, and Up and Running.

Reptiles & Amphibians

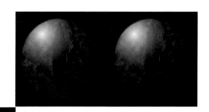

Snakes

These Arms Are Snakes

Seattle, Washington, USA

A post-hardcore band with some street cred who, according to various bloggery, had their name dissed by famous former Dead Kennedys front-man Jello Biafra. Jello allegedly called These Arms Are Snakes a prime exam-ple of "bad emo band names." While Jello's band name and stage name both represent politically charged punk history, and the name These Arms Are Snakes represents, uh, snake-like arms, surely there are better targets. May I suggest *actual* emo bands...maybe the Promise Ring, Jejune or Knapsack? Not that I have any opinions about band names.

Ghost Heart Snake

Marietta, Georgia, USA

In Chinese acupuncture, the Ghost Heart is the 4th of 13 ghost points along the inner arm near the wrist and is used to clear the heart and quiet the spirit. Meanwhile, Ghost Heart Snake wriggles further south with their 2007 song "(I Like the Way Her) Butt Moves."

The Deadly Snakes

Toronto, Ontario, Canada

The band originally formed in 1996 for a one-off gig at a friend's birthday party in the basement of a market-dis-trict laundromat. After four albums and national and international tours, they called it quits in August 2006.

The anaconda rules the snake king-dom, sometimes reaching well over 20 feet long and weighing over 400 pounds. **THE ANACONDAS** play punched-up surf music out of Amsterdam. During their 2003 tour of the States, they traveled 10,000 miles in 28 days to play 24 gigs in 21 towns. Their 2005 album *Snakin' All Over* is a pun on the title of a #1 UK hit from 1960, "Shakin' All Over," by Johnny Kidd & the Pirates.

Hot Snakes

San Diego, California, USA

Perhaps inspired by the title of Zappa's *Hot Rats* album. Formed in 1999 by Rick Froberg and John "Speedo" Reis (both formerly of Pitchfork and Drive Like Jehu) while Reis's main band, Rocket from the Crypt, was on a break from touring and recording.

Impotent Sea Snakes

From Atlanta, Georgia, this goth-metal-drag-glam band is, by their own admission, "a mind-boggling theatrical musical orgy the likes of which few could imagine." They have appeared on HBO's *Real Sex*, the Playboy Channel's *Sexcetera* and Germany's *Peep!*

The Impotent Sea Snakes' rock-circus stage show involves smoke bombs, fire-eating, glitter, whips, tat-toos, piercings, lots of makeup, impressively kinky costumes, a bassist named Snatch Nasty, singers 13, Princess Christy and Pat Briggs (likely name, "Pat"), guitarists Tess Tease and Buck Futt, and songs such as "Let Go O' My Thang." Special guests on their 2003 *Everything in Excess* album include soul-funk deity Isaac Hayes, Faster Pussycat's Taime Downe and porn legend Jenna Jameson. Their website warns visitors: "People, this *is* the band our mothers warned us about."

While a lot about the band's traits might compare to those of sea snakes (a seductive slinkiness, an otherworldly dangerousness, a potential venomousness), impo-tence is nowhere to be found.

69

NAMES
STILL AVAILABLE

These Arms Are
Feather Boas

The Got Milk Snakes?

Snake Oil Changlings

Void Where Constricted

The Diamondback
Fiancées

Medusa's Hairnet

Snakebite Snack
Vendors

Eastern Choral Snakes

The Herpetological
Blisters

Playing for Scales

Manic Snake Charmers

Oprah's Cobra

Viper Sao Paulo, Brazil

Vipers are dangerous. Rockers like to appear dangerous. Vipers tend to live 10 to 15 years. This Brazilian speed-metal band has been at it since 1985.

The Vipers Skiffle Group
London, UK

They were signed by George Martin in 1956 during the British skiffle craze. Later, under the shortened name the Vipers, the group added Hank Marvin, Jet Harris and Tony Meehan, who would go on to form the Drifters and the Shadows.

Viper Rash
Boston, Massachusetts, USA

"We're all about immediate gratification." Is this what caused the rash? You can't hold back? Song title: "God Doesn't Care."

Cobra Beijing, China

Formed in 1989, Cobra was the first all-female rock band in China. Bassist Yang Ying is also a member of the Chinese National Song and Dance Ensemble and one of the foremost *erhu* (ancient two-string violin) players in the world.

Cobra Starship
New York City, New York, USA

Guitarist Ryland Blackinton: "Gabe [Saporta, vocals] actually has about 15 different stories he tells people, but there is one in particular that I actually believe. He used to have two vintage leather jackets, one that said 'Cobra' and the other that said 'Starship Disco.' You could probably find them on eBay." Hit soundtrack single: "Bring It (Snakes on a Plane)."

Sweet Cobra
Chicago, Illinois, USA

In the 2003 remake of the 1979 comedy *The In-Laws*, Michael Douglas plays father of the groom, a CIA agent who involves the father of the bride, Albert Brooks as a nervous podiatrist, in a dangerous mission. While in the presence of a nutjob international smuggler (David Suchet), Brooks must pretend to be a legendary bad guy known as the Fat Cobra (ostensibly for his, uh, fat cobra). The conflictedly gay arms dealer cannot contain his lust for, and curiousity about, the Fat Cobra. In attempting to separate Brooks from Douglas and have him to himself, Suchet utters poutingly, "Are you coming, sweet Cobra?"

Iceage Cobra
Seattle, Washington, USA

Guitarist Jordan West: "We started the band in Spokane and all the other bands names sounded the same, like Fine For Now, Currently at the Moment, Common Error, Few and Far Between. We just wanted something that sounded tough. Lemmy thought, 'What band's name would appear across the back of a biker's jacket?' and came up with Motorhead. We kind of used that same process. At the time, the only Cobra band we'd heard of was the Detroit Cobras, but then after we chose our name, all the Cobra bands came out of the woodwork."

Bushmaster Washington, DC, USA

Another band named for another potentially deadly snake. This one features Hendrix-inspired Gary Brown, formerly of the Spoilers, on lead guitar and vocals.

Copperhead

San Francisco, California, USA
Psychedelic rock band formed around guitarist John Cipollina following his tenure with Quicksilver Messenger Service in 1970s.

Amarillo, Texas, USA
Southern rock band who took their name from the Steve Earle song "Copperhead Road."

Cleveland, Ohio, USA
Thrash-metal band, 1999–2004.

Brighton, UK   Female-fronted heavy rock cover band.

Nelson, New Zealand
Cover band, "just about everything except rap, punk, thrash and classical."

Whitesnake   Leeds, UK

Having recorded two albums as replacement vocalist for Deep Purple, David Coverdale split to form Whitesnake in 1977. Through decades of touring and recording, Coverdale has remained the only constant in the band. *The Simpsons* writers had fun with this rotating lineup of hair-band alumni during a "Treehouse of Horror" Halloween special. In it, Dick Clark celebrates the turn of the millennium in Springfield instead of in Times Square. Clark introduces the featured band as Whitesnake, but various band members, old and confused, think they are in Poison, Quiet Riot or Ratt.

The Chicago Kingsnakes

Chicago, Illinois, USA
The Chicago Kingsnakes have been performing live R&B since 1983. The kingsnake derives its name from its willingness to kill and eat other snakes.

New Fangs

Seattle, Washington, USA
No snakes, just vampires.

LUXURIOUS PYTHON hails from Almonte, Florida, and adds their own modern sound to the grand tradition of '70s rock swagger, featuring the tried-and-true lineup of guitar, bass, drums and Hammond B-3. A luxurious python skin about 7 feet long can be had for a mere US $180. Luxurious live pythons run from US $200 to a few thousand.

Lizards

Flying Lizards   London, UK

Flying lizards don't fly, but they do leap from trees and glide. This is pianist David Cunningham's project with fellow improvisers David Toop and Steve Beresford. Cunningham in a 1984 interview with writer Mick Sinclair: "This is terribly pretentious, but I've always toyed with the idea that the Flying Lizards represented rock and roll from some sort of alternative universe. It amuses me to think of a possible universe where James Joyce is a really popular author."

Cocktail Lizards

Philadelphia, Pennsylvania, USA
Cocktail lizards, lounge lizards, coffee-house lizards...they began as an acoustic duo.

Roadkill Lizard

Fletcher, Oklahoma, USA
Self-addressed question: "What would happen if Salvador Dali made music?" Songs include "Robot Girls Unite" and "Psychic Swine Hotline."

"Combining '60s-inspired garage rock, surf twang, bluesy swagger, and manic punk energy, Chicago's own EMERALD LIZARDS have arrived to re-inject the Roll into Rock! Howling frontman Ayman Samman has his roots in the deep underground of Egyptian Heavy Metal."

The Jesus Lizard

This Chicago band takes its name from the common name for the Central American basilisk, a lizard that is light enough and fast enough that it can run on the water. By contrast, Jesus Lizard's music is heavy noise-rock and wouldn't stay afloat long.

Former Scratch Acid singer David Yow formed the group with ex-Cargo Cult guitarist Duane Denison in 1987, adding David Sims on bass and Mac McNeilly on drums. The crew had a penchant for four-letter album titles: *Pure* (1989), *Head* (1990), *Goat* (1991), *Liar* (1992), *Lash* (1993), *Show* (1994), *Down* (1994), *Shot* (1996), *Blue* (1998) and *Bang* (2000).

Yow routinely exposed his genitals for dramatic effect during performances and was arrested for dropping his trousers onstage during Lollapalooza 1995. In his book *Our Band Could Be Your Life: Scenes from the American Indie Underground, 1981-1991*, Michael Azerrad describes Yow's vocal stylings as being "like a kidnap victim trying to howl with duct tape over his mouth."

Inner Lizard
Los Angeles, California, USA

The term "inner lizard," like "reptile brain," is used to refer to the part of the brain that deals with our most primal instincts and drives, our most animal self. Curiously, the band Inner Lizard uses autoharps, sleighbells and electric mandolins, which register with my "dog brain" and my human brain, but fail to arouse my reptile brain.

King Lizard   London, UK

Jim Morrison was the "lizard king." King Lizard is a glam-metal quartet formed in 2002. From a Purerawk.co.uk interview:

Nix: OK, so how did you come up with the name?

Flash: I was sitting there thinking of a name for the band for a long time, and we went through various names. There was Star Scream, Graveyard Tramps, Dog House...

Nix: Actually, Graveyard Tramps is awesome!

Flash: I like it too! When I do a side project, it's going to be Graveyard Tramps, so don't steal it! I came up with King Lizard because I wanted a name that sounded like a monster or something big.

Alice: Big like my cock.

Flash: King Lizard is also a kind of play on words for penis, as well. It's kind of like a big reptile. Not that I've got scales on my cock.

Sky: Or small arms, because that would be weird.

The Chameleons
Manchester, UK

This '80s dream-pop band was not chameleon-like, but they were consistently interesting and inventive.

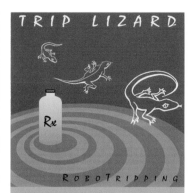

Washington, DC's TRIP LIZARD finished in the top ten at the Hard Rock Café's 2002 national Battle of the Bands competition and have gone on to appear at east coast festivals and open for such national acts as Gov't Mule and Better Than Ezra. Their 2004 CD, *Robotripping*, mixes rock, rap, ska and high-energy funk.

Blacklight Chameleons
New York City, New York, USA

Mid-80s psychedelic rock. Chameleon Blacklight is a kind of UV-reactive tattoo ink that causes skin art to glow vividly under blacklight.

The Gila Monsters
Venice Beach, California, USA

Gila monsters are large, thick-tailed, venomous lizards native to the southwest US and northern Mexico. Gila refers to the Gila River and is pronounced *Hee-la*. The Venice Beach-dwelling Gila Monsters play rock and R&B. Big Nick and the Gila Monsters, from Scottsdale, Arizona, play the blues and may actually be gila monsters.

Pinkeye D'Gekko
St. Louis, Missouri, USA

Pink-eyed gecko. Albino geckos often have pink eyes. 2004 CD: *Dry Clothes for the Drowning*.

Frogs and Toads

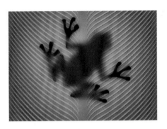

Amfibian New Jersey, USA
A post-Phish evolution for lyricist Tom Marshall.

Armored Frog
Eugene, Oregon, USA
Self-described "slow motion provocateurs." Favorite song title: "Drunk on Aphids," from *Weasel on a Weathervane* (2005).

Box of Frogs London, UK
From the expression "mad as a box of frogs," crazy and agitated. Formed in 1983 by former Yardbirds Chris Dreja (guitar), Paul Samwell-Smith (bass) and Jim McCarty (drums), with John Fiddler on vocals. Their two albums include guest appearances by Jimmy Page, Jeff Beck and Rory Gallagher.

The Carpet Frogs
Toronto, Ontario, Canada
Short wind-breaking while sitting on the carpet, causing a *ribbit* sound, is blamed on "the carpet frogs." These really talented guys are perhaps best known as the backup band for both Randy Bachman and Burton Cummings, but the Carpet Frogs backed hundreds of big-name acts as the house band for Lulu's Roadhouse, a mid-sized performance venue in Kitchener, Ontario.

Ethel the Frog Hull, UK
Another Monty Python-derived name. This one from a skit in which a BBC1 "news" program inexplicably called *Ethel the Frog* looks at gangland violence by examining the reign of terror by the Piranha brothers, Doug and Dinsdale, as well as their capture and sentencing to 400 years in prison.

Nano Frog
Patchogue, New York, USA
A) a frog 10^{-9} times the size of a standard frog, or B) a late '90s electronica trio.

Salty Frogs
Salt Lake City, Utah, USA
Energetic Celtic fusionists who invite you (saltily) to "Have Fun or Piss Off!"

Toad Switzerland
A 1970s prog-rock band whose song "Stay" was a hit on Swiss charts.

The Battletoads
Houston, Texas, USA
Battletoads was a video game created in 1991 to compete with the Teenage Mutant Ninja Turtles games.

The **Amphibious Jones** boys are Zappa-esque Denver art-rockers (in a good way). Latest CD: *Critters of Habit*. Drummer Stephen Mercer: "The band name came with the help of a Tom Robbins book called *Half Asleep in Frog Pajamas*. Unofficially. James [guitar, vocals] will still never say."

Toad the Wet Sprocket

Named for a fictitious band in Eric Idle's "Rock Notes" sketch on Monty Python's *Contractual Obligations* album. As an earnest rock reporter, Idle announces that "Rex Stardust, lead electric triangle with Toad the Wet Sprocket, has had to have an elbow removed following their recent successful worldwide tour of Finland. Flamboyant, ambidextrous Rex apparently fell off the back of a motorcycle. 'Fell off the back of a motorcyclist, most likely,' quipped ace drummer Jumbo McCluney upon hearing of the accident. Plans are already afoot for a major tour of Iceland." Idle wanted a name "so silly and unusual no one would ever consider it for a group."

It was meant to be a temporary name used only for their first gig. "We were gonna think of something better," confessed Glen Phillips, singer for the Santa Barbara, California, folk-rock foursome. "We were going to think of a good name...but it just never happened."

The band released five studio albums, two of which went platinum. Their name served them perhaps as well as their musicianship, leading to frequent inclusion of their tracks on compilation albums and film and television soundtracks. The band gave Eric Idle a copy of their 1996 platinum record award for *Dulcinea* as token of their gratitude.

Lava Toad

San Francisco, California, USA

The protruding edge of lava as it advances is called the lava toe. Lava Toad offers us songs such as "Wet for Jesus," "If Jesus Had a Gun" and "Go, Baby Jesus," noting, "Christians often find our biblical accuracy upsetting."

The Smokin' Toads

Toronto, Ontario, Canada

The mid-90s house band at Toronto's Brunswick House bar. Australian medical authorities warn that, despite tales to the contrary, smoking dried cane toads produces no hallucinogenic effects and can seriously harm the smoker's health.

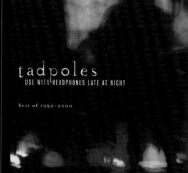

Todd Parker (guitar, vocals) used the name **TADPOLES** for his mostly solo 4-track recordings in the late '80s: "I'm a fan of simple names (the Beatles being a favorite), and I was thinking of something relating to my initials, T.P., and just arrived naturally at Tadpoles." TADPOLES the New York City psychedelic-rock band began in 1990 when Parker joined forces with filmmaker-drummer Michael Kite Audino to combine lighting, film clips and music in "multi-sensory" live performances. With additional members, Tadpoles soon became regulars on the Manhattan club scene and went on to record six albums later in the decade. The band went on indefinite hiatus in 2000.

Turtles and Tortoises

Blue Turtle Seduction
South Lake Tahoe, California, USA
"High-Altitude Bohemian Tribal Funk Grass." You know, hippie music.

Deep Turtle   Pori, Finland
Most turtles burrow. These turtles burrow deeper, where they play noise-core in unusual time signatures.

Hot Pink Turtle
Kansas City, Missouri, USA
Hot Pink Turtle sounds like a vaguely sexual expression rather than the name of a Christian rock group with a curiously titled collection of tunes called *Ticklewigglejigglepickle*. Wait, that sounds sexual, too.

Trampled by Turtles
Duluth, Minnesota, USA
Bluegrass-folk-alternative quintet. "So slow he was trampled by a herd of turtles."

Tortoise
Chicago, Illinois, USA
In a weird evolution, Tortoise began life as Mosquito in 1990, becoming Tortoise in 1992. Musical styles: punk, dub, space rock, avant-garde jazz, electronica.

Tortoise Corpse
Wales
A deceased thrash-metal band.

The Turtles

Howard Kaylan and Mark Volman formed a surf group called the Crossfires from Planet Mars while high-school classmates in Westchester, California. Their outstanding natural harmonies led to a recording contract, a change in musical direction and a name change. As the Tyrtles, they would play Byrds-like folk-rock. Though the intentionally misspelled name failed to catch on, the properly spelled Turtles broke into the *Billboard* Top 10 with a cover of Dylan's "It Ain't Me Babe" late in the summer of 1965.

With the help of various backing musicians and producers, the duo experienced numerous chart successes, but none as big as their 1967 #1 hit "Happy Together," which knocked the Beatles' "Penny Lane" from its perch and remained in the top spot for three weeks.

Volman and Kaylan un-Turtled themselves in 1969 (their record company owned the name until 1984) and soon joined Frank Zappa's band, the Mothers of Invention, using the stage names "the Phlorescent Leech [Volman] and Eddie [Kaylan]," or "Flo and Eddie" for short.

They went on to record several albums under the name Flo & Eddie as well as providing backing vocals on albums by T-Rex, Roger McGuinn, Ray Manzarek, Stephen Stills, Alice Cooper, Blondie, Bruce Springsteen, the Knack, Psychedelic Furs, Paul Kantner, Duran Duran, the Ramones and many other artists.

Gators and Crocs

Killer Crocs of Uganda are high-school buddies from Austin, Texas, who nearly 20 years later, "inspired by Halloween beer and tech-career drudgery refound the passions that drew them to the Live Music Capital of the World." There is a *National Geographic Ultimate Explorer* episode entitled "Killer Crocs of Uganda," which documents what happens when the Nile crocodile's food sources are depleted and human settlement encroaches their habitat. Crunchtime!

Alligator
Dublin, Ireland (alternative rock); Portland, Oregon (electro-pop instrumental); Vigevano, Pavia, Italy (thrash metal).

Alligator Attack   Brazil
Hey, it works both ways: "Environmental officials found the skinned and salted corpses of some 740 alligators in a nature reserve in the Amazon jungle, apparently destined for lunch in regional restaurants." *Reuters*, April 2, 2008

Alligator Pears
Seattle, Washington, USA
Another name for avocados.

Alligator Stew
Los Angeles, California, USA
Toured with Lynyrd Skynyrd in 2003. Album: *A First Taste of Alligator Stew*.

The Balham Alligators

Balham calls itself the "Gateway to the South." South London. The story goes that Geraint Watkins (keyboard, accordion, organ), Robin McKidd (fiddle, guitar, vocals), Kieran O'Connor (drums, percussion), Gary Rickard (guitar, vocals), and Pete Dennis (bass) met in a London pub 1983 and decided to counter the canned-drums-and-synths bands du jour with a mix of Celtic, R&B, rock, zydeco swamp music and swing.

The band toured widely until illness took the life of O'Connor in 1991. The Balham Alligators have released six albums and collaborated with such artists as Nick Lowe, Van Morrison, Mark Knopfler, Carl Perkins, George Harrison, Dr. Feelgood, and Bill Wyman and His Rhythm Kings.

Watkins started a band named the Wobblers in 1992, and McKidd formed the Companions of the Rosy Hours, but the Alligators have continued to reform on a regular basis to give south London an infusion of Cajun party music, Balham-style.

The Crocodiles
Sydney, Australia

Lead singer Jenny Morris sang with New Zealand all-girl band the Wide Mouthed Frogs in the '70s, moved to Sydney in '81, later sang backing vocals for INXS and co-wrote "You I Know" with Neil Finn of Crowded House. Don't know if Crocodile Hunter Steve Irwin ever saw this band.

Crocodile God
Liverpool, UK

Sobek was the Crocodile God of Egyptian mythology. Human body, crocodile head, fertility, power, protection. Self-description: "Crocodile God have been around since 1992, and putting out records since 1994. The songs are mostly about splitting up with girlfriends...."

Crocodile Teeth
Florence, Alabama, USA

Just two guys, one on vocals and acoustic guitar, one on "everything else." The demo "Trees and Power Lines" is worth risking the crocodile's teeth.

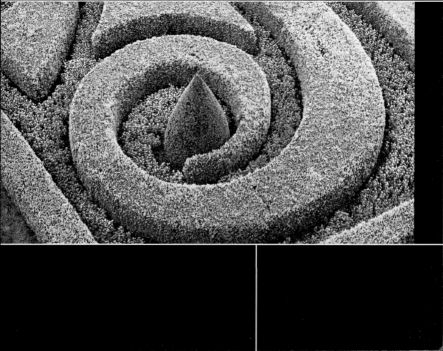

The Plants

Black Oak Arkansas

Black Oak Arkansas was formed in 1965 in their hometown of Black Oak, Arkansas, by Jim "Jim Dandy" Mangrum (vocals), Rickie Reynolds (guitar), Stanley Knight (guitar), Harvey Jett (guitar), Pat Daugherty (bass) and Wayne Evans (drums).

The group originally called themselves the Knowbody Else. Written accounts say that they stole their first PA system from a local high school, were subsequently charged and sentenced to 26 years at a nearby prison farm, received a suspended sentence, and high-tailed it to the hills to lie low, rethink and rehearse.

The Knowbody Else moved to Memphis in 1969 and recorded an album on Stax Records. A switch to Atco Records brought with it the name change to Black Oak Arkansas. Recent population surveys put that town's population at under 300.

The band had its biggest success with the single "Jim Dandy," a 1973 remake of LaVern Baker's 1957 hit. Kiss's first American tour was as an opening act for Black Oak Arkansas in 1974.

When Trees Leave

Deep Forest
Lille, Nord-Pas-de-Calais, France
Electronic world-music by Eric Mouquet and Michel Sanchez. From deepforestmusic.com: "The first Deep Forest album was supposed to be a project in honor of Earth Day...the name Deep Forest highlights the mission to save the tropical rainforests around the world. The music also features vocals from cultures that live in the rainforests."

National Forest
Manchester, UK
Lots of electronica in the forests.

Future of Forestry
San Diego, California, USA
Band leader Eric's mission statement: "My vision for Future of Forestry is to kind of create a community of musicians that want creativity to grow like a deep forest. Remember the Psalm (96) about the trees of the forest singing?"

The Timber Kings
Victoria, British Columbia, Canada
Harmonious logger rock.

A Minor Forest
San Francisco, California, USA
Slogan: "A Minor Forest Supports the Destruction of Mankind."

Forest Television
Agua Dulce, California, USA
If a tree is watching television in the forest, but nobody sees it, does it still count for the Nielson ratings?

Tree
Westwood, Massachusetts, USA
Though Tree is a curiously earthy name for a punk-metal band with a guitarist named Ooze, perhaps the connection is better explained in their 1994 album title, *Plant a Tree or Die*.

Braintree
Arlington Heights, Illinois, USA, and Auckland, New Zealand
No such thing as a braintree (though it's a good idea). Well-known Braintree, Massachusetts was named for Braintree, Essex, UK, whose name origin remains hazy.

Ghost Tree
Santa Cruz, California, USA
Their MySpace page says the music sounds like "hot sex on a Fijian island." Ghost Tree is the name of one of the world's most dangerous surfing waves, located near Monterey Bay, California.

Gravity Tree
Newark, California, USA
If you're not experiencing enough gravity, this is where you pick more of it. These prog-rockers' first album asks the burning question *Life or Dessert?*

Porcupine Tree started in 1987 as a home-studio project for Steven Wilson (vocals, guitars, keyboards). Today they are an in-demand, Grammy-nominated quartet with a string of diverse albums, including *Lightbulb Sun*, *Stars Die*, *Arriving Somewhere...*, and *Fear of a Blank Planet*. Their live performances incorporate cutting-edge electronic music and spectacular visual displays. There is no such thing as a porcupine tree, however. Young porcupines climb trees when less than a week old, but the adults' taste for bark often means the end of the tree.

Fever Tree Houston, Texas, USA

The late '60s rockers bounced between airy ballads to fuzzed-out psychedelia. Some of their material was written by the Holzmans, whose previous credits included tunes for *Mary Poppins*. A fever tree is a type of acacia common to southern Africa. Early European travelers believed contact with the tree led to feverish illness. In truth, the swampy lowlands where many fever trees grow provide ideal breeding sites for mosquitoes, which carry malaria.

Plastic Tree Ishikawa, Japan

Drooping cherry trees are popular in Japan. Crimson Queen and Bloodgood maples, too. Plastic Trees? Japanisdoomed.com calls them "one for fans of the lighter side of J-Rock."

Taken By Trees Sweden

Victoria Bergsman left the Concretes in 2006 to be Taken By Trees. They took her to *Open Fields*. For more aggressive behavior demonstrated by trees, check out the forest in *The Wizard of Oz* and the Ents in *Lord of the Rings*.

Treepeople Boise, Idaho, USA

They burned up the Seattle alternative scene until two of the four original members left for The Halo Benders. The Boise National Forest covers about 2.6 million acres northeast of the city.

Ego Tree Tallahassee, Florida, USA

Two of the band's five members are lawyers, which would in some circles explain the ego. Recent CD: *pionk*.

Tree of Woe Stevens Point, Wisconsin, USA

In a desert scene from the film *Conan the Barbarian*, evil necromancer Thulsa Doom (James Earl Jones) commands that Conan be crucified on the Tree of Woe. There is also a professional wrestling move by this name.

Treefort Northampton, Massachusetts, USA

"Treefort has been around longer than anti-virus protection." Treefort's first album was titled *Girls Allowed*.

NAMES
STILL AVAILABLE

Treemuggers

OaK Computer

Dogwood Apologists

Forgotten Ginko Trees

A Grove of Myrtles

Maples
Missing Shoes

Beech Blanket
Splinters

Leafblowers
of the Apocalypse

Forest Gimp

The Quaking Aspens

Gang of Tree

I Can't See It

CARBON LEAF is an acoustic-electric alternative band from Richmond, Virginia. They have recorded at least a half dozen albums and toured steadily since the mid-90s, opening for the likes of David Gray and the Dave Matthews Band. Their 2004 release, Indian Summer, made it to #5 on the Adult Album Charts. Their recent album, Love, Loss, Hope, Repeat, merited a cover story in *The Green Room* magazine. Carbon Leaf were the first unsigned artists ever to play the American Music Awards.

Treebeard Ottawa, Ontario, Canada
AKA Fangorn. He appears in the *Lord of the Rings* trilogy as the oldest of the treepeople, the Ents. He stands 14 feet high, takes forever to make a decision, and may have been based on Tolkein's pal C.S. Lewis. Also the name of a Sheffield, UK-based folk-rock group.

The Bamboo Steamers
Boston, Massachusetts, USA
Album: *The Many Lovemaking Sounds of…* Song: "Miss You Like an Eyeball."

Leaf
Bolton, UK, and Utrecht, Netherlands
The Bolton band's name was "chosen by a friend." Previous incarnations include Monkeys Ate My Soul. The Utrecht-based acoustic-pop group released their first album in 2007 and their first single, "Wonder Woman," was a Top 10 hit in the Netherlands.

32 Leaves Phoenix, Arizona, USA
It has been suggested that the band's name refers to the number of rolling papers ("leaves") in a package. However, the band's lead singer is quoted as having said that the name means "nothing really…just the title of a poem we found and liked."

Acacia London, UK
A '90s electronica collaboration between Guy Sigsworth (Frou Frou, Bomb the Bass, Imogen Heap, Björk, Seal) and Alexander Nilere. Songs: "Maddening Shroud" and "Cocaine Psychosis." Sigsworth has since produced and collaborated with Madonna, Britney Spears and Alannis Morissette

Orchestra Baobab Dakar, Senegal
Started out as the Star Band but became the house band of the popular Baobab Club in Dakar.

Tonal Oak Ann Arbor, Michigan, USA
Evidently not a pun on Tone Loc. From the artist's website: "…and under every witty tree, and under every tonal oak, the place where they did offer ocean-going weed to all their offerings…." And there is a painting entitled *Tonal Oak Landscape* by Amedee Joullin (1862-1917).

Wishbone Ash Torquay, Devon, UK
Band members wrote lists of words on two sheets of paper and co-founder Martin Turner had to pick a word from each list. The result was Wishbone Ash. Oh, and then they opened for Deep Purple.

Nice Ash
Wolfeboro, New Hampshire, USA
Singer's name is Ash Fischbein. Not a reference to the Nice Ash cigar brand.

Redwood Switzerland
This band's 2007 album, *We're All Going to Die*, became a Top 20 hit in Switzerland, even with tunes entitled "Plywood" and "Song for a Lesbian."

The Pinetops
Winston-Salem, North Carolina, USA
The Pinetops recorded their only album *Above Ground and Vertical* (1998) with Don Dixon (R.E.M., Matthew Sweet, the Smithereens). Pinetops is also a town in Edgecombe County, NC, home of the Pinetops 300, a "top ten tractor pull sanctioned by the National Association of Tractor Pulls."

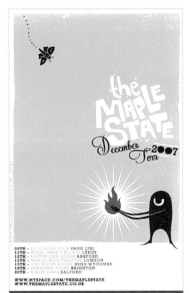

Manchester's **the Maple State**, comprised of brothers Gregory and Christian Counsell, William Pearson and John Goodwin, formed while at college in 2004. Their first EP received rave reviews and landed them tours with Motion City Soundtrack, Fightstar and Minus the Bear. In 2007, countless club dates and a few EPs later, the band added Richard Higginbottom on guitar. The result has been a more energetic sound and stellar press. *New Musical Express* called the EP *Say, Scientist* "faultless."

Pine Madison, Wisconsin, USA
Self-exploration: "Ask yourself one thing: have I ever yearned so badly for something that I would stop at nothing to obtain it? It is this emotional drive that the word 'pine' defines…." This from a punk band?

Dogwood
San Diego, California, USA
The band was Half-Off. After a few shows, a family member suggested "Dogwood," in reference to the type of wood used to construct the cross on which Jesus was crucified.

Willowtree Stockholm, Sweden, and Berlin, Germany
Engaged in internet battle with the band Roaring Silence over rehearsal space issues. Roaring Silence has accused Willowtree of liking IKEA furniture and listening to Tool.

White Willow Norway
Progressive rock since 1995: "We have long songs and short songs, sometimes complicated, sometimes easygoing. Sometimes crunchy guitars, sometimes hazy flutes and Mellotrons. Sometimes suicidal, sometimes euphoric. We are sometimes angry men, and sometimes fairy godmothers. We are White Willow, and proud of it!"

The Walnuts
San Diego, California, USA
Personal history: "The story of the Walnuts is an epic tale of death, love, pain, loss, self-destruction, struggle and the pure beauty of making music an art form of our own expression. It all started back in the time of cave people, when music was created by impulse and curiosity. We were there."

The **Morningwood tree** grows in New York City. Caught you skimming. *Rolling Stone* reviewer Jonathon Ringen writes: "Morningwood's dirty name perfectly suits the glammed-out, Times Square-in-the-Seventies vibe of its debut…Singer Chantal Claret's voice overflows with personality, veering from bubblegum cuteness…to full-on raunch…as former members of the Wallflowers, Spacehog and Cibo Matto generate a catchier-than-chlamydia mix of power-pop hooks and effects-heavy riffage."

The Walnut Dash Essex, UK
Not strictly a tree reference, but "they may well be Britain's tallest band, with an average height of 6 foot 3." Songs include "Going Straight," "Your Mum," and "Stupid O'Clock."

The Axe That Chopped the Cherry Tree
Denver, Colorado, USA
With an experimental extra-loud metal axe. From the legend that, as a youth, first president George Washington chopped down a cherry tree, fell under suspicion and declared to his father, "I cannot tell a lie…."

The White Birch Oslo, Norway
They take a lot of time between albums: "TWB believes in music that is made like diamonds…the pressing of mountains of coal into intensely focused drops of honest nature…."

Sumac Los Angeles, California, USA
Late '90s folk-pop quintet whose first album was titled *This Is Junk Rock*.

Hazel Portland, Oregon, USA
Not without a sense of humor, this pop-punk band was known to appear with its own dancer and medicine man. Their second album: *Are You Going to Eat That?*

Soul Cactus Orlando, Florida, USA
Cajun zydeco party music. Album: *Smell the Love*. Songs: "Too Close to the Liquor Store" and "I'm Drunk and I'm Working."

Skullfish Cactus
Chicago, Illinois, USA
Legend of Zelda game references? Toured with Smashing Pumpkins and Jesus Lizard.

81

Bush

Formed in 1992, the band named themselves Bush after their home district of Shepherd's Bush, West London.

Bush proved far more successful in the US than in the UK. [Not meant as a joke. Or maybe it is.] They managed to tap into a post-Nirvana grunge market still viable in America at the time. A persistent annoyance was the need to release albums as Bush X in Canada due to the prior existence of the '70s Canadian band Bush. The copyright holder of the name, guitarist-producer Domenic Troiano, eventually agreed to Bush's clear use of the name in exchange for their donations to two Canadian charities.

Their 1994 debut album, *Sixteen Stone*, went six-times platinum in the US. Its follow-up two years later, *Razorblade Suitcase*, went to #1 in the US and to #4 in the UK.

Many of the band's songs have been used in film soundtracks, and lead singer Gavin Rossdale has had roles in *Zoolander*, *Little Black Book*, *The Game of Their Lives*, *Constantine*, and other films.

Get Thee to a Shrubbery

Sugarbush
Birmingham, Alabama, USA

Sugarbush is a sweet-leafed plant that flourishes in the southeast United States. "Sugarbush is also a band of guys…who want to crash your party, drink your whiskey and break your techno CDs in half so that we can get drunk and listen to the new *Hank 3*."

Bustle in Your Hedgerow
Brooklyn, New York, USA

Getting their Led out. This Led Zeppelin cover band takes their name from the "Stairway to Heaven" lyric.

THE TRIMMED HEDGES
are Andy Juhl, Dominique Davis, Brian Davis and Evan Bremer. *The Seas Elected* is the first full-length album from this Minneapolis-based experimental-rock quartet. Their 2006 EP *Abandoned Cities* drew this response from KyndMusic/ RightAction reviewer Dave Terpeny: "The Trimmed Hedges are an impressive quartet that seems to understand how to encapsulate the folk, blues and psychedelic roots of prog-rock into a modern art rock sensibility."

Hedge Dweller
Cornwall, UK

Hedge Dweller as in hedgehog or peeping Tom or homeless person? Anyway, the guitarist has gone off to London, so they'll be looking for a third to pay hedge rent.

Hedgecreep
Memphis, Tennessee, USA

Review by *Sleazegrinder*: "Hedgecreep is a fantastic band name. Hedgecreep! You can see it, right? Some sweaty dude behind the bushes at the park, peeping at rollerskating teenies through cokebottle glasses. Awesome. Hedgecreep (the band) is from Memphis, and they play fuzzy, dizzy, Sleestack-motherfucker drug rock."

The Shrubs
Watford, UK

"After being sacked from the Stump for being too serious, Nick Hobbs formed his own band…." The Shrubs' 1986 single: "Full Steam into the Brainstorm." Debut album: *Take Me Aside for a Midnight Harangue*.

The Shrubbers
Milwaukee, Wisconsin, USA

The Shrubbers put down their pruners in 2000, came indoors and formed the Modern Machines.

Shrubbies
London, UK

Their 1999 album bears the curious title *Memphis in Texas* and contains the song "Twiddle Your Thumbs Mum."

Vocalist and lead guitarist Craig Nicholls' father played in a Sydney, Australia, Elvis cover band called the Vynes. Craig co-opted the name (with proper spelling) after the press habitually misspelled his band's previous name, Rishikesh, named after a city in India where the Beatles went to study meditation with Maharishi Mahesh Yogi. After paying their dues locally, **the Vines** broke in the UK in 2001 with the release of their first single, "Factory." Their first album, *Highly Evolved*, followed in 2002 and climbed to #3 on the UK Album charts, #5 in Australia and #11 in the US. They have enjoyed both success and critical acclaim since and recently released their fourth album, *Melodia*.

NAMES
STILL AVAILABLE

Creambush

Wicked
Pruning Tools

The Boxwood
Stranglers

Way Off Gorse

The Deadly
Nevergreens

My Privet Life

Missing Forsythia

The Shrub Chubbies

Quince Jones

Yew & Myrtle

Bets Best Hedged

Bramble On

Azalea Arson
Cambridge, Ontario, Canada
Protect your flowering shrubs! Songs from their debut EP: "Guns Don't Kill People, Husbands Who Come Home Early Do" and "John Madden Never Liked Football."

Azalea City Penis Club
Bristol, UK
A modified Azalea City Tennis Club? Anyway, it sounds painful. Keep it in your pants.

The Lilac Time
Herefordshire, UK
The name comes from the Nick Drake song "River Man."

Lilac Ambush
Goucester, Massachusetts, USA
Lilac bush, lilac am-bush. Lilac bush becomes vengeful, lies in wait.

Periwinkle Sydney, Australia
Became Dappled Cities.

The Hollies Manchester, UK
This 1960s beat band apparently took their name while hanging Christmas holly, not as a reference to Buddy Holly, as is often thought. The name was supposed to be a temporary fix. The original lineup consisted of lead singer Allan Clarke, guitarists Graham Nash and Vic Steele, bassist Eric Haydock and drummer Don Rathbone. Steele and Rathbone were soon replaced by Tony Hicks and Bobby Elliott. Elton John is the session pianist on the group's 1968 hit cover of "He Ain't Heavy." Dissatisfied with the commercial sound of the Hollies, Graham Nash joined supergroup Crosby, Stills & Nash.

Creeping Myrtle
Seattle, Washington, USA
Creeping myrtle thrives in the rainy northwest. Their 1999 album, *Ode to the Urchin,* contains these well-titled tunes: "A Good Mope," "Departure Never Leaves" and "The Nether Reaches of Florid Dandyism."

83

Hothouse Flowers

School friends Liam O'Maonlaí and Fiachna O'Braonáin began their musical partnership as street buskers in Dublin in 1985, calling themselves the Incomparable Benzini Brothers. They were joined by Peter O'Toole and as a group became Street Entertainers of the Year.

They adopted a new name, borrowing from trumpeter Wynton Marsalis's 1984 album *Hot House Flowers*. Their early performances led *Rolling Stone* to call them "the best unsigned band in Europe." Not for long, as U2's Mother Records released their first single, "Love Don't Work This Way," leading to a contract with London Records, then to an album that became the top debut effort in the history of Irish music.

Despite lineup changes, and personal and professional troubles that led to a hiatus in the mid-90s, O'Maonlaí and O'Braonáin have kept the Hothouse Flowers alive and vital, with new music and new gigs and tours through 2008.

Back to the Garden

Soundgarden
Seattle, Washington, USA

The band named themselves after a wind-channeling pipe-sculpture garden called the Sound Garden in Seattle's Magnuson Park. Soundgarden introduced unusual time signatures and open tunings to grunge and metal elements to the alternative-rock.

Savage Garden
Brisbane, Australia

The name comes from a line in Anne Rice's novel *The Vampire Chronicles*: "The mind of each man is a savage garden...."

The Seeds
Los Angeles, California, USA

Muddy Waters called this 1960s blues-rock band "America's own Rolling Stones." Lead singer Sky Saxon joined the Yohowha religious sect in the 1970s. Best known for their 1966 hit "Pushin' Too Hard."

The Flower Pot Men
London, UK

A 1967 psychedelic harmony-vocal band named for the BBC kids' program *Flower Pot Men*, but with period allusions to pot and flower power. Very soft-edged considering the band contained Nick Simper (bass) and Jon Lord (organ), who went on to Deep Purple the following year.

Motorflower
Boise, Idaho, USA

Motörhead meets flower power. Newest album: *Under the Daisy*. Motorflower has toured with the Wallflowers.

The Wallflowers
Los Angeles, California, USA

Named for the estranged and homely, the Wallflowers are led by Jakob Dylan, who became something of a charismatic heartthrob via the band's videos. In the band's early days, Dylan refused to allow his name to appear in the publicity notices, as he didn't want to bring the Son of Bob Dylan issue to bear on his band. Their 1994 album, *Bringing Down the Horse,* hit #4 on US Album charts.

Soul Flower Union Osaka, Japan
Formed in 1993, SFU (as they are often called) blend psychedelic rock, traditional Okinawan music, world music and Chin-Don (Japanese street music).

The Flower Kings were formed in 1993 by veteran Swedish guitarist Roine Stolt as a touring band to support his solo album, *The Flower King*, but remained together after the tour. Their 1999 album, *Flower Power,* contains one of the longest progressive-rock tracks ever recorded, the 18-section, nearly 60-minute "Garden of Dreams." Their latest album is 2007's *The Sum of No Evil.* "By incorporating jamming and new twists to every show, Flower Kings have built a devoted fan base of 'Flowerheads' that follow them all over the globe."

Blossom Toes
London, UK

Late '60s psychedelic pop from a band originally called the Ingoes. Name changed when signed to Marmalade Records. Guitarist Jim Cregan later joined Stud, followed by stints in Family, the Cockney Rebels and Rod Stewart's band. Brian Godding and Brian Belshaw formed the band B.B. Blunder.

Gin Blossoms
Tempe, Arizona, USA

Named for the colloqial term for rosacea, reddening of the skin, often accompanied by bumpiness. Alcohol consumption can aggravate the condition. The band saw a photo of legendary comedic actor (and drinker) W.C. Fields with nose in full bloom. The caption read, "W.C. Fields with gin blossoms."

Based in Regina, Saskatchewan, Canada, **Sonic Orchid** has been performing together since 2002. Their recent full-length debut album is entitled *Love & War*. The Saskatoon *Star Phoenix* had this to say about the band's live set: "Sonic Orchid really knows how to whip up an audience. With a delicious blend of kick-ass rock and raw, steamy sex appeal, Sonic Orchid is intense and is guaranteed to keep you primed. Frontwoman [Christine] Gasparic is no wallflower, playing guitar and commanding respect with her stage persona."

Blossomhead
Queensland, Australia

Blossomhead adds it up: "74 minutes, 24 songs, 11 musicians…7 years in the making, 1 epic album." It's entitled *Dream Beautiful*.

The Voom Blooms
Loughborough, UK

Drummer Thom Mackie claims he woke one morning with the band's name inexplicably etched in his mind. Frontman George Guildford recalls, "One night at about 3 AM, Thom texted me to say, 'We are called the Voom Blooms.'"

Krokus Solothurn, Switzerland

The band name Krokus comes from the word *crocus*, a flower common to regions of southern Europe. In early spring 1975, band founder Chris von Rohr saw a field of crocuses from a train window while returning from the L'Ecole des Chefs in France. He had decided to abort his career in the culinary arts, "and it was around this time the idea for a metal band was formed." All Krokus's albums have gone platinum in Switzerland.

Black Orchid

A favorite name for metal bands. Several in the UK, US, Australia, France, Spain, Mexico…

The Bluebells Glasgow, Scotland

Early '80s jangly guitar pop from vocalist Robert Bluebell (Robert Hodgens), who later joined Up and subsequently the Poems. Guitarist Craig Gannon briefly joined the Smiths. They had three Top 40 hits in the UK. One of them, "Young at Heart," later went to #1 after its use in a Volkswagen commercial.

NAMES STILL AVAILABLE

Flowerplower

Roses Are Rent

Crypt Orchid

The Advantageous Mowers

Lilies of the Valium

The Bloodshot Irises

Vinyl Flora

Peony Fetishists

The Sex Pistils

Weed the People

Fred Savage Garden

The Rhododendonnas

Tripping Daisy
Dallas, Texas, USA

Psychedelic grunge from the '90s. Albums: *Bill* (1992), *I Am an Electric Firecracker* (1995), *Jesus Hits Like the Atom Bomb* (1998) and *Tripping Daisy* (2000). The band broke up following death of guitarist Wes Berggren. Members went on to play with the Polyphonic Spree, Secret Machines and When Babies Eat Pennies.

Pansy Division
San Francisco, California, USA

Pansy = sissy = queer = a founding band of queercore rock movement. Pun on "panzer division," a German Army armored division.

The Posies
Bellingham, Washington, USA

They initially considered "the Poppies" as name but used Posies instead, "kind of play on Poseurs." Core members Jon Auer and Ken Stringfellow started as duo in 1986. Stringfellow is a member of R.E.M.'s touring band

Desert Rose Band
California, USA

Named for, uh, desert roses. "Desert rose" is the name geologists give to crystalized, rosette-shaped gypsum-barite formations. Highly talented country-crossover band featuring the Byrds' Chris Hillman, John Jorgenson, Herb Pedersen, et al.

The Stone Roses
Manchester, UK

Singer Ian Brown and guitarist John Squire formed the band in the mid–80s as a punk group called the Patrol. The name comes from the title of a 1959 spy thriller by Sarah Gainham.

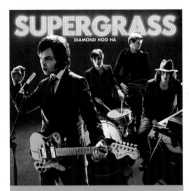

Formed 1993 in Oxford, UK, **Supergrass** first called themselves Theodore Supergrass, with the idea of creating a fictitious band leader, an animated character, who could do interviews. Due to the prohibitive costs of such animation, the idea was scrapped, along with the name Theodore. Their debut single, "Caught by the Fuzz," was based on a real incident involving singer-guitarist Gaz Coombs. In 1995–96 they won the NME Best New Band award, the Q Awards' Best New Act prize, the BRIT Awards' British Breakthrough Act prize and were nominated for the Mercury Prize in Best Album category. Supergrass has released six studio albums, including 2008's *Diamond Hoo Ha.*

Black Roses Derby, UK

Black roses do not exist. However, very deep red roses are often referred to as black and associated with death. There was a 1988 film entitled *Black Roses*, with a hard-rock band of the same name.

Boris the Sprinkler
Green Bay, Wisconsin, USA

Rumored to be Australian and Dutch bands by the same name. The Wisconsin band's debut album was titled *8-Testicled Pogo Machine*. Their name is a pun on the Who song "Boris the Spider," from *Meaty Beaty Big and Bouncy*.

The Grass Roots
Los Angeles, California, USA

The name applied to several bands assembled to perform material by Dunhill Records songwriting duo Steve Barri and P.F. Sloan. The first band hired were formerly called the Bedouins. The second group hired had previously performed as the 13th Floor. These Grass Roots groups scored 1 platinum album, 2 gold albums and 13 gold singles, most of them between 1966 and 1975.

Brady Bunch Lawnmower Massacre
Melbourne, Australia

Country-punk fusion from Melbourne's busiest singer-cartoonist, Fred Negro (apparently his actual name). Negro has fronted such acts as I Spit on Your Gravy, the Fuck Fucks, Squirming Gerbil Death, the Twits, They Might Be Negroes, and 57 Pages of Pink. It is tempting to dedicate this book to him.

Formaldehyde Dandelion
Gore Bay, Ontario, Canada

Formed in 1994 in a small town on Manitoulin Island. This band's name combines two of our favorite things.

The Weeds
Stittsville, Ontario, Canada

EP called *Groove Juice*. Songs have color titles: "Pink," "Indigo," "Grey," "Blue" and "Topaz."

Weed Patch
Los Angeles, California, USA

Mood swing in the weed patch: 2003 debut album, *Maybe the Brakes Will Fail*; recent album, *Some Kinda Happy*.

Food & Drink

Food & Drink

Where To Eat

The Main Ingredient

The Main Ingredient took off in 1970 with a series of Top 40 US R&B hits, but the trio, comprised of Donald McPherson, Tony Silvester and Luther Simmons, Jr., had been singing together in Harlem since 1964 as the Poets and then the Insiders. Perhaps the main ingredient in their turn-of-the-decade success was the addition of orchestral strings, which became an essential part of '70s soul.

When lead singer McPherson died suddenly of leukemia, Silvester and Simmons decided to continue with former backup vocalist Cuba Gooding, Sr. in the lead role. The new Main Ingredients soon released the #3 Pop chart hit "Everybody Plays the Fool." While they never charted as high again, they maintained a presence in the R&B Top 100 through the mid-70s, when Silvester left to produce, Gooding left for a solo shot with Motown, and Simmons left to work as a stockbroker.

Grand Buffet
Pittsburgh, Pennsylvania, USA
Grand Buffet's often satirical white rap-rock lyrics fill every hole in the steam tray. The duo of Jackson O'Connell-Barlow (aka Iguanadon, Grape-a-Don, Plaps) and Jarrod Weeks (aka Lord Grunge, Viceroy, M-Dog) held a release show for their recent CD, *King Vision*, at the American Legion Hall in Squirrel Hill, PA, but they have toured with such name acts as Of Montreal, MGMT and Suicide Girls.

All You Can Eat Buffet
Brick, New Jersey, USA
Skaboys from NJ: "Our singer came up with our name and we thought it was good." Actually, a Las Vegas hotel manager named Herb Macdonald is often credited with the first commercial use of the term "all you can eat," having posted it in an ad in the mid-1940s. The French cooked up the modern buffet-style meal in the 18th century but failed to explore its all-you-can-eat potential.

Food Will Win the War
New York City, New York, USA
Harmonious folk-rock from NYC. The slogan "Food Will Win the War" was used by the US goverment during both World Wars to encourage farmers to produce more food and conserve supplies as part of the war effort.

Trilobite Café
Nashville, Tennessee, USA
Heavy rock with keyboards, bass, drums and violin. Tennessee spent a few million years underwater, so trilobite fossils abound. Not recommended as a menu item.

Sad Café   Manchester, UK
Carson McCullers' novella *The Ballad of the Sad Café* was published in 1951. The British soft-rockers Sad Café recorded a steady stream of albums from the mid-70s through 1981 and had a Top 5 UK single with "Every Day Hurts" in 1979. SAD cafés opened in Toronto, Helsinki and London in the late '90s, offering Seasonal Affective Disorder sufferers blasts of spirit-lifting full-spectrum lighting with their lattes.

The Dinner Is Ruined Band
Toronto, Ontario, Canada
Started by Rheostatics drummer Dave Clark, the band has recorded eight albums, starting with *Burn Your Dashiki* and including *Worm Pickers Brawl* and *Elevator Music for Non-Claustrophobic People*. The band has also backed Tragically Hip singer Gordon Downie on his solo efforts.

Lavay Smith & the Red Hot Skillet Lickers
San Francisco, California, USA
Ouch! That's good.

The **"pancake fair"** community breakfast is a tradition

in many countries. Pancake Fair centers on the music of Californian Mike C. Webb, whose late '60s and early '70s influences (Creedence Clearwater Revival, Steely Dan, Humble Pie) shine through in both his song-writing and musicianship.

Antic Café
Tokyo, Japan

Sometimes billed as An Café or Antique Café. The band endorses the Japanese fashion label Sex Pot Revenge.

Jimmy Eat World
Mesa, Arizona, USA

According to guitarist Tom Linton, in a 1999 interview with Chris Blackburn, the band's name came from "a picture that my little brother drew — probably five years ago. My brother Jim beat up my younger brother Ed...and Ed drew this picture that said, 'Jimmy Eat World,' and it was a picture of him eating the world. My brother Jim is kind of a big guy."

I Spit on Your Gravy
Melbourne, Australia

The lead singer is Fred Negro, formerly of the Fuck Fucks. The lead guitarist is "General Sausage Fingers." The scantily but punkily clad backup singers are called the Spitettes. Don't say you weren't warned.

Funeral Diner
Moon Bay, California, USA

Just the place to go if you are dead but peckish and want a screamo band to serenade you while you decompose. Song title: "My Fist Smells Like Graveyard."

Eat London, UK

Listen to your mother: Eat. They released the album *Sell Me a God* on the Cure's label in 1989, then tried to eat each other. Or at least rip each other to shreds. A second album, *Epicure*, with two new guitarists, appeared in 1992. One critic called *Epicure* "one of the decade's greatest rock albums that no one has heard."

Starvin Hungry
Montreal, Quebec, Canada

They sound ravenous. Kind of like starvin hungry Arctic Monkeys. Kind of like the collective soul of starvin hungry but tragically hip arctic monkeys coming at you in a rusted-out Peugeot with no spare tire. In a good way.

NAMES
STILL AVAILABLE

Velveeta Underground

Dark Side of the Spoon

Björk's Fjörk

Cialis's Restaurant

Gobsnack

Houses of the Cannoli

Gluttony's Kitchen

The Lost Lunches

Fine Young Casseroles

Aunt Jezebel's Crab Shack

Flaming Pie Shop

Bistro Boys

The Egg

While the reason this progressive-rock trio settled on the name the Egg in 1969 remains a mystery, it is known that a London nightclub insisted they change their name from Uriel, the name they had previously used as a quartet (with Steve Hillage on guitar). In the Hebrew faith, Uriel is one of four angels who preside over the four corners of the earth. He's responsible for fire, thunder, earthquakes and perhaps guitarists. The nightclub's booking agents thought Uriel sounded too much like "urinal." Thus, organist Dave Stewart (not the Eurythmics David A. Stewart), bassist-vocalist Mont Campbell and drummer Clive Brooks became Egg.

Though plagued by label changes, they released three albums between 1970 and 1974: *Egg*, *The Polite Force* and *The Civil Surface*. Stewart went on to play with Hatfield and the North (named from a road sign) and National Health (named for the, uh, national health plan). Campbell also spent time as a member of National Health. British author Jonathan Coe's bestselling novel *The Rotter's Club* took its title from Hatfield and the North's second album.

Breakfast Specials

The Toasters
New York City, New York, USA
The Toasters started in 1981 and bill themselves as "the Ramones of Ska" and "the longest-running ska band in America." Early albums produced by Joe Jackson. Other Toaster bands include Toaster Fork! and Throwing Toasters.

The Square Egg
New York City, New York, USA
Inspired by Ronald Searle's book *The Square Egg and the Vicious Circle*. Song title: "Whatever Happened to Crack."

Sunny Side Down
Kansas City, Missouri, USA
They say Missouri loves company.

Toast
Guitarist Paul Trottier: "'Toast' has a comically fatalistic charm ('Uh-oh, we're toast') as well as the classic imagery of toasting champagne glasses. It has worked well for us. We're proud to say, 'We're Toast!'" The Chicago north shore band released *Ekstreemleeburnt* in 2004. Toast boxers, thongs and barbecue aprons are also available.

The Disco Biscuits
Philadelphia, Pennsylvania, USA
A name suggested by band friend Rob Hainey. Later realized that their music didn't really go with the name, but they have evolved to fit it by mixing jam-band flow with electronic beats.

Big Biscuit Express
Ventura, California, USA
"The Biscuit originates from Biscuitonia 5, a small planet located in sector 13 of the Orsini/Gagliardi nebula."

Green Eggs & Sam
Washington, DC, and Honolulu, Hawaii, USA
From the 1960 book by Dr. Seuss, *Green Eggs and Ham*. DC jam band: "The trio began in the winter of 2002 when two ordinary Budweiser-drinking guys [on bass and drums] adopted Sam [harmonica, guitar, vocals]." I'm told there's also a wedding band in Honolulu with a 96-year-old singer and some performance involving key-lime Speedos and hula hoops.

Half Man, Half Biscuit
Birkenhead, UK
He's a man, he's a cookie. Serving acerbic post-punk since 1984. Frontman Nigel Blackwell writes gritty, often satirical songs about working-class life. New album, *CSI: Ambleside,* parodies the *CSI* TV series.

Limp Bizkit
Jacksonville, Florida, USA
There's the story that the name came about when singer Fred Durst's dog Bizkit was temporarily hobbled by an injury, but more dependable sources suggest that the name came from a stoned roadie who commented that his brain felt like "a limp biscuit."

"Voyage Through the Lava Lamp is more than an album," writes band leader Robin Reda from his office at Zebra Valance Records in Los Angeles. "It is the soundtrack to your lava lamp. That's right, put it in your changer and gaze into the lava." **The Electric Marmalade** is the psychedelic '60s in all its tie-dyed glory, baby, with Reda on 12-string Rickenbacker and vocals, Devin Thomas (Wild Child, Oingo Boingo) on organ and Dave Beyer (Melissa Etheridge, Christopher Cross) on drums.

The Rolling Scones
Bakersfield, California, USA
"We are basically a tribute band to Weezer. Oh, and we eat spaghetti."

Sausage   Bay Area, California, USA
A Les Claypool enterprise. The original lineup of Primus got together in '94 and recorded *Riddles Are Abound Tonight*. Mr. Claypool's various band incarnations include Les Claypool's Frog Brigade, Les Claypool & the Holy Mackerel, Colonel Claypool's Bucket of Bernie Brains, and Oysterhead.

Baconflex   Denmark
"Electro glam and Tricky disco with cynical catchy tunes. Silverfoxdancer and DiscoPapa are the foundation of Baconflex, while prominent vocalist Merete Grr adds foxy tones and spicy attitude to programming."

Unexplained Bacon
Warwick, New York, USA
This jam-rock band was named after a quote from Homer. In *The Simpsons* episode "Treehouse of Horror XII," a computer tries to murder Homer in order to have Marge all to itself. It lures him downstairs in the middle of the night by cooking bacon. A sleepwalking Homer comes downstairs declaring, "Mmm...unexplained bacon!"

Hot Waffles
Cypress, California, USA
Comedy-folk-metal fusion from the Waffle brothers, Tim and Chris. Songs: "Have You Kicked an Emo Kid's Ass?" and "George Lucas Raped Our Childhood."

Breakfast Society
Cologne, Germany
The German word for breakfast is *Frühstück*. Album: *Breakfast on the Roof*.

Angry Man Breakfast
New York City, New York, USA
Swanson prepared foods offers a Hungry Man Breakfast. And "Hungry men ar angry," wrote D. Ferguson in *Scottish Proverbs* in 1641. Drummer-percussionist Todd Turkisher and multi-instrumentalist-sound manipulator Paul Socolow have, together or independently, played with David Byrne, Philip Glass, Tito Puente, Astrud Gilberto and Tiny Tim. Songs include "My Favorite Teeth" and "Trouser Ritual."

Bad Dream Good Breakfast
Seattle, Washington, USA
Orchestral indie rock with a 12-piece live band.

NAMES
STILL AVAILABLE

The Rolling
Doughnut Pimps

Mostly Muesli

Papa's Got a
Brand New Bagel

Granola Gay &
the Atomic Breakfast

Wafflehaus

Transcendental
Omelettes

A Hit with
the Breakfast Club

Sir Francis Bacon's
Sizzlin' Strips

The Cerealist Manifesto

Whole Lotta Latte

Adam & the Croissants

Yo La Ten
Go for Yogurt

Hot Chip

The electro-pop quintet Hot Chip was formed in 2000 by sixth-form classmates Alexis Taylor and Joe Goddard from Putney, in southwest London, and includes Owen Clarke, Felix Martin and Al Doyle.

The band is also known for its DJ talent. All five members of Hot Chip took part in BBC Radio One's *The Essential Mix* radio program, hosted by legendary DJ Pete Tong, on December 29, 2007. As Hot Chip, they combine guitars, keyboards, synthesizers, drums and samplers. Live, they often improvise songs on the fly, creating completely new versions in an almost jazz-like manner.

In a *DustedMagazine.com* interview, Joe Goddard discussed the band's name, "You know the feeling when you put a chip or French fry into your mouth and it's much too hot and it burns your tongue? It's a really immediate, undeniable, exploding feeling. We wanted to make music like that."

The Lunch Menu

Hotdog Manila, Philippines
Started by brothers Dennis and Rene Garcia in the mid-70s, Hotdog is one of the pioneers of the "Manila Sound," defined as "a very light kind of pop music that uses Taglish language and is full of juvenile sentiments."

Corndogs
Lillehammer, Norway
Started as the Rascals in 2003 but changed their name to the Corndogs when they realized the name Rascals was taken. Debut album: *Fastback on the Fast Track.*

Evil Weiner
Carrboro, North Carolina, USA
Popmatters.com: "Bill 'Billy Sugarfix' McCormick is the genteel man behind small-wonder band Evil Wiener... Despite the foreboding sound of the band's name, Evil Wiener's music is fantastical pop, rough-hewn gems... McCormick's day job as a substitute schoolteacher may also inform his sense of child-like innocence, as explored on the records from which this tribute release takes its basis, last year's *Evil Wiener Presents Billy Sugarfix's Lost Gumdrop Kingdom,* and the band's first full-length album, *Haunted House of Our Love.*"

Hot Club Sandwich
Olympia, Washington, USA
Combining the legendary Quintette du Hot Club de France with a triple-layer sandwich. Members also play in other bands Dysfunction Junction, Los Flacos, the Klezmer Mountain Boys, the SuperSones, the Coasters and the Djangomatics.

Los Angeles rockers **Wicked Relish** are Servet Fidan (vocals), Mike Villasenor (keyboards), Brian Ferrero (guitars), Gabe Rueda (bass) and Al Rueda (drums). Their most recent album is *Strange Friends*, perhaps referencing their encounters at their many club gigs along Hollywood's famed Sunset Strip. Fidan on the name: "We were kicking around names, and I was reading some article on Temple of the Dog. In the article, it described Chris Cornell's voice as being like a 'wicked relish' to Gossard's guitars. We get some crap about the name once in a great while — the wicked part — but we love it and most others do too."

The Blair Hordeski Sandwich
Portage la Prairie, Manitoba, Canada
Blair Hordeski is a singer-songwriter. His Sandwich includes Crash Test Dummies guitarist Murray Pulver.

Cheeseburger
Brooklyn, New York, USA
Stooges-influenced garage rock to eat cheeseburgers by. Their song "Cocaine" was featured in the *Grand Theft Auto IV* video game.

Steamed Clams
Barrow-in-Furness, UK

Intentionally silly, raw garage-rock played by school chums since 2002. Songs: "Elmo the Emo Emu," "Fashionable Knitwear" and "The Herman Verghner Appreciation Song."

Red Flannel Hash
Long Island, New York, USA

These guys started playing in high school in the early '70s, then reformed in Upstate New York in 1997. "Folks have read all sorts of things into this over the years. Quite simply, Red Flannel Hash came from a recipe on a New England calendar. It doesn't sound very good, but I must confess none of us have made it, so I can't say for sure. Something about leftover corned beef and beets!

Chicken Gravy
Brooklyn, New York, USA

Funky soul-jazz with musicians from four countries. Album: *It's Better with Chicken Gravy*.

Spam Allstars Miami, Florida, USA

Yes, Spam was a food first, long before email and text-messaging. This is Latin dance-funk played by a nine-piece band with horns and adding turntables by DJ Le Spam (Andrew Yeomanson). Albums: *Pork Scratchings* (1999), *Pigs in Space* (2000), *Spam Allstars Contra Los Roboticos Mutantes* (2004) and *Spamusica* (2006).

Irish Stew of Sindidun
Belgrade, Serbia

Celtic punk from Serbia. Started as traditional Irish music cover band, but they began writing their own songs. What they now play is a mixture of punk-rock and various other genres, "mused by Irish music motives." The band is part of a large Celtic-music sub-culture in Serbia that includes the bands Orthodox Celts and Tir na n'Og, with many songs centered around the love of Guinness and Celtic FC. The name Sindidun comes from a song by the Orthodox Celts on their album *Green Roses*.

NAMES
STILL AVAILABLE

Dropkick Nachos

Chicken Henny

Hot Tuna
Seniors Special

Vegetarian
Still Life Creation

Meatloaf's Encore

St. Paul Reuben

Mr. Roboto
Sushi Surprise

Slow-Cooked
Pokey Gumbo

Portishead
Portabella Ziti

Mama Casserole

Microwave
Zappa Grouper

The Hoagies

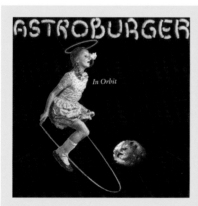

Astroburger is one of Norway's foremost alternative-pop bands. During their "2001: A Pop Odyssey" campaign, they released one 7-inch single a month. Twelve singles containing 26 songs. The most recent of their four full-length albums is *They Came From the Sun*. The band is helmed by the iconic donBingo, alter ego of band founder Geir Stadheim, a fixture in Oslo's independent arts community. More than 20 musicians have contributed as regular members of Astroburger since its formation in 1987.

Bowling for Soup

This Denton, Texas-based band's name is derived from comedian Steve Martin's "Bowling for Shit" sketch from his 1978 comedy album, *Wild and Crazy Guy*, itself a reference to the TV show *Bowling for Dollars*.

Their song "Girl All the Bad Guys Want" was nominated for a Grammy Award in the Best Performance by a Pop Duo or Group category. Frontman Jaret Reddick: "Now we're no longer known as the fat guys from Texas. Now we're the Grammy-nominated fat guys from Texas."

"Actually, we're all terrible bowlers," says Riddick. "We did a local Bowl-a-thon a few years ago, and we were picked to win because of our name. I think Chris bowled a 70. [And] I'm not a soup eater. But [guitarist] Chris loves the Wisconsin cheese soup. And I do like minestrone. But isn't that more of a stew?"

Select album titles: *A Hangover You Don't Deserve* (2004), *Bowling for Soup Goes to the Movies* (2005) and *The Great Burrito Extortion Case* (2006).

Soup or Salad?

Soup

Who would imagine the global desire to name your band after liquid food? Some Soups: Toulouse, France (pop); Volda, Møre og Romsdal, Norway (alternative-electronica); Berkeley, California (punk-rock); Oklahoma City, Oklahoma (blues-rock-jam). The latter sounds like it could get soupy.

Soupshop Vienna, Austria

From their band bio: "Once upon a time there were Dino (vox) and Jelio (guit /vox) and they happened to end up in a small, dingy joint of a restaurant on the nice island of Crete. This place opened at 4 in the morning and the only item on the non-existent menu was greasy goat soup, which was supposed to be the ultimate hangover cure. Well, the soup worked, and after several heavy drinking binges which ended at this 'Soupshop,' the name for the band was born."

Duck Soup

Copenhagen, Denmark
and Austin, Texas

Duck Soup is the title of a classic 1933 Marx Brother's film. The Danish Duck Soup is a ska-reggae band. The Texan Duck Soup calls itself the "Unofficial Band of the PGA."

Turtle Soup

Red Bank, New Jersey, USA

Winners of Top Jam Band and Top Groove Band awards at 2007 Asbury Music Awards. They played an eco-singles event called Green Singles Social Group, which is a safe, turtle-ish thing to do. *Turtle Soup* is the title of the Turtles 1969 album.

Hailing from Leeds, UK, **Loudmouth Soup** play a "gumbo of country, folk, psychedelia, vaudeville and various other unlikely sounds." *Leeds Music Scene* had this to say about a recent performance: "Loudmouth Soup's sound shows strong country influences, like [that of] the Band and Ryan Adams' more untempo moments. Their songs are introduced with a welcome wry humour, and they quickly have the crowd in their thrawl...." The title song from their debut album, *Skydiver*, is used as the theme music for the *A Bear's Tail* series on Channel 4. "Loudmouth soup" is a slang expression for alcoholic drink.

Soup Dragons Bellshill, Scotland
Named after a character in the BBC animated series *The Clangers*, which aired from 1969 to 1974. "The program featured a number of small creatures living in peace and harmony on — and in — a small, hollow planet far, far away, nourished by Blue String Pudding, and Green Soup harvested from the planet's volcanic soup wells by the Soup Dragon."

Gazpacho Oslo, Norway

Ambient prog-rock from Norway. From Keyboardist-producer Thomas Andersen on the band name: "We are a very unlikely mixture of people really, not the average types you'd expect to see in the same band…so we thought 'Gazpacho,' which really is the bastard of soups…Not that I'm soup obsessive or an expert in the field…with Gazpacho you get a surprise, something unexpected…."

Three Weed Salad

Austin, Texas, USA

Acoustic blues…funk…jam…looking to find a bass player…some odds and…live jams on MySpace…a whistler!…a pet bird? *Woah*, killer salad, dude. Song: "She's Out There with Coffeeboy."

"**Power Salad** is a comedy music group regularly heard on the nationally-syndicated *Dr. Demento Show* as well as on college and independent radio stations in the US and the Netherlands. The group evolved out of Akron, Ohio's radio comedy group Zot Theater in the late 1980s and has released three CDs of funny music." Tunes are written by Craig Marks and Chris Mezzolesta, and performed by Mezzolesta. Albums: *Force Doesn't Work on a Crustacean, Cinnamony Sea Anemone* and *Sweat Equity*.

Angry Salad

Boston, Massachusetts, USA

A 1990s pop band that had a college radio hit with their cover of "99 Red Balloons." Album: *Bizarre Gardening Accident*. They renamed themselves Star64 after being dropped by Atlantic Records. Guitarist Alex Grossi has also played with Quiet Riot, Bang Tango and numerous other bands.

The Salads

Newmarket, Ontario, Canada

Pop-punk band of friends since high school. Previous incarnations of the band: Lynx, Speechless, Pearl Necklace, the Curious George Invasion, 3 Sexy Guys on Stage, and Nacho Mama. Supposedly named by a friend of the band. "The Salads get their name from none other than the classy idea of rolling a mixed joint of weed and hash to make a 'salad.'"

Particle Salad

San Francisco, California, USA

Particle-accelerated salad. Ambient electronic music. One of several musical collaborative projects by Mark Fassett, who is also involved in Liquid State, Inglas, warrenpeece, 42 Shades of Gray, and Papa Bueno.

Rat Salad

Hollywood, California, USA

"Rat Salad" is an instrumental tune off Black Sabbath's 1970 album, *Paranoid*, and Rat Salad is a Black Sabbath cover band that bill themselves as "Hollywood's Best All-Male, English-Speaking Black Sabbath Cover Band." Begging the question…

NAMES
STILL AVAILABLE

Consommé Ted

Prince's Get
2 Ramen Soup

The Vichyssoise

Goat's Head Soup

Cream of
Magic Mushroom

Rock Lobster
Bisque

Ono Miso Ono

Lee J. Cobb Salad

Geek Salad

Waldork Salad

Brain Salad
Surge Effect

Rasta Salad

95

Moby Grape

Moby Grape is the punchline for the joke "What's big, purple and swims in the ocean?"

Many rock critics still consider Moby Grape to have been one of the best bands to come out of the San Francisco area at the height of the psychedelic '60s. Unlike in most bands, all five members wrote material and sang, and their musical styles moved freely between folk, country and driving blues-rock.

The impact of their 1967 self-titled debut album was perhaps diluted when their record company, Columbia, decided to conduct a marketing experiment by releasing ten of the album's 13 songs as singles. The album nonetheless peaked at #24 on the Pop Album charts. The Grape performed at the Monterey Pop Festival in the summer of '67, but legal issues kept them out of the film based on that legendary event.

The band's melodic three-guitar line-up included wild-eyed frontman Skip Spence, who had played drums on Jefferson Airplane's first album. Several musicians' biographies mention Spence's enthusiasm for LSD. He is said to have attacked a bandmate's hotel-room door while under the influence during the recording of the band's second record, *Wow/Grape Jam*. He was later diagnosed with schizophrenia.

A Nice Fruit Plate

The Applejacks USA and UK
Applejack is a traditional cider drink with a high alcohol content. The American Applejacks were an instrumental group who released some singles in the late '50s. Their "Mexican Hat Rock" broke into the Top 20. The British Applejacks were a quintet with vocals and had three British chart hits in 1964, including "Like Dreamers Do," written by a very young Paul McCartney. The early ad line for Kellogg's Apple Jacks cereal was "A bowl a day keeps the bullies away."

Not the only group ever to have been named **Fruit**, but among the best is Adelaide, Australia's gutsy female trio of Mel Watson, Susie Keynes and Sam Lohs. Formed in 1996, Fruit won Best Up-and-Coming Live Act at the 2001 Australian Live Music Awards and in 2003 took home the Best Live Album prize.

Apples in Stereo
Denver, Colorado, USA
The "Apples" part is said to have come from "Apples and Oranges," the last Pink Floyd song written by the late Syd Barrett. Though the band played as the Apples, they often used the old-school LP tagline "in stereo" on posters and in promotional material. Gradually, it became part of their name.

Appleseed
San Diego, California, USA
The seed of an apple. Johnny Appleseed was born John Chapman in 1774. He is remembered and celebrated for having brought the apple to many parts of the American Midwest. Less known is the fact that he was a Swedenborgian missionary spreading a branch of Christianity based on the writings of Emanuel Swedenborg, a Swedish scientist-turned-mystic who claimed to have witnessed God and been given the power to visit both heaven and hell at will and to speak to both angels and demons.

The Appleseed Cast
Lawrence, Kansas, USA
Perhaps the only band to move from Los Angeles to Kansas. Bandmember Chris Crisci: "There's a thousand bands per square mile in LA." One blogger claims Crisci took "Appleseed" from the title of a 2004 anime movie, the English translation of *Appurushido*. "Cast" presumably came from the credits.

Bad Apple

Los Angeles, USA, and Cairo, Egypt

The LA Bad Apples play "apple-core" alternative power-pop. The Cairo Bad Apples note that "Oriental tabla (drum), beat boxers, choir kids and Spanish guitar solos can all be found crawling up the explosive stage."

Black Apple

Chicago, Illinois, USA

The Arkansas Black apple (depicted on the band's website) is "one of the crispiest and most dense apples around," according to Produce Oasis.

Green Apple Quick Step

Seattle, Washington, USA

A term for diarrhea in the southern United States: what happens when you eat apples that aren't ripe and have to run for the facilities. This post-grunge band peaked in the mid-90s with a couple of albums, some MTV videos, and tours with Stone Temple Pilots, Rage Against the Machine, and Iggy Pop. Songs from their first album, *Wonderful Virus* include "Ludes and Cherrybombs" and "Eating on All Fours."

The Morbid Tavern Apple Choir

Unknown, Urbanmythland

After the Mormon Tabernacle Choir. This name regularly makes it onto lists of weird band names, but I have yet to unearth proof of their actual existence.

Bruised Apple

New York City, New York, USA

Acoustic duo. Self-description: "intelligent yet sensitive lyrics soothe the listening senses…." Please also read the article "Impedance Parameter Characterizing Apple Bruise" by Eszter Vozáry, Péter Lásló and Gábor Zsivánovits, from the University of Horticulture and Food, Budapest, Hungary.

The Silver Apples

New York City, New York, USA

Psychedelic electronic music duo featuring synthesizers and drums. Played in the late '60s. Reunited in the late '90s. The name comes from the Yeats poem "The Song of Wandering Aengus," which contains the lines "The silver apples of the moon/The golden apples of the sun."

Buckcherry

Los Angeles, California, USA

Guitarist Keith Nelson is quoted as saying, "There was this transvestite named Buckcherry who always used to bum cigarettes off me outside the shows. He was a nice guy, but a complete Hollywood freak." He means it in the nicest way. Nelson, singer Josh Todd and fellow bandmembers are well known for getting their collective freak on.

Wild Cherry

Steubenville, Ohio, USA

Famous for their 1976 hit "Play That Funky Music (White Boy)," Wild Cherry's name was taken from a package of cough drops by the band's guitarist and lead vocalist, Rob Parissi. The band was named Best Pop Group of the Year by *Billboard* magazine, and they went on to record three more albums in the late '70s. In 1990 Vanilla Ice (Robert Matthew Van Winkle) sampled "Play That Funky Music" in a song with the same title but failed to credit Parissi. The copyright infringement is said to have cost Mr. Ice a cool half-million.

Black Grape

Manchester, UK

Sour grapes in their band situation with Happy Mondays in 1993 led vocalist Shaun Ryder and dancer Bez to break away and form Black Grape with rappers from the Ruthless Rap Assassins and a guitarist named Wags. Their debut album went to #1 on the UK charts and their subsequent album to #11.

San Francisco Bay *Guardian* reviewer Howard Myint noted this Santa Barbara, California, band's distinctive "cathedral of reverb" sound and guitarist Jared Stivers' "bee-in-the-bonnet lead." Key to the **CHERRIES'** sound is its female vocalist. Known simply as Annalee, she weaves world-weary melodic lines above the crunch of guitar, bass and drums. Their 1998 CD title *Crotchrocket* apparently refers to the motorcycle depicted in the liner photos and labeled "Crotchrocket."

Walker &
the Brotherhood of the Grape
New York City, New York, USA

The Brotherhood of the Grape is the title of John Fante's 1977 novel about growing up in an Italian-American family. Poet Charles Bukowski wrote of him, "Fante was my god." Walker Hornung (the Walker in Walker &...) is a big Bukowski fan.

Banana Blender Surprise
Houston, Texas, USA

With the instant classics "Ode to Mergatroyd" and "Stay Away from My GE Deluxe." A remastered 2-CD retro-spective entitled *Paint the Town Brown* was released in 2006. The recipe is a secret.

Bananarama London, UK

The unnamed band's demo was "Aie a Mwana," a song by Black Blood, sung in Swahili. In an interview with DJ Ron Slomowicz, bandmember Keren Woodward explains, "It came from the Roxy Music song ['Pajamarama'], and 'Bananas' was just sort of one of those things. We were 18 and our first single was sung in Swahili and we thought that bananas were tropical... and I think someone sort of threatened us, if you don't get a name by the end of the day we're going to call you the Pineapple Chunks, which would have been a lot worse."

Melt-Banana Tokyo, Japan

Founded by friends attending Tokyo University of Foreign Studies. The Japanese noise-pop trio (with drummer du jour) has released eight albums and 23 EPs. These include 2005's *13 Hedgehogs* and 2007's *Bambi's Dilemma*.

The funk-rock horn band **Deep Banana Blackout** was formed in 1995 by former players from Connecticut's Tongue & Groove and Long Island's Pack of Matches. According to guitarist Fuzz: "We originally had a generic funk band name, you know, something with the word 'funk' in it...Zzzzzzzzz. One day, Jen [singer Jen Durkin] came to a gig and told us of a dream she'd had in which I was sitting on a rock and said to her, 'We must call the band "Deep Banana Blackout!"' We started saying into the mics that night that we were Deep Banana Blackout. We had so much fun goofing with it, and it was so much better than the name we were using, we just kept using it after that."

Banana Boy
Victoria, Australia

"Originally we were going to call it 'Two Blokes in the Throes of Middle-Aged Crisis Plus a Young Stunner Who Sings Like Aretha Franklin Having a Go at Dance Music,' but on reflection it sounded a bit drawn out...and also we don't happen to have a young stunner who sings like Aretha Franklin." Slang term for a guy with a curved penis.

The Banana Convention
Saginaw, Michigan, USA

All the fun and twice the potassium.

Banana Fish Zero
New York City, New York, USA

They cite their record label as Visa and Mastercard. *Banana Fish* is a manga that ran in Japan from the mid-80s to mid-90s. The plotline: An American soldier in wartime Vietnam goes crazy and guns down his friends. Since that time, the only words he has spoken are..."Banana Fish." J.D. Salinger's story "A Perfect Day for Bananafish" appeared in the January 31, 1948, edition of *The New Yorker*.

The Rockin' Berries
Birmingham, UK

A British Invasion band that missed the troop plane. The Berries had some solid UK hits in the mid-60s but failed to crack the US market. They eventually evolved from a light pop, vocal-harmony group into a cabaret-style musical comedy act.

Blueberry Spy
Massachusetts, USA

I spy, with my little eye, a blue fruit concealing weapons of mass destruction. Their 1995 album *Sing Sing* contains the songs "Just Drink the Hemlock" and "Shooting Birds at Mimes."

Blueberry
New York, New York, USA

"Gwen Snyder [vocals, keyboards] lives on her own planet — the planet Blueberry. And if you have even the tiniest drop of soul in your sauce you're really going to like it there. It's a place where lush folds of velvet vapor rise like street steam after a summer rain." All true, and high in antioxidants, too.

The Raspberries
Cleveland, Ohio, USA

In a 2007 phone interview with the *Ventura County Star*, former band-member Eric Carmen explained: "Are you familiar with the Little Rascals [from the *Our Gang* series]? There was a character in some of the episodes names Froggy. Anyway, in one episode, every time something would happen, he'd say, 'Aw, raspberries!' in that froggy voice. We'd been rehearsing for about a month and had tried to come up with a name, but we hadn't found anything we liked. Any time anyone came up with an idea, it was met with things thrown at them, booing and hissing, or whatever. We were really getting down to the wire — our first date was coming up in about a week and we hadn't named the band yet. That [*Our Gang*] episode was on, and I came into the rehearsal with my latest idea and they all hated it, and I said, 'Aw, raspberries!' and that was how it happened."

Strawberry Whiplash
Glasgow, Scotland, UK

Sweet-with-a-kick duo Laz and Sandra. Laz's other project is called Bubblegum Lemonade, named after (Mama) Cass Elliott's 1969 solo album *Bubble Gum, Lemonade & Something for Mama*.

NAMES
STILL AVAILABLE

Pomegranate Counters

I Sawyer Huckleberry

The Gitchee Papayayas

Tangelo Dundee

Enter the Dragonfruit

Persimmons in Mono

The Fig Nubians

Onanapple

Cranberry Shingles

A Boysenberry Beret

Rage Against the Tangerine

The Grape Peeler Diaries

Strawberry Switchblade from Glasgow, Scotland, are essentially friends Jill Byron and Rose McDowall. James Kirk, from the band Orange Juice, came up with the name. He had used it as the title of a fanzine, which he had since stopped producing. McDowall loved the name and didn't want it to die, so Kirk gave it to her. "I had the name Strawberry Switchblade, so I had to form a band...."

Wild Strawberries
Toronto, Ontario, Canada
Smultronstället, the Swedish title of Ingmar Bergman's 1957 film, means "the wild strawberry patch." Canada's Wild Strawberries are Roberta Carter Harrison and Ken Harrison. Their 2005 album is *Deformative Years*.

The Strawbs London, UK
Excited by the skiffle craze in late-50s Britain, Dave Cousins and Tony Hooper started a jug band called the Gin Bottle Four. This evolved into a bluegrass trio that rehearsed in the Strawberry Hill area of Twickenham, leading them to call themselves the Strawberry Hill Boys. By the mid-60s, their local fans referred to them simply as "the Strawbs." And by 1967, with a change of lineup, the name was formally adopted.

Strawberry Slaughterhouse Denmark
Albums: *Teenage Torturechamber* and *Suck — and the Art of Surviving Suburbia*.

Strawberry Minds
Moulins, France
Better than Suspicious Strawberry Minds.

Ego Plum
Los Angeles, California, USA
Did the music for a fashion show by Gidget Gein, the original bass player for Marilyn Manson. Song titles: "Return of Cannibal Chimp" and "The Amputots."

The Electric Prunes
Los Angeles, California, USA
The band formed in 1966 and went through personnel shifts as Jim & the Lords and the Sanctions. RCA sound engineer David Hassinger, who had recorded mid-60s Rolling Stones, suggested another name change might help. The Electric Prunes was a joke name that gained popularity with the band while recording "Ain't it Hard" at Leon Russell's studio.

Stick in your thumb and pull out a band named

PLUM:

Austin, Texas (power pop);

Poland (heavy rock);

Edinburgh, Scotland (alternative ambient/electro)

The Virgin Prunes Dublin, Ireland
The name "Virgin Prunes" comes from Dublin slang for outsiders and freaks. The lead singers, Gavin Friday (Fionan Hanvey) and Guggi (Derek Rowan), had a gang with Bono (Paul Hewson) of U2 as lads and gave him the nickname "Bono Vox of O'Connell Street." Dik Evans, The Edge's brother, played guitar for the band.

Blind Melon
Los Angeles, California, USA
Blind Melon is a term that bassist Brad Smith's father used to describe a couple of hippie neighbors back in Mississippi.

Hectic Watermelon
San Diego, California, USA
This instrumental trio, featuring guitarist-composer John Czajkowski, drummer Darren DeBree and bassist Harley Magsino, labels their music "Post-Zappa Commando Fusion." Czajkowski claims the band's name was stolen from a four-year-old child. Violinist Jerry Goodman plays with the band on their acclaimed 2006 album *The Great American Road Trip*.

Smackmelon
Boston, Massachusetts, USA
A heavy metal band that should not be confused with Smack Mellon, a Brooklyn foundation established to nurture the visual arts.

Honeydew Revue
Austin, Texas, USA
From Kyle Ryan at *The Onion*'s A.V. Club: "This Austin band wins for Best Opening Line of a Band Bio: '34.7 hundred years ago, in the mountains of Echinacea, an elf gave birth to a baby elf.'"

Kid Creole & the Coconuts
New York City, New York, USA

A crazily tight, zoot-suited, new-wave-calypso band led by Kid Creole (August Darnell). Album title: *Fresh Fruit in Foreign Places*.

Coconut Rough
Christchurch, New Zealand

The name is based on a popular candy in Australia and New Zealand. Bassist Bones Hillman later joined Midnight Oil, replacing Peter Gifford.

Grapefruit (1960s)
London, UK

This grapefruit came from an apple. Terry Doran at the Beatles' Apple Publishing offices in London met guitarist-vocalist John Perry and connected him and the Swettenham brothers (drums and guitar) with bassist-vocalist George Alexander. Together they formed Grapefruit. Alexander was born Alexander Young. He elected to stay in the UK when the Young family emigrated to Australia, where his brothers Malcolm and Angus went on to found AC/DC. Apple's Doran became Grapefruit's manager. They were introduced to the public by John Lennon and released two albums before disbanding in 1969. Perry can be heard in the chorus on the Beatles' single "Hey Jude."

Acid Lemon
Turin, Italy

Psychedelic flashback fruitiness. Paolo Messina and Simona Ghigo go retro and play Vox guitar and Farfisa organ, respectively, in their Italian homage to the British Invasion. Not to be confused with Acid Lemon Juice, the London-based Portuguese electronica duo.

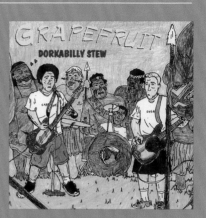

A younger **GRAPEFRUIT** grew out of Hawaii's fertile 1990s post-punk scene. Very few people listened to vinyl records in 1995, but that didn't stop the band from selling over 500 copies their single *Loopy on Bus Fumes*. Fresh out of high school in Kailua, they hit the road: "[We] played shows in and around San Francisco, Bakersfield, LA and San Diego, beginning each set with the words 'We're Grapefruit!' (Crowd silence.) 'From Hawaii!' (Crowd roars.)" The band went on to open for Green Day and to be part of a Vans Warped Tour.

Bang Lime
Oakland, California, USA

Bing cherry, bang lime? A side-project for drummer Joules Scott-Key and bassist Josh Winstead of Metric. Winstead plays guitar and sings in Bang Lime.

All Natural Lemon & Lime Flavors
New Jersey, USA

Rock rule #1427: Music fans want real fruit, not fruit flavors. Interesting music that failed to cause a blip on rock radar.

The Lemon Fog
Houston, Texas, USA

This mid-60s surf band turned into psychedelic-garage-folk rockers. That's what happens when your fruit gets foggy.

The Lemon Pipers
Oxford, Ohio, USA

This psychedelic pop group had a #1 hit in 1967 with the song "Green Tambourine," but they didn't like it. At least not at first. Producers Jerry Kasenetz and Jeff Katz from Buddah Records had found Ivan & the Sabres in central Ohio and convinced them (with a record contract) to change their name and move to NYC. Once there, they were given simplistic, relatively meaningless tunes to record (or else). Though "Green Tambourine" is often referred to as the first real bubblegum single and many other songs were foisted upon them, the Lemon Pipers' two albums contain occasional tracks that highlight their natural Byrds-like sound.

Strawberry Alarm Clock

Strawberry Alarm Clock's record company didn't like their original name, Thee Sixpence, and told them to come up with a new name. Keyboard player Mark White wanted something like "Strawberry Fields Forever." The band holed up in their rehearsal studio (White's parents' guest house) to think of something to go with "Strawberry." During a half-defeated lull between suggestions, they heard a broken but still ticking alarm clock "making some kind of wacky noise" in the background. The guys all turned to look at it simultaneously. The name fit the psychedelic tone of the times, and the record company loved it.

Their biggest hit, "Incense and Peppermints," climbed to #1 on the *Billboard* charts in 1967, but it was intended as the B-side of the single, with "Birdman of Alkatrash" as the A-side. The band had written "Incense and Peppermints" as an instrumental, but the record's producer brought in lyrics by an outside songwriter. The band failed to embrace this lyrical contribution, and neither of its two singers, Lee Freeman and Mark Weitz, wanted to sing the song. A teenage singer named Greg Munford, in the studio but not a member of the band, was drafted as lead vocalist on the track.

The Lemonheads
Boston, Massachusetts, USA

Lemonheads are a kind of candy produced by Ferrara Pan Candy Company (also Orangeheads, Cherryheads, Grapeheads, etc.). Lemonheads co-founder Evan Dando liked the idea of his band as sour on the outside and sweet on the inside. "Sometimes I think I kept it just because Iggy Pop said he liked the name," Dando said in a 2006 interview. "I had dinner with him in a restaurant in Japan, and he told me how much he loved the name. Now, that's worth something."

Tangerine Dream Berlin, Germany

Edgar Froese formed the Ones in 1965, but after a few gigs, including Salvador Dali's house, the band turned into the Tangerine Dream, famous today for its use of atmospheric instrumentation.

Tangerine Zoo
Boston, Massachusetts, USA

In their heyday, they opened for Jimi Hendrix, Van Morrison and Deep Purple. Started as Ebb Tides, then became the Flower Pot. Record execs didn't like "pot" reference, so in 1967 they chose the healthy fruit-and-animal alternative Tangerine Zoo. They were invited to play Woodstock but had prior booking.

The Orange Humble Band
Sydney, Australia

Formed in 1995 by Lime Spiders and Someloves founder Daryl Mather.

Orange Range
Okinawa, Japan

A great mantra. The remix of their 2004 single "Kirikirimai" was on the *Fantastic Four* film soundtrack.

Agent Orange
Placentia, California, USA

A chemical herbicide most notably used by the US military to clear jungle areas concealing enemy troops during the Vietnam War. An estimated 19 million gallons were dropped on South Vietnam during that conflict. The band is skate-punk cum surf revival. They formed in 1979 and are still going.

Moldy Peaches
Port Townsend, Washington, USA

Adam Green and Kimya Dawson... Mount Kisco, NY '94, Port Townshend, Washington '99, New York City '00... four albums, then the success of their single "Anyone Else But You" from *Juno* soundtrack. The duo now make sporadic appearances to perform their signature cute songs with hard edges, such as "Little Bunny Foo Foo," "Steak for Chicken," and "Downloading Porn with Dave."

Peaches & Herb
Washington, DC, USA

Producer Van McCoy paired Francine "Peaches" Hurd Barker with Herb Fame (Herbert Feemster) to form Peaches & Herb in 1965. Peaches disliked touring and was replaced by Marlene Mack. (There have been five Peaches.) Best known is Linda Greene. The '70s disco duo recorded "Shake Your Groove Thing" (#5) and "Reunited" (#1). Due to the instability of the music business and unpaid royalties, Fame spent much of his career as a police officer. A lawsuit in 2001 awarded Fame and Greene back royalties and allowed Fame to retire from the force.

Papaya Paranoia

Tokyo, Japan

Musician-cartoonist Ishijima Yumiko and "office lady who wants to play music" Michiko Morinaga. Yumiko on her choice of name: "I selected it with no special meaning in mind, just for its special sound, PA-PA-YA-PA-RA...."

The Papaya Kings

New York City, New York, USA

Papaya King is a famous NYC juice and frankfurter stand (since 1932): "Our Frankfurters are tastier than filet mignon." This garage-surf band released *Don't Fear the Reverb* in 1998, including songs such as "Man or Mancini" and "Zombie Creep."

The Mango Tea-Cups

Groningen, Netherlands

Teeing up the tea-funk.

Mangoswell Paris, France

Café pop and reggae.

Pineapple Protein

Corpus Christi, Texas, USA

Enough juicy protein to open for rap-core band (Hed) p.e. [Hed Planet Earth].

The SANTA CRUZ, CALIFORNIA-based **Super Pineapples** play ska-punk with a tropical punch. They are named for the giant pineapples that grew in global locations during the Late Cretaceous Period.

Their eponymous 2004 CD includes the tunes "Clean Up on Aisle Five" and "Being Original Is Nothing New." A new CD and DVD are planned for...uh, soon.

The Pineapple Thief

Somerset, UK

In a 2002 directors' poll ranking the best films of all time, the 1948 Italian film *The Bicycle Thief* ranked #6. The UK prog-rock band the Pineapple Thief was founded by Bruce Soord, formerly of Vulgar Unicorn, in 1999.

Passion Fruit

Madrid-Amsterdam-Berlin

Three young women from three countries doing Eurodance pop. Their 1999 tune "The Rigga Ding Dong Song" went to #1 in Mexico and reached the Top 10 in 14 countries. Two of the trio died in a plane crash in 2001.

PINEAPPLES FROM THE DAWN OF TIME

"Surf punk pranksters" from the mid-80s. Song title: "Freaky Acid Planet." The Pineapples returned in 2000 as nine-piece band known for their live costume-party antics. Alluding to their longevity, their MySpace quote reads, "Helter Skelter...Mine's an Alka Seltzer!"

Brisbane, Australia

Meat Beat Manifesto

Started by Jack Dangers (John Corrigan) and Jonny Stephens in 1987 in Swindon, UK. While the band has always focused on electronic music, it has included several instrumentalists over the years and has made inroads into the jazztronica genre.

Dangers and Stephens parted ways in 1994 when Dangers moved to San Francisco, taking MBM with him. After 11 albums, Meat Beat Manifesto continues to be a consortium of musicians, singers and turntablists, with Dangers taking lead role as recruiter, composer and keyboardist.

Dangers on the band name: "It's just a bunch of words strung together to form a name, much like the Butthole Surfers. What does that mean? Does that mean they surf on butt holes? After a while, the name doesn't really say anything. It's a moniker. Throbbing Gristle. It's good to have a memorable name. Tortoise. What does that mean? Where did you get your name from? 'Well, I have a pet tortoise.' Who knows?"

Your Entrée

The Meat Joy
College Park, Maryland, USA
Band members all came from an art-school background. They named the band after a performance-art piece by Carolee Schneemann in 1964. This group performance involved raw fish, chickens, sausages, wet paint, plastic, rope, shredded scrap-paper…

Red Red Meat Chicago, Illinois, USA
A '90s band known as much for, uh, urine fights with other bands as they were for their music. After breakup in 1997, band members went on to form Califone and Sin Ropas.

THE MEAT PUPPETS' name is the title of a song on their first album. They chose it in 1980 over another choice, the Bastions of Immaturity. The band started out writing and playing punk tunes, but the material soon evolved into their unique blend of psychedelic rock, punk and country. The current Meat Puppets lineup features Curt Kirkwood (guitar, keyboards, vocals), Cris Kirkwood (bass, keyboards, "guit-jo," vocals) and recent addition Ted Marcus (drums, percussion). Their latest album, *Rise to Your Knees*, was recorded in their adopted hometown, Austin, Texas. It is the first album of new songs from the Puppets since 2000.

The Meatmen
Detroit, Michigan, USA
Founded in the late '70s by Tesco Vee, 4th-grade teacher and contributor to the punk fanzine *Touch and Go*. "The name came from Tesco's old friend B.F. [who] belched after eating meat, making him the meat man." The Meatmen are known for their graphic and lyrical offensiveness.

Barbeque Bob & the Spare Ribs
New York City, New York, USA
Rockabilly blues with self-deprecating songs such as "Thinking with the Wrong Head" and "Too Bored to Live, Too Dumb to Die."

Barbe-Q-Barbies Helsinki, Finland
All-female hard-rock quintet. "[Our] lyrics tell of bad men and wicked women, alcohol, and the rest of life's little perks."

Captain Beefheart & His Magic Band
Humboldt County, California, USA
Captain Beefheart is the pseudonym of Don Van Vliet (born Donald Glen Vliet), said to have been a child prodigy as an artist and sculptor. Some accounts suggest the name Beefheart came from an uncle's description of a penis ("looks like a big 'ole beef heart") In a 1970 *Rolling Stone* interview, Van Vliet requests he not be asked why or how he and Frank Zappa came up with the name. Childhood friends, Zappa and Beefheart began working on a movie script called *Captain Beefheart vs. the Grunt People* as teenagers.

DustyGroove.com on **the Greasy Beats'** self-titled CD: "They got the name of the group right on this one because the music here is greasy and gritty...The overall groove is rich and full, almost with Memphis soul touches at times, but cut down with the leanness of the modern deep funk generation." The Los Angeles-based Greasy Beats feature some of the most in-demand musicians in Southern California, having performed or recorded with the Black Eyed Peas, Sergio Mendez, Big Daddy Kane, Cake, Mos Def, Alicia Keys, Joss Stone, and Justin Timberlake, to name just a few.

Porterhouse Bob & Down to the Bone

Los Angeles, California, USA

Barrelhouse boogie and New Orleans zydeco, with lots of food songs: "Po'k Chops," "Slammin' the Ham," "Pass the Lickin' Sauce," and "Doin' the Fat Thing."

Veal

Vancouver, British Columbia, Canada

From artist's bio: "Although Veal, the word/meat/concept, is a dark metaphor for a misguided generation, Veal the band is simply three guys committed to expanding the parameters & definitions of pop music." The band started in Vancouver, where guitarist-vocalist Luke Doucet was living as a member of Sarah McLachlan's touring band. As a solo artist, Doucet was named Musician of the Year at the 2001 West Coast Music Awards.

Four Fried Chickens and a Coke

Kansas City, Kansas, USA

An 11-piece horn-driven R&B revue formed in 1997. In the 1980 movie *Blues Brothers*, John Belushi and Dan Aykroyd's characters are tracking down members of their old band and place this unusual order at the restaurant where one of them is working.

The Pink Meat

Brooklyn, New York, USA

Gritty girlcore from all-female trio Taly Martisius, Sam West, and Bug. Lots of lyrical meat/sex innuendoes. Martisius formerly played guitar in the San Francisco band Virgin Mega Whore (a Virgin Megastore pun).

Jimmie's Chicken Shack

Annapolis, Maryland, USA

The band's name is taken from the name of a restaurant where Malcolm X used to hang out. Jimmie's Chicken Shack started as a duo with vocalist Jimi Haha and guitarist Jim McD. They then added drummer Jim Chaney (3 Jims=Jimmies) and bassist Che Lemon.

Dark Meat Athens, Georgia, USA

Blues, punk, psychedelic jam, jazz and Zappa-Beefheart-styled musical explosions. At live performances, the band can swell to as many as 30 players, with the horn section going by the name the Vomit Lasers.

Vegetarian Meat

Dayton, Ohio, USA

Singer-guitarist Alex McAulay has written a number of teen novels (*Oblivion Road, Lost Summer, Bad Girls*), all with MTV books.

NAMES
STILL AVAILABLE

Big Slabs of Tofu

Filet Alright

Dio Diablo Combo

Yngwie Malmsteen's Smorgasbord

The Vealies

Eggplant & Kraut Tour

Sub Primus Rib

Lamb Fried Down on Broadway

Kooks Special

Red Hot Chili Cheesesteak

Paella Fitzgerald

Meat of the Month

105

Prefab Sprout

Formed in 1977 by singer-song-writer Paddy McAloon and drummer Michael Salmon. McAloon has offered numerous stories regarding the origin of the band's curious name. A favorite is one in which he claims to have misheard the line "hotter than a pepper sprout" in Nancy Sinatra and Lee Hazlewood's song "Jackson."

However, when pressed he has admitted to interviewers that he devised the name as a teenager, in homage to the weird band names of his turn-of-the-70s youth. Other names considered are said to have included Grappled Institution, Dry Axe, and Village Bus.

Prefab Sprout was based in Witton Gilbert, County Durham, UK, and driven by its leader's quirky imagination. All but one of their nine albums made it into the UK Top 25, with four entering the Top 10.

The band included brother Martin McAloon on bass, Wendy Smith on guitar and vocals and Fiona Attwood on backing vocals. Salmon left and was replaced by drummer Neil Conti. Prefab Sprout had more drummers (11) than Spinal Tap (8)!

Choice of Vegetable

Heavy Vegetable
Encinitas, California, USA
Formed by guitarist-singer Rob Crow, lead singer Eléa Tenuta, bassist Travis Nelson and drummer Manolo Turner. Songs: "Lactose Adept" and "Abducted by the Work Aliens." Crow was also involved in the bands Thingy, Snotnose, Optiganally Yours and Alpha Males.

Beangrowers St. Julians, Malta
When a festival organizer demanded a band name for the posters, the band got a friend to go and give him any name she could think of.

Black Eyed Peas
Los Angeles, California, USA
On their name: "Black Eyed Peas are food for the soul."

2 Beans and a Grape (often referred to as 2BG) formed in 2002, with John Borgman on bass and vocals, Lyle Geoffrey Brown on drums and Marc Sveen on guitar. John and Geoff are stepbrothers and have played together since grade school. 2BG performs their original rock-funk-pop songs in and around Santa Cruz County, California.

Goober & the Peas
Detroit, Michigan, USA
Jack White from the White Stripes was a one-time drummer. "Goober peas" is what Confederate soldiers in the American Civil War called emergency rations of boiled peanuts.

KoRn
Bakersfield, California, USA
Heavy, heavy band who called their second album *Life is Peachy*. One name story is that someone just blurted it out in a name-storming session. The other story in circulation involves two gay men at a party.

Screaming Broccolli
Staten Island, New York, USA
See *steaming broccoli*. Artistic misspelling. We are encouraged to "Rock with the Broc!"

Hard Broccoli
Annapolis, Maryland, USA
A project of musical-theater guy Doug Schenker. Song: "Post Nuclear Surfin' Song."

Chilli Willi & the
Red Hot Peppers London, UK
Pub rock 1971–1975. Debut album: *Kings of the Robot Rhythm*. Drummer Pete Thomas later joined Elvis Costello as one of the Attractions.

Black Cabbage
Guelph, Ontario, Canada
At least eight members, with five songwriters, make Black Cabbage "the Wu-Tang Clan of Canadian folk-rock." Black cabbage is also known as Cavolo Nero and is a common Italian vegetable.

Of Cabbages & Kings
New York City and Chicago

This side project for members of the Swans, Foetus and Prong centered around guitarist Carolyn Master and bassist Algis Kizys. The name is from Lewis Carroll's 1872 verse "The Walrus and the Carpenter": *The time has come/ the Walrus said/ To talk of many things/ Of shoes—and ships— and sealing-wax—/ Of cabbages—and kings—/And why the sea is boiling hot—/And whether pigs have wings.*

Eggplant Danceoff!
Sandown, New Hampshire, USA

Unable to get their big purple vegetables on the floor, three members have started a new band, the Brave Little Abacus.

Eggplant Queens
Bellmore, New York, USA

Glam band with three singers: Huevos Rancheros, Yo Yo Yolk and Sunnyside. On guitar, we have Eggdrop, with Eggpants on bass and Scramberg on drums. More egg than eggplant.

The Green Onions
Harrisburg, Pennsylvania, USA

"Green Onions" was a huge hit for Booker T. and the MGs in 1962. This band of high-school classmates got together in 2001 and are currently scheduled to open for the Gin Blossoms.

Lettuce
New York City, New York, USA

A great 7-piece funk-soul band. "They were fond of showing up with their instruments at underground jazz clubs like Wally's (usually at other musicians' gigs) and asking, 'Will you let us play?' Hence the birth of the name Lettuce."

Philly Style magazine had this to say about hometown band the **Parsnip Revolt**: "Earnest, wistful and undeniably radio-friendly, the Parsnip Revolt offer soulful feel-good rock melodies with widespread appeal." Guitarist Jake Williams on the name: "If you look back on the history of the parsnip, it was a staple on most dinner plates until the potato was introduced. The potato ruled for long enough. It's time for the parsnip to revolt. The Parsnip Revolt!"

Mayhem Lettuce
Port Byron, Illinois, USA

"Mayhem Lettuce rules the cosmos. It's 2 guys, often with beards, who like it when it rocks. Sometimes they go to space. Other times, they get spooky. You never know. You just never know." One guy's sister was making a salad, and he said that her lettuce-chopping style looked more like mayhem.

The Offbeets
Leesburg, Florida, USA

Appeared as themselves in the 1965 B-movie *Daytona Beach Weekend* and contributed to the We the People album *Mirror of Our Minds* in 1966.

Smashing Pumpkins
Chicago, Illinois, USA

The name refers to pre-Halloween prank of smashing jack o'lanterns. Frontman Billy Corgan's first band was a goth group called the Marked.

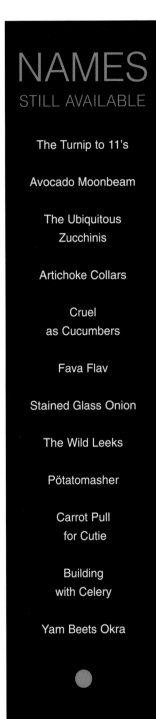

NAMES
STILL AVAILABLE

The Turnip to 11's

Avocado Moonbeam

The Ubiquitous Zucchinis

Artichoke Collars

Cruel as Cucumbers

Fava Flav

Stained Glass Onion

The Wild Leeks

Pötatomasher

Carrot Pull for Cutie

Building with Celery

Yam Beets Okra

Sweet

Drummer Michael Tucker and singer Brian Connolly played together in R&B and psychedelic-rock band called Wainwright's Gentlemen in Middlesex, UK, before forming the Sweetshop with bassist Steve Priest and guitarist Andy Scott.

The band shortened its name to the Sweet when they discovered another band named the Sweetshop. Signing to RCA Records, they hooked up with the songwriting team Chinn and Chapman. RCA pitched the group as a bubblegum-pop band with chart-focused singles such as "Wig Wam Bam," "Funny Funny," "Alexander Graham Bell" and "Little Willy."

Sweet's compromise was to put their harder rock sound on the B-sides. They had their first real rock hit with "Blockbuster" in 1973, followed by '70s radio classics "Ballroom Blitz" and "Fox on the Run."

There was a resurgence of interest in the band in the '90s when their songs appeared on soundtracks for films such as *Wayne's World* and *Dazed and Confused*.

The Dessert Cart

Cake Sacramento, California, USA
Cake members eschew the let-them-eat-cake attitude and are active environmentalists and involved in community-minded causes. At concerts, the band has taken to giving out trees for its audience members to plant.

The Sea & Cake Chicago, Illinois, USA
The name comes from drummer John McEntire's misinterpretation of the Gastr del Sol song "The C in Cake."

My Friend the Chocolate Cake
Melbourne, Australia
"My Friend the Chocolate Cake comes from a record by a band from Sydney called Ya Ya Chorale…I had an EP of theirs and I was sharing this house, and all the women in the house always referred to it. I think it was an anti-dieting joke. Every second day I hate it and every other day I like it."

Figgy Duff Newfoundland, Canada
Named after the traditional Newfoundland pudding. The band combined traditional Newfoundland folk music with rock influences.

Humble Pie Essex, UK
Ex-Small Faces singer-guitarist Steve Marriott joined forces with Peter Frampton. The two chose the name to escape the media tag of "supergroup."

The Pietasters
Washington, DC, USA
"Some British neighbors used to refer to the heftier guys in the band as 'Pietasters,' British slang for fat guys."

Sherbet
Sydney, Australia
Formed in 1969 by guitarist Clive Shakespeare. Later reformed as the Sherbs.

FruitCake-SuperBeing from Dallas, Texas: "Founded in 1998, FruitCake-SuperBeing [are] an ode to blues, rock, electronica, soul, dance and hip-hop. FruitCake-SuperBeing is a melting pot of those genres, using samples, guitar, bass, live drums, harmonica, keyboards and energetic vocals…

On stage this group puts across a persona…characters straight out of a tale of barbeques and redemption in the South." Albums: *Developmental Texas How Now* and *Electronically Challenged Blues Hop From Texas*.

Amalgam in the Middle

The Imaginary Cookies

A project of Canton, Ohio, multi-instrumentalist Scott Paris with friends Chris Egert and Joe Middleton. Paris on the name: "My wife is my muse and when I need a project name she inadvertently helps me pick one. We were burning candles that smelled like fresh baked cookies. I made a comment that I wanted to go out for coffee because of the scent. She suggested that I have some imaginary coffee with my imaginary cookies and it clicked." Album: *Amalgam in the Middle*. Scott Paris also records as a solo artist.

Sugarcubes

Reykjavík, Iceland

Most famous for launching Björk's career. Einar Örn Benediktsson: "We needed a pop band...to make money so we could put out records and books. We decided to *make* a pop band to do so. It became the Sugarcubes."

Sugarcult

Santa Barbara, California, USA

Singer-guitarist Tim Pagnotta called the lesbians who lived in a nearby apartment "the Sugar Cult girls."

The Mighty Lemon Drops

Wolverhampton, West Midlands, UK

Originally called the Sherbet Monsters.

Big Sugar

Toronto, Ontario, Canada

Formed in the early 1990s by singer-guitarist Gordie Johnson out of the Bourbon Tabernacle Choir. Spin-offs: Grady, Train 45, and Truths & Rights.

Sugarloaf

Denver, Colorado, USA

Originally Chocolate Hair. Changed name after getting a recording contract. Sugarloaf is a mountain outside of Boulder, Colorado.

Dolly Mixture

Cambridge, UK

All-female new wave band who were dating members of the Damned. Dolly Mixture is manufactured by the British-based Handy Candy Company.

The Wondermints

Los Angeles, California, USA

Have toured as Brian Wilson's band. The band likes the wonderments of the universe. Their lyrics often mention things such as trilobites and DNA.

Pudding Attack

Oklahoma City, Oklahoma, USA

Songs: "Neon Nihilism" and "Jackie the Stripper." Album: *Miniskirt Cash Machine*.

Vanilla Fudge

Long Island, New York, USA

Began as the Electric Pigeons, later shortened to the Pigeons. Became the Electric Fudge in spring 1967. "The name had been suggested by a female vocalist in a local band [who] had a real passion for the novelty Drumstick-brand ice-cream cones, especially the Vanilla Fudge-flavored ones."

NAMES
STILL AVAILABLE

Blind Lemon Cake

The Last Macaroons

Godley Good
Crème Pie

Manassas
Molasses

That Cranberries Tart

Savoy Truffle Cake

The Tiramisu Tears

Sunny Day
Cookie Club

The Licorice Whips

Scary Spice
Lamé Flambé

The Jolly Gobstoppers

A Band of Pudding

The Bourbon Tabernacle Choir

The core lineup of Toronto's Bourbon Tabernacle Choir consisted of Chris Brown, Jason Mercer, Andrew Whiteman, Chris Miller, Gregor Beresford, Gene Hardy, Dave Wall and Kate Fenner, with numerous collaborating musicians.

According to a CBC TV interview, Chris Brown divined the name from a dream he had. As is so often the case, the name was meant to be used for one show only. In this case, a lunchtime performance at a local high school, where they performed the only song they knew, an original entitled "The Sermon," with Andrew Whiteman providing a hellfire-and-brimstone rant. The Choir went on to release three albums and develop a devoted cult following.

Their indie hit "Put Your Head On" attracted the attention of film director Bruce McDonald, who included it on the soundtrack to his 1991 film *Highway 61*.

Enough to Drink

Hot Chocolate London, UK
They made a reggae version of John Lennon's "Give Peace a Chance" before leader Errol Brown realized he needed permission. It turned out Lennon liked Brown's version and signed the group in the final days of Apple Records. In 1970 Hot Chocolate had hits with "Love Is Life," "Emma," "You Could Have Been a Lady" and "I Believe in Love," and wrote hits for Herman's Hermits and Mary Hopkin. But it was in the disco era that Hot Chocolate went nova with "You Sexy Thing" and "Every 1's A Winner."

The Tea Party
Windsor, Ontario, Canada
Named for the infamous hash sessions of famous Beat generation poets Allen Ginsberg, Jack Kerouac and William Burroughs. Mixing blues rock with Middle Eastern influences, their music was dubbed "Moroccan roll."

Big Al & the Kaholics
Jacksonville, Florida, USA
One of Florida's most popular live bands. Big Al has opened for Tesla, Spin Doctors, Badfinger, the B52's, the Beach Boys and other national acts.

Iron & Wine Austin, Texas, USA
Stage name of Samuel Beam. Iron & Wine was taken from a dietary supplement, Beef Iron & Wine. He decided to drop the Beef.

The Dixie Dregs
Augusta, Georgia, USA
Guitarist Steve Morse and Dixie Grit bassist Andy West called themselves the Dixie Dregs, when they became leftovers from Dixie Grit. Albums: *Night of the Living Dregs, Dregs of the Earth* and *California Screamin'*.

Totally Blind Drunk Drivers
Estonia
Polished power-pop. Known simply as Blind in Estonia.

Ultra Violet Booze Catastrophe
Montreal, Quebec, Canada
Late '90s punk. EP: *Electric Honky*.

Beer Goggles Adelaide, Australia
EPs: *5.8% alc/vol* and *Boredumb*.

Beverley Beer Bellys
Vellejo, California, USA
From the 1960s US television series *The Beverly Hillbillies*.

From British Columbia's secluded Lasqueti Island, **24-Hour Church of Beer** is a power trio consisting of Rev. Tim (bass, lead vocals), Mutha Superior G (guitar, vocals) and Brother Lazarus (drums, vocals). But "divine collaborative shows" sometimes include "DJ PJ, DJ Hash, Lari, Reverend Forrest Jackson, keyboard genius Sean Lehay, Hurricane Betty, and the White Trash Gospel Choir." CD: *The Incredible Impoliteness of Being*.

The Human Body

Some of Its Parts

Blood on the Hidden Tracks

Hit My Crazy Bone

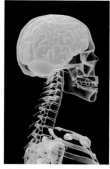

The Human Body

Some of Its Parts

Small Faces

One of the great mid–60s London bands, with Steve Marriott, guitar; Ronnie Lane, bass; Kenney Jones, drums; and Jimmy Winston, keyboards (later Ian McLagen). They started as a blues band, became mods, then went psychedelic.

Steve Marriott: "[A] 'Face' was a top mod, a face about town, a respected chap! The name came from a girl called Annabelle I knew from Chelsea...We were trying to think of a name, and she said, call yourselves the Small Faces 'cause...we were all little and had little boat races. It was great for us because it fitted in with wanting to be faces anyway."

After several hit singles, including "Itchycoo Park," "Lazy Sunday" and "All or Nothing," and four albums, the last the psychedelic concept album *Ogden's Nut Gone Flake* in 1968, Steve Marriott left to form Humble Pie with Peter Frampton. The rest of the band became Faces in 1969 when Ron Wood and Rod Stewart joined the band after leaving the Jeff Beck Group.

Meet the Head
Chicago, Illinois, USA

"Things we sing about: failed relationships, reconstructive eye surgery, baseball riots, crumbling neighborhoods, cops, scapegoats, movies we love, and the art of drunken bitterness after you've been fired."

Nuclear Forehead
Fall City, Washington, USA

Settled on the band name Nuclear Forehead after overhearing a remark describing someone's forehead. Songs "Butter is Lipgloss" and "Peroxide Brain Damage."

Bad Brains Washington, DC, USA
Started out in 1975 as Mind Power, a jazz fusion group, but a more aggressive style and singer brought the name change: Bad Brains, from the Ramones song "Bad Brain."

The Nerves
Los Angeles, California, USA

All three members wrote songs. Bassist Peter Case (who later formed the Plimsouls): "[The name the Nerves] comes from being in the mainline...when you write a song you want the greatest possible number of people to hear it. That's what every writer dreams about, and why not go for it?"

Naked Eyes Bath, UK
Childhood friends Pete Byrne and Rob Fisher fronted this '80s synth-pop band. They'd previously been in the band Neon with future members of Tears for Fears. Pete Byrne: "At one point we had all [the EMI] marketing people – about 20 people – just sitting around thinking about [the name]...It was crazy...It just came to me one day."

London's **Mad Staring Eyes** won the Best Unsigned Band competition of out 2,000 hopefuls at Glastonbury Festival 2005. Drummer Oli Darley: "The name Mad Staring Eyes was one of those late-night moments of inspiration that usually hit you when you about to fall asleep. The band name, album title (*Bored of Looking Cool*) and cover art are all connected...we hide everything except our eyes because we're bored of trying to look cool. As the first line says, *I'm so bored of looking cool/ I think I'll smash my face into this wall.*"

many sides of the
FLATFOOT SHAKERS

Victoria, Australia's **FLATFOOT SHAKERS** have toured extensively, playing festivals across Australia and in Sweden, Belgium, Germany and Switzerland. They were also featured performers at the Rockabilly Rave in England and twice at Viva Las Vegas in Las Vegas, Nevada. They bring their love of vintage '50s rockabilly to their recordings, including recent albums *Many Sides of the Flatfoot Shakers* and *Let's Go to the Planet Bop*.

Third Ear Band London, UK
Emerged from the Giant Sun Trolley and the People Band in the late '60s. They recorded soundtrack music for Roman Polanski's 1972 film of *Macbeth*. Name likely stems from their Raga influences.

Spooky Tooth London, UK
Previous bands: the Teenagers, the Ramrods, the V.I.P.s and Art. Art became Spooky Tooth when American Gary Wright joined the band in 1968. Guitarist-vocalist Luther Grosvenor went on to play in Stealers Wheel and Mott the Hoople.

Baby Teeth Chicago, Illinois, USA
Lead singer-keyboardist "Pearly Sweets" (Abraham Levitan): "We did wear all white for the first few years we were a band, but we got tired of it and all our white clothes got dingy."

Stiff Little Fingers
Belfast, Northern Ireland
"Stiff Little Fingers" was a track by London's the Vibrators.

Finger Eleven
Burlington, Ontario, Canada
Started in 1989 as the Rainbow Butt Monkeys. The name Finger Eleven comes from one of their own lyrics: *When everything is pushing you in one direction and your instinct drives you in another — that's finger eleven.*

Voodoo Armpit
South Pembrokeshire, Wales, UK
Several members also play in the band Rystik Grwf.

Stump London, UK
Anglo-Irish experimental '80s rock. Albums: *Mud on a Colon, Quirk Out* and *A Fierce Pancake*.

Toenut Atlanta, Georgia, USA
Donuts and foot fetishes don't mix. Self-description: "Weirdo rock and roll."

Big Toe San Diego, California, USA
Amputee Mark Goffeney plays classic-rock bass and guitar with his feet. Yes, there is video.

Fierce Nipples
Hudson Valley, New York, USA
Described by a reviewer as "uneasy listening."

Nomad Nipples
Trondheim, Norway
Tired of playing death metal, punk and hard rock, they decided to create "a totally schizophrenic masterpiece."

Love Handles Finland (indie rock); London, UK (jam rock with horns); Melbourne, Australia (covers); Baltimore, Maryland, USA (covers).

NAMES
STILL AVAILABLE

The Pancreatics

Deviant Septum

MC 900ft Colon

Eyes Afloat

Kidney Economics

Cerebellum Antebellum

Earboom Echo

The Why Brains

United Prostates of America

Small Feet

Liver & Bunions

Nipplepixies

113

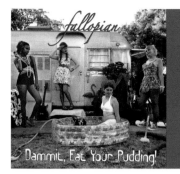

Dammit, Eat Your Pudding!

Fallopian is physically connected to Santa Monica, California. "Once upon a time there was a girl...and a girl...and a girl...and another girl...and they formed the wonderful, most extravagant and spectacular band to ever put on a dress." Their new album, *Dammit Eat Your Pudding!*, features the garage-punk classic "Sex with a Tree."

The Plasmatics

This New York City band was formed by anti-artist Rod Swenson after his MFA degree from Yale. He was into art as a confrontational medium. (He also made pornographic films.)

Wendy O. Williams ("WoW") answered the newspaper ad for Swenson's "theater" project and became the band's lead singer. The idea was to create a shock-rock band that would disturb the status quo and anyone in their proximity.

The band was known to chainsaw guitars and take sledgehammers to television sets. Williams performed topless, usually with electrical tape over her nipples to avoid being charged with obscenity. On November 16, 1979, they blew up a car on stage. Going a step further, they blew up police cars during the song "A Pig is a Pig."

They were banned in London, arrested in Cleveland and Milwaukee, and Williams was nominated for a Grammy for best female rock vocalist in 1985.

Williams retired from music in 1991 and became a health-food advocate while working for a natural foods co-op. She committed suicide in 1998.

Iron Prostate
New York City, New York, USA
Started punk in their 40s. Songs: "Rock'n'Roll Nursing Home," "Bring Me the Head of Jerry Garcia," "Hell Toupee." Album: *Loud, Fast and Aging Rapidly.*

Belly Boston, Massachusetts, USA
Tanya Donnelly was in the original Breeders (with Kim Deal) and Throwing Muses (with stepsister Kirstin Hersh) before forming Belly in 1991. Donnelly chose the name because she thought the word was "both pretty and ugly."

Abdominal Cavity Mikkeli, Finland
Death-grind-metal by S. Brutalizer. EP: *Cranial Dust.*

The Bad Livers
Austin, Texas, USA
Bluegrass punk trio famous for playing Miles Davis, Metallica, Mississippi John Hurt, Slayer, the Misfits...

Lynyrd's Innards
Chicago, Illinois, USA
Obvious Lynyrd Skynyrd pun. Short, insanely fast songs.

Ovarian Trolley
San Francisco, California, USA
Sisters Laurie (bass, vocals) and Jennifer (drums, vocals) Hall played in a band called Glorious Clitoris before forming Ovarian Trolley with guitarist Buck Bito.

Blood on the Hidden Tracks

Heart
Bellevue, Washington, USA
Fronted by sisters Ann and Nancy Wilson. The band had been called Army, then changed its name to White Hart, from Arthur C. Clarke's 1957 story collection, *Tales From the White Hart*, and then simply Heart. The Wilson sisters and Sue Ennis had an acoustic side project called the Lovemongers in the '90s. Nancy Wilson is married to director Cameron Crowe and has scored a number of his films.

Joan Jett & the Blackhearts
Ardmore, Pennsylvania, USA
The name Blackhearts comes from the name of the record label Joan Jett started with Kenny Laguna in 1979, when none of the major US labels would release her solo debut (already released in Europe), following the breakup of her teenage band, the Runaways. The album *I Love Rock'n'Roll* was released in 1982, the title track a cover of a song by the Arrows.

Purple Hearts Romford, UK
Started as the Sockets but switched their name to Purple Hearts, the street name for an amphetamine-barbiturate mixture popular with '60s mods.

The Black Heart Procession
San Diego, California, USA
Started in 1997 by Three Mile Pilot members Pall Jenkins and Tobias Nathaniel when that band took a hiatus. "The two settled on the Black Heart Procession as a name because it captured three elements they wanted embedded in their music: darkness, heart and a driving, marching sound."

Blessed by a Broken Heart
Montreal, Quebec, Canada
Christian retro glam hair screamo rap nu metal with emphasis on photos of the boys in the band.

Tom Petty & the Heartbreakers
Gainesville, Florida, USA
Previous Petty bands include the Sundowners, the Epics and Mudcrutch (which included future Heartbreakers). The name Heartbreakers was suggested by producer Denny Cordell. Tom Petty is said to have preferred the King Bees.

The Heartbreakers
New York City, New York, USA
Late '70s punk band formed by Johnny Thunders and Richard Hell after leaving the New York Dolls and Television.

The Youngbloods
New York City, New York, USA
Named after lead singer Jesse Colin Young's second solo album, 1965's *Youngblood*. Best known for their hit "Get Together," later used in a National Council of Christians and Jews TV and radio ad campaign.

Type O Negative
Brooklyn, New York, USA
Sort of tongue-in-cheek goth-metal. Nickname: The Drab Four. Their first compilation album: *The Least Worst of….*

Blood Obsession
Albany, New York, USA
Originally called themselves Infanticide. Songs: "Self-dismemberment," "Menstrual Soup," "Beauty in Decapitation." Sound blood obsessive?

NAMES
STILL AVAILABLE

Coronary
in a Coal Mine

The Crafty Arteries

Heart Transplant
for Cutie

The Blood Typists

Hemoglobal Warfare

Blood Pudding
from Hell's Kitchen

Brain Vein 3000

The
Hemophilanthropists

My Bloody Overtime

Aorta Kill You

Dulcet Pulse

The Blood Vassals

THE PLEASURES
OF MERELY
CIRCULATING

An energetic post-punk trio from Marfa, Texas, **the Pleasures of Merely Circulating** somehow blend Iggy Pop with rockabilly to create their own compellingly original sound. Singer-guitarist Jeanne Sinclair fronts for fellow Pleasures Robert Helpern and Chris Cessac. They can be viewed on YouTube and sampled on MySpace. The band's name is the title of a poem by American poet Wallace Stevens (1879–1955), who spent the bulk of his life working for an insurance company.

The Cincinnati-based electro-pop duo **Bad Veins** was started in 2006 by Benjamin Davis and Sebastien Schultz. Davis: "There's something intuitive about the name Bad Veins and our flowers that we have on everything. The anatomy of a flower is similar to the anatomy of a person. They are both complex and delicate, intricately connected inside, like electronics and wiring are. The idea links us and our gadgetry together." And it's also reminiscent of the name Bad Brains.

The Shins

Formed in 1997, in Albuquerque, New Mexico, as a side-project for singer-songwriter James Mercer, then of the band Flake Music. That band also included drummer Jesse Sandoval, bassist Marty Crandall and guitarist Neal Langford, all of whom would spend time as part of the Shins' performing band.

Relocation to Portland, Oregon, two solid albums and endless touring — often with friends Modest Mouse — served to build the band a significant global fan base. The band's third album, *Wincing the Night Away*, debuted at #2 on *Billboard*'s Album charts.

The name the Shins is derived from the name of a fictional family (the Shinns) in the Broadway musical *The Music Man*, one of Mercer's father's favorite plays.

Cold Blood
Oakland, California, USA
Started as the Generation and became Cold Blood in 1968. Drummer Sandy McKee has claimed the name was kind of a slang way of saying the band was always "cool," and that it was not referencing Truman Capote's bestselling book *In Cold Blood*, released just two years earlier.

3 Inches of Blood   Vancouver, British Columbia, Canada
Medieval warfare themes. Fans come to shows in Viking helmets. One vocalist does high falsetto; one screams. Self-description: "Born out of a love for pure metal, weaned on a diet of fantasy and mythology, 3 Inches of Blood have been slaying the infidel and defending the faith for nearly eight years."

Hit My Crazy Bone

Skeletal Family
Keighley, West Yorkshire, UK
This gothic-horror band started in 1982 and took their name from a track off David Bowie's 1974 album, *Diamond Dogs*.

Skeletonbreath
Brooklyn, New York, USA
Art-rock instrumental trio of violin, bass and drums.

The Bones   Karlskrona, Sweden
Tag: "Wasted Since '96." Singer goes by the name Beef Bonanza. Songs: "She Hates Me (Yeah Yeah Yeah)," "Screwed, Blued and Tattooed."

Boneshaker
Pau, Aquitaine, France
Championing the culture of the biker chick. "Boneshaker" was a name given to the earliest pedaled bicycles, manufactured in the late 1860s, obviously referring to their extremely uncomfortable ride.

Chubby Nuthin' & the Bone
Chicago, Illinois, USA
Started by brothers Luke and Mike Wilhite: "Our sound is like taking an ice-cream churn filled with groove, shaking it up and funking with it so it will diddle your happy place."

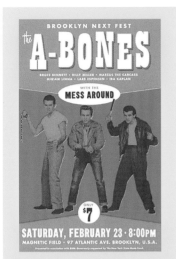

BROOKLYN, NEW YORK'S **A-Bones** are named after a song by the Trashmen, a '60s surf-rock band from Minneapolis. The A-Bones were formed in 1984 by vocalist Billy Miller and drummer Miriam Linna, who had previously been the editors of the crazy pop-culture journal *Kicks*. Albums: *The Life of Riley* (1991), *I Was a Teenage Mummy* (1992), *Music Minus Five* (1993), *Crash the Party* (1996). Two band members also played with Yo La Tengo.

The Skulls
Los Angeles, California, USA
With vocalist Steven William "Billy Bones" Fortuna. Guitarist Marc Moreland went on to form Wall of Voodoo.

Live Skull New York, New York, USA
Album cover for *Bringing Home the Bait* features a cow brain. Members eventually split to pursue other bands, including Of Cabbages and Kings, Come, Chavez, and Fuse.

White Skull Vincenza, Torino, Italy
From an interview with frontman Tony "Mad" Fonto: "I gave the name White Skull to the band…it is mystical. I'm a collector of skulls. For me, the skull is the place where good and evil live together, all the power is inside. You could [be] crazy, mad or normal, depends what you have inside."

The Skulls Vancouver, British Columbia, Canada
Zep cover band became a punk band after seeing the Ramones live in '77. Band split up in '78, with singer Joey Shithead (Joey Keithley) forming D.O.A. and other members forming the Subhumans. They were there for the birth of Canadian punk.

Jawbox Washington, DC, USA
The band lived in a house in Silver Spring, Maryland, wrote all of its songs in the basement, and made records in Arlington, Baltimore and Hoboken. Their first show was opening for Fugazi.

Bone-Box • Americana roots music from Manchester, UK, fronted by Jay Taylor (guitar, vocals): "I had this beautiful old dictionary of disused Underworld slang from the Victorian era with me before I was due to go on stage at our first show in London. The promoter asked me the name of the band…I stuck my finger in the dictionary and it landed on 'Bone-Box.' It turned out to be a word for someone's jaw, so you'd say, 'I'm going to smack you in your bone-box.'" Albums: *Death of a Prize Fighter*, *Working the Ribald Ratio* and *Bridge of Brotherhood and Unity*.

NAMES
STILL AVAILABLE

Bone Ami

Sternum Drang

Rib Cage Rumble

Coccyx Grind

The Bone Apart Conquests

Skullucifer

Metacarpal Eleven

Spine on the Enemy

The Teflon Hip

Fiona Ankle

60 Cycle Humerus

My Bones Points

From Helsinki, **Knucklebone Oscar** belongs to the same Finnish underground scene as the Flaming Sideburns and Sweatmaster. Oscar has been touring and recording actively in Finland for over ten years.

His latest release is *Back From the Jungle!* "Oscar`s music is best described as electrifying 'ADD-blues'...Oscar and his quartet are determined to bring you the most exhausting, kick-ass live show of your life, with hard grinding guitar pyrotechnics, hyper-active moves, trash voodoo mystique, masked marvels, jungle specialties, axes, wailing megaphones and freaks of nature."

Spinal Tap
Los Angeles, California, USA

The band...the film...the legend! In the context of the movie, the band is started by childhood friends David St. Hubbins (Michael McKean) and Nigel Tufnel (Christopher Guest), who start as a skiffle band called the Originals but later have to change their name to the New Originals, then the Thamesmen, before choosing the name Spinal Tap to reflect their change in sound. Spinal Tap is spelled with no dot on the i and an umlaut on the n – a parody of heavy-metal umlaut bands. Shearer McKean and Guest have toured as Spinal Tap on several occasions and have also issued recordings as Spinal Tap and as the Folksmen, from the film *A Mighty Wind*.

Spinecracker
Toronto, Ontario, Canada

Formed after the breakup of Skaface and King Apparatus. Released one album: *Kill the President*.

Spineshank
Los Angeles, California, USA

Formed out of Basic Enigma in 1995. From a VoxOnline.com interview with guitarist Mike Sarkisyan: "The Spineshank name started out meaning backstabbing, but it took on a life of its own. The kids understand it — they get it. It's more of a feeling now...it's become an emotion." Lead singer Jonny Santos quit to form Silent Civilian.

Hipbone Slim & the Kneetremblers London, UK

Tag: "Bald Man With Too Many Bands!" How many bands, you ask?: Louie and the Louies, the Snags, the Waistcoats, the Nine Ton Peanut Smugglers, Sir Bald & His Wig-Outs, Juke Boy Barkus & Baldie McGhee, and the Legs. Slim has also recorded with members of the Milkshakes, Jackie & the Cedrics, Mummies, Finks, Bomboras, Huntingdon Cads, Johnny Bartlett and Holly Golightly. All on his label, Alopecia Records.

The Femurs
Seattle, Washington, USA

Started by Rob "Femur" (Rob Schaffer), drummer for Loveless and the Goodnight Trail. Began as a solo project but has expanded to a duo with the addition Colin "Femur." The second album from the Femurs is called *Jack Cafferty Vs. Chuck Scarborough*, titled after their favorite NYC news anchormen.

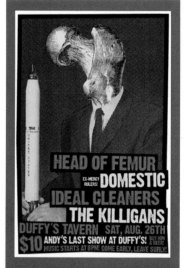

The Chicago band **Head of Femur** evolved out of the band Pablo's Triangle and has toured as an 8-piece (2 guitars, trumpet, trombone, violin, drums, keys, 4 vocalists & percussion) with such acts as Bright Eyes and Rilo Kiley. "The name Head of Femur comes from when Elvis Presley appeared on the *Ed Sullivan Show* and the cameramen were told to film Elvis's pelvis no lower than the head of femur, a location the band says is the point where rock and roll becomes sex." Debut album: *Ringodom or Proctor*.

Woe 'R Us

Woe, Misery & Sorrow

Tragedy, Pain & Failure

The Black Sorrows

Melbourne's Black Sorrows evolved out of Jo Jo Zep & the Falcons. Frontman Joe Camilleri (aka Jo Jo Zep, Joey Vincent) had also played with the King Bees and Adderley Smith Blues Band (from which he was reportedly fired for sounding too much like Mick Jagger). Despite their name, the Black Sorrows were supposed to be a non-serious, "fun" outlet for Camilleri.

During the band's early years, musicians came and went in a musical revolving door of Melbourne blues-rock talent. The first two Black Sorrows albums were mostly rawly recorded covers. But 1987's *Dear Children* delivered a solid collection of band originals and put them in the Top 20 on the Australian Album chart.

The Black Sorrows has had six Top 40 hits singles in Australia, with "Chained To the Wheel" charting the highest at #9. Their most recent album is *Roarin' Town* (2006). A compilation, *The Essential Black Sorrows*, was released in 2007.

The Jo Jo Zep song "So Young" was covered by Elvis Costello.

Woe 'R' Us

Grief Boston, Massachusetts, USA
AllMusic.com on Grief's innovation in metal: "Grief's sludgy doom metal, however, brought extremely slow riffs to the metal underground." Members also affiliated with Bane of Existence and Disrupt.

Absolute Grief
Rimouski, Quebec, Canada
This goth-metal band started out as *Faithful Time*.

Grief Society Bedford, UK
Self-description: "Obsession, emotional blackmail, stalking and loneliness are features throughout...."

Sad Breakfast Mexico City, Mexico
Band name actually comes from the acronym for *Standard American Diet*.

Sadness Kills the Superman
Birmingham, UK
From the Black Sabbath song "Spiral Architect": *On a black snow sky/ Sadness kills the superman/Even fathers cry*.

The Sad Lives of the Hollywood Lovers Harrisonburg, Virginia, USA
Last song recorded by the band: "The Prayers and Tears of Arthur Digby Sellers," on the album *The Mother of Love Emulates the Shapes of Cynthia*. Band broke up because it was taking too long to say the titles at gigs.

Sweet Misery France
Album: *That Which Does Not Kill Us Makes Us Stronger* (2005). Proceeds go to animal rights. Big on not banning pitbulls.

Sad Music for Happy Humans, Portland, Oregon: "Once there was a boy. He found words to not suit the complexity of thoughts and thought, 'There must be another language, one in which I can say what I mean, and yet people can still hear what is within them, thereby leaving all parties satiated.' This boy, he tried nosepicking, armpit farting, hiccuping and more. Still his thoughts lay untranslated. One day a Kleptor from Romagulan VII visited his world and showed him something new and fantastic: MUSIC! From that day forth, this boy spoke in no other language."

Absolute Misery
Belleville, Ontario, Canada
Solo project of Matt Zuchowski (aka DarkDread), as distinguished from his drone-based metal projects Funerary Dirge, DoomSquirrel, Goatbomb and Alone in Silence.

Church of Misery
Shinjuku, Tokyo, Japan
MySpace tagline: "Let there be doom!!!" Songs almost exclusively about serial killers.

The Miserables
Oakland, California, USA
Singer goes by Mr. Miserable. Songs: "Ugly Dose of Daylight" and "Hole in the Sky."

The Misery Loves
Nutley, New Jersey, USA
They should incorporate: The Misery Loves Company, Inc.

Seed of Sorrow Norway
Started as a side project in 2004 by Eivind and Thomas. Eivind was taking a break from his band FBS (Fucking Bull Shit).

The Sorrows Coventry, UK
One of the '60s British Invasion bands that didn't quite make it. (Maybe their name?) Their song "Take a Heart" peaked at #21 in the UK.

Joyful Sorrow Toledo, Ohio, USA
"Christian Screamo Metal."

Tragedy Portland, Oregon, USA
Formed in 2000 from members of Deathreat and His Hero Is Gone.

The American Tragedy
Shreveport, Louisiana, USA
Named as a juxtaposition to the American Dream. Trey: "[The name] was better than Diesel Dollar 19 or Ghost Chickens or My Friend Glen or Ash...." J.C.: "My dad won't admit it, but he likes it, too. But my mom, she hates it. Mom watched N'Sync on television, she wants us to do something like that."

Atragedyinprogress
Talgarth, Wales, UK
"Interestingly the small mountain town of Talgarth sits in the shadow of the Black Mountains, lurking in this shadow you have A Tragedy in Progress."

Life Long Tragedy
San Francisco, California, USA
Songs: "This Year's Disease" and "The Bottomless Hole."

Paperback Tragedy
Baltimore, Maryland, USA
Performed for five years as Brat before changing name: "We felt the name Brat didn't give a good enough representation of us and our style. If you never heard us or heard Brat, you would check us out expecting to hear a 14-year-old-girl punk band. And even though Will does sing like a girl, we are all not 14!"

Divine Tragedy
Pittsburgh, Pennsylvania, USA
Songs: "When Civilization Falls," "Zombageddon," "Ashes." Album: *Final Dawn* (2007).

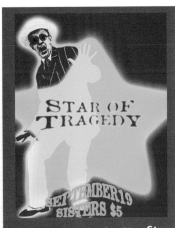

Oklahoma City's hard-rocking **Star of Tragedy** features drummer Starr Raven on lead vocals. About life's tragedies: "Friday, after I got off work...I took the dogs out for a pee break. My little French bulldog was leaning over the edge to check out a frog in the pool, when the next thing I knew, she fell in...bulldogs can't swim good, so I had to jump into a 12-foot inground pool full of green water to save her. Unfortunately, my phone was attached to my belt...and as I was saving her, it fell off somewhere in the deep end, never to be recovered. So, needless to say, I lost most of my important numbers."

NAMES
STILL AVAILABLE

Woe Babies

Like Miserable on Rice

Sorrowmarrow

The Why Botherers

Bruising for a Losing

Crap Out Kids

The Long Listless

Hail to the Grief

My Sad Friends

Failure School Dropouts

The Tragic Beans

Pep Club Silencers

Evripidis & His Tragedies
Barcelona, Spain
Euripides (ca 484–407 BC) was third of the ancient Greek tragedians. The Spanish Euro-pop band centers around Athens-born Evripidis Sabatis and his "girlfriends."

One of the Loudest Tragedies Ever Heard…
Los Angeles, California, USA
A band assembled by producer-vocalist Johnny Fisher in 2002, with a female rhythm section, bassist Natalia Bolanos, drummer Claudia, and fashion photographer Mark Zarnow on guitar.

Greyhound Tragedy
Edmonton, Alberta, Canada
Led by producer Steve Loree (guitar, vocals) formerly of cowpunk outfit Jr. Gone Wild, Deadbeat Backbone, Fat Dave Crime Wave and others. Greyhound Tragedy is a reference to post-career racing dogs.

Tacoma Hellfarm Tragedy
Guelph, Ontario, Canada
From *Wavelength* interview: "We used to rehearse on Darryl's parents' horse farm, in an old century barn. His parents…would have all of their friends up from the city to party and it soon became known as the 'Hellfarm'…The 'Tragedy' is that back in the 1800s on the farm, something went horribly wrong and family members killed family members in some sort of murderous rage…The Tacoma part came from a design firm in Guelph called Tacoma Steckly."

Tragedy Ann
Ventura, California, USA
Christian rock band punning on the classic fabric doll Raggedy Ann.

Pain
Stockholm, Sweden
A side project for Hypocrisy singer Peter Tägtgren.

A Band Called Pain
San Francisco, California, USA
African-American heavy metal band. Guitarist Shaun Bivens: "My cousin [singer] Allen Richardson brought KISS's *Love Gun* album over to my house. After listening to it, I said, 'We should be KISS for Halloween.' And then we decided to start a band."

Painkiller Hotel
Aurora, Illinois, USA
"The band decided on the name Painkiller Hotel for the musical references it evokes. The moniker may sound harsh to some, but it is the subtle conjuring up of late '60s and early '70s rock that rings in most ears."

Agony Face
Milan, Italy
They claim to play "surrealistic death metal."

The Faded received the Los Angeles Music Awards' Alternative Band of the Year prize two years running (2005 and 2006). "Their music blends early glam rock, techno-punk, early alternative, and today's energy to create a powerful new sound."

Failed Teachers is a manic punk guitar-drums duo from Lucerne, Switzerland, and, yes, they used to be teachers. "After they gave up their well-paid pedagogue jobs…they have produced teaching methods and didactical means to drag the weed-smoking Neo-Hippie-Youth… back onto the hard tarmac of street-punk." Albums: *Failed Teachers*, *The Big Exam (Live)*, *Men's Room Romance*.

Failure
Los Angeles, California, USA
Hardly a failure, co-founder Ken Andrews (vocals, guitar) produced the theme song for the Bond film *Casino Royale*. He and Greg Edwards (bass, vocals) met through classified ads. Failure has opened for Tool and Nine Inch Nails. Other Failures: Pomona, California (punk); Aalten, Netherlands (punk rock); Copenhagen, Denmark (hard rock); Allentown, Pennsylvania (ska punk); Ames, Iowa (punk).

The Failures Union
Buffalo, New York, USA
Former bands: Lemuria, the Exit Strategy, the Grade Grubbers. Songs: "Defection or Suicide" and "Friends in Jail."

Failure by Design
Ormskirk, UK
Went through five drummers before breaking up in 2006.

Failed Humanity
Ipswich, UK
Members later joined Extreme Noise Terror and Criminal. Album: *The Sound of Razors Through Flesh* (2001).

Shiny Happy People

The Unbearable Lightness
of Being Gleeful

Yeah Yeah Yeah (Yeah Yeah!)

Shiny Happy People

The Verve

Several original members of this Manchester, UK, band met in junior high school. Occasional member Simon Tong, also a school friend, later joined Blur.

They started out as simply Verve, but following their participation in the 1994 Lollapalooza tour, the band was sued for trademark infringement by Verve Records and had to change their name to "The Verve."

They are best known for their hits "Bittersweet Symphony," "The Drugs Don't Work" and "Lucky Man." "Bittersweet Symphony" was used in several ad campaigns against the band's wishes. Because a sample from "The Last Time" by the Rolling Stones was used in the song, credits given to Richards and Jagger provided their (now ex-) manager Allen Klein sufficient ownership to sell rights to the Verve's composition.

Singer Richard Ashcroft has also worked as a solo artists and is married to ex-Spiritualized keyboard player Kate Radley. Band members have played in the Shining, the Beta Band, Black Rebel Motorcycle Club, the Music and other side projects.

Ready for the World
Flint, Michigan, USA
Mid–80s hits "Oh Sheila" and "Deep Inside Your Love." The band formed in high school and was discovered by Detroit radio personality "the Electrifying Mojo."

Smilers   Estonia
From the Rod Stewart album *Smiler*. Started in Helsinki. Huge in Estonia. Song: "Football Is Better Than Sex."

Smile Brigade
Seattle, Washington, USA
Ironic band name. Songs: "Today Has Not Been a Goldmine," "Doombox," "Devastating," "Ashes and Graves."

The Giggles
Bloomington, Indiana, USA
Won the Indy Music Scene Jr. Battle of the Bands in 2006. Still recording their debut album. Songs: "Robots Don't Cry" and "Alarm Clock, I Hate You." Good pop.

The Giggle Club
Los Angeles, California, USA
Featured on the cover of *Lil Miss Thang!* magazine.

Happy the Man
Harrisonburg, Virginia, USA
Named after the Genesis song "Happy the Man." In 2000: "After breaking up in 1979 the members of Happy the Man pursued various other projects and it was during one of these side trips that guitarist Stanley Whitaker, besieged by adoring Happy the Man fans at a festival in Mexico, decided to put the band back together."

Happiness Factor
Dallas, Texas, USA
First album: *Self-Improvement?* Lots of tongue-in-cheek songs about the many ways things suck.

The Happiest Guys in the World
New York City, New York, USA
Garageband bio: "We realized that the world needs very, very happy music more than ever…." Songs: "To Be or Astronaut To Be," "I Am the Ground Hog (And It's My Day)," "You Can Make It If You Try, Try, Try," "Welcome Aliens!"

How to Win at Life
FOUNDED IN 2000 by singer-guitarist Benjamin Leon and keyboardist Joseph Morais, How to Win at Life has played venues all over California, including top clubs such as B.B. King's in LA and Blake's in Berkeley. The band's new rhythm section features Chris Wiebe on bass and Greg Ogan on drums. Their recent album is entitled *The Defibrillator*.

The Wonder Stuff are from Stourbridge, West Midlands, UK. Pre-Wonder Stuff band names included Flowers From Eden and Wild and Wandering. (The drummer was kicked out of the Lemon Drops for not cutting his hair.) Lead singer-guitarist Miles Hunt is the nephew of Bill Hunt, who played keyboard for the '70s rock bands Wizzard and Electric Light Orchestra. Formed in 1986, the Wonder Stuff broke up in the '90s but has reformed occasionally since, though Hunt and Malcolm Treece (guitar, vocals) are the only original members to play under the name.

Vision of Sunshine
Los Angeles, California, USA
Released a self-titled LP in 1970, very rare, on AVCO Embassy Records. From collector site Waxidermy.com: "'Vision of Sunshine,' the opening song on side B, opens with a young boy singing, 'May the long time sun shine upon you, all love surround you, and the pure light within you, will guide you on your way.'"

The Like
Los Angeles, California, USA
The band was started in 2001 by three girls aged 15 and 16. The name comes from the conversational tic of saying "like" all the time. Drummer Tennessee Thomas's mother is said to have suggested it.

Joyside Beijing, China
Joyside was the subject of Kevin Fritz's 2006 documentary *Wasted Orient,* about the band's first national tour of China in 2001. Bio quote: "They dig pure rock'n'roll, give great big kisses to devil, and run wild on the burning side."

Miss Bliss
Dexter, Michigan, USA
Originally formed in 1992 and called Second Coming. "Miss Bliss" is the title of a song by Incubus. Miss Bliss is shoegazy, not Incubus-y.

Blissful Intentions
Amarillo, Texas, USA
Blissful Intentions does screamo. Broke up when both singers moved to Detroit.

The Giving Tree Band
Chicago, Illinois, USA
Self-directed mandate: "The Giving Tree Band members consider it their duty, as musical artists, to serve. They view songwriting as an opportunity to explore ways to increase understanding and to improve the overall well-being of people and the environment." Four multi-instrumentalists who play "non-toxic instruments."

Ashley Said Yes!
Denver, Colorado, USA
Guys who met working at a comic-book store.

NAMES
STILL AVAILABLE

The Freakin' Happys

Giddy Uppers

The Effervescents

That's So Like Possible

The Smile Highs

Joybuzzer

The Going Places

Alpha Club Go!

The Spreadjoys

Chakra Fun Do

The Love Loves

Hugs for Emos

125

FROM HOUSTON, TEXAS • **Bright Men of Learning**: "As our moniker suggests, we are smart, capable dudes. But all praise is due Him. And by HIM, I mean Jebediah (pronounced Jeb-ah-DIE!). Jebediah is our spiritual leader and advisor. He guides in all action – and inaction. If we do not respond, it is His will. If we do not speak, it is He who has silenced us. If we do not play for two months, it is because our singer's still in law school, and is very, very busy." Enthusiastic, straight-ahead rock. Album: *Bright Men of Learning.*

Yes London, UK

The band's original guitarist, Peter Banks, had the idea that a three-letter name would stand out on posters. The band saw many great musicians go through its ranks, including the classic lineup of Jon Anderson, Chris Squire, Steve Howe and Alan White, but also Bill Bruford, Tony Kaye, Rick Wakeman, Geoffrey Downes, Trevor Horn, Patrick Moraz, Trevor Raben and others. The double-album *Tales from Topographic Oceans* (with four 20-minute-plus songs) and its tour are said to have been the inspiration for *This is Spinal Tap.*

Yeah Yeah Yeahs

New York City, New York, USA

Name taken from NYC vernacular. Drummer Brian Chase also plays in the Seconds. Guitarist Nick Zinner has played with Bright Eyes and Head Wound City. Singer Karen O. and Zinner used to share an apartment with Metric's Emily Haines and Jimmy Shaw.

Right Said Fred

East Grinstead, UK

Brothers Fred and Richard Fairbrass, with friend Mark Hollins. Named after a 1962 novelty hit by Bernard Cribbins. Their own novelty hit was 1991's "I'm Too Sexy."

Hooray! For Everything

Pittsburgh, Pennsylvania, USA

"The name Hooray! for Everything comes from an episode of the *Simpsons* and is a tribute to our enduring love of the show."

Fun Boy Three Coventry, UK

This post-Specials offshoot helped launch Bananarama's career via their hit single "T'ain't What You Do (It's the Way That You Do It)" featuring the female group on backing vocals.

Fun People

Buenos Aires, Argentina

Originally named Anesthesia, as a tribute to late Metallica bassist Cliff Burton and his song "Anesthesia Pulling Teeth." Renamed Fun People following legal problems from use of the word anesthesia.

Let's Active

Winston-Salem, North Carolina, USA

The name came from a "nonsense-English" t-shirt bought in Japan. Led by songwriter Mitch Easter, producer for R.E.M.

Exciter Ottawa, Ontario, Canada

Started in 1978 as Hell Razor, but changed name in 1980 to Exciter, after the Judas Priest song.

The Exciters

Queens, New York, USA

A 1960s American girl group, though later joined by Herb Rooney, singer Brenda Reid's husband. First hit was the #4 single "Tell Him" in 1962. Also released the original "Do Wah Diddy Diddy," later a hit for Manfred Mann.

Shake Some Action!

Seattle, Washington, USA

Named after the 1976 album by San Francisco's the Flamin' Groovies.

Out of Halifax, Nova Scotia, Canada, comes the indie duo the **Superfantastics**, with Matthew MacDonald on guitar and Stephanie D'Entremont on drums. "Since the release of their acclaimed debut LP, *Pop-Up Book*, the Superfantastics have toured Eastern Canada steadily...showcased at festivals such as CMW, NXNE and the Halifax Pop Explosion. Recently, the group was nominated for two Nova Scotia Music Awards, Best New Artist and Best Alternative Album, as well as an East Coast Music Award for Best Music Video." Their new EP is *Choose Your Destination.*

Your Family Tree Or Mine?

Mom, Dad & the Relatives

Oh, Baby Baby

Siblinghood

Artefacts from the Teen Age

Your Family Tree or Mine

Sly & the Family Stone

Sly Stone was born Sylvester Stewart. He sang gospel in the his family's group the Stewart Four in the '50s and doo-wop as part of a mixed-race high-school group called the Viscaynes.

He later worked as a DJ for Oakland, California, radio stations KSOL and KDIA, and as record producer for the Beau Brummels, the Mojo Men, and the Great Society. He adopted the name Sly Stone in 1966 when he started a band called the Stoners. His brother Freddie started a band called Freddie & the Stone Souls. At the suggestion of saxophonist Jerry Martini, the two bands combined to become Sly & the Family Stone.

Four of the five Stewart siblings joined the band and changed their names to Stone. Sly & the Family Stone became one of the hottest acts in America, with a long string of hit singles and an appearance at Woodstock in 1969.

The band was inducted into the Rock and Roll Hall of Fame in 1993.

Mom, Dad & the Relatives

The Beautiful Mothers
Seattle, Washington, USA
Beautiful Mothers strangle lyrics. "Strangled amongst the energy and sound are lyrics written with poetic style found in the literary works of L'autreamont, Beaudelaire, and Hesse."

The Mamas & the Papas
Los Angeles, California, USA
Papa Denny Doherty: "We were all just vegging out watching TV and discussing names…John was pushing for 'The Magic Circle.' *Eech*, but none of us could come up with anything better, then we switch the channel and it's the Hell's Angels on this talk show...and the first thing we hear is, 'Now, hold on there, Hoss. Some people call our women cheap, but we just call them our Mamas.' Cass jumped up: 'Yeah! I want to be a Mama!' And Michelle is going, 'We're the Mamas! We're the Mamas!' I look at John. He's looking at me, going, 'The Papas?' Problem solved."

Mother Hips
San Francisco, California, USA
Former incarnations include Pippi Longstocking and Trunk-of-Funk. Their name is a simple anagram of Mother Ship, a frequent point of reference in the songs of Parliament and Funkadelic. Album: *Kiss the Crystal Flake* (2007).

My White Bread Mom
Columbus, Ohio, USA
Song: "Counter Culture Daddy Warlord."

Mother Mother   Vancouver, British Columbia, Canada
Started as just Mother but found there were other Mother bands. Current name echoes a lyric from Marvin Gaye's "What's Going On?"

Joe Mama Band
Queensbury, New York, USA
Recent album: *Green Pepper Air Freshener*.

Vocalist Helen Nishimura and guitarist Matty schemed up the band **Soccermom** in 2002 while working together in a French fashion boutique that catered to prostitutes and strippers in Venice Beach, California. They have played well-known LA clubs such as the Whisky, the Roxy and 14 Below. "Like all great bands, first they create a scene, then they show up late."

Mother Love Bone
Seattle, Washington, USA

Started as Lords of the Wasteland. The name Mother Love Bone is said to have been randomly assembled from a list of words frontman Andrew Wood liked. Wood died of a heroin overdose just prior to the release of their debut album, *Apple*. Members went on to form Pearl Jam, Temple of the Dog and Love Battery.

The Mothers of Invention
Los Angeles, California, USA

They were called the Soul Giants when Frank Zappa joined the band, but renamed the Mothers on Mother's Day 1964. The name was expanded to the Mothers of Invention to appease MGM Record's concern over Mothers being slang for "motherfuck-ers." The new name was derived from the expression "necessity is the mother of invention."

Gay Dad London, UK
Brit-pop band formed by former music journalist Cliff Jones. Despite a fashion-able look, provocative name and top producers, the band was largely panned by the press and soon disbanded.

Gear Daddies
Austin, Minnesota, USA

Suffering from GAS (gear acquisition syndrome). Their song "Zamboni" appeared on soundtracks for Disney's *Mighty Ducks* movies.

Daddy Cool Melbourne, Australia
The name comes from the 1957 song "Daddy Cool" by US group the Rays. Daddy Cool included their version of the song on their debut album, *Daddy Who? Daddy Cool*. Their previous bands included the Pink Fairies and Sons of the Vegetal Mother.

Meet...The Relatives is the debut album for Orange County, California, band the Relatives. *OC Weekly* hailed the Relatives as "gooey power pop with a dangerous garage-rock edge." Their sophomore release is 2004's *Dirty Little Secret*.

Big Bad Voodoo Daddy
California, USA

Blues legend Albert Collins signed a poster for guitarist-singer Scotty Morris: "To Scotty, the big bad voodoo daddy." Morris explains, "I thought it was the coolest name I ever heard, on one of the coolest musical nights I ever had, so when it came time to name this band, I didn't really have a choice. I felt like it was handed down to me."

Red Aunts
Long Beach, California, USA

All-female '90s punk band with short songs, such as "Sleeping on the Wet Spot," "Built for a Barstool," "Lethal Lolita."

Uncle Tupelo Belleville, Illinois, USA
Formed by Jay Farrar, Jeff Tweedy and Mike Heidorn after the breakup of the Primitives. Uncle Tupelo is a fat, old Elvis-like character in a cartoon drawn by Chuck Wagner, a friend of the band. Farrar and Heidorn went on to form the band Sun Volt, while Tweedy formed Wilco with the other members of the band.

NAMES
STILL AVAILABLE

Moms with
Just Cause

My Donor Dad

Papatropolis

Bloody Cousins

Really Great Uncles

Stepmothers
of Tomorrow

The Bad Daddies

Gene Pool Floaters

The Mothers of Tuition

Noose Aunts

Dissonant
Relatives

The Father
Knows Beast

Babyshambles

Another band that started as a side project. This time by Libertines frontman Pete Doherty in 2004. Babyshambles now appears to be his primary focus – well, apart from headline-grabbing drug arrests and a bit of a solo career. The new album, *Shotter's Nation*, received top marks.

The band consists of singer-songwriter Peter Doherty, Drew McConnell (bass), Mick Whitnall (lead guitar), Adam Ficek (drums). Babyshambles was a name given to Doherty by the Queens of Noize. The name is a reference to the pear-cider drink Babycham. His Libertines bandmate Carl Barât had been called Papashingles.

Doherty is as famous for his substance-abuse problems, dating Kate Moss and hanging out with Amy Winehouse and Elton John as for his music. His detractors have even suggested that Babyshambles was formed largely to generate more cash to fund Doherty's drug addictions.

Lyrically, Babyshambles songs tend to deal with fairly dark subject matter. Titles include "Crumb Begging Baghead" and "The Lost Art of Murder."

Oh, Baby Baby

The Babys London, UK
Late 1970s rockers. The name was chosen because record companies were looking for teen bands. The names Cry Babys and Big Babys were proposed, half-jokingly.

Big Bang Babies
Hollywood, California, USA
A '90s glam-rock band whose name has fun with the multiple meaning of "bang." Guitarist Keri Kelli went on to play for Ratt, Alice Cooper, Skid Row and Slash's Snakepit.

Blake Babies
Boston, Massachusetts, USA
After a reading by poet Allen Ginsberg at Harvard, the band asked Ginsberg to name them. Ginsberg suggested Blake Babies, inspired by William Blake's *Songs of Innocence and Experience*.

Backyard Babies Nässjö, Sweden
Credited with starting the sleaze-rock revival in Sweden. Way to go, guys. Debut EP: *Something to Swallow*.

Baby Strange
Boston, Massachusetts, USA
The title of a T. Rex song from the album *The Slider*.

Peter & the Test Tube Babies
Brighton, UK
Oi punk band formed in 1978. They one-up the Sex Pistols with their song "The Queen Gives Good Blow Jobs." Albums: *Soberphobia, Pissed & Proud, Mating Sounds of South American Frogs* and *Fuck The Millennium* (released in 2000).

Zuckerbaby
Calgary, Alberta, Canada
The name Zuckerbaby comes from a German art film made in 1985 and written and directed by Percy Adlon.

The Cribs
Wakefield, West Yorkshire, UK
Consists of three brothers, twins Gary and Ryan Jarman and younger brother Ross, recently joined by Johnny Marr (the Smiths). Latest album: *Men's Needs, Women's Needs, Whatever* (2007).

Children of Bodom Espoo, Finland
The name refers to the unsolved murder of three teenagers at a place called Lake Bodom. Album: *Are You Dead Yet?*

The Subteens are a piss-and-vinegar punk band from Memphis, Tennessee. "For lack of anything better to do, the Subteens formed in the fall of 1995. According to the band, things pretty much went downhill from there. Singer-guitarist Mark has been known to perform in his skivvies and a football helmet (for when he falls off the stage)." Recent album: *So That's What the Kids Are Calling It…*(2004).

Someday Tricycle's debut album, *Mystic Knights of the Pretty Sun*, has drawn comparisons to many of the "B" bands — the Byrds, Big Star, Badfinger, the Beatles, and the Beach Boys. Having started in Jacksonville, Florida, the band currently resides and records in Portland, Oregon.

The Offspring
Garden Grove, California, USA
Frontman Bryan Holland and bassist Greg Kriesel met on the cross country team. Guitarist Kevin Wasserman was the school janitor they befriended to buy alcohol. The name Offspring refers to Holland's pursuits (a "spring off" to many things). Such as his hot sauce company, Gringo Bandito.

The Prodigy Braintree, Essex, UK
Keyboardist-composer Liam Howlett chose the name Prodigy in tribute to his first synthesizer, the Moog Prodigy.

Boys Brigade
Toronto, Ontario, Canada
Named after a Christian youth organization formed in the 19th century, with the motto "Sure and Stedfast" [archaic spelling still used]. Malcolm Burn (keyboards, vocals) went on to production fame working with Daniel Lanois.

The Fat Boys
Brooklyn, New York, USA
Buffy the Human Beatbox was a pioneer in making mouth sounds to emulate hip-hop percussion.

Ugly Kid Joe
Isla Vista, California, USA
The band's name riffs on the name of glam-metal band Pretty Boy Floyd. Albums: *As Ugly as They Wanna Be, Menace to Sobriety, Motel California*.

Every Mother's Son
New York City, New York, USA
Marketed as a clean-cut bubblegum band: the son every mother wants.

The Woodentops
Northampton, UK
The name of a BBC TV children's series from the 1950s.

The Ataris Anderson, Indiana, USA
The Ataris lead singer Kris Roe used to collect Atari video games.

Goo Goo Dolls
Buffalo, New York, USA
The Goo Goo Dolls achieved breakthrough success with the single "Name" in 1996. Early on, a club owner insisted they change their name from Sex Maggots, as the local newspaper would not print it. Their current name came from a *True Detective* ad for a toy called a Goo Goo Doll. "We were young and…had a gig that night and needed a name…If I'd had five more minutes, I definitely would have picked a better name."

Marcy Playground
New York City, New York, USA
Named for the playground at lead singer John Wozniak's grade school in Minneapolis.

NAMES
STILL AVAILABLE

Neighborchild

Baby Eats Gravy

99 Pablums

Weeds
in the Kindergarten

The Skids Kids

One Two Many

Breastfeeder
Flashback

Carpetcreepers

Playtime
for Progeny

Live Cricket
Mobile

Pram Rally

Power Outage
Children

Scissor Sisters

The Scissor Sisters are Jake Shears (lead vocals), Ana Matronic (vocals), Babydaddy (bass, guitar, banjo, keyboards), Del Marquis (guitars) and Paddy Boom (drums). They formed in New York City in 2001 as sort of a glam-funk-disco-revival band.

They've received limited attention in the mainstream US music media, but they are huge in the UK and Europe. Their self-titled debut album (2004) and subsequent release, *Ta-Dah* (2006), both reached #1 on the *Billboard* UK Album charts. Their first Top Ten single was a disco cover of Pink Floyd's "Comfortably Numb." The band collaborated with Elton John on their dance-club hit "I Don't Feel Like Dancing."

The name Scissor Sisters comes from the sexual position of "leg-scissoring" that enables genital-to-genital rubbing between two female partners. Vocalist Jake Shears worked as a stripper at a club called IC-Guyz in New York.

Scissor Sisters albums have been banned from Wal-Mart because of their lyrical content.

Siblinghood

Gutter Twins
Los Angeles, California, USA
A collaboration between Greg Dulli (Afghan Wigs, the Twilight Sisters) and Mark Lanegan (Screaming Trees, Queens of the Stone Age). Lanegan on their name: "It seemed appropriate, especially considering the shape we were in when we started."

No Way Sis   Glasgow, Scotland
Oasis cover band led by Joe and Gerry McKay. Other Oasis cover bands include Blurasis, Champagne Supernova, Oasish, Definitely Might Be, Gallagher, NoAces, Pasha & the Wonderwalls, Supersonic...

Sadista Sisters   Edinburgh, Scotland
The Sadista Sisters were Teresa D'Abreu, Judith Alderson, Jacky Tayler and Linda Marlowe, a 1975 feminist, black-comedy, rock extravaganza that ran at the Edinburgh Festival before playing a successful run in London. Dave Stewart joined them for a tour of Germany before forming the Tourists and the Eurythmics with Annie Lennox.

Twisted Sister
New York City, New York, USA
Guitarist Jay Jay French was around when Gene Simmons was transforming Wicked Lester into KISS and wanted to create a glitter-drag band inspired by Bowie and the New York Dolls. French: "[First vocalist] Michael [Valentine] was a full-throttle drinker, and he rang from a bar saying he'd come up with this great name. But when he came home he'd completely forgotten making the call...if I hadn't picked up the phone, we may never have called ourselves Twisted Sister."

Sister Morphine
Minneapolis, Minnesota, USA
Promoted as the "Twin Cities' sleaziest hair rock n roll/metal." Named after the Jagger-Richards-Marianne Faithfull song.

Swing Out Sister   Manchester, UK
The name came from the 1945 film *Swing Out, Sister*. Band members claim they chose it because the only thing the band could agree on was that they all hated that name.

Melbourne's **My Twin Sister Lulu** is not really a drag queen, but rather a cross-dressing singer-songwriter, the alter ego of unshaven, foul-mouthed, beer-swilling, testosterone-fuelled Paddy. *Wine, Woman and Song* has been described as *"A Clockwork Orange* meets Monty Python." "With titles like 'Why Did You Marry Such a Stupid Cow,' 'I Always Fall Asleep in Meetings' and 'Masturbating to the Sound of Your Own Voice,' Lulu and Paddy balance precariously on a fine line between comedy and anger management. Both side-splitting and heart-wrenching."

Sister Hazel Gainesville, Florida, USA
Named after Gainesville aid worker
Sister Hazel Williams. From an interview with frontman Ken Block: "She
doesn't care what religion, what race,
what orientation, if you're a prostitute
or a drug addict or anything, she'll give
you a safe, warm place to dust off,
regroup, and get back on your feet."

Brother Voodoo
Edmonton, Alberta, Canada
Named after the Marvel Comics character, a Haitian voodoo sorcerer who
assists Doctor Strange.

The Blues Brothers
New York, New York, USA
Started as a Dan Ackroyd and John
Belushi skit on *Saturday Night Live* in
1978. SNL band leader Howard Shore
suggested they call themselves the
Blues *Brothers* as a joke on their dis-
similar appearance. Paul Shaffer
helped assemble the all-star band.

Big Brother
& the Holding Company
San Francisco, California, USA
Named by promoter Chet Helms,
combining Big Brother from the top of
a list and the Holding Company from
near the bottom. Janis Joplin was in
the band before leaving to form the
Kozmic Blues Band.

The Funk Brothers
Detroit, Michigan, USA
Nickname of the Motown session musi-
cians from the late 1950s to 1972.

The Radar Brothers
Los Angeles, California, USA
Members also play in Mt. Wilson
Repeater and Dengue Fever. Songs:
"Like an Ant Floating in Milk" and "A
Dog Named Ohio."

PunkNews.org on this high-energy
Boston-based band: "**Turpentine
Brothers** is the brainchild of guitarist Justin Hubbard of the Kings of
Nuthin' and drummer Tara McManus
of Mr. Airplane Man. While the duo
started off moonlighting old country
standards, their creation soon became
something comparable to Reigning
Sound, the Mystery Girls and the
Deadly Snakes. Integral to their current sound is the swirling, wild organ
work of Zack Brines."

Flying Burrito Brothers
San Fernando Valley, California, USA
Gram Parsons had used the name for
his side sessions while in the International Submarine Band in Boston. It
came to refer to an informal group of
former Submarine Band players and
hot Los Angeles musicians.

Doobie Brothers
San Jose, California, USA
Guitarist Tom Johnston attributes the
name to friend Keith "Dyno" Rosen,
who noted the guys' fondness for
"doobies." Related album: *What Were
Once Vices Are Now Habits* (1974).

Righteous Brothers
Los Angeles, California, USA
Got their name while with the vocal
group the Paramours. A man shouted,
"That was righteous, brothers."

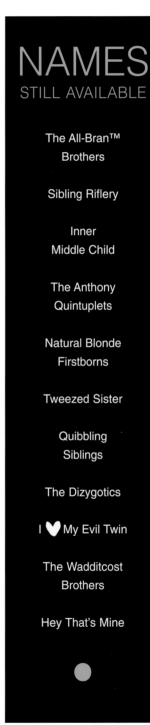

NAMES
STILL AVAILABLE

The All-Bran™
Brothers

Sibling Riflery

Inner
Middle Child

The Anthony
Quintuplets

Natural Blonde
Firstborns

Tweezed Sister

Quibbling
Siblings

The Dizygotics

I ♥ My Evil Twin

The Wadditcost
Brothers

Hey That's Mine

Imperial Teen

San Francisco's Imperial Teen is fronted by ex-Faith No More guitarist-vocalist Roddy Bottum, with Will Schwartz (guitar, vocals), Lynn Truell (drums, vocals) and Jone Stebbins (bass, vocals). Their latest album is *The Hair the TV the Baby and the Band*, an inventory of what the band has been doing in the five years since their previous record: working in a hair salon, writing TV scores, having a baby and playing in another band.

The name Imperial Teen has no real significance. "We were actually called something else, but we were sent a cease-and-desist notice... There was another band that we didn't know about with that other name, so we scrambled and came up with Imperial Teen. It sort of fit the identity of the band, especially back then."

America's oldest gay publication, *The Advocate*, praised the band in a 1999 article: "With lyrical allusions to wearing lipstick and male pronouns used to address love objects, Imperial Teen serves up a gay sensibility that ordinarily surfaces only from straight bands like Pulp and Pizzicato Five." Roddy Bottum (Roswell Christopher Bottum III) came out in 1993.

Artefacts from the Teen Age

The Adolescents
Fullerton, California, USA
One of the original West Coast punk bands, formed in 1979 by members from Social Distortion and Agent Orange. Well known in the skate-punk genre with songs "OC Confidential" and "Skate Babylon."

The Teen Idles
Washington, DC, USA
A short-lived (1979-80) but hardly idle punk band featuring Ian MacKaye and Jeff Nelson, still in high school but after a stint as the Slinkees and before they formed Minor Threat. The Teen Idles set a precedent for all-ages shows in punk venues by suggesting that under-age concert goers mark a black X on their hands at licensed shows in California.

Frankie Lymon & the Teenagers
Harlem, New York, USA
The group included five boys in their early to mid-teens. Their first single, "Why Do Fools Fall in Love" (1956), was their biggest hit, followed by "I'm Not a Juvenile Delinquent" and "Out in the Cold Again." Lymon became a heroin addict and died at age 25.

All-American Rejects
Stillwater, Oklahoma, USA
One member of the band suggested the the All-Americans, another suggested the Rejects (though rumors suggest the influence of Green Day's 1997 song "Reject"). Breakout hits with "Dirty Little Secret" and "Move Along."

Teenage Head
Hamilton, Ontario, Canada
Formed in 1979 and often called Canada's Ramones, the band took their name from the 1971 album *Teenage Head* by San Francisco's the Flamin' Groovies. The band appeared as themselves in the B-movie *Class of 1984*.

Teenage Fanclub
Glasgow, UK
Their cover of Camper Van Beethoven's "Take the Skinheads Bowling" is featured in the Michael Moore documentary *Bowling for Columbine*. Previous bands: Boy Hairdressers, BMX Bandits. Formed in 1989 around the three lead singers, Norman Blake, Raymond McGinley and Gerard Love.

Philadelphia, Pennsylvania's **Teenage Girls** offer the following warning for their album *Cheerleader Offering*: "This album presents some of the most obnoxious pop-infested catchy rock songs ever recorded in a well-articulated, wickedly sinister format." Tracks include "Extraterrestrial Encounter at the Elk's Lodge" and "Trixie's All-Star Banquet."

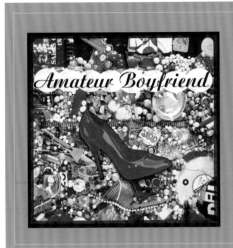

Singer-keyboardist Sean Bates needed a backing band for a gig on a Seattle cable access show. Those hastily assembled musicians became Ruby Minor. The addition of other new members led to **Amateur Boyfriend** — song title, 2003 debut album title, band name.

Teenage Bottlerocket
Laramie, Wyoming, USA

Formed by twin brothers Ray and Brandon Carlisle following the breakup of their previous band, Homeless Wonders. From a *PunkRockReview*.org interview: "When we started Teenage Bottlerocket in 2001, we were really into the Ramones. I think a conversation might have taken place between Ray and I that went something like, 'This band is going to be leather jackets, Chuck Taylors, all Ramones.'"

The Boyfriends
London, UK

From *The Guardian*: "As for the name, Wallace explains that they're all prime boyfriend material because 'we're nice to mothers — both our own and other people's. And none of us is entirely ugly.'"

D Generation
New York City, New York, USA

Also known as DGen. Songs: "No Way Out" and "Vampire Nation."

Generation X London, UK

Started in 1976 as Chelsea, added Billy Idol as singer and changed their name to Generation X. The name comes from Charles Hamblett and Jane Deverson's 1965 book based on their interviews with anti-establishment youth. Idol's mother had a copy. Gen X broke up in 1981, with Billy Idol going on to a solo career and Tony James forming Sigue Sigue Sputnik.

Girlschool
London, UK

This female heavy-metal band started in 1975 as Painted Lady, but changed to Girlschool in 1978, seemingly growing younger name-wise. Part of the new wave of British metal. In recent years, they have played the reunion circuit with bands such as Alice Cooper, Twisted Sister and Motörhead.

Boys Like Girls
Boston, Massachusetts, USA

They are straight. Former bands: the Bends, Fake ID, Lancaster, and the Drive.

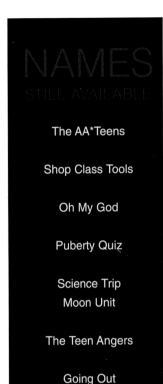

NAMES
STILL AVAILABLE

The AA*Teens

Shop Class Tools

Oh My God

Puberty Quiz

Science Trip
Moon Unit

The Teen Angers

Going Out
with Trevors

Over The Hills

Third Period
Ditch

The Adolflescents

Humbert Humbert
Girls School

Prom Plan 182

135

New York City's **Sonic Youth** got their name from singer-guitarist Thurston Moore's idea of combining "Sonic" from MC5's Fred "Sonic" Smith with the reggae trend of using the word "Youth" in their names. Founding members include Moore, Lee Ranaldo (guitar, vocals) and Kim Gordon (bass, guitar, vocals). Gordon and Moore played earlier gigs together as Male Bonding, Red Milk and the Arcadians. The band often includes Mark Ibold on bass and Steve Shelley plays drums.

Mathclub Hollywood, California, USA
Members met working in a music store. "Making math club cool."

Rational Youth
Montreal, Quebec, Canada
Formed by Tracy Howe and Bill Vorn in 1981. The name was a pun on the National Youth, short-form for the National Youth Orchestra. Howe was a former member of the Normals, a band that included Men Without Hats frontman Ivan Doroschuk.

Musical Youth
Birmingham, UK
A pop-reggae boy band said to have been inspired by the Jacksons and New Edition. Their 1982 hit "Pass the Dutchie" was based on the Mighty Diamonds' "Pass the Kouchie" (about marijuana), the title and chorus subtly altered to "dutchie," in reference to a type of cooking pot rather than, uh, you know…pot.

Wasted Youth
Los Angeles, California, USA
This hardcore punk band is known for speed. Its 10-song 1981 debut album, *Reagan's In,* is less than 15 minutes long. You don't want to waste time, even if you're Wasted Youth.

This Is Serious, Mum
Melbourne, Australia
An anonymous satirical band who perform in masks. Albums include *Beasts of Suburban, Hot Dogma* and *Great Truckin' Songs of the Renaissance*.

The Young & the Useless
New York City, New York, USA
With a name that mocked the glamorous TV soap *The Young & the Restless*, this early '80s punk band included Beastie Boy Adam Horovitz and shared a practice space with the Beastie Boys, who were playing as a punk band at the time. The success of the Beastie Boys eventually meant the end of the Young & the Useless. EP: *Real Men Don't Floss*, on Ratcage Records.

The Dontcares Stockholm, Sweden
Self-explanation: "The Dontcares… Rex $uperior (vocals, guitar) and Zed Divine (drums)…had the urge to play fast Rock'n'Roll…joined by two local wackos…Unholy Sabertooth Hell Fire Tiger (bass) and Glimmer Twin (lead guitar)…pretty soon they had a handful of fans in and around Stockholm… released debut single on Dirtnap Records…featured three songs, 'Spit in the Ass,' 'Going, Screaming, Burning' and the classic, 'Evil Sexmachine.'" ■

The Penfifteen Club is based in Los Angeles. The band's recent album, *Feel It*, is tightly arranged pop-punk with an healthy infusion of hard-rock sexual swagger. Singer-guitarist Luke Tierney: "I was informed by my little sister that there's an old prank involving the name. It entails asking a kid if he or she wants to join your club. If they say yes, then you tell them the club is called the Penfifteen Club and that you have to write it on their hand to initiate them. Then you write (preferably in thick black ink) PEN15. They get to go back to class with the word PENIS written on them. After hearing that story, we decided to go with the longer, and subsequently more cryptic name, the Penfifteen Club."

Love and Lust

My Chemical Romance

Newark, New Jersey's My Chemical Romance are a theatrical gothish band who were labeled emo quite early on. They reject the label, but their lyrics *do* tend to be confessional and angst-ridden, and frontman Gerard Way does look like the quintessential emo.

Their name is taken from Irving Welsh's *Ecstasy — Three Tales of Chemical Romance*, a 1996 collection of three novellas. Welsh is perhaps best known as the author of *Trainspotting*. It has been suggested that Welsh created a new literary genre with his drug-addled characters: the chemical romance.

The band formed shortly after the events of September 11, 2001, and addressed the attack and its outcome in their song "Skylines and Turnstiles."

Albums: *I Brought You My Bullets, You Brought Me Your Love* (2002), *Three Cheers for Sweet Revenge* (2004) and *The Black Parade* (2006).

Tainted Love

White Trash Debutantes
Los Angeles/San Francisco
Trashy punk since 1989, with high-profile singer Ginger Coyote. The band invited tarnished Olympic figure-skater Tonya Harding to join the band.

World's End Girlfriend
Nagasaki, Japan
Katsuhiko Maeda started his World's End Girlfriend band project when he was 13.

Love Spirals Downward
Los Angeles, California, USA
Started in late '80s by Ryan Lum with vocalists Kristen Perry, Suzanne Perry and Jennifer Wilde. Shortened their name to Lovespirals in the late '90s.

Romeo Void
San Francisco, California, USA
Early '80s new-wave band consisting largely of visual artists. Known for singles "Never Say Never" and "A Girl in Trouble (Is a Temporary Thing)."

Good Men Gone Bad
Stuttgart, Germany
Formed in 1992, the band contributed the soundtrack to Jochen Ehmann's 1995 animated film, *Hobo*.

The Useless Playboys
Richmond, Virginia, USA
Evolved from the True Detectives. Drummer Scott Minor joined Sparklehorse.

Army of Lovers   Sweden
Frontperson Alexander Bard is a drag queen who claims to be the love child of John F. Kennedy and Marilyn Monroe, raised on Mars and brought back to Earth to spread a message of love. Their name is taken from a 1979 documentary by West German gay-rights activist Rosa Von Praunheim.

Tattooed Love Boys
London, UK
Named after the title of a song off the Pretenders' debut album.

SMALL CHANGE ROMEOS
LONG WAY FROM TOMORROW

San Francisco's **Small Change Romeos** write politically aware songs with strong narrative elements. Songwriters Chris James and Mike Ruy are backed by drummer Matt Berg, bassist Robert Wright and keyboardist John Patterson. Their two albums have featured contributions from members of Crazy Horse, Tesla, Starship and Spearhead.

Dyslexic Love features classic garage-rock from electrical engineer and guitarist Tim Bertulli's home studio in Calgary, Alberta, Canada. Bertulli offers, tongue firmly in cheek, a review excerpt from the *Manila Standard*: "There's not one sexual reference, satanic verse, pornographic image, or foul slur. That's something you can't find everywhere."

Pretty Tied Up
Leicester, Midlands, UK
Hard-rock with female lead vocals. Named for the Guns N'Roses song "Pretty Tied Up (The Perils of Rock N' Roll Decadence)."

The Slipshod Swingers
Los Angeles, California, USA
Albums: *Orange Lamborghini, Woes and Hail Mary's, Transistor Radio*.

Trailer Park Casanovas
Torrance, California, USA
"Whether they are singing about cars, pills, booze or tattoos, the Trailer Park Casanovas epitomize American ideals, lost love, cheap sex and beer. Their lyrics are a train wreck of tastelessness, honesty and irony…."

Clumsy Lovers Coquitlam,
British Columbia, Canada
Albums: *Still Clumsy After All These Years, Barnburner, Smart Kid*.

The Trammps
Philadelphia, Pennsylvania, USA
Best known for their 1977 hit "Disco Inferno," used in the soundtrack to *Saturday Night Fever*.

Urge Overkill
Chicago, Illinois, USA
Named for a line in the 1978 Parliament song "Funkentelechy." Known for their cover of Neil Diamond's "Girl, You'll Be a Woman Soon," used in the movie *Pulp Fiction*.

The Go-Betweens
Brisbane, Australia
Formed in 1977 by guitarists Robert Forster and Grant McLennan and moved to the UK in the '80s. Collaborated with Sleater-Kinney. Won the 2005 Australian Recording Industry Association Best Adult Contemporary Album award for their last album, *Oceans Apart*.

Icky Boyfriends
San Francisco, California, USA
With the 2005 double-CD *A Love Obscene* (pun on John Coltrane's *A Love Supreme*). Songs include "There's a Burrito in My Jockstrap" and "Passion Assassin."

Carbon Dating Service
Saskatoon, Saskatchewan, Canada
"Last year we did a 24-hour bandswap. We went out to dinner with about 30 people, picked a few band leaders and drew names out of a hat to pick new bands. Then each band had 24 hours to come up with three new songs and one cover to play a show the next night." Raised over $2000 for charity.

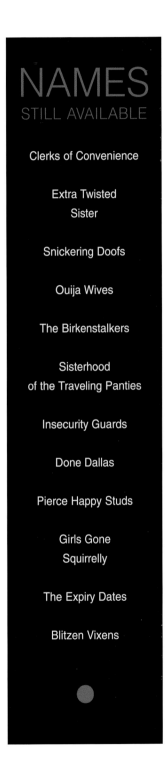

NAMES
STILL AVAILABLE

Clerks of Convenience

Extra Twisted
Sister

Snickering Doofs

Ouija Wives

The Birkenstalkers

Sisterhood
of the Traveling Panties

Insecurity Guards

Done Dallas

Pierce Happy Studs

Girls Gone
Squirrelly

The Expiry Dates

Blitzen Vixens

KISS

Rhythm guitarist Paul Stanley (Stanley Harvey Eisen) and bassist Gene Simmons (Chaim Witz) started a band called Wicked Lester in New York City, 1971. Auditions brought them drummer Peter Criss (Peter Criscuola) and lead guitarist Ace Frehley (Paul Frehley).

Stanley suggested the name KISS when Criss mentioned one of his former bands, the Lips. The stylized lightning-bolt SS in their all-capped name intentionally bore likeness to the Nazi SS (*Schutzstaffel*) insignia, a scandal-worthy gesture given Stanley, Simmons and Frehley's Jewish backgrounds.

Using KISS as an acronym for Kids In Satan's Service was a gimmicky afterthought.

KISS's makeup was inspired by the New York Dolls and by Simmons' obsession with comic books. The band created way-larger-than-life stage personas: Stanley, the Starchild; Simmons, the Demon; Frehley, the Spaceman; and Criss, the Catman.

Live performances featured fire-breathing, blood-spitting, smoking guitars and wild pyrotechnics. And they may have made more money from merchandising than any other band in rock history.

Untainted Love

Paramore
Franklin, Tennessee, USA
The name is "our friend's mother's maiden name." Singer Hayley Williams: "And Paramore is French for 'secret love,' and in Spanish it means 'for love.'" More or less.

Modern Romance
London, UK
An '80s dance-pop with horns by ex-members of the Leyton Buzzards. Formed as a subversive vehicle for satirical songwriters Geoff Deane (vocals) and David Jaymes (bass), who switched from punk to pop and ended up scoring a string of Top 40 hits.

The Romantics
Detroit, Michigan, USA
The band adopted the name the Romantics because they formed on Valentine's Day 1977. Biggest hits: "What I Like About You" and "Talking in Your Sleep."

Ambitious Lovers
New York, New York, USA
Formed by guitarist-singer Arto Lindsay and keyboardist Peter Scherer, with works based on the seven deadly sins and featuring collaborations with Marc Ribot, Vernon Reid, Bill Frisell, Caetano Veloso, Nile Rodgers and other notable musicians. Three albums: *Greed, Envy* and *Lust*

A Shore Scenic Romance
Pataskala, Ohio, USA
Self-description: "One of those bands that just won't die no matter how much you try to kill them."

Beloved (US) North Carolina, USA
Christian metalcore. Ex-members of Beloved went on to play in bands such as Classic Case, Dead Poetic, Advent and the Almost.

The Beloved London, UK
The video for "Sweet Harmony" shows a naked John Marsh in a group of women, also naked, carefully shot and edited so as to provoke controversy but not censorship.

The Dreamlovers
Philadelphia, Pennsylvania, USA
This R&B quintet formed in 1956 and also performed under the names the Romancers and the Midnighters. Biggest hit: "When We Get Married."

Melbourne's **Kisschasy** formed in 2002 with ex-members of Tenpin and So Many Ways. The game Kisschasy is basically tag with kisses. "We needed a name that was about fun and immaturity...the first six months or so [it was] 'Did you say Kisschasy!?'"

Love & Mathematics is a quartet from Vancouver, British Columbia, Canada. The band is named for a song off Broken Social Scene's 2003 album *Feel Good Lost*. The *Edmonton Journal* called their music "eerily gorgeous." Vancouver's leading entertainment paper, *The Georgia Straight*, said, "esoteric atmospherics, layering repeated guitar, bass, and keyboard lines to build a lush wall of swirling tone. It's an approach that the band pulls off with aplomb."

Kiss Kiss Milton, New York, USA
The name Kiss Kiss is derived from a 1960 collection of short stories by Roald Dahl. Debut album, *Reality vs. The Optimist*, released on Eyeball Records in 2007.

Movie Star Kiss
Los Angeles, California, USA
Fronted by Ronnie Day and Ryan Michael, formerly of Supercrush.

Love Tambourines Tokyo, Japan
Listen while I beat…my love tambourine. Smooth Japanese soul-pop from the '90s.

Loverboy Calgary, Alberta, Canada
Rejected by every major US label until Canadian sales caught their attention. Stadium-rock hits: "Turn Me Loose," "The Kid is Hot Tonight," "Working for the Weekend."

Young Love
New York City, New York, USA
Frontman-songwriter Dan Keyes: "I knew if I had another band, it would be called Young Love. It's not two words just randomly thrown together. The name is an idea, and all of my songs reflect that."

The Considerate Lovers
Tromso, Norway
Even their song titles are considerate: "Winter Ain't So Cold When You Got Someone on Your Mind." Great band from well north of the Arctic Circle.

Cupid's Inspiration Stamford, UK
Cupid only had one arrow: 1968's "Yesterday Has Gone."

I'm with Cupid
Brooklyn, New York, USA
Pun on the t-shirt slogan "I'm with Stupid." Members also in the Fakers.

The Pin-Up Girls
Manila, Philippines
First Philippine band signed to a US label. Songs: "Jackson Pollock 9" and "Spacegrrl Superb."

The Valentines
Harlem, New York, USA
A doo-wop group formed in 1952 in the Sugar Hill district of Harlem, first as the Mistletoes, then the Dreamers, and finally settling on the Valentines in 1954, inspired by the song "My Funny Valentine."

NAMES
STILL AVAILABLE

The More Adores

Bachelor Buttons

My Gentlemen
Collars

The Chocolate Hearts

Weddable
Women

The Prom Knights

Bridal Wave

The I
in Understand

Rampant Cupidity

Ironing Men

The Respectomatics

High Fidelity
Husbands

141

Gene Loves Jezebel

Formed in 1980 by twins Michael and Jay Aston, with Ian Hudson and a drum machine, in Porthcawl, South Wales. They called themselves Slav Arian, but changed their name when they moved to London in 1981.

The name of the band was based on the twins' nicknames. They regularly frequented a club called St. Martins, where Jay had been dubbed "Jezebel" because of his long hair. Michael had a limp from a badly healed leg break, thus was given the nickname "Gene," from musician Gene Vincent, who was crippled in a motorcycle accident in the '50s.

Michael moved to the US in 1989, but the other members continued to record and perform with Jay under the name Gene Loves Jezebel. Michael eventually assembled a band in the US that also tours as Gene Loves Jezebel, and the two bands have fought over the band name, royalties and song rights since the late '90s.

Naming Names

Bertha Does Moosejaw
Ottawa, Ontario, Canada
Moosejaw being a mid-size city in Saskatchewan. The "does" being a reference to the porn classic *Debbie Does Dallas*. Bertha being a fictitious person. Songs "Sex with the Dead" and "Peco the Taco Monkey."

Blow Up Betty
Adelaide, Australia
An "all-chick" pop-punk band formed in 2003. Debut album: *Asking for Trouble* (2007).

Brutally Frank
Joplin, Missouri, USA
A psychobilly punk trio who play very fast songs on simple themes: "The Bottle," "Bottled Happiness," "Liver."

Carter the Unstoppable Sex Machine
Lambeth, South London, UK
Formed in 1987 by singer Jim "Jim Bob" Morrison and guitarist Les "Fruitbat" Carter from the band Jamie Wednesday. Reportedly named for Fruitbat's aptitude and stamina.

Unruly Helga
Los Angeles, California, USA
Fronted by singer Deena Kamm. Unruly Helga sounded better than Unruly Deena.

X-Legged Sally
Belgium
Albums: *Eggs and Ashes*, *The Land of the Giant Dwarfs* and *Bereft of Blissful Union*.

Smashed Gladys
Toronto, Ontario, Canada
Female-fronted '80s glam-rock. No Gladys. Moved to New York and recorded two albums. Members went on to play for Yellow Scab, Higher Octane, Cycle Sluts from Hell and the Throbs.

Plastic Bertrand
Brussels, Belgium
Previous bands: Boy Scouts, Hubble Bubble, Roger Junior and the Pelicans. Collaborated with ABBA's Anni-Frid Lyngstad on *Abbacadabra*, a musical tale for children.

A Quincy, Massachusetts, trade-union-supporting, sports-team-loving, Celtic punk band formed in 1996. The band's name was taken from an old drunk-tank lock-up in Boston: "You don't want to wind up in **Dropkick Murphys** after last call." Their latest record, *The Meanest of Times*, rose to #20 on the US Album charts.

The Melvins were started by singer-guitarist Buzz Osborne (King Buzzo) in Washington state in the early '80s and were a big influence on Nirvana. Kurt Cobain auditioned for the band on bass but was so nervous he forgot his bass lines. The band is named after a grocery clerk at a Thriftway in Montesano, Washington, where Osborne also worked. Melvin was greatly despised by his fellow employees. The band is now based in San Francisco.

NAMES
STILL AVAILABLE

Right Said Wilma

The Dryland Cousteaus

Lulu's Boyfriend Dick

Emmageddon

Nicole to Newcastle

Trashmouth Kennys

A Band Called Doris

Savage Jordan

Breakfast at Tiffany's Cubicle

A Smith & Wesson Jones

All the Cloying Chloes

Jeff Leppard

Jennyanykind
Carrboro, North Carolina, USA
Critically acclaimed grunge rockers turned indie-Americana band.

John Fred & His Playboy Band
Baton Rouge, Louisiana, USA
Born John Fred Gourrier, John Fred started his Playboy band in 1956. Best known for their song "Judy in Disguise (with Glasses)," a 1968 novelty hit based loosely on "Lucy in the Sky with Diamonds."

Gary Lewis & the Playboys
Los Angeles, California, USA
Drummer Gary Lewis, son of comedian Jerry Lewis, was in a band called the Playboys when promoters promoted his name in hopes of capitalizing on his famous bloodline. Guitarist Dave Walker was the real musical leader and sang most of the vocals.

Juicy Lucy London, UK
Changed their name from the Misunderstood because they were looking to move away from psychedelic sound to "something more contemporary and commercial." Took their name from a character in Leslie Thomas's 1966 novel, *The Virgin Soldiers*.

Less Than Jake
Gainesville, Florida, USA
"We got the name from our drummer Vinnie's parents' bulldog, Jake. His parents would go out to dinner and bring back food just for the dog. Vinnie had to give up his spot on the couch for the dog. So everything was less than Jake, and so are we. It is also a phrase: 'Everything is Jake' is a term 1920s gangsters used to suggest that everything was cool, no problems. So Less Than Jake implies that something is wrong or uncool."

143

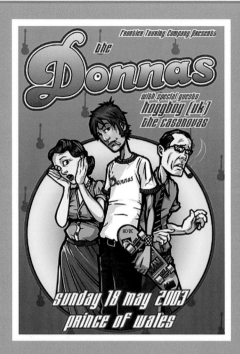

THE DONNAS

This all-female Palo Alto, California, band performed in high school as the metal-queen Electrocutes. The Donnas developed as a side project that allowed them to play less metal-based songs. At one stage, band members all adopted the name Donna (like the Ramones). They have released six albums on their own Purple Feather Records, including the latest, *Bitchin'*, in 2007. Their song "Take It Off" was featured in the 2004 movie *Dodgeball*.

Nick Cave & the Bad Seeds
London, UK

Nick Cave moved to London from Australia following the breakup of the original Birthday Party band. He likely named his new band after the parable of the bad seed and the good seed in Matthew 13 of the New Testament. The band performs as themselves in Wim Wenders' 1988 film *Wings of Desire*, about angels in Berlin.

Furious George
Manhattan, New York, USA

Fronted by George Tabb (Roach Motel, Atoms for Peace, False Prophets, Gynecologists, Iron Prostate), with Stevie Ramone on bass and Michael Harper on drums. Tabb: "I was called 'Furious George the Jew' as a kid, and the name kinda stuck. Then I forgot about it, but was reminded of it by a girl named Rebecca. So that's how we got the name. And now Curious George wants it. Fucking little monkey."

Dean Ford & the Gaylords
Glasgow, Scotland, UK

Formed in 1961 by guitarists William "Junior" Campbell and Patrick Fairley as simply the Gaylords, the name of a once notorious Chicago street gang. Additional vocalist Thomas McAleese took the stage name Dean Ford. Manager Peter Walsh later changed the band's name to the Marmalade (an idea that came to him over breakfast), and they had a number of hit singles in the late 1960s and 1970s

The McCoys
Union City, Indiana, USA

Most famous for their 1965 hit "Hang on Sloopy." The band was guitarist Rick Zehringer (later known as Rick Derringer), his brother Randy on drums and bass player Dennis Kelly. Rumor has it they won't play with Juliana Hatfield.

Ednaswap
Los Angeles, California, USA

A female-fronted alternative band whose name came from a performance nightmare. Frontwoman Anne Preven dreamt she was in a truly bad band called Ednaswap, and they were booed off stage. Preven has written songs for Sinead O'Connor, Madonna and Natalie Imbruglia.

Welcome
to the Couch

My Beautiful
Brain Laundrette

Madness:
The Two-Step Beyond

Welcome to the Couch

My Beautiful Brain Laundrette

Simple Minds

Vocalist Jim Kerr and guitarist Charlie Burchill started a punk band in Glasgow in 1977, calling themselves Johnny & the Self Abusers. But they soon became more interested in various aspects of new wave, changed their style and took the name Simple Minds, from a lyric in David Bowie's "Jean Genie": *He's so simple-minded he can't drive his module/He bites on the neon and sleeps in the capsule.*

Their unique, immediately recognizable sound is a layered wash of guitar and synthesizers, with a strong rhythmic pulse and Kerr's darkly romantic vocals. They have recorded 15 albums to date, the most recent, *Black & White 050505.*

The band's biggest single, "Don't You (Forget About Me)," written by Keith Forsey for *The Breakfast Club* soundtrack, was first offered to Brian Ferry and Billy Idol, who both declined it.

The band has maintained a political awareness throughout its history and wrote the #1 UK single "Belfast Child" in response to violence in Northern Ireland. They recently performed at the concert for Nelson Mandela's 90th birthday.

American Head Charge
Minneapolis, Minnesota, USA
Early incarnations of the band include Flux, Gestapo Pussy Ranch, and Warsaw Ghetto Pussy. Bassist Chad Hanks says he likes three-word band names. I guess he also likes the words charge, head and American. But in that order they sound like a consumer credit psychosis. I have an idea for a band name.

Fix My Head
Oakland, California, USA
Songs: "I Sharted My Pantaloons" and "Garbage Existence."

My Head for a Goldfish
Vincenza, Italy
Hardcore experimental trio formed in 2006. Not sure what this means in Italian.

The Mindbenders
Manchester, UK
Their name was inspired by the 1962 film *The Mind Benders*, a spy thriller about a scientist who voluntarily undergoes brainwashing experiments. Best known for their hits "Groovy Kind of Love" and "Game of Love." Guitarist Eric Stewart later helped form 10cc.

Dream Academy   London, UK
Their first two albums produced by David Gilmour. Biggest success with their first single, "Life in a Northern Town."

Dream Syndicate
Los Angeles, California, USA
Previous band called Goat Deity. Drummer Dennis Duck suggested the name Dream Syndicate, a reference to the early '60s New York experimental ensemble whose members included the Velvet Underground's John Cale.

50¢ HEADRUSH
selfish, foolish, freedom

Detroit's straight-ahead power-pop rockers **50¢ Headrush** formed in 1999. Vocalist Kevin Bovee came up with the name after sitting up too fast and getting a headrush and thinking it was like getting a cheap buzz. Bovee is joined by guitarist Jeff Szymanski, bassist Ken Krawczyk and drummer Billy Beardsley. Their latest album is *Selfish, Foolish, Freedom.*

Dream Theater
Long Island, New York, USA
Started under the name Majesty in 1985 as a project for some prodigiously talented Berklee College of Music students. A pre-existing Majesty in Las Vegas caused them to change their name. Dream Theatre was suggested by drummer Mike Portnoy's father. It was the name of an old movie theater in Monterey, California.

Dream Warriors
Toronto, Ontario, Canada
Started as the duo King Lou and Capital Q in 1988, later adding Spek and DJ Luv. Achieved international success with "My Definition of a Boombastic Jazz Style" in 1990.

Freddie & the Dreamers
Manchester, UK
Before becoming a singer, Freddie Garrity worked as a milkman. Biggest hits: "I'm Telling You Now" and "You Were Made For Me." Garrity and Dreamers bassist Pete Birrell went on to host their own children's TV series, *The Little Big Time*.

Velvet Dreamfield
Cincinnati, Ohio, USA
Garageband bio: "Velvet Dreamfield signify a fictional character that symbolizes the personalities of every member in the band. All of the instruments together are the sound of Velvet's voice. Many of the songs that we play are from Velvet's perspective...."

Asleep for Dreaming
Kansas City, Missouri, USA
Short-lived band went on to form We Are Voices, former bassist joined Chariot.

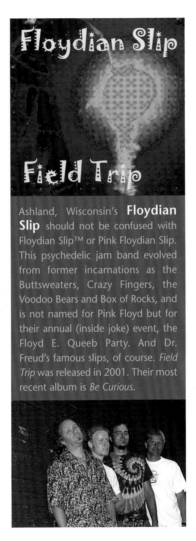

Ashland, Wisconsin's **Floydian Slip** should not be confused with Floydian Slip™ or Pink Floydian Slip. This psychedelic jam band evolved from former incarnations as the Buttsweaters, Crazy Fingers, the Voodoo Bears and Box of Rocks, and is not named for Pink Floyd but for their annual (inside joke) event, the Floyd E. Queeb Party. And Dr. Freud's famous slips, of course. *Field Trip* was released in 2001. Their most recent album is *Be Curious*.

Awake and Dreaming
Toronto, Ontario, Canada
We've all done it. These guys do it as a five-piece rock band.

Woke Up Falling
Portland, Oregon, USA
Reviewer Simon Rogers: "Dreamy lyricism with angels and death as recurring images." Albums include *Dividing Blue from Blue* and *It's Only Your Ghost*.

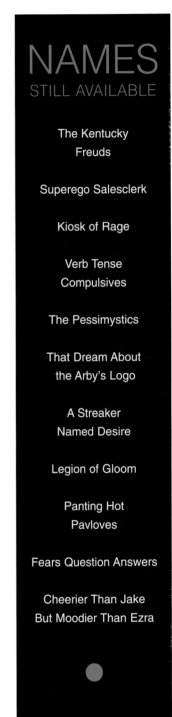

NAMES
STILL AVAILABLE

The Kentucky
Freuds

Superego Salesclerk

Kiosk of Rage

Verb Tense
Compulsives

The Pessimystics

That Dream About
the Arby's Logo

A Streaker
Named Desire

Legion of Gloom

Panting Hot
Pavloves

Fears Question Answers

Cheerier Than Jake
But Moodier Than Ezra

147

Masters of Reality
Syracuse, New York, USA

Named after the 1971 Black Sabbath album, *Master of Reality*. Formed in 1981 by Chris Goss. Goss has produced Kyuss, Queens of the Stone Age, Soulwax, Melissa Auf der Maur and others. Spin-offs: Goon Moon, Boogeymen, Creepjoint.

Masters of the Obvious
Chicago, Illinois, USA

Also known as M.O.T.O. Formed in New Orleans in 1981 by Paul Caporino, moved to Boston and then Chicago in 1987. Caporino is anti-CD, preferring cassettes and vinyl. In this bit from the *Chicago Tribune*, he confronts the obvious: "The low point came when he played a 1995 show 'and nobody showed up. I pretty much decided not to play live and just make records because we were worse than not popular,' he says. 'We were almost a nonentity, vapor.'"

Anger Is a Gift   Essex, UK

The name comes from a softly spoken lyric in Rage Against the Machine's song "Freedom." Often attributed to Aristotle, from his discussion of the morality of philanthropy, but misconstrued.

Tempercalm
Glasgow, Scotland, UK

Their song "I Need a Co-Pilot" was featured in the 2005 Xbox 360 game *Saints Row*.

Love/Hate
Los Angeles, California, USA

Hair-metal band formed in 1985 with lead singer Jizzy Pearl. Songs: "Boozer," "Dope," "Wasted in America."

New York City's **Hate in the Box is** "candy-coated horror rock — a five-piece, all-live, whirl-a-gig of musical mayhem; a perfect picture of innocence lost and childhood memories shattered...Theatrical and comical, they are an anime rock band brought to monstrous life, fronted by an American Gothic Lolita from the darkside, a living, breathing Technicolor Nightmare." Featuring Rainbow Blight, Optimus Crime, Teddy Krueger and Lil' Johnny Hyde. Previously called Broken Toys. Shouldn't have wound that Jack in the Box so tightly.

Confrontation Camp
New York, New York, USA

Funk-metal and rap collaboration with Public Enemy's Chuck D (under the name Mistachuck) and Professor Griff, with Kyle "Ice" Jason. Album: *Objects in the Mirror Are Closer Than They Appear*. Kyle in *Rolling Stone*: "We address issues, we confront the issues. We're not running and hiding from any one particular thing."

Low Low Low La La La Love Love Love
High Peak, Derbyshire, UK

Known as Low Low. Started in 2003 by Ellis (drums, percussion) and Kelly Dyson (songwriter), now a six-piece band. The name comes from a pre-Low Low song in which the choruses were "low low low la la la" and the last chorus went into "love love love."

Fear
Los Angeles, California, USA

An LA punk unit formed in 1977 by Lee Ving and Durf Scratch. Bassist Flea was in the band briefly before joining Red Hot Chili Peppers. John Belushi got them a spot on *Saturday Night Live* in 1981. Their song "I Don't Care About You" was covered by Soundgarden and Guns N'Roses.

Fear Factory
Los Angeles, California, USA

Started as Ulceration but changed name in 1990 to something that better reflected their industrial sound. Albums include *Soul of a New Machine*, *Obsolete*, *Digimortal* and *Demanufacture*.

Tears for Fears
Bath, UK

Duo formed by Roland Orzabal and Curt Smith in 1981, whose earlier bands included Graduate and History of Headaches. Tears for Fears comes from a form of primal scream therapy developed by Arthur Janov. Janov's theories are also in lyrics for the hits "Shout" and "Everybody Wants to Rule the World."

Madness: The Two-Step Beyond

Mad Caddies
Santa Barbara, California, USA

Formed in 1995 by high-school friends as the Ivy League but discovered another band with the same name. Songs: "Macho Nachos" and "Nobody Wins at the Laundromat."

Mannequin Depressives
Calgary, Alberta, Canada

"Retro-80s-esque…electro-madness." Latest album: *Girls Are Evil* (2008). A pun on manic depression. Band members confess to interest in mental disorders. The music is not at all depressing.

System of a Down
Glendale, California, USA

Formed in 1995 by Serj Tankian (lead vocals, keyboards, rhythm guitar) and Daron Malakian (vocals, lead guitar) after the break up of their previous band, Soil. Daron: "I thought of the name from a poem that I had written. It was originally called 'Victims of the Down,' but Shavo didn't really like the word 'victims' in the title, so I thought up 'System of a Down' and it just clicked...Plus, now our album will be under the S section, next to Slayer!"

Biff Hitler & the
Violent Mood Swings   Ireland

Song: "I Want to Walk You to Your Horse (and Possibly Hold Your Hand)," a parody of Irish courting rituals. Keith Richards' band mates on his *Dirty Work* album include a trio of Stones roadies who go under the name the Biff Hitler Trio.

Manic Sewing Circle
Chicago, Illinois, USA

Ska-punk band formed by high-school kids in 2004. Two albums: *Nobody Gets What We're Saying* (2005) and *Summer Spins* (2007).

Suicidal Tendencies
Venice, California, USA

A thrash-metal and skate-punk band formed in 1981. Their 1983 hit, "Institutionalized," one of the first hardcore punk videos to receive substantial MTV airplay. It was also used in the movie *Repo Man* and on the TV show *Miami Vice*. Vocalist Mike Muir's brother Jim was one of the Z-Boys, the legendary skateboard team banned from playing in LA until the 1990s due to alleged gang affiliations.

Madness

Madness started as the North London Invaders in 1976, became the Invaders, then briefly changed their name to Morris & the Minors (named for the Morris Minor automobile). The name Madness pays homage to one of their favorite ska-reggae artists, Prince Buster; it's the title of a song off his 1963 album, *Feel the Spirit*.

The band were leaders in the late-70s ska-revival movement and scored some 17 Top 10 singles in the UK. Their biggest hits were "My Girl," "Baggy Trousers," "Our House" and "One Step Beyond." Two musicals have been written based on the songs of Madness: *One Step Beyond* had a brief run at the Theatre Royal Stratford East in 1993, and *Our House* ran in London in 2002 and 2003.

They have reformed a number of times since the 1990s, as Madness and under the name the Dangermen. They have also collaborated with Prince Buster, Elvis Costello, UB40, Ian Dury and the Pet Shop Boys.

Their 2008 album is *The Liberty of Norton Folgate*.

SEROTONIN hails from Washington state's Puget Sound. "Serotonin's newest album, *You Can Watch My Monsters Die*, showcases the band's introspective lyrics within its...mutating styles. The music takes you on a ride through morphing blends of soulful groovy funk, boot-stomping bluegrass, a splash of psychedelic jazz, all the while maintaining a steady dose of driving rock."

Ego Cleveland, Ohio, USA

What else but the mighty prog-rock power trio! Songs: "Ego Trip" and "Illage Vidiot." Are there venues for prog-rock in Cleveland?

Agoraphobic Nosebleed

Springfield, Massachusetts, USA

Self-declaration: "Like flatulence in a wind tunnel, the listener must simply submit to being decimated." Extremely concise songs using drum machines to record songs with over 1,000 beats per minute, with some songs only 5 seconds long. *Alternative Press* review quote: "Until singers can grow extra heads and someone invents a drummer who can outplay the Gatling gun, this is the shit."

Neurosis

Oakland, California, USA

Experimental psychedelic metal formed in 1985 by ex-members of Violent Coercion. Songs: "Obsequious Obsolescence," "United Sheep," "Burning Flesh in Year of Pig."

Neurotic Outsiders

Los Angeles, California, USA

A '90s hard-rock side project for John Taylor (Duran Duran), Matt Sorum (the Cult and Guns N'Roses), Duff "Rose" McKagan (Guns N'Roses) and Steve Jones (Sex Pistols).

The Obsessed

Rockland, Maryland, USA

Formed in the 1980s then reformed in the '90s, when the band's recordings were made. Led by guitarist Scott "Wino" Weinrich, who has also been involved with Saint Vitus, Spirit Caravan and the Hidden Hand.

WIDESPREAD PANIC is an Athens, Georgia, jam band formed in 1986 and named for the band's founder, guitarist Michael "Panic" Houser. Houser died of cancer in 2002, but the band continued with stellar guitarist Jimmy Herring. Widespread Panic is renowned for its tireless touring schedule (250 live shows a year) and for never playing the same show twice.

Panic! At the Disco

Las Vegas, Nevada, USA

Took their name from the lyrics of the song "Panic" by the band Name Taken, from Orange County, California: *Panic at the disco/ Sat back and took it so slow/ Are you nervous? Are you shaking?* Panic at the Disco is known for its hits, oui, but also for its mock Victorian circus shows complete with contortionists and dancers.

The Panic Division

San Antonio, Texas, USA

Formed by three members of the post-hardcore group Carbon 12 Theory. Song "Polysix" is named after one of their keyboards.

The Panic Channel

Los Angeles, California, USA

Formed after the third breakup of Jane's Addiction. Features Jane's Addiction guitarist Dave Navarro, bassist Chris Chaney, drummer Stephen Perkins, and Skycycle vocalist Steve Isaacs. The name refers to the electronic media's desire to induce panic to maintain ratings.

Straightjacket Fits

Dunedin, New Zealand

Formed by ex-members of the DoubleHappys and the Orange. Their early songs "Life in One Chord" and "She Speeds" were minor NZ hits.

Bark Psychosis

East London, UK

Ambient electronica formed from the early '90s. Side project: Boymerang.

Acrotomophilia Gemert, North Brabant, Netherlands

Named after the term for sexual attraction to amputees. Songs: Well, never mind.

Necrophobic

Stockholm, Sweden

Death-metal band formed in 1989 and big on Viking mythology and anti-Christian lyrics. Named themselves after the song "Necrophobic" from Slayer's 1986 album, *Reign in Blood*.

Them

Belfast, Northern Ireland, UK

Formed in 1964 when Van Morrison left his previous band, the Golden Eagles, and joined the Gamblers, who were promptly renamed by keyboardist Eric Wrixon for the 1954 horror film *Them*. Their biggest hit was "Gloria." Morrison left in 1967 after money and management squabbles. Them continued without Morrison until the early 1970s.

The Kooks

Brighton, UK

Formed by students at the Brighton Institute of Music in 2004 and named after the song "Kooks" on David Bowie's 1971 album, *Hunky Dory*. Already (justifiably) huge in the UK.

Beyond Insanity

East Alton, Illinois, USA

Previous incarnations include Lepidus and Driven by Pain. Self-declaration: "The band is not together right now. There were certain complications between the practice space, and alcoholism, and overbearing timeshare with other bands and women."

Brink of Insanity

New Milford, Connecticut, USA

Short-lived high-school hardcore band. Their 2006 demos include the songs "Warface" and "Brink of Insanity." The drummer and guitarist have collaborated in Circuit Breaker.

Mental as Anything

Sydney, Australia

Founding members Martin Plaza and Reg Mombassa met at the East Sydney Technical College art school (now the National Art School) and formed the band in 1976. All of the early members became accomplished painters. Promoter Paul Worstead chose the name Mental as Anything from a list given to him by the band — in this case specifically describing fellow artist Ken Bolton after one of their early party performances.

Pamper the Madman

Des Moines, Iowa, USA

The phrase is used in *The Vampire Lestat* by Anne Rice, during a passage in which Lestat is having an existential crisis.

Formed in 1982 but largely inactive since the early '90s, Dublin's **Paranoid Visions** toured with the Sex Pistols and the Damned on their reunion tours in 1996 and 2001, respectively. The 2007 album *40 Shades of Gangreen* is their first new recorded material in 16 years.

NAMES STILL AVAILABLE

The Manic Librarians

Sharp as Marbles

Primal Yodel Therapy

Electroshock Rainbows

Mad as a Blank Tape

Incited by Blue

Jimmy the Wolverine

My Expanding Shrinks

They Are in My Phone

Are You Using Your Head?

Long Sleeves Tightly Bound

Life in a Complex

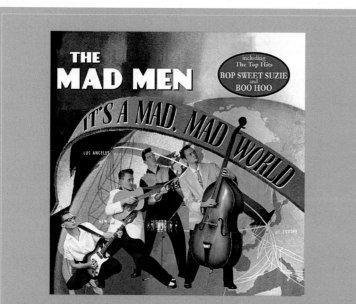

The Mad Men come from Zagreb, Croatia, and are touted as the best rockabilly band from Eastern Europe. The oldest band member was 26 and the youngest 19 when they recorded their debut album, *It's a Mad Mad World*. The record was recorded in Berlin at Lightning Recording Service studio on vintage valve recording equipment for a genuine '50s sound. The recording engineer-producer was Ike Stoye, of Ike and the Capers and Spo-Dee-O-Dee fame.

Harbinger Complex

Fremont, California, USA

"Walk inside your mind, filling your body with an unknown substance... You have experienced the Harbinger Complex." In the 1960s, singer Jim Hockstaff and company recorded a handful of singles that featured an aggressive fuzz guitar sound and can almost be described as proto-punk. They opened for Big Brother & the Holding Company, Van Morrison, the Animals and Sly & the Family Stone, among others, but mostly played the local clubs, pizza parlors and roller rinks

The Conniption Fits

Fairlee, Vermont, USA

Formed in 2004 by ex-Motorplant singer Steve Blanchard and now based in Boston, Massachusetts. Blanchard said his mother used to use the expression "don't have a conniption fit." The band was chosen to score the music for the upcoming video game *Mechwarrior: Living Legends.*

Head Like a Hole

Wellington, New Zealand

This '90s alternative-rock band always had metal influences. They took their name from title of a Nine Inch Nails' song from 1989's *Pretty Hate Machine.*

The Deviants London, UK

Late '60s psychedelic-rock from art students inspired by the Fugs to create a band. Also called the Social Deviants. Fronted by Mick Farren and occasionally resurrected as a group. Spin-off groups include the Pink Fairies and Twink. Later albums with various lineups include *I luman Garbage* (1984) and *Eating Jello With A Heated Fork* (1996).

Edge of Sanity

Finspång, Sweden

Recorded a couple of albums, but band members' other bands are comical for sheer number: Bloodbath, Brejn Dedd, Darkcide, Demiurg, Diabolical Masquerade, Godsend, Incision, Infestdead, Karaboudjan, Katatonia, Maceration, Masticate, Nightingale, Odyssey, Overflash, Pan.Thy.Monium, Ribspreader, Route Nine, Star One, Steel, Total Terror, Unicorn, Sorskogen, Frameshift, Another Life, Stygg Död, Incapacity, Marduk, Infestdead, Ophthalamia, Darkified, Facebreaker, Scypozoa, Kill, Solar Dawn, the Deadbeats, the Nasty Flames, Fistel, Carve, Paganizer, Berenice Bleeding, Deranged, Foreboding, Eaten, Those Who Bring The Torture, Putrevore, Revolting.

Shriekback London, UK

Experimental new wave band formed in 1982 by Barry Andrews (League of Gentlemen, XTC), Carl Marsh (Out on Blue Six) and Dave Allen (Gang of Four). Albums include *Naked Apes & Pond Life* (2000), *Oil & Gold* (1985) and *Jam Science* (1984). Newest record: *Glory Bumps* (2007) Spin-offs: The Elastic Purejoy, King Swamp, Moonstrance.

Jocks & Surfers

Poets & Beatniks

Heroes & Superheroes

Rock and Role Playing

Jocks & Surfers

OK Go

OK Go began in Chicago in 1998 but now call Los Angeles home. Singer Damian Kulash met bassist Tim Nordwind at Interlochen Arts Camp in Michigan when they were 11.

They took their band name from an Interlochen art teacher who used to say, "OK...go!" to start each sketching session (not track-meet event).

The band's second album, *Oh No*, was recorded in Malmö, Sweden, and produced by Tore Johansson (the Cardigans, Franz Ferdinand) in the fall of 2004. A cheap ($10) homemade video for the first single, "A Million Ways," was released unofficially via the internet and downloaded over 9 million times, making it the most downloaded video of all time.

Members of OK Go — Kulash, Nordwind, drummer Dan Konopka and guitarist-keyboardist Andy Ross — are known for their appearance as well as their music, often wearing vests, ties, dress shirts, suspenders, dress pants of loud colors and/or clashing patterns. Styles they claim are influenced by Oscar Wilde, "Republican assholes" and "other people too wealthy to know how crazy they look."

The Starting Line
Philadelphia, Pennsylvania, USA
Started as Sunday Drive but discovered that Sunday Drive was the name of a Christian rock band.

Go! Team   Brighton/London, UK
"The name came from an article I read about plane crashes. The Go Team are the people who clear up the wreckage – so it's fucking morbid really." An Olympia, Washington, band called the Go Team was a side-project for Calvin Johnson (Beat Happening) and Tobi Vail and Billy "Boredom" Karren (Bikini Kill). Collaborating musicians included Kurt Cobain.

Stars of Track and Field
Portland, Oregon, USA
The name is the title of the first track on Belle and Sebastian's 1996 album, *If You're Feeling Sinister*.

Dexy's Midnight Runners
Birmingham, UK
Named after the amphetamine Dexedrine, known for keeping users up all night — the midnight runners. Singer Kevin Rowland (ex-Killjoys) is said to have imposed a no-drink, no-drugs policy on band members, having himself struggled with cocaine addiction.

Fastball

This Austin, Texas, band began as Magneto USA but changed their name when they signed to Hollywood Records. *Fastball* is the title of a baseball-themed porn film: "It's like a really raunchy *Bull Durham*." Their 1998 album, *All the Pain Money Can Buy*, went platinum in the US and remained in the *Billboard* Top 200 for a year.

The Olympics
Los Angeles, California, USA
A doo-wop group formed in 1957 by lead singer Walter Ward. A cover version of their song "Good Lovin'" was a hit for the Young Rascals in 1965.

Baseball Furies
Chicago, Illinois, USA
The Baseball Furies are a gang in the 1979 thriller *The Warriors*, from the 1965 book by Sol Yurick and based on the Greek Furies and events in Xenophon's *Anabasis*.

High School Football Heroes
Long Island, New York, USA
Album: *Close Only Counts in Horseshoes and Hand Grenades*.

Chad the Quarterback
Espoo, Finland
"We are a punk-rock band from Finland. But we make songs about life in high school in Minnesota. It's weird." Albums: *Chad Loses Boner, Chad Goes to College,* and *…Of the High School Football Team*.

Slapshot
Boston, Massachusetts, USA
In the 1980s, Slapshot issued an open challenge to play any other band at street hockey.

Five for Fighting
San Fernando Valley, California, USA
The name refers to the ice-hockey penalty for fighting. It's the stage name of singer-songwriter John Ondrasik.

Two for Flinching Perth, Australia
A ska-punk band formed in 2004. Lead singer Hayley Willson formed the Blast Off Girls following the breakup of Two for Flinching in 2007.

Big Thumb Bowlers
Tucson, Arizona, USA
People with big thumbs have difficulty with off-the-rack ten-pin bowling balls. Albums: *Recorded at Gunpoint, All These Random Jims*.

Let's Go Bowling
San Joaquin Valley, California, USA
Formed in 1986 by bassist Mark Michel (Kyber Rifles) and keyboardist Derren Fletcher. Albums: *Music to Bowl By, Freeway Lanes* and *Mr. Twist*.

The Headpins Vancouver, British Columbia, Canada
Founders originally played in Chilliwack. Randy Bachman's (Guess Who, BTO) wife, Denise McCann, sang with the band.

Dribbling Darts
Auckland, New Zealand
Originally called Dribbling Darts of Love, from Shakespeare's *Measure for Measure*: "No. Holy father, throw away that thought / Believe not that the dribbling dart of love / Can pierce a complete bosom. Why I desire thee."

Fatkid Dodgeball
Columbus, Ohio, USA
"Whatever else is going on in your life, being at a Fatkid Dodgeball concert will make that go away for a while…you will get your face rocked." Getting hit in the face by a dodgeball has a way of clearing your head.

Brass Knuckle Surfer
Atlanta, Georgia, USA
Instrumental ambient space-rock since 2003. Members have also played in the Black Kites, Hiatus, Soft Collision, Foundry, the Brew and Novocaine.

NAMES
STILL AVAILABLE

Javelin Catcher

Pickup League
Potentates

The Quarterback
Sneaks

Goalie Dreams

High Inside Ball 3

For Free Referee

Beckham
Bent Mine

Turf Surfers

The Way Original
Gnarly Baggies

Squid in the Tube

Six-String Bikini

The Well-Waxed
Woodies

Released in 2007 on NeatGuy Records, *They Came from Beneath the Surf* is the second CD of instrumental surf rock from California's **Pavlov's Woody**. Best known for documenting the "conditioned response," Russian physiologist Ivan Petrovich Pavlov won the 1904 Nobel Prize for his work on the nature of digestion. The term "woody" refers to the wood-paneled vans popular with surfers in the early '60s. At least I think it does.

Phantom Surfers
San Francisco, California, USA
Songs: "Batwoman vs. Ratfink," "A Slot Car Named Desire," "Stumps of Mystery."

Surf Coasters
Tokyo, Japan
Dick Dale, often dubbed "King of the Surf Guitar," has referred to the band's founder, Shigeo Naka, as the "Prince of the Surf Guitar."

Surferosa
Oslo, Norway
The band's name is inspired by the Pixies' 1988 debut album, *Surfer Rosa*.

Thee Andrews Surfers
Ghent, Belgium
Punning on the Andrews Sisters. Primarily an instrumental side-project for members of Fifty Foot Combo.

Surfer Roadkill Ra! Ra! Ra!
London, UK
Started as a side-project for Biodrone. Songs: "Surfing with a Shotgun," "I Came, I Surfed, I Conquered."

Butthole Surfers
San Antonio, Texas, USA
"Butthole Surfer" was a song performed by the band known variously as Nine Foot Worm Makes Own Food, the Dick Clark Five, Abe Lincoln's Bush, Fred Astaire's Asshole, etc. An emcee at an early gig forgot the band's name and used the song title to announce them. It stuck, so to speak. The term is a graphic reference to male homosexuals.

The Beach Boys
Hawthorne, California, USA
Mike Love named the band the Pendletones, after the plaid Pendleton wool shirt that was a West Coast fashion trend in the 1960s. Dennis Wilson was the only member of the group who surfed. The name was changed to the Beach Boys by a young promotions man named Russ Regan to tie in with their first single, "Surfin'."

Surfaris Glendora, California, USA
Surf + Safari = Surfari. Their 1963 surf masterpiece "Wipe Out" was actually the B-side of a 45 rpm single.

Bikini Kill
Olympia, Washington, USA
Riot Grrrl punk originals involved in the feminist fanzine *Bikini Kill*, after which the band was named. Spinoffs: the Fakes, Spider & the Webs, Boo Boo & the Corrections, and Le Tigre.

Tabarnacos Surfers
Montreal, Quebec, Canada
Surf sounds of the St. Lawrence River. Based on the mild French-Canadian curse *tabarnak* (tabernacle). Tabernacos are southbound Quebeckers.

Poets & Beatniks

Real MEN write Poetry

The Dust Poets
Brandon, Manitoba, Canada

The band has now become "one of Manitoba's hottest and most geographically challenged folk-pop groups." The mandolin-trumpet-trombone player now lives in Sackville, New Brunswick, where his wife "got a real job;" three other band members live in Ontario; while frontman Murray Evans remains in Manitoba.

As the Poets Affirm
Ottawa, Ontario, Canada

Began as a trio in 2001 but has expanded to seven players. Their second album, *The Jaws That Bite, The Claws That Catch*, topped Canadian college radio charts in 2004.

Men Poets   Texas, USA
Album: *Birth of the Cool*. A nod to Miles Davis's seminal 1957 album, *Birth of the Cool*.

The Last Poets   Aix, France
Where else would you look for them?

Dog The Dead Poets
Newark, USA, and Plymouth, UK

Poets who are dead. Their song "Cobain" pays homage to the poet Kurt.

Poetryclub
Bayern-Berlin, Germany

Inspired by a visit to the Walt Whitman monument. The project involves 12 singers and 15 musicians under the direction of lyricist "Cosmic."

Poetry in Motion
Minooka, Illinois, USA

The title of a 1982 documentary film featuring readings by 24 well-known [sic] poets. Poetry in Motion® was a program developed in 1992 by the Poetry Society of America and New York City Transit to place poems on the sides of subway cars and buses.

Poets of the Fall

According to the band, the name Poets of the Fall came from the idea of opposites being necessary to form a whole. To Olli Tukianen, Marko Saaresto and Markus "Captain" Kaarlonen, poets represent the positive side of things and the fall, the negative, different ends of the spectrum. We can only assume that Finnish poetry is magically uplifting. And they are a bit cagey about what they mean by "the Fall": the crisp autumn season or the fall of humanity. What's poetry without slippery metaphors?

Founded in Helsinki in 2003, the Poets of Fall, or POTF as they are often known, gained wide exposure in 2004 after composing the song "Late Goodbye" for the video game *Max Payne 2*. The song earned them the Game Audio Network Guild (G.A.N.G.) Award for Best Original Vocal Song, Pop category. In 2006 Poets of the Fall won Best Finnish Act at the MTV Europe Music Awards and had the most played single on Finnish radio, "Carnival of Rust."

POETS & PORNSTARS

Better than poets without pornstars. Their fans are called Sex Ninjas. This big-club Los Angeles group was led by British-born singer-guitarist Hal Ozsan, with lead guitarist Tom Domaracki, keyboardist Randy Austin, bassist Sally Hope and drummer Dave Plesh. Ozsan recently left the band, and the search for a new singer has begun. The group released its self-titled album in 2005 — revamped and rereleased by Adrenaline Records in 2007.

NAMES
STILL AVAILABLE

The Ferlinghetti Straps

Rhymes with Poetry

A Tree

The Wealthy Poets

Call Before
You Dig

Poets with Cars

Beatnik Accountants

Tropical Beatniks

Back in
Black Beret

The Gauloise-
Wah Pedals

Goatees of
Death Metal

Groovy Bongos
Betty

Poetry 'n' Lotion
Tampa, Florida, USA
Produces fewer greenhouse gas emissions. Interview quote: "We're all really great singers. We just don't have vocals." Songs: "Serpentstance," "Sweet Relish."

The Beat Poets
Ireland
Gary Snyder, Allen Ginsberg, Lawrence Ferlinghetti, Gregory Corso, Neal Cassady, Diane di Prima, Anne Waldman, et al.

Vogon Poetry
Utrecht, Netherlands
In Douglas Adams' *A Hitchhiker's Guide to the Galaxy*, an alien race known as the Vogons produce the third-worst poetry in the universe. (Earthlings produce the worst.)

Ten Second Epic
Edmonton, Alberta, Canada
An epic is a long narrative poem that celebrates the feats of its hero. "An epic is a long journey that has a great impact in your life, so the name basically means, take every ten seconds of your life and live them like they mean so much more. It was our attempt to be deep and meaningful when we were 16 years old, and even though it's a really tough name to say, we still like it quite a bit."

Beatnik
Wellington, NZ, and Liverpool, UK
The term *beatnik* was first applied to members of the nonconformist Beat Generation in 1950s America. Beatnik(s) bands also reside in Innsbruck, Austria; Barcelona, Spain; Marion, Indiana; and elsewhere.

New World Beatniks
Florida, USA
"I just kind of put some names together," says guitarist Ronnie Levine. The first use of the term "beatnik" is generally attributed to writer Herb Caen in a 1958 issue of the *San Francisco Chronicle*, combining "beat" from Beat Generation and the Russian (or Yiddish) suffix "-nik," meaning someone or something associated with the, well, whatever the main term is: beatnik, sputnik, nogoodnik. Anyway, Florida is definitely New World, and the US served as key turf for the Beat Movement, so...how about New Beatnik World?

The Cappuccino Beatniks
Prince Edward Island, Canada
The Cappuccino Beatniks and their ilk once had to themselves the creativity that goes with powerful caffeine-creation equipment, but according to coffee-espresso-maker-tips.com, cappuccino machines have invaded all strata of society. "No longer just a diversion or a taste treat for yuppies and beatniks, cappuccino has become a mainstream staple...."

Beatnik Turtle
Chicago, Illinois, USA
Horn-fueled original rock band Beatnik Turtle claims that they took their name because "it was the last domain name available." They further note that their name should never be pluralized: "Beatnik Turtles ain't a band, people! I mean, talk about a stupid name!" According to their mandate, Beatnik Turtle Inc. is the world's leading supplier of Beatnik Turtle products, information and services.

The 1999 CD *Danger Bongo Crossing* from New York's **Bossa Nova Beatniks**. The Beatniks were the Flyboys until a 1991 practice session at which their bassist stepped up to the microphone and quipped, "And now for the bossa nova beatnik sound of Tom Gould [lead singer]." Gould took the cover photo in Kenya. A bongo is a chestnut-coated, spiral-horned antelope.

Beatnik Flies
Silver Spring, Maryland, USA
Doing the benefits and fighting the power at farms, beaches, clubs and coffeehouses for three decades. No flies on these guys.

Beatnik Filmstars   Bristol, UK
Much cheekier than most of the other beatniks. And more prolific. From 2007: *Cat Scan Aces*, *Left Hooks (Songs That Got Nowhere)*, *Shenaniganism (Tape Hiss & Other Imperfections)*, and a six-CD box set of older material.

Rodeo Beatniks
Pennsylvania, USA
Not sure about the rodeo part, but they have the coffeehouse thing going and perform something they call "funkry & western, blues grassy, edgy-folk rock."

Dreamtime Beatniks
Kingsbridge, UK
A group of musicians and producers working with David Michael Aslow to create "intelligent techno and tribal house music." The term "dreamtime" is said to have been coined by anthropologists Spencer and Gillen in 1899 to refer to the creation beliefs of Australia's indigenous peoples. "The Dreaming" is now the preferred term, denoting a time before time when all things were created. It also involves the concept of the past, present and future all existing simultaneously, but you may need a couple of double espressos and a magic biscotti to wrap your head around it.

Superbeatnik
Montpellier, France
Angry Superbeatnik with new CD, *No Hand Hold*.

Beatnik Termites
Cleveland and Baltimore, USA
Formed in 1987 with Pat "Termite" Kim on lead guitar, the band's sound features "doo-wop vocals, buzzsaw guitars and surf-punk drumbeats." The late Kurt Cobain is said to have cited the Beatnik Termites as one of his favorite bands.

BeatnikBrown
Philadelphia, Pennsylvania, USA
Formed in 2003, this jam-band quartet's primary focus is improvising funky live music, performing both original songs and "uniquely interpreted covers." Through spring and summer, they appear at each month's First Friday celebration, in front of the Well-Fed Artist Gallery in the city's art district.

Get Cape. Wear Cape. Fly.

Get Cape. Wear Cape. Fly is the stage name of Essex, UK, artist Sam Duckworth (aka Slam Dunkworth) and his band. Duckworth admits to being heavily influenced by Billy Bragg (also from Essex) and has covered Bragg's song "A New England." Bragg appears on the song "Interlude" on Duckworth's 2008 album, *Searching for the Hows and Whys*. Previous album: *The Chronicles of a Bohemian Teenager* (2006).

"The name Get Cape. Wear Cape. Fly, isn't meant to suggest superhuman powers. "I didn't want to use my own name and wanted something different," explains Sam. "It was actually a headline in a computer gaming magazine I found the night before my first solo performance. I've used it ever since."

Get Cape. Wear Cape. Fly has toured with the Flaming Lips, the Magic Numbers, OK Go, Funeral for a Friend, the Kooks and others.

Heroes and Superheroes

Gym Class Heroes
Geneva, New York, USA
MC Travis "Schleprok" McCoy and drummer Matt McGinley became friends during Grade 9 gym class. McGinley: "Travis was playing drums in a band and I was in another band. We played at a friend's party together. During one of our songs Travis came up and started rapping over it, and we thought it sounded really cool. We've been Gym Class Heroes ever since."

Action Heroes   Devon, UK
Previously Harry & the Hormones, they claim to have considered the names Buff Orpington's Burger Volcano and Super Models. Members went on to form Babyhead, the Rumble Strips and Zen Hussies.

Schoolyard Heroes
Olympia, Washington, USA
Songs: "Plastic Surgery Hall of Fame," "Dude, Where's My Skin?" A parental advisory regarding the band's material led bassist Jonah Bergman to remark in *Spin*: "We love everyone…it's not about worshipping the devil. It's a Halloween dance every night."

Fuzzy Nerds   Athens, Greece
Fuzzy Nerds are either a type of candy or a Greek indie trio.

N*E*R*D
Virginia Beach, Virginia, USA
Created by Pharrell Williams and Chad Hugo, with vocalist Shae Haley of the Neptunes, when they decided to use Spymob as their backup band to recreate their sound live in 2001. N*E*R*D stands for No-one Ever Really Dies.

Eugenius
Glasgow, Scotland
Started as Captain America in 1990 but changed name due to threat of legal action by Marvel Comics. Eugenius is a pun on lead singer Eugene Kelly's name.

Brainiac
Dayton, Ohio, USA
Brainiac is one of Superman's arch-enemies. Founders Tim Taylor (guitar, keyboards, vocals) and Juan Monasterio (bass) met playing cello in 5th grade and eventually played their first show as We'll Eat Anything.

Miracle Wimp
Waipahu, Hawaii, USA
The title of a book by Erik P. Kraft that follows Tom Mayo (aka Miracle Wimp) as he "navigates his way through wood shop, dating, driving…."

Backseat Superstars
Atlanta, Georgia, USA
Retro '80s hair band. Song: "White Trash Gutter Girl."

Super Sonic Soul Pimps
Seattle, Washington, USA
"Alien mother, pimp for a dad…3 hybrid children…the Super Sonic Soul Pimps…." Who shave their heads and wear shiny gold jumpsuits.

The Super Friendz
Halifax, Nova Scotia, Canada
Formerly known as Rhinoplasty. *Superfriends* was a Hanna-Barbera TV cartoon show about the DC Comics heroes. It aired from 1973 to 1986 in the US.

Atlanta, Georgia's **Nerd Parade** are Randy Garcia, Abby Wren, Rich Wilson, Chris Sheldon and John Jacobus. The name is the title of one of Wilson's solo albums. "Abby, John and I were sitting in the studio…One of them suggested we use *The Nerd Parade* as the band's name in honor of my solo record and what it stood for." On their appearance: "We dress up in various ways — maybe a dorky sweater, blazer or hat. Abby wears schoolgirl or nurse-like dresses because they are fun, easy and sexy…I would hate to have a totally uniform look in this band because we are not totally uniform people."

Supersuckers
Seattle, Washington, USA
Upon forming in Tucson, Arizona, "we were initially a five-piece called the Black Supersuckers — a name found in some quality adult literature we had laying around in our impeccably clean band house!" The band has backed Steve Earle and Willie Nelson.

Supertramp
Los Angeles, California, USA
The band was called Daddy for a few months in late 1969, then changed to Supertramp, a name taken from Welsh poet William Henry Davies' 1908 book, *The Autobiography of a Super-Tramp*.

Turbonegro
Oslo, Norway
They chose between two names: Nazipenis and Turbonegro. Founding member Thomas Seltzer: "A turbonegro is a large, well-equipped, armed black male in a fast car, out for vengeance. We are his prophets." Lead guitarist Euroboy: "It's actually two Latin words. It means fast and black, and we thought that was a cool name for a band, because our music is very fast and very dark."

Avengers
San Francisco, California, USA
Formed in 1977 and fronted by Penelope Houston. Their first album was produced by Sex Pistols' guitarist Steve Jones.

Psychedelic Avengers
Hanover, Germany
A collaborative project with over 40 artists in various countries.

Purple Avengers
Brisbane, Australia
The title of an episode of Hanna-Barbera's *The Great Grape Ape* cartoon, featuring the 40-foot-tall purple gorilla Grape Ape.

Psyclone Rangers
Allentown, Pennsylvania, USA
Psyc + Lone + Rangers. Led by vocalist Jonathan Valania and guitarist Scott Dantzer. Valania is now a music columnist with the alternative magazine *Magnet*.

The Hollow Men
Leeds, UK
Named after a T.S. Eliot poem published in 1925. Members went on to play in Spacehog, Fever Hut, Black Star Liner and the Buzz Aldrins

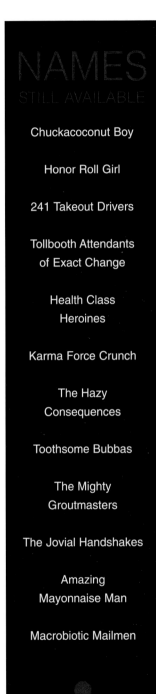

NAMES STILL AVAILABLE

Chuckacoconut Boy

Honor Roll Girl

241 Takeout Drivers

Tollbooth Attendants of Exact Change

Health Class Heroines

Karma Force Crunch

The Hazy Consequences

Toothsome Bubbas

The Mighty Groutmasters

The Jovial Handshakes

Amazing Mayonnaise Man

Macrobiotic Mailmen

161

The Exploding Boy
Stockholm, Sweden

The song "Exploding Boy" appears on the Cure's rarities and B-sides album *Join the Dots*. Johan Sjöblom (Prune, Fake Moss) and Les Andersson (Kodji, Run Level Zero) started their Exploding Boy in January 2006.

Echoboy Nottingham, UK
Formed by Richard Warren as a trio in 1998 after the demise of his former band, the Hybrids, Echoboy is now a two-drummer, seven-man extravaganza.

Electro Hippies
St. Helens/Wigan, UK

Late '80s lo-fi punk songs about vegetarianism and animal rights. Vocalist-guitarist Jeff Walker quit the band to join Carcass.

Artis the Spoonman
Seattle, Washington, USA

A percussive spoon player, street performer, who apparently can play two flutes simultaneous with his nose. The song "Spoonman," about Artis's unique talents, was Soundgarden's first major hit.

Batman Parade
Cupertino, California, USA

From an interview on Soundpick.net: "Well, someone made up this thing...you take the name of your very first pet and add it to the first street you ever lived on [and] that is your stripper name...So when we asked Davin what his stripper name would be, he told us that his very first pet was a hamster...that he named Batman Parade."

the exceptional gentlemen

state of grace

The Exceptional Gentlemen
Other considered names for this Waterloo, Ontario, Canada, band included Me & My Sweater Vest and the Cups. Bassist Steve Breen lost his patience when a strong lobby developed for "the Marvin Gaze." After one particularly wild gig, the band saw an inebriated female fan safely home, her honor intact, thus earning them the compliment "exceptional gentlemen."

Frozen Ghost
Toronto, Ontario, Canada

The title of a 1945 horror movie about a plastic surgeon and a wax museum.

Velocity Girl
College Park, Maryland, USA

The band took its name from a 1986 Primal Scream single B-side. They recorded three full-length albums on the Sub Pop label: *Simpatico!*, *Copacetic* and *Gilded Stars and Zealous Hearts*. The band had an atypically clean sound for a '90s band. Spin-offs: Starry Eyes, Air Miami and Julie Ocean.

Kleenex Girl Wonder
Downers Grove, Illinois, USA

Solo project of multi-instrumentalist Graham Smith. Album: *Graham Smith is the Coolest Person Alive.*

Mudgirl
Vancouver, British Columbia, Canada

Singer Kim Bingham's project after the breakup of Me, Mom & Morgentaler. Backed by members of Rhymes with Orange. "Mudgirl" is the title of a short story that Bingham wrote about "a waif made of mud."

Girl Scout Hand Grenade
Flint, Michigan, USA

Female-fronted industrial death-metal formed in 2002. Conversely involved in fundraising for their local food bank.

Violent Femmes
Milwaukee, Wisconsin, USA

Earlier incarnations included Ruthless Acoustics, Trance & Dance Band and Rhomboid. The VF formed in 1980, named for — well, the lies run deep. May have been named for a fictitious band that bassist Brian Ritchie claimed his brother played in. The pickup horn section for live gigs is known as the Horns of Dilemma.

Chemical Brothers
Manchester, UK

The duo of Ed Simons and Tom Rowlands began as DJs, calling themselves the 237 Turbo Nutters (their house number and a reference to their Blackburn raving days). Eventually chose the Chemical Brothers, after their own song "Chemical Beats."

Mighty Mighty Bosstones
Boston, Massachusetts, USA

Formed in 1985, the Bosstones' name is a pun on Boston. Discovering that there was already a 1950s a-cappella group by that name, they became the Mighty Mighty Bosstones, the suggestion of a bartender friend.

Enough About Me, Let's Talk About My Hair

On the Outs
with the In Crowd

Dyed & Coiffed Up

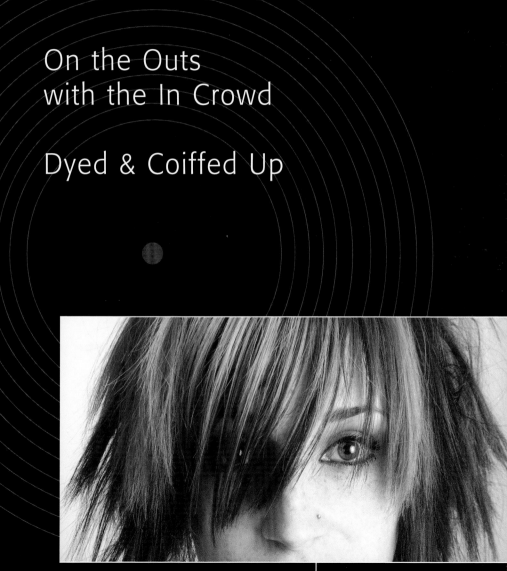

Enough About Me, Let's Talk About My Hair

On the Outs with the In Crowd

Public Image Ltd.

In 1978, following the breakup of the Sex Pistols, Johnny Rotten reverted to his real name, John Lydon, and created Public Image Limited (PiL) with dub bassist Jah Wobble, guitarist Keith Levene (the Clash) and temporary drummer Jim Walker. The music they created was anti-pop experimental dub dance fusion. The popular press declared it self-indulgent, but the band's first album rose to #22 in the UK, and *New Musical Express* called PiL "arguably the first post-rock group."

The name Public Image Ltd. was inspired by Muriel Spark's 1968 novel. Lyndon had been reading the works of the Scottish novelist while on holiday in Italy. "I checked out some of her other books when I got home. One of them was called *The Public Image*. It was all about this actress who was unbearably egotistical. I thought, 'Ha! The Public Image. Limited.' Not as a company, but to be limited — not being as 'out there' as I was with the Sex Pistols."

Elvis Costello & the Attractions
London, UK

Prior to his band with the Attractions, Costello (Declan Patrick MacManus) had played in Clover and Flip City. The name Attractions was chosen as an ironic comment on the band's motley appearance. The Attractions released an album without Costello in 1980, entitled *Mad About the Wrong Boy* and consisting of tracks written primarily by keyboardist Steve Nieve.

Pretty Things London, UK

Formed by guitarist Dick Taylor and singer Phil May in 1963, their name taken from Bo Diddley's song "Pretty Thing." Taylor was in Little Boy Blue & the Blue Boys, which became the Rolling Stones, but quit to form his own band.

Dirty Pretty Things
London, UK

Stephen Frears 2002 film *Dirty Pretty Things* chronicles the story of London immigrants pressured to sell their organs for money. The band was formed in 2005 by Carl Barât and other former members of the Libertines. There were already two bands using the name Dirty Pretty Things, one in Salisbury and one in Australia, but those bands agreed to change their names.

Drop Dead, Gorgeous
Denver, Colorado, USA

A punctuation pun on the expression "drop-dead gorgeous." Albums: *In Vogue* (2006) and *Worse Than a Fairy Tale* (2007). Recently signed to Geffen.

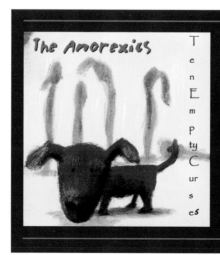

The Anorexics

T e n   E m p t y   C u r s e s

"Very little is known about the **Anorexics** apart from they originate from Coventry, England. They have done very few live shows and almost no interviews. All that can be said is that their lineup is constantly under review and they mostly consist of one man, Neil J. Taylor, who writes and records in the lazarette (the part of a boat where they used to stash the lepers) of an ancient Scottish trawler as it drifts around the Mediterranean Sea."

Atlanta, Georgia's **Ultrababyfat** was formed in 1993 by childhood friends Shonali Bhowmik and Michelle Dubois. They started out as Babyfat, but changed their name to Ultrababyfat in 1998 with the addition of new members — and because of a bar band with the name Babyfat. There 2006 album is *No Ringo No*.

Drunk Dead Gorgeous
Keewanee, Illinois, USA
Another pun on "drop-dead gorgeous." Songs: "Comfortably Miserable," "Nostalgiaholic," "This Moment and Death."

The Lovelies
Milwaukee, Wisconsin, USA
Formed in 1996 and fronted by Liv Lovely (Liv Mueller).

Pretty the Quick Black Eyes
Austin, Texas, USA
Evolved out of the 1990s emo band Mineral. Fueled by "black-and-tans and a lethal dose of pessimism"

Beauty's Confusion
Philadelphia, Pennsylvania, USA
Songs have been featured on *Oprah* and in the Sega game *Full Auto*, "the world's most destructive racing game"

Beautiful Disaster
Reistertown, Maryland, USA
Female-fronted pop-punk since 2005. Songs: "Fragile Fool" and "Stupid Me."

Anorexic Beauty Queen
Syracuse, New York, USA
Song: "You've Got a Cute Little Skull."

Skinny
Cleveland, Ohio, USA
Formerly called 2 Skinny Dorks. Also the name of a London, UK, trip-hop band whose most successful song was "Failure."

Naked Skinnies
Columbus, Ohio, USA
Fronted by singer-guitarist Mark Eitzel before Eitzel formed American Music Club.

Thin Lizzy
Dublin, Ireland
Formed in 1969 and named for the Dandy comic-book robot Tin Lizzie, whose name was in turn inspired by a nickname for Ford's Model T car. The name became Thin Lizzy early on when a show promoter mistook the word Tin for Thin because of band member's Irish accents. Famous for their dual lead-guitar sound and the classic rock tune "The Boys Are Back in Town."

Bimbo Toolshed
San Francisco, California, USA
Female-fronted sleaze-punk rock led by singer Swoopo Bravo. Album: *Sex! Violence! Trash!* Sounds like: "You just got slapped in the face and had an orgasm at the exact same instant...."

NAMES
STILL AVAILABLE

The Slimmerthans

Jawdrop Knockouts

Beauty School Janitors

The Spa Tans

Fat Camp Losers

The Magic Bust

Slick Grace

The Perennial Chat-Ups

Cheekbone High

Clique Freqs

Cosmo Nots

The Thick

Cute Is What We Aim For
Buffalo, New York, USA

Started in their teens as a side-project for Cherry Bing singer Shaant Hacikyan. According to former bassist Fred Cimato, he and Hacikyan were talking about their then-nonexistent band, and Hacikyan said, "I need a band name. It's gotta be cute [one of his favorite words], we're aiming for cute here." So cute is what they aimed for.

Bad Flirt
Montreal, Quebec, Canada

Singer-songwriter Jasmine White-Gluz started the band in 2002 as a solo project and "as an ode to her fantastically bad techniques at talking to boys." The band expanded in 2005 and is now a six-piece.

Demimonde Slumber Party
Eugene, Oregon, USA

Frontwoman Melissa Lubofsky is also vocal about being vegan. Debut album: *Green*.

Jet Set Willy
Cambridgeshire, Midlands, UK

The name of a game for the ZX Spectrum home computer, released in 1984. The object of the game is to get the exhausted miner Willy to tidy up his house after a huge party.

The Clique   Houston, Texas, USA
Late '60s sunshine pop from a studio band based around producer-songwriter Gary Zekley. Most famous for their song "Superman," covered by R.E.M. on their *Life's Rich Pageant*. Zekley went on to form Yellow Balloon.

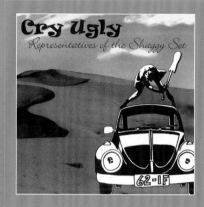

The Amsterdam trio **Cry Ugly** was formed in 1996 by Andrew Vroomans. The band won the Buytenpopfestival in Zoetermeer in 1997, earning studio time to work on their debut album, *Book of Dreams*. Their second album, *Representatives of the Shaggy Set*, was released in 2005.

Big Ugly
Stratford, Connecticut, USA

Ugly is in the eye of the beholder, but lead singer-bassist Dominick Mauro is a huge dude.

Broken Social Scene
Toronto, Ontario, Canada

Began in 1999 as K.C. Accidental, formed by Brendan Canning and Kevin Drew as an ambient project, pulling in friends from other Toronto bands. Now has 19 members. The name of the band reflects its amorphous structure. Members also play in Do Make Say Think, Metric, Stars, the Weakerthans, Valley of the Giants, the FemBots, Junior Blue, the Dears, the American Analog Set, and other bands.

All Sexy But Ginger
Northallerton/Bedale, UK

A Spice Girls reference? Formed in 2003, the band won of a battle of the bands at the Richmond Live Festival in 2006, for which they received the David Reed Trophy, named for the director of the Swaledale Cheese Company.

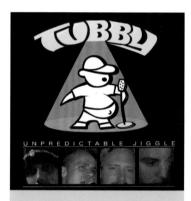

San Diego's **Tubby** has toured with Fishbone and Blue Öyster Cult. They were a *High Times* "Featured Unsigned Band" and took first place at the Worldfolk National Battle of the Bands in Las Vegas in 2006. Neil MacPherson, keyboards: "I was asked to put together a band for the Sandbar, so I called a bunch of people I'd always wanted to play with. We met the night of the gig, and I realized we hadn't bothered to come up with a name. The Sandbar had an even smaller stage back then, so I was practically sitting on this big plastic storage tub. Hence, Tubby was born...we still can't agree on a better name."

SUPAPHAT hails from Sacramento, California, and evolved from the bands Mama's Gravy and Nothing. They derive their name from a cartoon character created by the band for their album covers and promotional materials, a heavyset retro-70s funkster with an orange afro and sideburns: Supaphat (pronounced soup-a-fat). Albums: *Lose Myself* (2007) and *Ride with Me* (2005).

The Tragically Hip
Kingston, Ontario, Canada
The name comes from the title of a comedy sketch in ex-Monkee Michael Nesmith's hour-long video Elephant Parts. Nesmith in turn borrowed the phrase from the song "He's So Cool" by American singer-songwriter Carolyne Mas. The Hip have won 9 Juno Awards and were inducted into the Canadian Music Hall of Fame in 2005.

Girl Talk
Pittsburgh, Pennsylvania, USA
Though the name origin may seem straightforward, it's the stage name of [male] musician Gregg Gillis, who says, "It's actually a reference to some obscure line in a Jim Morrison poetry book. I don't even know which one anymore...It kind of sprung up amongst friends as a joke"

Boring Normals
Midlothian, Virginia, USA
Started as a solo project by Rob Williams in the late '90s after the breakup of Joe Buck, which reformed as Joe Buck, Jr. in 2007.

Charm Farm Detroit, Michigan, USA
Formed in the '90s by singer-songwriter Dennis White (aka Static Revenger), who was part of Inner City, a techno-dance outfit in the late '80s. Charm Farm is best known for their remix of "Superstar." White went on to work with Madonna and has had several successful dance songs as a solo artist

SECRET AGING MEN
gather under cover of night in the town of Alpharetta, Georgia, near Atlanta, "cooking up their own soul-satisfying bouillabaisse of various traditional and progressive instrumental sounds." Band members are Rick Meyer (electric, acoustic, synth guitars), Ed McAdory (keyboards), Sam Hall (bass) and Sal Caltabiano (drums, percussion). Their most recent album is *Night Mowing*.

Inner Beauty Contest
Long Beach, California, USA
EP: *The Better to See Them With*. Songs: "Starting Quarrels, Breaching Dams," "Snuffing Out the Candle Before It's Lit."

Weigh Down
New Haven, Connecticut, USA
Formed in 1998 from the remains of Seagrave and Leaves of Lothlorien, they began as *the* Weigh Down but became just Weigh Down around 2002.

Poor Get Fat
Barrie, Ontario, Canada
Debut album: *Underfed*.

Above Average Weight Band
Sotham, Warwickshire, and Otley, West Yorkshire, UK
Both play classic rock and are available for weddings. The name is a pun on Average White Band.

Split Enz

Friends Tim Finn and Mike Chunn met art students Phil Judd, Noel Crombie and Rob Gillies at Auckland University in 1971. Finn and Judd developed a songwriting partnership and formed a band called the Split Ends – later revising their name to Split Enz, slyly slipping in a patriotic NZ for New Zealand.

The band saw numerous musicians come and go, notably the permanent addition of Eddie Raynor on keyboards. And Crombie's main role was as the designer of costumes, stage sets, posters and album covers, and later director of videos. Foregoing the pub circuit, Phil and Tim decided they would play only theatres and concert halls, for proper theatrical presentation of their work. The approach was unusual to '70s rock crowds, and the sensitive Judd took any negative criticism to heart.

In 1977 Tim Finn's younger brother Neil replaced Judd, and Split Enz began the second phase of its evolution, with chart hits and top industry awards, including, in 2005, induction into the Australian Recording Industry Association Hall of Fame. The brothers Finn also received the Order of the British Empire for their musical contributions in Split Enz, Crowded House and as solo artists.

Dyed and Coiffed Up

Beauty School Dropouts
Nashville, Tennessee, USA

"We were actually looking at a font website and came across a font called Beauty School Dropout and thought it would be a great band name." The font was designed by Nick Curtis in 1997.

Scissors for Lefty
San Francisco, California, USA

Band member Bryan Garza is left-handed. The name was suggested by a friend. Also considered: Unsad.

4 Non Blondes
San Francisco, California, USA

Rumored to have chosen the name after a perfect blonde family who gave them dirty looks in a public park.

Blonde Redhead
New York City, New York, USA

Their name is the title of a song by DNA. The trio of eerie-voiced Kazu Makino and twin brothers Simone and Amadeo Pace perform lyrics in English, Japanese, French and Italian.

Blondie
New York City, New York, USA

Formed by guitarist Chris Stein and vocalist Deborah Harry in 1976, both former members of the Stillettos. The name is said to have come from a motorist calling out to Harry. Inducted into the Rock and Roll Hall of Fame in 2006. In summer 2008 Blondie traveled the US and Europe with their Parallel Lines 30th Anniversary Tour, and Capitol/EMI released an expanded anniversary edition CD of that classic album.

The Long Blondes
Sheffield, UK

"Before we had a name, we actually had a song called 'Long Blondes.' It was about groupie girls with long blonde hair that go around trying to steal everyone's boyfriends. Though they are not blonde, it has been said that they formed the band first, then learned to play instruments.

Platinum Blonde
Toronto, Ontario, Canada

The band was conceived by British émigré Mark Holmes, who worked as an apprentice hairstylist. Their first three records all went multiple platinum in Canada. The band chose their name as a knowing nod to the Hollywood glamour machine. Jean Harlow plays the lead role in the 1931 Frank Capra film *Platinum Blonde*.

Atomic Blonde
Nashville, Tennessee, USA

This all-female hard-rock quartet started as the fragile-sounding Glass Lily. In renaming themselves, they wanted to combine the word Atomic with another word. The Blonde refers to the hair of their singer, Dacia. Their song "Babydoll" is featured in the video game *Air Guitar Rock Star*.

Concrete Blonde
Los Angeles, California, USA

Began as Dream 6, a band formed in 1982 by singer-bassist Johnette Napolitano and guitarist James Mankey. Label-mate Michael Stipe (R.E.M.) suggested the name Concrete Blonde.

Jonathan Bree and Heather Mansfield formed **the Brunettes** in Auckland after leaving their previous bands, Yoko and the Nudie Suits. The Brunettes use unusual instrumentation, such as glockenspiel, banjo and Optigan (optical organ), and tour as both a quintet and a ten-piece "orchestrette." Albums: *Holding Hands, Feeding Ducks* (2002), *Mars Loves Venus* (2004) and *Structure & Cosmetics* (2007).

Blonde on Blonde
Newport, South Wales, UK
Named themselves after the 1966 Bob Dylan album. They played the Isle of Wight Festival in 1969.

The Wig Titans
Los Angeles, California, USA
Roots-rock with three songwriters who share lead vocals. Bassist-vocalist Mary Fleener is also a graphic novelist.

Secret Beauty Cream
Pasadena, California, USA
Also known as Bob Owen & Double Secret Beauty Cream.

Lee Press-On & the Nails
San Francisco, California, USA
Big-band swing led by bandleader Lee Presson, who also played keyboards in the Oingo Boingo tribute band Dead Man's Party.

Lipps, Inc.
Minneapolis, Minnesota, USA
Lipps Inc, lip synch. Studio recording by Steven Greenberg with vocals by 1976 Miss Black Minnesota, Cynthia Johnson. Had a big disco hit with "Funkytown."

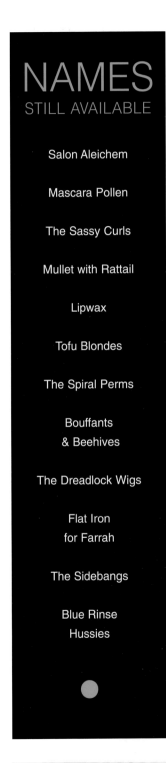

NAMES
STILL AVAILABLE

Salon Aleichem

Mascara Pollen

The Sassy Curls

Mullet with Rattail

Lipwax

Tofu Blondes

The Spiral Perms

Bouffants
& Beehives

The Dreadlock Wigs

Flat Iron
for Farrah

The Sidebangs

Blue Rinse
Hussies

Big Fuzz is a side-project for Deep Banana Blackout guitarist Fuzz. The band's 2004 album is entitled *Exercising the Demons*. Fuzz also plays in Caravan of Thieves, Tom Tom Club (side-project of Talking Heads) and Rolla (with wife, singer Carrie Ernst). He's joined on this sweaty funk-rock project by bandmates Rob Somerville (sax), Rob Volo (trombone), Benj LeFevre (bass), Andy Sanesi (drums) and Barry Seelen (keys).

"exercising the demons"

Matching Mole Canterbury, UK
Robert Wyatt formed the band in October 1971 after he left Soft Machine. Wyatt: "Matching Mole was a pun on the French title of William Burroughs' novel *The Soft Machine — La Machine Molle*." Wyatt was in the process of assembling a new lineup for the band in 1973 when he fell from a window and became paralyzed. He continued to make music and later collaborated with Henry Cow.

Looking Glass
New Brunswick, New Jersey, USA
Had a #1 US hit in 1972 with "Brandy (You're a Fine Girl)," later covered by the Red Hot Chili Peppers.

Lipstick Conspiracy
San Francisco, California, USA
Transgender power-pop whose first performance was at a 2003 benefit for the San Francisco Sex Workers Film Festival.

Haircut 100 Beckenham, Kent, UK
Singer Nick Heyward went solo in 1983. Drummer Blair Cunningham joined the Pretenders and also played with Paul McCartney. The band was reunited in 2004 for the VH1 television series *Bands Reunited*.

Haircuts That Kill
Los Angeles, California, USA
Short-lived 1984 band. Singer Chuck Mosley joined Faith No More. Recordings existed only on cassettes.

The Combovers
Brisbane, Australia
A collaboration between Luke Reichelt and Michael Simms. Album: *Pasta of Muppets.*

The Crew-Cuts
Toronto, Ontario, Canada
They sang from 1952–1964. Deejay Bill Randle in Cleveland, Ohio, coined their name after seeing their similar haircuts.

50-Cent Haircut
Los Angeles, California, USA
The band was practicing at a garage in a rough neighborhood when the barbershop around the corner began advertising "50 cent haircuts." Singer Jay Souza: "A song has to be able to stand on its own with a single voice and a single instrument, and if it can't do that, then it's not really a great song. The song is 'the thing' first and foremost — and then we rock it. We thought the name 50 Cent Haircut suited that ideal."

The Beards
Adelaide, Australia
Tagline: "Bearded music for bearded people." Songs: "Beard Revolution," "It Only Takes a Fortnight to Grow a Decent Beard," "A Wizard Needs a Beard" and "Big Bearded Bruce."

The Flaming Sideburns
Helsinki, Finland
Finpop.net interview with drummer Jay Burnside: "At first we were planning to call ourselves Los Cyclones, but then our guitar player at the time, Vilunki 3000, came up with this logo for us. It's a photo of Elvis with his sideburns flaming. We had to name ourselves in order to fit the name with our logo!"

The Men They Couldn't Shave
Nordby, Norway
Tagline: "Nordicana — Norwegian roots band playing warm country rock while trying not to freeze to death in the cold north." Presumably from "the men they couldn't *save*."

All the Fashion

Our Biggest Sale of the Season

Accessorize! Accessorize!

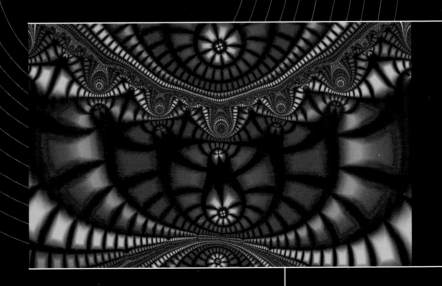

All the Fashion

Style Council

Style Council was formed in London in 1983 by singer-guitarist Paul Weller (the Jam) and keyboardist Mick Talbot (Merton Parkas). Weller sought a change of direction from his previous mod-revivalist power trio. A change of style.

His determination to explore funk, soul, R&B, even rap, disappointed Jam fans, especially because he had departed at the height of that band's popularity. The line "kick out the Style, bring back the Jam" in the Tears for Fears song "Sowing the Seeds of Love" is a direct reference to Weller's perceived betrayal.

Mick Talbot's synthesizers and clavinets distanced Weller from the stripped-down sound of his former band. Style Council also turned their collective attention to social commentary and political activism. Their debut gig was at 1983's May Day Show for Jobs and Peace in Liverpool. They played Band Aid, Live Aid and benefits for striking miners. They were vocally anti-Thatcher.

The band had its biggest successes with "My Ever Changing Moods," "Walls Come Tumbling Down" and "Speak Like a Child."

It was Paul Weller in his Curtis Mayfield period.

Our Biggest Sale of the Season

Depeche Mode
Basildon, Essex, UK
Formed in 1980 by former members of the French Look, Norman & the Worms, Composition of Sound and No Romance in China. Named Depeche Mode after a French fashion magazine, with *dépêche* literally meaning update or dispatch. The band liked the idea of "fast fashion." Founding member Vince Clarke went on to form Yazoo and Erasure.

Images in Vogue Vancouver, British Columbia, Canada
An early incarnation included Kevin Crompton, who left to form Skinny Puppy. The band considered changing their name to the Spell but discovered an Australian band using the name, so named their second album *The Spell* instead. Spin-offs include 69 Duster, Naked in the Garden and National Velvet.

Elegant Simplicity
Manchester, UK
Tagline: "Mellotron and guitar-driven songs of misery, juxtaposed with uplifting melodiousness."

Fashiøn
Birmingham, UK
Formed in 1978. Three albums: *Product Perfect*, *Fabrique* (reissued as *The Height of Fashion*) and *Twilight of Idols*.

Fashion Victims
Scottsdale, Arizona, USA
Formed by Cary Miller in New Jersey in 1998, but relocated to Arizona to work with recording engineer Shelly Yakus (John Lennon, U2, Tom Petty, Dire Straits).

Rockville, Maryland's **Dog Fashion Disco** play eclectic hardcore and metal with satirical lyrics reminiscent off Zappa or Mr. Bungle. Guitarist Greg Combs' cousin is given credit for having conjured the three words during a name-storming session. Their most recent album is 2006's *Adultery*. Other albums: *The Embryo's in Bloom*, *The Anarchists of Good Taste*, *May of the Dead*. Spin-offs include Polkadot Cadaver, Phantom Communique, the Alter Boys and Ideamen.

Menswear London, UK
Mid-90s Britpop, with the name sometimes written Menswe@r. Best known for the 1996 single "Being Brave." Guitarist Chris Gentry went on to form Vatican DC.

House of Large Sizes
Cedar Falls, Iowa, USA
Formed in 1987 by married couple Dave Deibler and Barb Schlif and named after a chain of clothing stores for plus sizes in the US Midwest. Live album: *Idiots Out Wandering Around* (I.O.W.A). Barb and Dave currently own and operate Mohair Pear, a vintage clothing store in Cedar Falls.

**The House
That Gloria Vanderbilt**
Algonquin, Illinois, USA
They made *The Onion*'s 2006 Worst Band Names list. Gloria Vanderbilt notoriously developed one of the first lines of designer blue jeans. She also inherited scads of money, acted, painted, wrote, married at least four times and gave birth to CNN anchor Anderson Cooper.

The Beau Brummels
San Francisco, California, USA
Named after the early 19th-century dandy Beau (George Bryan) Brummell. (Brummell claimed that it took him five hours to dress.) The name was also chosen, in part, to be close to the Beatles in LP racks, The Beau Brummels wore British-style "mod" clothes.

Supermodel Stalker
Brooklyn, New York, USA
Boom Box Repair Kit released their debut album, *The Glory Of*, in 2002 under the band name Supermodel Stalker.

Models Melbourne, Australia
A merger between members of Teenage Radio Stars and JAB in 1978. Debut album: *Alphabravocharliedeltaechofoxtrotgol*. Toured with the Ramones, the B52's, the Vapours and XTC.

New Model Army Bradford, UK
Named after the new army established by Oliver Cromwell after the English Civil War. Guitarist-songwriter Justin Sullivan: "The New Model Army was the army that won against the king. From that army came all the first ideas about democracy. It's actually a very important part of American history as well. But the name, for instance, in Ireland, means something completely different, because Cromwell later took the army to Ireland and committed all sorts of atrocities...We've never played Drogheda, the town that Cromwell razed. The interesting thing about revolutions is, they all follow the same pattern. There's always a revolution followed by a period of anarchy — with a huge ferment of ideas and idealism — followed by a military dictatorship."

Mannequin Men
Chicago, Illinois, USA
With *Fresh Rot* on Flameshovel Records.

Jack's Mannequin
Orange County, California, USA
Started as a side-project for Something Corporate pianist Andrew McMahon. He had considered the band name the Mannequins, but had gone off "the" names. He decided to combine the title of a song he had written, "Dear Jack," with Mannequins, arriving at Jack's Mannequin.

The five members of Denver-based **Mannequin Makeout** brought a crazy art-school approach to their music, with cheesy Casio keyboards, Theremin, circuit bent toys, eccentric arrangements and go-for-it vocals by Brittany Gould. The band dispersed in 2007. Members have gone on to form La Scala, Games for May, Action Packed Thrill Ride, Faceless Soiree and Married in Berdichev.

Wax Mannequin
Hamilton, Ontario, Canada
The stage name of singer-songwriter Chris Adeney. Wicker and wire mannequins were around in the 1700s. The late 1800s saw extensive use of hand-carved wax mannequins. The Parisian mannequin manufacturer Pierre Imans is said to have brought lifelike emotion to his figure's posture and facial features.

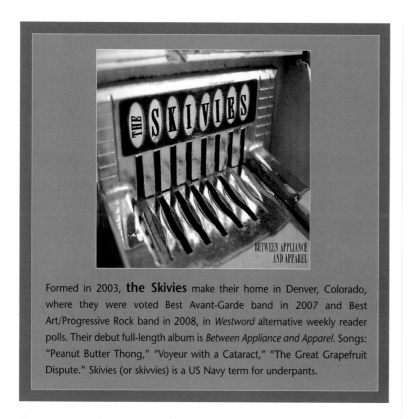

BETWEEN APPLIANCE AND APPAREL

Formed in 2003, **the Skivies** make their home in Denver, Colorado, where they were voted Best Avant-Garde band in 2007 and Best Art/Progressive Rock band in 2008, in *Westword* alternative weekly reader polls. Their debut full-length album is *Between Appliance and Apparel.* Songs: "Peanut Butter Thong," "Voyeur with a Cataract," "The Great Grapefruit Dispute." Skivies (or skivvies) is a US Navy term for underpants.

Die Mannequin
Toronto, Ontario, Canada
Singer-guitarist Care Failure's (Caroline Kawa) band after the demise of the Bloody Mannequins. Die Mannequin's two EPs, *How to Kill* and *Slaughter Daughter,* are compiled on the disc *Unicorn Steak.* Canadian director Bruce McDonald made a documentary about the band, *The Rawside of Die Mannequin,* which premiered in 2008.

The Five Satins
New Haven, Connecticut, USA
Male doo-wop group formed in 1954 and best remembered for their single "In the Still of the Night."

The Chiffons
New York City, New York, USA
The silky Chiffons had their first hit with the Gerry Goffin/Carole King-penned song "One Fine Day." Their single "I Have a Boyfriend" was interrupted on Dallas station KLIF to make the first radio announcement of the assassination of President John F. Kennedy on November 22, 1963.

The Orlons
Philadelphia, Pennsylvania, USA
Formed in 1960, this all-female vocal group backed Dee Dee Sharp on "Mashed Potato Time" and "Gravy (for My Mashed Potatoes)." They had their own Top 10 hits with "The Wah-Watusi," "Don't Hang Up" and "South Street." Orlon is a synthetic textile fiber trademarked by DuPont.

Velvet Crush
Providence, Rhode Island, USA
Crushed velvet, velvet crush. Formed in 1989 by singer-bassist Paul Chastain and drummer Ric Menck. Their 1994 album, *Teenage Symphonies to God*, is the *AllMusic Guide* pick of their seven albums.

The Velvet Underground
New York City, New York, USA
Considered by rock critics to be among the most influential bands of the late '60s. The band name was the title of a book that John Cale found upon moving into his NYC apartment. Michael Leigh's *The Velvet Underground,* published in 1963, looks at such "underground" practices as mate-swapping, group sex, homosexuality, sadmasochism, etc., in the new age of contraception.

The Velours
London, UK
Old-school, plush, velvet-like blues.

Suede   London, UK
Formed in 1989 and one of the most steadily successful British bands of the '90s, with four albums reaching #1, #3, #1 and #1 on the UK charts between 1993-1999. To create suede, the flesh side of leather is rubbed to create a velvety nap.

Big White Undies
Gainesville, Florida, USA
Acoustic folk-rock with three-part harmony. Jam Band of the Year in 1995.

The Panties
Orange County, California, USA
The elastic has gone out of this waistband. R.I.P., Panties.

Black Panties
Seattle, Washington, USA
Lots of elastic left in these panties. A power-tube-sizzling rock quartet that isn't afraid to let its early '70s influences show.

The Hypnotic Panties
Annapolis, Maryland, USA
Great name. Four women and a drummer guy having bluesy, swinging fun.

Modern Skirts are based in Athens, Georgia, and a regular act at that city's famous 40 Watt Club. Their name comes from a lyric in the Stephen Malkmus song "Old Jerry." Mike Mills of R.E.M. has called Modern Skirts his favorite Athens band, and summer 2008 saw them open for that band in Europe. The group prides itself in well-constructed songs and natural harmonies. Recent album: *Catalogue of Generous Men.*

Ultra Bra Helsinki, Finland
In 1994 Olli Virtaperko and several friends entered a political song contest with "Shoot the Commissioners, Those Crazy Dogs" and won. Despite their English name, their four albums are sung in Finnish.

Red Jumpsuit Apparatus
Jacksonville, Florida, USA
The name Red Jumpsuit Apparatus was chosen by placing words on a wall and having a blindfolded band member choose. Other names considered: Umbrella Ninjas and Evil Slamina ("Evil Slamina being Live Animals spelled backwards").

Plain White T's
Chicago, Illinois, USA
Together since 1997, "playing to packed houses craving for that perfect pop-punk punch."

Tubetop Mama
Lansdale, Pennsylvania, USA
A cover band with a merch table full of tubetops.

The Dirty Skirts
Cape Town, South Africa
Won the *Blunt* magazine Doc Martens Demo Competition. The single "Homewrecker" off their 2007 album, *On a Stellar Bender*, reached #1 in South Africa. Their second full-length album, *Daddy Don't Disco*, brought with it a UK tour in 2008.

Skort Vancouver, British Columbia, Canada
Tagline: "We are not a joke band." Bernice, Krista, Sarah Jane and Rob bring us "Knee Socks" and "Smell My Hippie Love."

NAMES
STILL AVAILABLE

Nine Inch Heels

Houndstooth Knickers

Ball Gown Letdown

The Gimme Guccis

Flirty Little Halters

Thwart the Skort

Luxe Tux Lint Pluckers

Vera Wang Chung Tonite

Peep-Toe Pumps

My Morning Peacoat

Grease Stained T's

The Fabulous Dry Cleaners

175

DR. PANTS

GARDENING IN A TORNADO

Oklahoma City's **Dr. Pants** is the brainchild of David Broyles, who call's his genre "quirk-rock." The band's debut was the double-CD *Feezle Day*, containing 38 tracks. Their latest album, *Gardening in a Tornado*, was released in 2006. It's "a mind-blowing, lo-fi mix of power pop, folk, hip-hop, electronica and instrumental rock."

The Swinging Blue Jeans
Liverpool, UK
Five Top 40 hits, including #2 in 1963 with "Hippy Hippy Shake" and #3 in 1964 with "You're No Good."

Bob B. Soxx & the Blue Jeans
New York City, New York, USA
Early '60s group produced by Phil Spector. Bob B. Soxx was Bobby Sheen.

Pantsuit
New York City, New York, USA
All-female trio formed in 2003. Album: *The Path From the House to the Lawn*.

Elastica London, UK
Formed in 1992 by guitarist Justine Frischmann (Suede) and drummer Justin Welch (Spitfire, Suede), with bassist Annie Holland and guitarist Donna Matthews (Darling Buds). The band's debut album entered the UK charts at #1. Elastica broke up in 2001 after releasing the single "The Bitch Don't Work."

Sta-Prest
San Francisco, California, USA
Levis Strauss & Co. first produced their Sta-Prest wrinkle-free trousers in 1964. Active in the 1990s San Francisco queercore movement, the band Sta-Prest released an EP, *Vespa Sex*, and three singles. Spin-off bands include Feelings on a Grid and Puce Moment.

Actionslacks
San Francisco, California, USA
Also from Levis Strauss & Co., Action Slacks were another type of easy-care trouser. The band Actionslacks formed in 1996 and have remained in near constant motion since. Recent album: *Full Upright Position*.

Caution: Pants!
Chicago, Illinois, USA
Self-explanation: "Caution: Pants! worships a 90 ft. tall praying mantis named Pestor, from the planet Zanitoblerone"…but apparently they recently had a falling out that Pestor couldn't fix, and they split up.

The Green Pajamas
Seattle, Washington, USA
Songs: "Kim the Waitress," "All Clues to Megan's Bed," "Strung Behind the Sun."

The Shirts
New York City, New York, USA
The band got its name in 1975 when a founding member, Robert Racioppo, having just broken up one band to form a new one, expressed no interest in the naming process: "Call it anything — shirts, pants, shoes. The Shirts!" They opened for bands such as Television and the Talking Heads at CBGB, and eventually headlined.

The Suits XL
Quebec City, Quebec, Canada
Previous name: Sunny Side Up. The Suits XL is an ironic name: "We're not in the major leagues, but we've already had our share of business problems with 'suits.'" Album: *Quarter-Life Crisis*.

The Cardigans
Jönköping, Sweden
It sounded better than the Sweaters. Formed in 1992. Six studio albums with solid sales, songs used for video games and film soundtracks, and they played themselves on the graduation episode of *Beverly Hills 90210*.

My Morning Jacket
Louisville, Kentucky, USA
While lead singer Jim James was visiting his old friends, his favorite bar from his student days burnt down. He found a discarded jacket among the charred remains. Inside the jacket were the stitched initials "MMJ." James decided they stood for "My Morning Jacket."

The Blue Raincoats
TORONTO, ONTARIO, CANADA

The new project for Keri Steele from Hush Hush. "Famous Blue Raincoat" is one of Leonard Cohen's most famous (and covered) songs, from his 1971 album, *Songs of Love and Hate.*

The Merton Parkas London, UK
Formed in the Merton area of South London, where the Mods wore parkas. The band featured the brothers Talbot. Mick Talbot (keyboards) went on to form Style Council with Paul Weller.

The Psychedelic Furs
London, UK
Began as RKO in 1977, then Radio, then booked gigs as both the Europeans and the Psychedelic Furs, gradually favoring the latter. Their 1981 album, *Talk Talk Talk*, yielded "Dumb Waiters" and "Pretty in Pink," which inspired John Hughes' 1986 film of the same name.

Handsome Furs
Montreal, Quebec, Canada
The married duo of Dan Boeckner (Wolf Parade) and writer Alexie Perry. Named for the tile of a story by Perry.

Accessorize! Accessorize!

Smart Brown Handbag
Los Angeles, California, USA
Critically acclaimed but nearly invisible. Self-description: "The band who is perhaps best known for its almost complete anonymity over the course of its 10 releases…." This dream-pop trio's impressive catalog extends from 1994's *Silverlake* to 2006's *Harry Larry*. The story goes that a male friend was being taunted for carrying a purse-like bag, and a female friend defended him by insisting that it wasn't a purse, it was a "smart brown handbag."

Shoes Zion, Illinois, USA
Formed in 1974 by brothers John and Jeff Murphy and still going. Started Black Vinyl Records and the recording studio Short Order Recorder.

Sneaker Pimps Hartlepool, UK
A dub-electronica band started in 1995. The name comes from an article in which the Beastie Boys talked about hiring a man to track down classic sneakers.

Bootsauce
Montreal, Quebec, Canada
A hard-edged funk-rock band formed in 1989. Their debut, *The Brown Album*, scored modest hits with "Play with Me" and the Hot Chocolate cover "Everyone's a Winner." Both *The Brown Album* and its follow-up, *Bull*, attained gold status in Canada. Their third album, *Sleeping Bootie*, didn't fare as well. The record company released their final, self-titled album and a greatest hits collection prior to the band's breakup in 1996.

Nu Shooz Portland, Oregon, USA
The '80s husband-and-wife dance duo of John Smith and Valerie Day had several chart hits, including a #3 Hot 100 single with "I Can't Wait." Nominated for Best New Artist Grammy in 1987. Still active as a duo and with the New Shooz Orchestra.

Cameo
New York City, New York, USA
They were started in 1974 by Black Ivory's Larry Blackmon as the 13-piece New York City Players, echoing the famous Ohio Players. Perhaps because of this similarity, they soon changed their name to Cameo. The band possessed a deep-funk, dance-groove sound combined with Blackmon's signature nasal vocal style. Their hit "Word Up!" is an '80s funk classic.

The Swingin' Medallions
Greenwood, South Carolina, USA
Started as Pieces of Eight (with 8 members) but became the Swingin' Medallions upon signing with Smash Records in 1965. The band performed beach music in the then-popular west coast style.

177

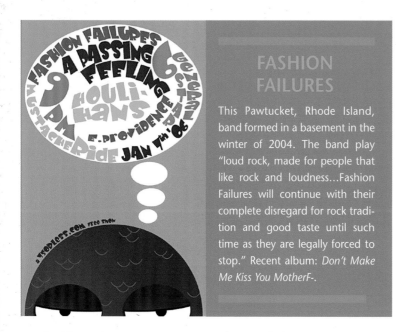

FASHION FAILURES

This Pawtucket, Rhode Island, band formed in a basement in the winter of 2004. The band play "loud rock, made for people that like rock and loudness...Fashion Failures will continue with their complete disregard for rock tradition and good taste until such time as they are legally forced to stop." Recent album: *Don't Make Me Kiss You MotherF-*.

Men Without Hats
Montreal, Quebec, Canada
Founded in 1980 by brothers Ivan and Stefan Doroschuk, the band played early bar gigs as Men With Hats, throwing their hats into the audience at the end of performances. This eventually led them to change their name to the less mundane Men Without Hats. The global success of the single "The Safety Dance" heralded a wave of hits lasting throughout the '80s.

The Cuff Links
Staten Island, New York, USA
Singer Ron Dante was also the lead vocalist in the fictitious band the Archies ("Sugar Sugar," etc.), which is why the Cuff Links hit "Tracy" sounds so similar. A true tradesman, Dante refused to tour with either bubblegum band.

The Bangles
Los Angeles, California, USA
An all-female group with multiple hits in the '80s, including "Manic Monday," "Walk Like an Egyptian" and "Eternal Flame." The band started as the Colours; then became the Supersonic Bangs, with the name taken from an *Esquire* article on hairstyles; then shortened themselves to the Bangs, until they discovered a New Jersey band of the same name; finally becoming the Bangles, the title of a track on the Electric Prunes' 1967 debut album, *I Had Too Much to Dream (Last Night)*.

The Chocolate Watchband
Cupertino, California, USA
Appeared in the 1967 film *Riot on Sunset Strip* and opened for the Doors. Though the Chocolate Watchband and the Strawberry Alarm Clock evolved around the same time, neither appears to have riffed off the other's name.

Golden Earring
The Hague, Netherlands
Known for all time as the "Radar Love" guys. George Kooymans, 13, and his neighbor Rinus Gerritsen, 15, called their band the Tornados but soon learned of another Tornados band. The boys had been opening their performances with the song "Golden Earrings," a hit for Marlene Dietrich in 1947 and Peggy Lee in 1948, so took the song title as their name, later dropping the s.

Staind
Springfield, Massachusetts, USA
Shaping nu-metal and alternative metal since 1995. The typo band has sold more than 15 million albums.

Fashion Bomb
Chicago, Illinois, USA
Industrial metal with black fingernails. Debut album: *Devils to Some, Angels to Others*.

Farewell to Fashion
Sebring, Florida, USA
Toured with such bands as Taking Back Sunday, Embodyment and Rookie of the Year. New singer acquired from Remembering Never.

End of Fashion
Perth, Australia
Band leader Justin Burford: "I want to break down the walls — within that context, that image, we can do anything we want, no matter whether it's super cheesy or punk, I want to kill fashion, see the end of it." OK, but check out their press photos.

Shock Your Mama

Innuendo & Out the Other

Sugar & Spice

Snakes & Snails

Sexual Acts & Preferences

Shock Your Mama

Innuendo & Out the Other

The Vibrators

This long-lived London punk band formed in February 1976 and opened for the Stranglers in March. Later that year they supported the Sex Pistols at the 100 Club, to great notice. By January 1977 they were headliners at London's Roxy Club, and two months later they were opening for Iggy Pop.

Their first single, "We Vibrate"/ "Whips and Furs," set the tone, and the debut album, *Pure Mania*, rose to #49 on the UK Album charts. Their final single on Epic Records, "Judy Says (Knock You in the Head)" was included in *Mojo* magazine's list of All-Time Best Punk Singles.

Frequent lineup changes kept the Vibrators out of the limelight through much of the '80s and '90s, but they continued to record — 11 albums! — and perform for the devoted. The turn of the millennium saw membership solidify as a trio with founding members Ian "Knox" Carnochan and John "Eddie" Edwards, and the addition of "Pete," from the Finnish band No Direction. The Vibrators began an annual touring schedule that would fatigue most younger bands.

Stiff Little Fingers took their name from the 1977 Vibrators song "Stiff Little Fingers."

Coach Said Not To
Minneapolis, Minnesota, USA
All-female trio inspired by a university brochure instructing college girls how to politely preserve their honor.

Let's French
Washington, DC, USA
"In 2005 three French exiles and one Parisian Russian émigré crossed the Atlantic with hopes of bringing about a violent revolution in the United States…advocating a three-hour work day, socialized medical treatment, and croissant for all."

Flesh for Lulu
Brixton, UK
Moody vegetarian band sees '60s pop singer Lulu eating a fast-food hamburger. Really.

Hot Nasties
Calgary, Alberta, Canada
Started in high school as the Social Blemishes but became the Hot Nasties a year later. High school is like that.

Barenaked Ladies
Toronto, Ontario, Canada
Chose their name to convey the thrill of seeing something forbidden. Their career was jump-started in 1991 when the then-mayor of Toronto had them removed from the city's New Year's Eve concert lineup because she felt their name objectified women.

Springbok Nude Girls
Stellenbosch, South Africa
Named for the scantily clad models who appeared on a series of '70s compilations known as the Springbok albums. Very popular in South Africa.

All that we wanted

The glam-rockers the **Pin Ups** are lead singer-guitarist Randy Roberts, keyboardist Bad Ronald, bassist Kriss Teen and drummer Peter "Parker" Minucci. *All That We Wanted* was recorded in 1995 and is still in print. Indie music promoter Musicians Exchange says of this New York City quartet, "Pin Ups…sound like Electric Angels, Sweet and Lou Reed."

Formed in 1988, Boston-based **Girl On Top** features a solid back beat, crunchy pop-punk guitars, and vocals by front-woman Karen DeBiasse. The band performs regularly in Boston, NYC and throughout New England. The independent romantic-comedy film *Getting Personal* includes 13 songs by Girl on Top.

Nudeswirl
New Brunswick, New Jersey, USA
Alternative-metal band who toured with bands such as White Zombie, Danzig and Mindfunk.

Stark Naked & the Car Thieves
Little Rock, Arkansas, USA
Tight, bluesy covers band whose logo is a naked man pushing the band in a convertible.

Sweaty Nipples
Portland, Oregon, USA
Brian Lehfeldt and Davey Nipples were two teenagers who decided "if we started a band we could maybe get into shows for free." They've played over 1,300 shows across the US with the likes of Bad Brains, Pearl Jam, Soundgarden, Ministry, Fishbone, Pantera, Radiohead, Korn and Alice in Chains.

Joy Zipper
New York City, New York, USA
The zipper is pulled shut.

Sex Clark Five
Huntsville, Alabama, USA
Their take on the British band name Dave Clark Five.

Mother Love Bone
Seattle, Washington, USA
A legendary Seattle band that lasted only two years, 1988–90. Legendary in part because of the players who moved on to fame, and in part because of the death of charismatic frontman Andrew Wood due to a heroin overdose just days before the release of the band's debut album, *Apple*. Stone Gossard and Jeff Ament helped create Pearl Jam. Bruce Fairweather joined Love Battery.

Sex Pistols London, UK
Perhaps the quintessential '70s punk band. They were the Strand, then the Swankers, then like several other bands, they were renamed by manager Malcolm McLaren. Among the rejected names: Le Bomb, Beyond and Teenage Novel.

Sex Machineguns Japan
The band admits that the name was meant to suggest that Sex Machineguns are more powerful than Sex Pistols.

Jetsex Paris, France
Sex and punk-rock with the jetset.

Sex Museum Madrid, Spain
Heavy beats from a band that has opened for Metallica, Sepultura, Sonic Youth and Deep Purple.

NAMES
STILL AVAILABLE

Betty & Erotika

Mr. Happy Muscle

Sex Water Pistols

Our Inflatable Friends

Orchestral Climaxes

Trampoline
Sex Club

Indoor Pearl
Divers Association

Thruster's Last Stand

Gently Ribbed Giants

The Nightly Nudes

Pommel Horse
Perks

A Waiter
Named Randy

181

The Breeders
Dayton, Ohio, USA

Pixies bassist Kim Deal and Throwing Muses guitarist Tanya Donelly thought they'd form a band and named themselves the Breeders after a folk-rock group Deal had formed with her twin sister Kelley in the '70s.

The Humpers
Long Beach, California, USA

Led by Scott Drake of the Suicide Kings. Broke in Yugoslavia with the release there of the album *My Machine*.

Several Girls Galore
Hastings-on-Hudson, New York, USA

They sound the opposite of how their name sounds.

The New Pornographers
Vancouver, British Columbia, Canada

Songwriter Carl Newman has said that he came up with the name after watching the Japanese film *The Pornographers*.

Porn Flakes
Baltimore, Maryland, USA

Leader Snackie Hillman came up with the name in Baltimore's Mount Royal Tavern circa 1989.

Porn on the Cob
Vancouver, British Columbia, Canada

"POTC came together as a djembe, a guitar and a rent bill to write lyrics on. It's been a fire of passionate shows ever since."

Originally from Glasgow, **Impure Thoughts** settled in Berlin after periods in Ireland, France, the Czech Republic, and many open-ended European locations. Since arriving in Berlin, the band has built up a strong fan-base through extensive touring and consistently great live shows. Their second album, *Lights Ahead*, was released on Germany's Cannery Row record label in 2006 and contains 14 songs full of energetic original tunes with searing guitars and strong vocal harmonies.

Pornhuskers
Kansas City, Missouri, USA

"Ten years ago a man by the name of Bob Tinfoil found himself traversing the country as a door to door salesman of marital aids…."

Roger's Porn Collection
Austin, Texas, USA

Roger plays bass.

Porno for Pyros
Los Angeles, California, USA

Ex-Jane's Addiction frontman Perry Farrell named his new band after seeing a fireworks ad in a porn magazine.

Hardcore Superstar
Gothenburg, Sweden

Several #1 singles and music awards in Sweden.

Mega Purple Sex Toy Kit Marin
Santiago Coruña Estrada, Spain

Old-school '60s rock with a ballsy Hammond B-3 to Purple things up.

Steely Dan Annandale-on-Hudson, New York, USA

Steely Dans are dildos used in William S. Burrough's controversial 1956 novel *Naked Lunch*. Students of the Beat writers, Walter Becker and Donald Fagen used the name as a in-joke, having no idea it would be forever linked to them.

Climax Camp for Girls
Alton, Illinois, USA

In the Nabokov novel *Lolita*, the title character attends Camp Q. In the 1962 film adaptation by Stanley Kubrick, Lolita attends a summer camp for girls called Camp Climax.

The Kinks London, UK

The Kinks name is said to have come from their flamboyant or "kinky" style of dress on stage. "Kinky" had less of a sexual connotation back then. The band was known to wear high boots and capes at a time when other British bands were still wearing trim-fitting mod suits.

THE SEATSNIFFERS RE-ISSUED

"THE SEATSNIFFERS" & "ALL OF THIS"

Antwerp, Belgium's **Seatsniffers** are probably Belgium's most popular roots-rock band, playing a blend of rockabilly, R&B and gutbucket blues with a punk-rock energy. In 2007 the Seatsniffers were the in-studio house band for the new Dutch TV show *De Garage*. The most recent Seatsniffers album is *Turbulence*.

Kinky Slinky

Oklahoma City, Oklahoma, USA
Reggae-funk in OK City. Sounds kinky. They call the music "Howdy Dread."

Black Tape for a Blue Girl

Brooklyn, New York, USA
A Projekt Records projekt. Gothy. Kinky in an ambiently darkwave way.

Asexuals

Montreal, Quebec, Canada
A punk band formed in 1983. Toured Canada and Europe, opening for Public Image Ltd. and DOA.

The B Sexuals

Sacramento, California, USA
Phil and Mike.

TokyoSexWhale

Ottawa, Ontario, Canada
Very heavy and whale-like, with a female bassist. There was a Hong Kong punk band called Tokyo Sex Whale.

Cherry Poppin' Daddies

Eugene, Oregon, USA
Rebelling against the Pacific Northwest grunge trend of the late '80s and early '90s, frontman Steve Perry sought to form a band that could raise some hell without lumberjack shirts and distorted amplifiers. Thus was born the Cherry Poppin' Daddies, a rocking funk-and-ska band. But with an intentionally racy name, wild costumes, half-naked female dancers, and an enormous, shapely, conservative-crowd-offending pickle statue.

Naked Lady Wrestlers

Crockett, California, USA
Album: *Not So Quiet on the Western Front*.

Buck Naked
& the Bare Bottom Boys

San Francisco, California, USA
Originally from Omaha, Nebraska, Buck Naked played music in a rockabilly vein. Thanks to certain lyrics and song titles, this was dubbed "pornobilly" by his detractors. Buck Naked (Phillip Bury) used to turn up on stage "wearing only cowboy boots, a cowboy hat, a guitar, and a strategically placed toilet plunger…Despite its name, the rest of the band were always fully clothed on stage.

Kings of Pleasure

Tucson, Arizona, USA
Retro jump-blues and swing guys doing their '50s best.

From Jamaica Plain, Massachusetts, comes the sweet electro-funk sound of **Lovewhip**, Boston Music Award winners and five-time nominees. Check out "Virtual Booty Machine," heard on TV's *Veronica Mars*. Erin Harpe (vocals, guitar), Jim Countryman (bass, vocals) and Pete Koopmans (drums) create "exciting dancehall-punk collisions," says the *LA Times*. Countryman on the name: "Love Handles wouldn't get us anywhere, and we like to whip people with Love on the dance floor."

Nashville Pussy

They can't call themselves... Well, they can and do, and positively exude the raw sexuality of it, with a lineup that's equal parts estrogen and testosterone — two women, two men, delivering aggressive below-the-belt rock and roll.

The Atlanta, Georgia, husband-and-wife team of guitarist-songwriter Blaine Cartright and guitarist Ruyter Suys have led Nashville Pussy through some 200-plus perform-ances a year for the past decade. With longtime NP skin-banger Jeremy Thompson on drums and more recent recruit 6-foot-plus Karen Cuda on bass, the band becomes a furious force of good-time decadence. Hips move, drinks flow, libidos do what libidos do.

Nashville Pussy's name comes from Motor City madman Ted Nugent's onstage banter prior to launching into "Wang Dang, Sweet Poontang," as captured on *Double Live Gonzo*. They understand the shock value of their name and feel no need to defend it.

The band has released four full-length albums: *Let Them Eat Pussy* (1998), *High as Hell* (2000), *Say Something Nasty* (2002), *Get Some* (2005).

Sugar & Spice

T.I.T.S. San Francisco, California, USA
With Kim Wet, Abbey Kreme, Wendy U Wannit and Mary Elizabreast.

Titty Bingo Houston, Texas, USA
A bingo caller's night out.

Boobarellas Brazil
Named for the 1968 film *Barbarella*, based on the French Barbarella comics.

Jeanie & the Tits
Orlando, Florida, USA
With Jean Smegma, Mary Mammary, Tina Bulimia, Buni Lamor.

Big Muff
New York City, New York, USA
An electric-guitar distortion pedal made by Electro-Harmonix. Also the recording alias of Itaal Shur.

Enos Presley and the guys from **44 Double D** offer up "sex-driven rock & roll with modern styling's of '70s glam punk, with a hint of rock-abilly and a pinch of goth." Their recent album is *Sex Is Evil*. Stu Gibson of *SleazeGrinder* magazine says, "Pile on the tremolo, bring on the big, curvy Gretsches and coat in grease for a delightful treat."

The Red Muffs
San Fernando Valley, California, USA
Real red muffs are perfect for every occasion.

Hole Los Angeles, California, USA
Best known as Courtney Love's band. Then as Melissa Auf der Maur's former band.

Tight Pink Holes
Geelong, Victoria, Australia
Shock-rock from down under.

Camel Toe Miami, Florida, USA
Funk-rock songs: "Midget in a Thong," "Camel Toe Party," "Havana Banana."

Labiators
Ashville, North Carolina, USA
Noise boys.

The Clits West Coast, Portugal
Electro-punk "riot-grrrl" band. Debut EP: *The World Is a Mess But My Hair Is Perfect*.

Clit 45 Long Beach, California, USA
Street-punk hardcore. Named for the popular firearm cartridge Colt .45.

The Clit Cops Berlin, Germany
Rude lyrics. Rude stage show. Isn't clit spelled with a K in German?

The Slits London, UK
Formed in 1976 from members of the Flowers of Romance and the Castrators.

Spread Beaver Japan
Featuring the late X Japan and Zilch guitarist Hideto "hide" Matsumoto.

Chapel Hill, North Carolina's **Snatches of Pink** has been playing swaggering, bluesy, '70s-style rock for over two decades. Comprised of songwriter Michael Rank on vocals and guitar, Marc E. Smith on guitar and backing vocals, Nikos Chremos on bass and John Howie Jr. on drums, the band has shared stages with the likes of the Ramones, Iggy Pop and Soundgarden. AllMusic.com reviewer Jo-Anne Greene gave their recent album, *Love Is Dead*, 4 out of 5 stars.

Saturday Night Beaver
Portsmouth, UK
Disco tribute band with an odd promise in its name.

Turbovulva
Hollywood, California, USA
Album: *Fanci Panti Parlor*. Other band is Strap-On Sweetie.

The Twats Washington, DC, USA
With Lord Taint, Cuntess Twat (vocals), Rusty Trombone and Sir Drunks-a-Lot.

The Twat Waffles
Binghamton, New York, USA
At least five friends with instruments and liquor.

Alabama Thunderpussy
Richmond, Virginia, USA
These guys are actually a serious metal band.

Oedipussy Manchester, UK
With Phil Parfitt of Perfect Disaster and Wolfgang Radio.

Analog Pussy Berlin, Germany
Jiga and Jinno relocated from Israel to Germany following the release of their 1990 album, *Psycho Bitch From Hell*.

Haunted Pu55y New York City
"Haunted Pu55y is likely the world's finest histrionic fear-metal band."

Dreadlock Pussy Netherlands
Dutch nu-metal groovecore whatever. No women in this one.

Tokyo Ghetto Pussy Germany
Jam & Spoon (Rolf Ellmer and Markus Loeffel) electronica well west of Tokyo.

Shirley Temple's Pussy
Seattle, Washington, USA
Stone Temple Pilots liked the STP logo (Scientifically Treated Petroleum). The first STP name they performed under was Shirley Temple's Pussy.

The PoCLITicals Maryland, USA
Four girls who look way too young for this name.

Glorious Clitoris
San Francisco, California, USA
Before they became Ovarian Trolley.

Vaginal Croutons
Côte-St-Luc, Quebec, Canada
"Girls," says singer Johnny Jackoff, "don't generally seem to be as fond of the name as we are."

VaginaSore Jr. Tampa, Florida, USA
Painful pun on Dinosaur Jr. They have gigs. They have a CD.

NAMES
STILL AVAILABLE

Happy As Pam's

Republic of Guzzonga

The Peeping Areolas

Poontangle
Conditioner

The Oval Orifice

Shivering Clits

British Labia Party

Smoochacoochie

The Vagina
Travelogues

Snatch
the Golden Fleece

100-Watt Twat

G Spot GPS

Revolting Cocks

The Revolting Cocks started in 1985 as a side-project for Ministry frontman Alain Jourgensen and Belgian musician Luc Van Acker, adding fellow Belgians Patrick Codenys and Richard 23.

The name origin is vague but seems to have come from someone ("some girls" or a bartender) referring to them as "revolting cocks." There is also a story about a Brussels-based street gang called the Revolting Cocks.

Known for their raunchy live performances and explicit lyrics, RevCo, as they were more discreetly known, had songs placed on the Parents Music Resource Center's "banned" list.

Trent Reznor (Nine Inch Nails), Billy Gibbons (ZZ Top), Rick Neilsen (Cheap Trick), Nivek Ogre (Skinny Puppy), Kirk Hammett (Metallica) and many other notable musicians have played on Revolting Cocks albums and/or performed with them live.

Albums include *Big Sexy Land*, *You Goddamned Son of a Bitch* (Live), *Beers, Steers and Queers*, *Finger Lickin' Good*, *Cocked and Loaded*, and *Cocktail Mixxx*.

Snakes & Snails

Jesus Penis Houston, Texas, USA
Experimental rock that only Jesus's penis would appreciate.

Micropenis Paris, France
Declaration: "Men & women want to cut the penis down to size."

Penis Fly Trap
Boston, Massachusetts, USA
More fun than a Venus flytrap and a handful of hamburger.

Penis Genius
San Francisco, California, USA
Vocalist/media critic Benjamin Vanderford was the guy behind the Iraqi beheading hoax. Album: *Fire Next Time*.

Steaming Wolf Penis
Seattle, Washington, USA
From Paperthinwalls.com: "Seattle anti-anti-joke jokesters Steaming Wolf Penis warrant exactly this one minute and twenty-three seconds of your time."

Dicks
San Francisco, California, USA
Frontman Gary Floyd was one of the first openly gay musicians in hardcore punk. Queercore band Limp Wrist pays homage to Floyd in the song "Ode."

Citizen Dick
Buffalo, New York, USA
Adopting the name of a fictional band in the 1992 film *Singles*. In the film, Matt Dillon's band members include Pearl Jam's Stone Gossard, Jeff Ament and Eddie Vedder. Citizen Dick is a reference to Seattle band Citizen Sane, which takes its name from the 1941 film *Citizen Kane*.

Compact Dicks Trondheim, Norway
Trying to play straight-faced hard rock while wearing eyeshadow, lipstick and backing a vocalist named Jack Boner.

Adickdid Eugene, Oregon, USA
Early '90s all-female trio who toured the West Coast and opened for Hole, Fugazi, Bikini Kill and Lunachicks.

Dick Van Dick
New York City, New York, USA
Pun on squeaky-clean actor Dick Van Dyke's name. Album: *dictastrophe*.

Pickled Dick have changed their name to Mike TV in an attempt to broaden their audience and expand their commercial options. Sellouts?! Guitarist Jhon Cosgrove: "We are still exactly the same band, but hopefully we can keep the band going rather than all having to join the Navy." They recently won the Jagermeister songwriting competition and their track "The Jager Song" is part of the Jagermeister ad campaign. Mike TV (less their Pickled Dicks) come from Chesterfield, Wolverhampton and Hammer Vale, UK.

"After decimating the Scandinavian music scene, **Foxycock** hopped on the first illegal Japanese fishing vessel and headed straight to Greenland. Not much of a music scene in Greenland, so they continued southwest to Nova Scotia. After an initial warm reception, they were brutally mocked and raped by polar bears and barely escaped with their lives, and a hit song!" Hollywood-based writers and musicians Josh Murphy and Douglas Smolens and friends offer, for your consideration, the album *Black Music for White People*.

Big Dick & the Extenders
Islamorada, Florida, USA
Woody's, "Exotic Adult Fun in the Keys," is proud to be the Florida home of Big Dick & the Extenders.

Dick Delicious & the
Tasty Testicles Atlanta, Georgia, USA
Winners of the first Howard Stern Award for Excellence in Music.

Rumpleforeskin
New Haven, Connecticut, USA
More than we need to know about Rumplestiltskin. Rumpleforeskin's Top 21 friends on MySpace are all porn spam vixens.

Buzzcocks Manchester, UK
Seminal Manchester pop-punk band. In Manchester street slang, "cock" means "my lad," as in "Gi' me a buzz, cock."

Cock Rock for Cannibals
Dallas-Ft. Worth, Texas, USA
"This is the music god told us to make, right after he told us who to vote for."

The Glamorous Stunt Cocks
Boston, Massachusetts, USA
In this case, the word stunt seems ill advised.

Locomotive Thundercock
Cleveland, Ohio, USA
"Ride the Cock and find yourself in the shittiest biker dive bar, rocking out with tuthless criminals who smell blood."

Monster Cock Rally
Oakland, California, USA
About to release their seventh studio album, *That Look in Your Eye*.

The Yuppy Pricks Austin, Texas, USA
"We're rich. We're assholes. We play punk-rock." New album: *Balls*.

Sgt. Pekker
Los Angeles, California, USA
Composer Arthur Jarvinen and friends create an "anti-thology" poking fun at sacred Beatles texts, with songs such as "Marsha, I Fear," "Man, My Guitar Playing Really Reeks," and "Golden Shower Curtain Rods."

Swollen Members
Vancouver, British Columbia, Canada
The first band who made me go *what!?* Right before they won a whack of Canadian music and video awards.

Test Icicles London, UK
Previous band name, Balls, wasn't witty enough.

Blueballs Deluxe
Arlington, Virginia, USA
"God Fearin' Gun Runnin' music."

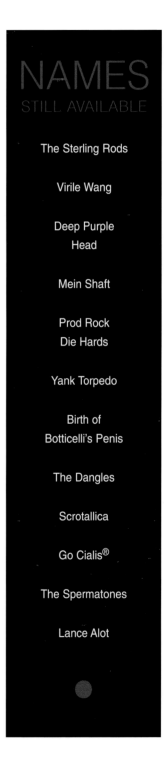

NAMES
STILL AVAILABLE

The Sterling Rods

Virile Wang

Deep Purple Head

Mein Shaft

Prod Rock Die Hards

Yank Torpedo

Birth of Botticelli's Penis

The Dangles

Scrotallica

Go Cialis®

The Spermatones

Lance Alot

Orgy

Formed in Bakersfield, California, by singer Jay Gordon and guitarist Ryan Shuck. Shuck had played in one of Gordon's previous bands, Sexart. The two have stated publicly that the band name is not in fact sex-related but refers the mix of different musical styles they present.

They added bassist Paige Haley, guitarist Amir Derakh and drummer Bobby Hewitt of Electric Love Hogs, rehearsed for a few months and, without ever having played live, released their debut album, *Candyass*. Driven by trade reviews and word of mouth, it made it to #32 on the US Album charts.

They first appeared live at EdgeFest in Tulsa, Oklahoma, in 1998, followed by a spot on the Family Values Tour, which also featured heavyweights KoRn, Limp Bizkit and Rammstein.

Sexual Acts & Preferences

Climax Los Angeles, California, USA
They climaxed in 1972 with the #3 single "Precious and Few."

Digital Orgasm Belgium
In 1997 the Lords of Acid, known for their grinding beat and explicitly sexual lyrics, released a *less* sex-oriented album under the name Digital Orgasm.

Moneyshot
Victoria, British Columbia, Canada
"…from house destroying parties…to the Warped Tour, from sold-out clubs to empty clubs, from touring with No Means No to opening for Nazareth… we've been there. Like an experienced lover, we know just the right way to make your toes curl."

Holy Fuck Toronto, Ontario, Canada
Group electronica with several major award nominations and a big European tour.

Fuck the Facts
Ottawa, Ontario, Canada
Grindcore-noisecore since the late '90s. Still recording, touring and selling hoodies.

The Fucking Champs
San Francisco, California, USA
Metal trio known for flipping around in odd time signatures and producing advanced guitar harmonies. Guitarist uses a custom 9-string guitar.

The Fuck Fucks
Melbourne, Australia
Another band assembled by my man, Melbourne cartoonist-musician Fred Negro. It seems a new city ordinance had come into effect regarding posters plastered to public poles. Pub owner Craig McEvan said to Fred, "The cops told me they'd fine the pub *not* the band, so ya could be called the Fuck Fucks or anything, but *we'd* get fined!" Fred thought to himself, *The Fuck Fucks, what a* top *name for a band!* "I was determined to form a band called the Fuck Fucks purely so I could get HUGE street posters printed up that would get the pub fined."

FuckEmos Austin, Texas, USA
Also playing as the Asshole Surfers. Many albums and, again, a range of merchandise.

"Faced with an entire generation of young people being raised on nothing but over-produced radio rock and emasculated thrift-store hipster whining, Bloomington, Indiana's **Tremendous**

Fucking (you can call 'em Tremfu if Mom's around) lives to grab an audience by the throat, smash their emo glasses, and go home with their girlfriends."

DOES IT OFFEND YOU, YEAH? is an Electro-dance-punk trio from Reading, UK. As of press time, they were scheduled to open for Nine Inch Nails on their 2008 North American tour. In an interview with NME.com, synth player Dan Coop explained: "Everybody thinks the name is some kind of statement, but it's a quote from David Brent in an episode of *The Office*…We needed a name to put as our [MySpace] profile name so [decided to] just put the first thing that was said on TV. We switched it on and Ricky Gervais said, 'Does it offend you, yeah? My drinking?' So we just went with that. No thought went into it whatsoever."

Fucking Orange
Denver, Colorado, USA
Kind of f-ing *metallic* orange. With the song "Fucking Green."

FuckVegas Italy
Happy together for four years of booming bass, crunching guitars and general mayhem. In celebration, the album *FuckFuckVegas*.

Fuckwolf
San Francisco, California, USA
On Kimosciotic Records: "There may be many 'wolf' bands gallivanting around the globe, some may even say the waters are already overpopulated, but obviously they have not heard this wolf. Fuck all the other wolfs… Fuckwolf is the pride of the pack. Combining the finer elements of mal-functioning dub and warehouse noise, Fuckwolf create an aural douche that will leave the most hardened listener salivating for more."

KY & the Backsliders
Gainesville, Florida, USA
Side project for Bob "Bobzilla" DuPerry Jr., bassist for Gainesville band Toy Grenades.

Ima Fucking Gymnist
Los Angeles, California, USA
Issued the 7-inch "…So Freakin' Juicy," played some gigs, then wussed out and became Ima Gymnist. Their blog: "We are proud of the things we've done with Fucking in our name and hope that w/o it we do WAYYY more!"

Dance Me Pregnant
Omaha, Nebraska, USA
Another of *The Onion* AV Club's Worst Band Names of '07. "A sonic tapestry…that serves to accentuate the scream of consciousness that is Dance Me Pregnant." Presumably a riff on the W.P. Kinsella novel (and Bruce McDonald film) *Dance Me Outside*, which explores life as a teenage metalhead on the Kidabanesee Reserve.

Goblin Cock
San Diego, California, USA
"Goblin Cock is a band from beyond time, beyond space, beyond your naive concept of dimension in Metal." They've opened for Blue Cheer. They perform in cloaks. And their MySpace page gives you a choice: "Kegrah the Dragon Killer" or "The Porpoise Song."

NAMES
STILL AVAILABLE

The Roamin' Orgies

Interdessertcourse

Square Root Threesome

Chin Picnic

Electropulse Orgasmotron 3000

My Kama Future

I Forget Where I Put It

A 9-Volt in the Netherlands

More Badfinger

Gay Pipefitters Local

Interracial Bake Sale

The Go Fish Girls

Machine Gun Fellatio

This Sydney, Australia, circus-rock crew has been opening eyes and ears since the late '90s. Band members include Brian Ferrysexual, Chit Chat von Loopin Stab, the Love Shark, Pinky Beecroft, Three K Short, the Widow Jones and special live guest Christa "KK Juggy" Hughes. Albums: *Bring It On!*, *Paging Mr. Strike* and *Machine Gun Fellatio on Ice*. In 2004, they opened for KISS and attempted to convince Gene Simmons to wear a prop vagina on his head.

The Circle Jerks

Los Angeles, California, USA
Formed in 1979, the band has done it all – except perhaps, you know, that name thing. They've toured and appeared with national-level acts, recorded 7 albums, been featured on dozens of compilations and film soundtracks, and recently scored two songs on the new *Jackass* video game. The Vans shoe company has produced a Circle Jerks tribute shoe.

Wank Los Angeles, California, USA
Album: *Get a Grip on Yourself*.

Lesbians on Ecstasy

Montreal, Quebec, Canada
"The Lesbians on Ecstasy are making electronic music of the lesbian variety."

Live Action Pussy Show

Köln, Germany
Three women and a male bassist. "One of Germany's great garage trash bands, their name alone is enough to cause lots of attention, a few giggles, and more than enough controversy."

Kung Fu Dykes

Virginia Beach, Virginia, USA
"From secret temples hidden deep underneath the Oceana Naval Base in Virginia Beach, Virginia, come the most mesmerizing women in rock: Kung Fu Dykes." In wild costumes, playing something called Samurai Rock.

Big Blow & the Bushwackers

Brisbane, Australia
I'm not sure they meant the name to be rude. "Just your typical high-energy world, roots and original music performed on mandolin, tuba, didgeridoo, accordion, more brass, lots of percussion and handmade instruments."

The Queers

Portsmouth, New Hampshire, USA
Formed by Joe Queer (Joe King) in 1982. The name Queers was meant to poke fun at what Joe called the "Art Fag" community in New Hampshire.

The Fags Seattle, Washington, USA
A 7-piece (including MC) excursion into gender-bending punk lunacy.

The Butchies are a lesbian trio from Durham, North Carolina, fronted by Kaia Wilson (guitar, vocals), with Alison Martlew (bass, vocals) and Melissa York (drums, vocals). The band on their 2004 album, *Make Yr Life*: "If after listening to this 10-track cream dream you don't feel like you just had one of the biggest epiphanies of your life, you clearly voted for Bush and are immune to evolution. *Make Yr Life* is undoubtedly the record that will facilely evolve the music world as we know it (Mothership not included)."

Gaye Bykers on Acid

Leicester, Midlands, UK
Kicked it off in 1984 "at the height of Thatcherite Britain." Alter egos Lesbian Dopeheads on Mopeds claim to be from New Zealand. The double name is said to have been a ruse allowing them to get paid for playing two slots on a festival gig, "and a good excuse to dress up in frocks." Insane number of recordings.

Gladrub Toronto, Ontario, Canada
From the Canadian Indie Band database: "Formed in Toronto in 1993, Gladrub sounds like 'Pavement on speed' doing a happy version of Joy Division."

Horror Chiller
Monster Thriller

Vampires

Ghosts

Ghouls

Cannibals

Monsters

Horror Chiller Monster Thriller

Vampire Weekend

New York's Vampire Weekend displays influences of Congolese soukous music, and its sound has been described as "Upper West Side Soweto."

The band formed in 2006. Lead vocalist-guitarist Ezra Koenig previously played saxophone in the free-jazz improvisation collective Total War and afro-pop band the Dirty Projectors. Other band members are Rostam Batmanglij (keyboard, guitar, vocals), Chris Tomson (drums) and Chris Baio (bass).

Their name is the title Koenig's amateur film, which revolves around a younger Ezra fighting off vampires in scary masks. (At the time of printing, the trailer was available at blog.limewire.com/posts/1138.)

Their self-titled debut was released on XL records in 2008, and three songs — "Oxford Comma," "A-Punk" and "Mansard Roof" — quickly charted in the UK. The group performed on *Saturday Night Live* in early 2008.

Koenig was also in the short-lived humorous rap group L'Homme Run.

Aural Vampire Tokyo, Japan
Exo-Chika takes on a vampire persona onstage. Raveman wears a slasher mask. And, yes, they play with the aural/oral ambiguity. The duo bonded through a mutual love of horror movies.

Vampire State Building Norway
Leather fetish costumes and lewd stage shows with ballet dancers. Spin-offs: Lonely Crowd, Zeromancer, Red Harvest.

Saltwater Vampires
Charleston, Illinois, USA
Album: *We Are Masterpieces Created by God.*

Vampire Rodents
Toronto, Ontario, Canada
Led by singer-guitarist Daniel Vahnke, with Victor Wulf (keyboards), Andrea Akastia (violin, cello), Jing Laoshu (percussion). Spin-offs: Ether Bunny, Dilate, Pillow. Vahnke now lives in Phoenix, Arizona.

Vampire Beach Babes
Toronto, Ontario, Canada
"Two parts Bauhaus, one part Duane Eddy." Albums: *Reckless Summer* (1999), *Attack of the Killer Bikinis* (2002), *Beach Blanket Bedlam* (2005).

The Vampire Lezbos float between worlds: Portland, Oregon, and Auckland, New Zealand. Guitarist-vocalist Dave: "It was 1984 and we wanted a name that alluded to our

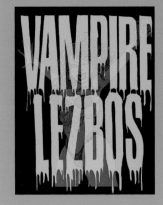

punk/new wave sound — especially in conservative Spokane [Washington] — and also a name that would help bring people out to our shows who hadn't already seen us. Plus, pissing off the local rednecks was in order, too." The name was taken from a Cramps song, which came from the 1971 Spanish-West German film *Vampiros Lesbos*, taglined "A Psycho-Sexadelic Horror Freakout."

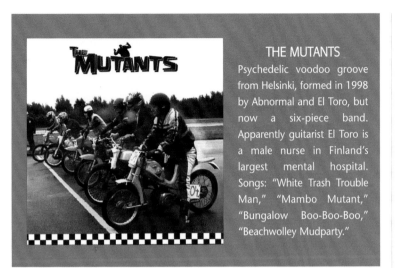

THE MUTANTS

Psychedelic voodoo groove from Helsinki, formed in 1998 by Abnormal and El Toro, but now a six-piece band. Apparently guitarist El Toro is a male nurse in Finland's largest mental hospital. Songs: "White Trash Trouble Man," "Mambo Mutant," "Bungalow Boo-Boo-Boo," "Beachwolley Mudparty."

Probably Vampires
Chicago, Illinois, USA

Keyboardist Dan Smart: "The name was basically created to satisfy the two-headed desire that most of us in the band had to let everyone know that we were a loud and in-your-face kind of band that wasn't about to treat its audience delicately...while at the same time assuring everyone that under no circumstances do we ever take our music too seriously."

Blood Sucking Freaks
Adelaide, Australia

From the title of director Joel Reed's 1976 horror/exploitation movie (also called *The Incredible Torture Show*): "theatre macabre, blood, gore and de-capitation abound as an evil magician and his eyeball-eating midget assistant ravage SoHo." Song: "Suck Me."

Fangboy & the Ghouls
Ventura, California, USA

Campy gothic punk-metal formed in 1995. Songs: "Pretty Little Dead Things," "We've Come for Your Daughters."

Shapes Have Fangs
Austin, Texas, USA

Dustin Coffey, Evan McGlothlin, Josh Willis and Skyler McGlothlin all grew up in the small East Texas town of Gun Barrel City. Influenced by the Kinks and the Zombies. Previous bands include Nautilus and the Fabulous Bread Winners.

The Gore-Gore Girls
Detroit, Michigan, USA

All-female big-beat rock. Took their name from the 1972 grindhouse classic *The Gore Gore Girls*, by thrill-king director Herschell Gordon Lewis.

Gorelord Oslo, Norway

Gore + warlord. Formed in 1999 by Frediablo (Necrophagia, Grimfist). Albums: *Zombie Suicide Part 666*, *Force Fed on Human Flesh*, *Norwegian Chainsaw Massacre*.

Doofgoblin
Charlottesville, Virginia, USA

Proudly advertise making *The Onion*'s Worst Band Names list in 2007.

Slash's Snakepit
Los Angeles, California, USA

Named for Slash's home studio (known as "The Snakepit," due to his fondness for snakes, and the studio's proximity to his pets). Slash wanted to call the band Snakepit, but the record company insisted they add his name to boost sales. Different lineups included ex-Jellyfish singer-guitarist Eric Dover and 3 of a Different Kind singer Rod Jackson.

The Flesh Eaters
Los Angeles, California, USA

Started in 1977 by Chris Desjardins, film-school graduate, private-school English teacher and writer for *Slash* magazine (which became a record label). *The Flesh Eaters* is a 1964 sci-fi thriller about a group of people stranded on an island where Nazi experiments have produced flesh-eating monsters.

The Creatures
London, UK

Siouxsie Sioux's post-Banshees band with former Banshees drummer Budgie.

Get Him Eat Him
Brooklyn, New York, USA

Formed in 2004 and led by *Pitchfork* writer Matt LeMay. According to LeMay, "The name comes from an idea our former keyboardist, Raf, and his friend Erin had for a cartoon show, in which these two seals named Get Him and Eat Him chase a fisherman. Get Him only says 'Get Him' and Eat Him only says 'Eat Him.'"

Devastator attacks with thrash-metal from Padova, Italy. They formed when Violent Overture split into two bands, Devastator and Motrok (though band members still seem to move between those two projects). Albums: *Alive from Devastation, Thrash'n'War* and 2007's *Alcoholic Invasion*. Songs: "Post Atomic Beer," "Chuck Berry Wants Hardcore," "I Hate Cover Bands."

The Ghost Is Dancing
Toronto, Ontario, Canada
Drummer-keyboardist Kevin Corlis: "Finally one day we had the thought, 'Hey, racehorses have cool names!' We downloaded a list of a few hundred names and went through them that night in the kitchen. We ended up with the Ghost Is Dancing. It took approximately one month and those five hours sitting in the kitchen to name our band after a horse. I voted against that name. It was 5-1, though, so I lost."

Ghosts London, UK
They were Roman Polanski, then worried about a lawsuit so became Polanski, then changed to Southpaw, found a US band named Southpaw, so became Ghosts and ironically moved from a moody electronic sound to bouncy pop.

Ghostland Observatory
Austin, Texas, USA
Duo of frontman Aaron Behrens and producer-drummer Thomas Turner, who dress in capes for their live shows. The name: "Aaron's brain is filled with ghostly sonatas and astral observations, so through thought they mixed and mingled in the strangest of fashions."

Godzuki
Detroit, Michigan, USA
Named after the animated mini-Godzilla from kids' TV show *The Godzilla Power Hour*, which aired in the US between 1978 and 1981. It's a science-art-themed side-project for members of His Name Is Alive, the Whales, the Ohms, the Volebeats, the Mystic Moog Orchestra and Teach Me Tiger.

Broadzilla
Detroit, Michigan, USA
The all-female power trio has won six Detroit music awards. Album: *Broadzilla vs. the Tramp-o-Lean*.

The Haunted
Gothenburg, Sweden
Self-titled debut was named Album of the Year by *Terrorizer* magazine.

Screaming Headless Torsos
New York, New York, USA
The brainchild of mad-scientist, virtuoso guitarist David "Fuze" Fiuczynski. Inspired by P-Funk and Living Colour and fronted by singer Dean Bowman.

Headless Human Clones
Portland, Oregon, USA
"In 1997 the *Times* ran an article predicting the creation of headless human clones for organ harvesting within ten years."

Igor & the Skindiggers
Winnipeg, Manitoba, Canada
"Igor unleashed this zombified quartet with a hunger for global domination, and flesh, on an unsuspecting world."

Big Head Todd & the Monsters are a laidback blues-roots band from Boulder, Colorado. Frontman Todd Park Mohr is Big Head Todd. "The name is a tribute to legendary blues-jazz 'heads' (Eddy 'Cleanhead' Vincent, etc.). They were scheduled to perform their first gig, but had no name. Todd came up with it at the spur of the moment and it stuck!" Top 20 hits with "Broken Hearted Saviour," "Resignation Superman" and "Bittersweet."

Cannibal & the Headhunters
East Los Angeles, California, USA
Scored a hit with "Land of a Thousand Dances" in 1965. Toured with the Beatles on their second North American tour. Named after singer Frankie "Cannibal" Garcia's nickname.

Fine Young Cannibals
Birmingham, England, UK
The trio of Roland Gift, David Steele and Andy Cox. Their name comes from the 1960 film *All the Fine Young Cannibals*, loosely based on the life of trumpeter Chet Baker.

Cannibal Corpse
Tampa, Florida, USA
Bassist Alex Webster just thought Cannibal Corpse was a catchy name. (Fun guy.) The band has been banned variously for cover art, lyrics and live performances. Albums: *Eaten Back to Life, Butchered at Birth, Tomb of the Mutilated, Gallery of Suicide*.

Fast Food Cannibals
Thüringen, Germany
Alternative rock-pop-electro-metal sung primarily in German.

According to *Zine Guide*, they're #2 in the top 500 bands featured in zinedom. **Electric Frankenstein** was formed in 1991 by brothers Sal and Dan Canzonieri (aka Danny Frankenstein) and singer Steve Miller in Whippany, New Jersey. "We came up with the name this way: AC/DC is another name for electricity and the Dead Boys were first named Frankenstein, so we got Electric Frankenstein." Their most recent album is *Burn Bright, Burn Fast!*

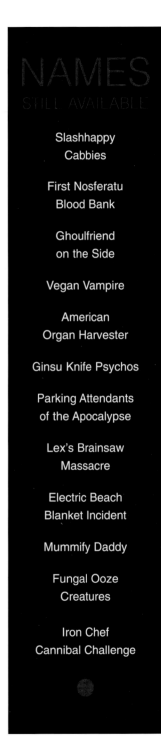

NAMES STILL AVAILABLE

Slashhappy Cabbies

First Nosferatu Blood Bank

Ghoulfriend on the Side

Vegan Vampire

American Organ Harvester

Ginsu Knife Psychos

Parking Attendants of the Apocalypse

Lex's Brainsaw Massacre

Electric Beach Blanket Incident

Mummify Daddy

Fungal Ooze Creatures

Iron Chef Cannibal Challenge

195

Chainsaw Curtis & the Creepers are a hard-working bar band from Footville, Wisconsin. Chainsaw Curtis is guitarist-vocalist Curtis Rodeheaver. The story goes that during a decrescendo chorus of "Mustang Sally" piano player Eddie Lusk introduced the backup band as "The Creepers! The Blues Creepers!" There are said to have been more than 30 Creepers over the years. The 2008 Tour of the Taverns edition of the Creepers features Danny Grayless on bass and Glenn Fischer on drums. Recent album: *Pantloads of Fun*.

Monster Taxi Miami, Florida, USA
Monster Taxi is Jason Klein, creator of neo-disco funk and channeling porno chic with songs like "Boogie Make a Splash" and "Cosmic Love Juice."

Thelonious Monster
Hollywood, California, USA
Thelonious Monk was a monster player. Debut album: *Baby, You're Bummin' My Life Out in a Supreme Fashion*.

Monster Magnet
Red Bank, New Jersey, USA
Previous incarnations as Dog of Mystery and Airplane 75. Took the name Monster Magnet in 1989, from a big red magnet manufactured by the toy company Wham-O in the '60s.

Mummies
San Mateo, California, USA
Garage surf-punk from the late '80s and early '90s. Songs: "That Thing From Venus," "Hairy Mairy." They wear matching tattered mummy costumes on stage. Members also played with the Batmen, the Orange Peels and the Phantom Surfers.

Destroy All Monsters
Ann Arbor, Michigan, USA
Anti-rock noise band started in 1973 by art students. The name comes from the Japanese horror movie *Destroy All Monsters*. There was also a comic book with the same title.

Bizarros
Akron, Ohio, USA
Started in 1976 by the sons of rubber factory workers. Often seen as the forgotten Ohio band.

Siouxsie & the Banshees
London, UK
Sex Pistols groupie and Bromley punk rocker Siouxsie Sioux (Susan Janet Ballion) formed the band with bassist Steven Severin to fill an opening on a Sex Pistols bill. Sid Vicious was the band's first drummer before joining the Sex Pistols as a bassist. Robert Smith of the Cure was a guitarist with the band on several occasions. The name combines Edgar Allan Poe's "Cry of the Banshee" and a tribute to the Sioux tribe, because Siouxsie Sioux hates cowboys.

KILLER BARBIES
Spain
This punk band fronted by singer-guitarist Silvia Superstar (Silvia García Pintos) has starred in two exploitation films by director Jess Franco, *Killer Barbys* and *Killer Barbys vs. Dracula*. Spelling was changed because of Mattel's copyright.

Dead, Grateful or Ungrateful

Dead Dead

Undead Dead

Dead, Grateful or Ungrateful

Dead Dead

The Dead Milkmen

Philadelphia's Dead Milkmen formed in 1983 with Joe Genaro (aka Joe Jack Talcum), Dave Schulthise (aka Dave Blood), Dean Sabatino (aka Dean Clean) and Rodney Linderman (aka Rodney Anonymous).

In Toni Morrison's *Song of Solomon*, the main character, Macon "Milkman" Dead III, derives his nickname from the fact that he was breastfed for far too long. "Joe came up with the band name in high school for a creative writing project, so the name actually existed before the band was a reality. When Dave and Joe started to write songs together, they actually considered the name Hüsker Du."

Key songs: "Taking Retards to the Zoo," "Bitchin' Camaro," "If You Love Somebody, Set Them on Fire," "The Thing That Only Eats Hippies," "Let's Get the Baby High" and their cult hit "Punk Rock Girl." Select albums: *Metaphysical Graffiti*, *Beelzebubba*, *Big Lizard in My Backyard*.

Post-Dead Milkmen bands include Burn Witch Burn, the Cheesies, the Town Managers, Touch Me Zoo, Butterfly Joe, the Low Budgets, and the Big Mess Orchestra.

Curl Up And Die
Las Vegas, Nevada, USA
"At first we were trying to start just like this fake, funny band. Stupid, spooky grindcore stuff. We saw a hair place called Curl Up and Dye, like D-Y-E. We thought that was a pretty funny name, and we changed it to D-I-E."

As I Lay Dying
San Diego, California, USA
They won the Ultimate Metal God award from MTV2 at the first annual "All That Rocks" special and were nominated for a Grammy Award for the song "Nothing Left."

All the Heathers Are Dying
Queens, New York, USA
I know what's killing the Heathers. Don't miss "Cowboatbrain."

A Place to Bury Strangers
Brooklyn, New York, USA
The Washington Post called them "the most ear-shatteringly loud garage/ shoegaze band you'll ever hear." They've opened for Jesus and Mary Chain, Black Rebel Motorcycle Club and Nine Inch Nails.

Rigor Mortis   Dallas, Texas, USA
They played the 2008 Ozzfest in Texas. Guitarist Mike Scaccia has also played with Ministry. Bassist Casey Orr has played with GWAR as the character Beefcake the Mighty.

The Undertakers   Wallasey, UK
Operating across the Mersey from Liverpool in the mid–60s, the Undertakers covered US hits at all the "jive hives."

Funeral Diner formed in 1998 in Half Moon Bay, California, and currently live in San Francisco. The band has toured extensively in Europe, Japan and North America. Their 2005 album, *The Underdark*, was based on Dungeons and Dragons themes. "Musically, it's more spread out, with longer songs and some new sounds, combined with the usual abrasive, screaming assault. The lyrics address the contradictions and personal conflicts that arise from living within a society in decline." Band members are currently involved in Lemonade, …Who Calls So Loud and Sterling Says.

Nottingham, UK's **Teenage Casket Company** was formed in 2004 by ex-members of Panic and China Doll. Guitarist Jamie Derelict: "I always had the idea of Teenage Casket Company being a cool and unique band name to have…I had the whole concept of the coffin with wings logo for years, too. It's what the name of a business would be if they specialized in making coffins for kids." Albums: *Dial It Up* and *Eat Your Heart Out*.

Dr. T. & the Undertakers
Miami, Florida, USA

"One night…I came in with this black bag…Bob Barbara made the comment of how I looked like a doctor carrying that bag…I simply responded, 'Just call me Dr T.' I added the Undertakers from an English group called the Undertakers, who wore black capes and rode English bikes to their gigs."

Funeral Crashers
New York, New York, USA

Formed in 2001, the band predates *Wedding Crashers*, but the name does have a cinematic reference: 1971's *Harold and Maude*, in which young Harold attends funerals of people he did not know. Debut album: *La Fin Absolue du Monde*.

Funeral Dress
Antwerp, Belgium

Formed in 1985 "and living the punk life ever since." Vocalist Dirk lived across from an undertaker and saw people coming and going from funerals every day.

Drive-in Funeral
Lafayette, Louisiana, USA

They clarify: "A drive-in funeral the personification of a lack of shock value the movies we watch, a mirror of our perverted society we all stand aside and try to make sense of it all." Huh?

Obscene Eulogy
Saint John, New Brunswick, Canada

Members are also affiliated with Coffin Birth, Beyond the Goat, Wizzard and Finntroll.

Sepultura
Belo Horizonte, Brazil

Formed in 1984, this was the first Brazilian metal band to have an international following. *Sepultura* is Portugese for *grave*. They chose the name after Max Cavalera translated the lyrics of the Motörhead song "Dancing on Your Grave."

Coffin Break
Seattle, Washington, USA

Centered around Pete Litwin on guitar and Rob Skinner on bass. Litwin went on to form Softy. Skinner formed Popsickle.

Graveland   Wroclaw, Poland

A much darker Graceland. "Epic pagan metal." Albums include *Carpathian Wolves*, *Dawn of Iron Blades*, compilation called *In The Glare Of Burning Churches*.

Headstones
Kingston, Ontario, Canada

Frontman Hugh Dillon who now fronts the Hugh Dillon Redemption Choir. Dillon has acted in a number of films, including *Hard Core Logo*, *Dance Me Outside* and *Trailer Park Boys: The Movie*.

Cemetery Superfly
Arlington, Massachusetts, USA

Began as Supernaut in the 1990s. Reformed as Cemetery Superfly in 2006 and named after a bizarre encounter with a ghost.

Bodysnatchers   London, UK

All-female ska-revival band, 1979–1981.

The Dead Bodies
Shelby Township, Michigan, USA

Albums: *CCCCXX or Cock Cock Cock Cock Xanadu Xanadu* (2008), *Mr. Spookhouse's Pink House* (2007).

Heaps of Dead
Peterborough, Ontario, Canada

Mixing material from their 2007 Crushing Ontario Tour.

Deadsy   Los Angeles, California, USA

Toured with Korn's Family Values Tour. Albums: *Deadsy*, *Commencement*, *Phantasmagore*.

The Deadthings
Saint Kilda, Melbourne, Australia

Formed in 2002 by Leigh Van Hell (guitar) and Julez C. Mephisto (vocals). Lots of tasteless songs about necrophilia, e.g. "Dead Girlz Don't Say No" and "Cemetery Mary." Album: *Dead Over Heels*.

199

The Deadly Deaths
Hamilton, New Zealand
Trio with lots of synths, formed in 2006. Previous bands: Dead Pan Rangers and Nimbus.

Dead Love Junkies
London, UK
Electronica duo of William "Jo Jo Bear" Andrews and Nicole "The Muse" Albarelli, formed in 2007. Songs: "Dead Love Stupid Junkie Girl," "Under My Skin."

Died Pretty
Sydney, Australia
Fronted by guitarist Brett Myers and singer Ron Peno after the breakup of the 31st. An early incarnation of the band was called the Final Solution and included Radio Birdman singer Rob Younger on drums.

Another Dead Juliet
Providence, Rhode Island, USA
"Some say we're a cross between Econochrist and the Refused."

Dead Girls Ruin Everything
Lawrence, Kansas, USA
"Formed from the ashes of Ultimate Fakebook and Podstar."

Dead Elephant Bicycle
Chapel Hill, North Carolina, USA
From the *Guilfordian*: "While singer Dylan Angell's lyrics were compelling, their unflinching bleakness may have been a little draining on the serotonin stores of the average listener…Opting for a kind of funerary minimalism, the musicians didn't so much play their instruments as lament over them. And indeed, as their set limped on, piling one dirge on top of another, members of the audience may have begun to feel as though their psyches were being rolled over repeatedly by, yes, a dead elephant."

Death by Kite
Copenhagen, Denmark
Power-pop trio formed in 2004. Their name appears in a lyric for the song "Scared of Heights."

Dead Peasant Insurance
Cleveland, Ohio, USA
Experimental electro-noise group with album titles such as *Horrible Noise*, *Long Pig* and *Burning Buildings*. "Dead peasant insurance" is a colloquial term for when a corporation takes out insurance on its employees and makes itself the beneficiary.

Death From Above 1979
Toronto, Ontario, Canada
Dance-punk duo of Sebastien Grainger and Jesse F. Keeler. They added 1979 to their name after a legal dispute with DFA Records in New York. (Death From Above was the nickname of LCD Soundsystem's James Murphy before the September 11th attack.) New projects: Les Montagnes and MSTRKRFT.

First Day Dead
Pittsburgh, Pennsylvania, USA
Grindcore and death metal. Album: *Sleep Gardening, The Heavily Relaxed*.

The influence of New Brunswick, New Jersey, band **Deadguy** on modern hardcore and metal was acknowledged in 2006 when their only studio album, *Fixation on a Co-Worker*, was inducted into the *Decibel* magazine Hall of Fame. Members have gone on to play in Human Remains, Kiss It Goodbye, Lifetime, Lord Sterling, No Escape, Playing Enemy and Rorschach. The band was named after a line in the 1991 John Candy movie *Only the Lonely*, about a Chicago policeman who falls in love with a woman who works in a funeral home.

Molten Lava Death Massage was formed by three students at the Hong Kong International School, Indy Shome (guitar, vocals), Andrew Chu (drums) and Ben Gagnon (bass). Shome used school equipment to record their debut album, *Eye of Ra*. School Music Club president Shome recorded, mixed, mastered and produced the entire album, with Gagnon (club vice-president) contributing his artistic skills to the cover design. According the city's premier English paper, the *South China Morning Post,* Molten Lava Death Massage is Hong Kong's best band name.

Theory of a Deadman North Delta, British Columbia, Canada
TOAD was signed to Nickleback frontman Chad Kroeger's label, 604 Records. The band chose its name from the original title of "Last Song," a track penned by leader Tyler Connelly about a man who writes his memoirs before committing suicide.

Grateful Dead
San Francisco, California, USA
Often simply "the Dead" to their faithful fans (Deadheads). Though there is historical debate as to which dictionary and what substance was being imbibed or ingested, the prevailing tale is that Jerry Garcia happened upon the term "grateful dead" in a dictionary and liked its sound and meaning. The rest is a long, strange trip.

Grim Reaper
Droitwich, UK
Formed in 1979 and fronted by singer Steve Grimmett and guitarist Nick Bowcott. From a 1985 interview with Grimmett in *Faces*: "We don't believe in it (Satanism) at all. It frightens me, to be quite honest. I've never really dealt with it or read up on it. It's just a hook...The name Grim Reaper lends itself superbly to a logo, but all the other satanic stuff on the album cover (pentagrams and other symbols of black magic) weren't our idea. In fact, it took me almost two months to find out exactly what they meant." Bowcott went on to write for *Guitar World* and works for the Marshall Amplification company.

NAMES
STILL AVAILABLE

The Dead Dead

Mortal Coil
Shuffle Band

Dead Talented

Funeral Homies

The Three
Casketeers

Who's Dead

Pulseless in Seattle

Penny for
Your Eyelids

The Undertaker's
Drawers

Sans Serif
Headstones

The Hearse Chasers

Six Feet Blunder

The Zombies

Formed in 1964 in St. Albans, Hertfordshire, UK, this British Invasion band was fronted by St. Albans Grammar School friends Colin Blunstone (lead vocals), with main songwriters Rod Argent (keyboards, vocals) and Chris White (bass, vocals). They all planned to go off to college but on a whim entered a local band contest sponsored by the *London Evening Post* and won a recording contract with Decca.

They chose their name for the competition. Chris White: "We chose it from desperation." Colin Blunstone: "My first reaction was horror. We did have alternatives, like Chatterley & the Gamekeepers, but we were desperate."

The band's first single, "She's Not There," was also their biggest hit. Other hits include "Time of the Season" and "Tell Her No."

Blunstone went on to join the Alan Parsons project and also released solo albums.

Argent and White continued under the band name Argent.

In 2008, to mark the 40th anniversary of the album *Odessey & Oracle*, the four surviving band members played the album live in a three-night concert series at London's Shepherd's Bush Empire Theatre.

Undead Dead

Am I Dead Yet
Belgium
Played their screamo tunes for 21 shows then died (as a band, anyway).

Buried and Still Breathing
Strafford, New Hampshire, USA
Formed by members of Cipher Zero, they similarly played a few shows and disintegrated.

Dead or Alive
Liverpool, UK
Formed in 1980, they are best known for their #1 UK single "You Spin Me Round (Like a Record)." Singer Pete Burns appeared on the TV show *Celebrity Big Brother*.

Buried Twice
Quad Cities Area, Iowa, USA
Death-metal with the toetag: "Brutal as brutal can be." Songs: "Dead Alive," "Mass Grave Pit," and "The Night Evelyn Came Out of the Grave."

Undead
New Milford, New Jersey, USA
Formed by Bobby Steele (guitar, vocals) after he was kicked out of the Misfits.

Born Dead Icons
Montreal, Quebec, Canada
Late '90s hardcore punk released on Dead Alive Records.

Hollywood Undead
Los Angeles, California, USA
"Donning bone-chilling masks so that their strapping good looks cannot take away from their musical artistry."

One Man Army
& the Undead Quartet
Gothenburg, Sweden
Albums: *21st Century Killing Machine*, *Error in Evolution* and *Grim Tales*. Founder Johan Lindstrand: "The band name is basically action meets horror. I'm very fond of the old *Rambo* movies. I think if you see the cover it's the beast that arises. You can see the One Man Army, the Rambo figure with its followers."

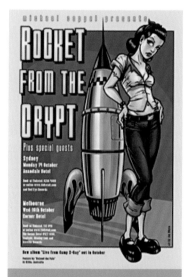

San Diego, California, singer-guitarist John Reis formed both **Rocket From the Crypt** and Drive Like Jehu in 1990 following the breakup of his band Pitchfork. Rocket From the Crypt is perhaps Reis's most commercially successful creation. The band derived its name from '70s Cleveland punks Rocket From the Tombs. RFTC went through several lineup changes but produced seven studio albums and a "farewell" live CD/DVD, the latter released in 2008.

"Finally, after years of clawing at the lids of their caskets, they are fully risen and walking among us. *Boneyard Lullabies* is a collection of shroud-pleasing tunes inspired by the real-death experiences of **Nick Noxious**... Horror fans familiar with Glenn Chadbourne's art will recognize the cast of characters and the landscapes they inhabit. Music fans will appreciate the wacky musical shenanigans of **the Necrophiliacs**..." As featured on Dr. Demento.

Dead Disco Leeds, UK
This all-female trio started in art school in 2005. They claim that the name just came out of words in a hat. Metric has a 2003 song called "Dead Disco," as does the Finnish band Lapko.

Dead Can Dance
Melbourne, Australia
Duo of Brendan Perry and Lisa Gerrard formed in 1981, moved to London. "To understand why we chose the name, think of the transformation of inanimacy to animacy. Think of the processes concerning life from death and death into life. So many people missed the inherent symbolism and assumed that we must be 'morbid gothic types,' a mistake we deplored and deplore."

School for the Dead
Northampton, Massachusetts, USA
Formed in 2001 and named after frontman Henning Ohlenbusch's debut solo recording. Bands members also have played in the Maggies, New Radiant Storm King, the Aloha Steamtrain, the Mammals, the Gay Potatoes, Lo Fine, the Figments, King Radio, Spanish for Hitchhiking, the Tea Lights, and Humbert.

The Deadutantes
San Francisco, California, USA
All-female psychobilly quartet. Members went on to play in Bad Shit and Drink Skate Destroy.

Brunch of the Living Dead
Brooklyn, New York, USA
NYC scene band featuring guitarist Sara Landeau of the Slips. *Brunch of the Living Dead* is also the title of a 2006 short film.

Dead Hooker Bridge Club
Miami, Florida, USA
Song: "Hung Like a Whale."

Abra Cadaver
Wellington, New Zealand
Meanwhile, north of the equator, four or five bands by this magical name terrorize US bars and clubs. The Hives' 2004 album, *Tyrannosaurus Hives*, has a song by this title.

Thundercorpse Akron, Ohio, USA
"Why the name Thundercorpse? Because 'the Beatles' was already taken! We're two guys that hated our normal jobs so we just decided to rock! "

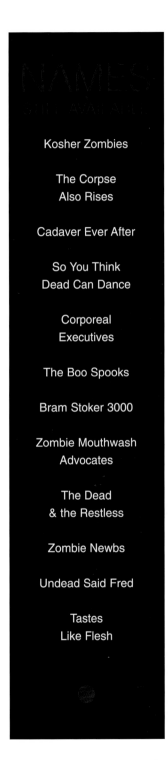

NAMES
STILL AVAILABLE

Kosher Zombies

The Corpse
Also Rises

Cadaver Ever After

So You Think
Dead Can Dance

Corporeal
Executives

The Boo Spooks

Bram Stoker 3000

Zombie Mouthwash
Advocates

The Dead
& the Restless

Zombie Newbs

Undead Said Fred

Tastes
Like Flesh

White Zombie
New York City, New York, USA
Formed in 1985 and led by singer Rob Zombie (aka Rob Straker, born Rob Cummings), who started as an illustrator. Named after the 1932 film *White Zombie*, starring Béla Lugosi.

The Amazombies
Seattle, Washington, USA
Female-fronted pop-punk trio started by bassist Noriko Kaji in 2000. Album: *Bitches & Stitches*.

Lord Groovy & the Psychedelic Zombiez Denver, Colorado, USA
This jam band has opened for Primus, the Spin Doctors and the Wallflowers.

Sabertooth Zombie
San Francisco, California, USA
"In the summer of 2004, a five-headed hydra was formed...Each head possessed...its own vile skill that enables Sabertooth Zombie to penetrate flesh and strike its sonic venom to the bone."

Fake Shark, Real Zombie!
Vancouver, British Columbia, Canada
The name is a reference to Lucio Fulci's 1979 film, *Zombi 2*, in which a shark and a zombie engage in combat. The band has a following and a record deal in Japan.

Zombie Girl
Edmonton, Alberta, Canada
A husband-and-wife duo whose second album, *Blood, Brains and Rock 'N' Roll,* was delayed when four separate printing companies refused to print artwork that contained copious amounts of blood and a brain on a plate.

Sydney, Australia's **Zombie Ghost Train** mixes '50s rockabilly and with '70s punk attitude, "zombified" clothes and freaky makeup. "Zombie Ghost Train are one of Australian rock's best-kept secrets. A powerhouse psychobilly band with a world-wide following...Zombie Ghost Train get their audience into a positive uproar, a must-see for any punters who like their live music rocking." Albums *Glad Rags & Body Bags, Dealing the Death Card* and *Monster Formal Wear.*

Zombie Prom Queen
Wellington, New Zealand
Lo-fi trash-blues duo of Tangent Precipitate and Voodoo T. Savage. Also affiliated with the Insatiable Opium Cowboys.

The Zombie Valentines
Madrid, Spain
Retro '60s rock group formed in 2005. Their surf song "Tormento" appeared on the compilation *Bikini Beat Vol. 2.*

Zombie Apocalypse
New York City, New York, USA
Zombiecore. They split an EP with Leeds-based Send More Paramedics. *Zombie Apocalypse* was the title of a 1998 album by NYC band Mortician.

Zombie Bazooka Patrol
Nashville, Tennessee, USA
Folk-punk in zombie makeup. Song: "Better Off Undead."

Bulimic Zombie Choir
Nijmegen, Gelderland, Netherlands
Song: "Zombistafari" (reggae tune about weed-smoking zombies).

Traffic Jam Zombies
Indianapolis, Indiana, USA
Short-lived quartet that formed from the remnants of Furnished Souls for Rent.

Zombiedaddys Örebro, Sweden
"Four zombies wake up at the local cemetery...After the killing and brain-eating they decide to start a band."

Zombies Ate My Neighbors
Dayton, Ohio, USA
A very aggressive band named after a Sega video game, released in 1993, in which teenagers have to kill vampires, demons, werewolves and zombies in a suburban setting.

Zombina & the Skeletones
Liverpool, England, UK
B-movie themes with Theremin and saxophones, featuring Zombina, Doc Horror, Kyle K'thulu, Ben Digo and X-Ray Speck.

Punch-Outs

Blow-Ups

Poisons

Popular Weaponry

Weapon of Choice
California, USA

Lonnie "Meganut" Marshall's Fishbone-esque collective of edgy, costumed funkateers came from the breakup of Marshall Law. Brother Arik Marshall briefly joined the Red Hot Chili Peppers, replacing guitarist John Frusciante.

A Is for Automatic Weapons
Norwich, UK

Well-armed screamo. Song: "Slay the Dragon."

Guns N'Roses
Los Angeles, California, USA

Tracii Guns' L.A. Guns and Axl Rose's Hollywood Roses melded in March 1985. All three L.A. Guns who joined GN'R soon quit and were replaced by Duff McKagan (bass), Slash (guitar) and Steven Adler (drums). After almost a decade of hits, hugely popular videos and record-setting tours, members left for such side projects as Slash's Snakepit and the Neurotic Outsiders, leaving Axl to work on his ten-year album project, *Chinese Democracy*.

Killing Joke

London's Killing Joke was formed in 1979 by Jaz Coleman (vocals, keyboards) and Geordie Walker (guitars). According to Coleman, their manifesto was to "define the exquisite beauty of the atomic age in terms of style, sound and form."

Their initial foray into primitive punk grew increasingly denser and more aggressive, edging toward metal. Bands such as Nirvana, Ministry, Nine Inch Nails, Tool, Metallica, Soundgarden, Foo Fighters, Faith No More and Korn have all acknowledged the influence of Killing Joke on their own music.

At press time, Killing Joke were set for a world tour that would see the band reunited in their original lineup and playing two nights per venue. At each stop, the first concert will feature a performance of their first two albums *Killing Joke* and *What's THIS For...!* in their entirety; on the second night they will perform the album *Pandemonium* as well as early singles. Killing Joke has released 13 albums to date.

WEAPON SHOP, the duo of Mysterious Hannigan and Obadiah Crumbwitty, disseminate their music from America's Pacific Northwest. The name Weapon Shop comes from the book *Weapon Shops of Isher* by science-fiction author A.E. van Vogt. According to Crumbwitty, "In the libertarian-leaning story, the idea of the Shops is that any man has the right of self defense, even against the imperial state. The shops even provide an alternative legal system to bypass the corrupt imperial system."

COCKED 'N LOADED

Formed in Alliston Rock City, Massachusetts, in 2003 and named for the platinum-selling L.A. Guns album *Cocked & Loaded*. Joel Simches, *The Noise* [Boston]: "Don't look for any deep meaning here. Just knock back some Jagermeister and rock the fuck out. Otherwise, you'll get a pool cue up the back of your head and a knee to the groin. This ain't music for chardonnay-sipping, politically correct, ponytailed pussyboys. This is real rock for real men…Yow!"

The Gun Club
Los Angeles, California, USA
The Gun Club was formed by Jeffrey Lee Pierce, singer-guitarist and former head of the Blondie fan club in Los Angeles; guitarist Brian Tristan, who later renamed himself Kid Congo Powers; bassist Don Snowden, a music critic for the *Los Angeles Times*; and drummer Brad Dunning. The group was initially called the Creeping Ritual. The name the Gun Club was suggested by Circle Jerks singer Keith Morris.

Guns N' Wankers UK
Formed by former members of Snuff (punk) and the Wildhearts (rock). Broke up when Snuff reformed. Other members went on to the Hormones and Dogpiss.

Armed & Hammered
Toronto, Ontario, Canada
Formed in 1989 by singer Mopa Dean, bassist for goth band Masochistic Religion. Dean left in 2000 to form the G-Men. Arm & Hammer is a brand of baking soda. Armand Hammer was a 20th-century American industrialist.

L.A. Guns
Los Angeles, California, USA
Glam-metal band formed in 1983 by guitarist Tracii Guns (Tracy Ulrich). Singer Michael Jagosz went to prison for a while and was briefly replaced by Axl Rose, before Rose left to form Hollywood Rose. The two bands combined in 1985 to become Guns N'Roses, but Tracii and Axl fought until Tracii left to reform L.A. Guns. These Guns have performed and recorded, with and without their founder, and scrapped over rights to the band name for over two decades. Members have also played in Dogs D'Amour, Girl, W.A.S.P., Contraband, Bang Tango and Brides of Destruction.

A Girl A Gun A Ghost
Savannah, Georgia, USA
Often conveniently abbreviated to AGAGAG. Song titles are pretty long too. Play fast, write long?

Warm Guns
Los Angeles, California, USA
Happiness is a warm gun, mama. "Probably the most unique aspect of the Warm Guns is that the lead singer [Lewis Carlino] is paralyzed from the waist down and lives his life, writes the music, and performs in a wheelchair."

207

Itchy Trigger Finger
Kilkenny, Ireland

"Itchy Trigger Finger are the only metal act in Kilkenny to have received arts funding for two years in succession."

Orange 9mm
New York City, New York, USA

Formed in 1994 after the breakup of Burn. A number of firearms take 9mm cartridges: Glock 17, Beretta M9, Beretta 92FS, Smith & Wesson Sigma, Uzi….

Magnum Birmingham, UK
Started as the house band for Birmingham's Rum Runner club (a gig later held by Duran Duran). Magnum has had several UK chart hits, both albums and singles, and despite a hiatus from 1995-2001, they have been performing and recording since 1972.

Velvet Revolver California, USA
Often considered Slash's *new* band, Velvet Revolver is a supergroup whose ranks have included former members of Guns N'Roses, Stone Temple Pilots, Wasted Youth, the Infectious Grooves and Silverchair. Slash hangs with people who have a thing for gun-related band names.

Celibate Rifles Sydney, Australia
Rolling Stone's David Fricke said of their 1986 album, *The Turgid Miasma of Existence*: "At a time when most punk outrage is just witless spleen at 90 mph, these Aussie spitfires have fired off a release that shakes with lyric force and experimental valor, not just speed and volume." They've released 14 studio albums.

Popgun is a fiery Oslo-based power trio. Bassist-vocalist Egil Stemkens: "The idea was to come up with a name that would tell people what the music was all about. We're the kind of guys who don't go off until that Fender Twin or Hiwatt amp is really struggling and that pure sonic heart-/gut-purified energy is really showing off! I think the name Popgun says it all: We combine a good melody line with kick-ass attitude." Their debut album, *A Day in a Day and a Half*, was released in 2006. Their most recent effort is *Manic Anti-Depressive*.

Thirty Ought Six
Columbus, Ohio, USA

Named after a cartridge for a powerful rifle. Latest album: *Amazing Attractions for Rebellion*.

The Bang Bang Heartbreak, UK
At age 18, conjoined twins Tom and Barry Howe landed with music impresario Zak Bedderwick, who trained them in secret as musicians and performers. An American documentary filmmaker captured the Bang Bang's progress, including them rehearsing their signature song, "Two Way Romeo." This is a rock story with a bizarre twist: exploitation, punk angst, alcohol, drugs, a love interest, and ultimately death as Tom attempted to rid himself of his brother. Existing recordings reveal a band that was punk before punk.

Bang Bang Bang
Washington, DC, USA

"Unlike Spinal Tap, the knobs on their amps do not go to 11. It's the tequila in the veins that give Bang Bang Bang that extra edge…."

Biff Bang Pow! London, UK
Glasgow's Alan McGee left Laughing Apple to move to London, where he started Biff Bang Pow!, a name taken from the title of a song by the Creation, one of his favorite bands.

The Blasters
Downey, California, USA

Founded by brothers Dave and Phil Alvin in 1979. Phil: "I thought Joe Turner's backup band on Atlantic Records…were the Blues Blasters. I just took the 'Blues' off…."

Bullet for My Valentine
Bridgend, Wales

Originally called themselves 12 Pints of My Girlfriend's Blood and later Jeff Killed John. They eventually settled on Bullet for My Valentine because "it's a name which refers to fictional evil yet loving lyrical content."

Bullets & Romance
Vacaville, California, USA

Former name: Gooser. Headlined the Sacramento "Jammies" three years while still in high school.

Bullets Over Broad
Philadelphia, Pennsylvania, USA

Members have gone on to play in the End of Radio and Riding Bikes in Venice. *Bullets Over Broadway* is the title of a 1994 film by Woody Allen.

36 Crazy Fists
Anchorage, Alaska, USA

The title of a 1977 Jackie Chan movie.

Blam Blam Blam
Auckland, New Zealand
The band had two hit singles in 1981: "There is No Depression in New Zealand" and "Don't Fight It Marsha, It's Bigger Than Both of Us."

Art of Fighting
Melbourne, Australia
A series of video games developed in the early 1990s. The band's recent album is *Runaways*.

Brawl Park
Brockton, Massachusetts, USA
"Major League hardcore at its best." Pummeling barre chords and baseball motifs.

Fisticuffs Bluff
Santa Cruz, California, USA
A short-lived band with the single "Leap Year Myths."

Five Knuckle Chuckle
Orangeville, Ontario, Canada
Mid-90s hardcore band that began as Noah Fence. The term "five-knuckle chuckle" refers to male masturbation.

Digital Knife
Portland, Oregon, USA
Album: *Mini-Van Nation*. Songs: "God Hates Straight Lines," "They Call Me Macadamia."

Daggers Manchester, UK
Young band doing a convincing job of reinventing '80s synth-pop. *New Musical Express*: "Brilliant...If there's any justice in the world, the Gary Numan-goosing, skyscraping electro-rock of 'After Midnight' and 'Magazine' will fill stadiums one day."

Shonen Knife Osaka, Japan
This all-female band has also performed as a tribute band called the Osaka Ramones.

Young Knives
Ashby, Leicestershire, UK
A play on "young knaves," found in a book they were thumbing through.

Crochetd Machete
Madison, Wisconsin, USA
"Super fun happy fact: Our name comes from one of Andrew's guitar student's mothers, who said if she ever had a band she'd name it Crocheted Machete. We liked it and removed an 'e'."

Bomb
San Francisco, California, USA
This mid-80s queercore band contributed a track entitled "B/E/A/F/A/G" to the 1990 compilation *J.D.s Top Ten Homocore Hit Parade*.

Detroit's **Dirtbombs** were formed as a side project by Mick Collins of the Gories in 1992. The band has been through 17 lineups since its inception. In September 2006, *Spin* magazine listed the Dirtbombs at #10 in their list of "Top 25 Live Bands Now" issue. The band has opened for acts such as Blondie, Mudhoney and Radio Birdman and have shared a bill with Blue Cheer.

Brainbombs Sweden
Greg Chapman for *Ugly American*: "The Brainbombs must lace their snuff riffs with devil dust because they have the insidious ability to infect your consciousness with an unrivaled vileness."

Hate Bombs Orlando, Florida, USA
At a cocktail party, Ken Chiodini's wife claimed a pair of catty women were lobbing "invisible hate bombs" at her.

Mad Bomber Society
Edmonton, Alberta, Canada
The Mad Bomber Society was formed in Edmonton in 1997 by Rich Bomber. Debut album: *Atomic A-Go-Go*.

Hollowpoint
"Following in the footsteps of their 2004 critically acclaimed release *Dust & Blood*, Hollowpoint's *Bait and Switch* does not miss a beat. Hailing from Tampa Bay, Florida, Hollowpoint features the strong vocals of bassist Todd Miller, the searing intensity of guitarist Shane Laughridge, and the rock-solid workhorse drumming of Tony Wysk."

A-Bomb Chop Shop
Chicago, Illinois, USA
Album: *From the Coffin to the Rave*.

This Bike Is a Pipe Bomb
Pensacola, Florida, USA
People have actually been held for questioning and entire city blocks cordoned off as the result of fans pasting promotional stickers on their bicycles. The band would have us know, "This Bike Is a Pipe Bomb is staunchly opposed to war."

Big Audio Dynamite
London, UK
Formed in 1983 by ex-Clash singer-guitarist Mick Jones. Their 1985 debut: *This Is Big Audio Dynamite*.

The lead singer's name is Slink Moss. He wanted to call the band Black Cat Rocket, after the fireworks brand, to suggest that the music was explosive. The band agreed to add Explosion to their name so that Slink could have his fireworks. "**Slink Moss Explosion** is an original group that seeks to infuse old country and blues with modern energy. It's new gunpowder in an old gun...We take the roots and make them fresh green leaves."

The Slow Poisoner
ANDREW GOLDFARB, SAN FRANCISCO: "I got my band name from a book entitled *A Memoir of Extraordinary Popular Delusions and the Madness of Crowds*, written by Charles Mackay in 1841. He has chapters on various incidents of public hysteria, including one called 'The Slow Poisoners' about a rash of poisonings, by incremental means, in France in the 1700s (wives were doing in their husbands; it became something of a fad). I thought this would be an over-the-top name for a band. For ten years, I led a group called the Slow Poisoners, but over that time we diminished from a quartet down to a duo, and when the last member other than myself finally disappeared, I simply scratched the 's' off the end of all our merchandise and soldiered on as a one-man band!"

HiFi Handgrenades
Detroit, Michigan, USA
Formed after the breakup of the Fags. Founder John Speck wanted to create "an honest, no-frills band echoing the melodic sound of the Descendents and Dagnasty, combined with the attitude of midwestern greats such as *Stink*-era Replacements and Naked Raygun."

The Boom
Boston, Massachusetts, USA
Formed in 1979 from the remnants of Kid Sonic & the Boom. In 1981 the Boom released their only single, "Nancy Packs a Piece," the cover for which depicted a likeness of first lady Nancy Reagan holding a .44 magnum.

Killswitch Engage
Westfield, Massachusetts, USA
The band came from the breakup of Overcast and Aftershock. "Killswitch... is like turning everything off. Like if someone's hand gets caught in something in a metal-working shop, the foreman will press one button that will turn off the machines."

Kill Switch...Klick
Seattle, Washington, USA
Sebasstian [sic] is said to have come up with the name while working at Microsoft as "a landscape grunt." The mower started to sputter and he thought, *Better hit the kill switch*. "This was at the same time Jeffrey Dahmer was all over the news...A random thought of Dahmer with a switch on the side of his head marked 'Kill' came to me...What if Dahmer had a Kill Switch that went 'Klick' and he instantly changed into the strange creature he eventually became."

Poison
Los Angeles, California, USA
Formed in Pennsylvania in 1983 under the name Paris. They moved to Los Angeles in 1984. The name Poison came about when they heard a group of protesting parents say that rock music was "poisoning" the lives of their children.

Crimes & Punishments

It Was My Evil Twin

I Fought the Law
and the Law Threw the Switch

Crimes

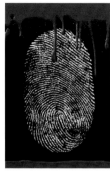

The Raconteurs

The Raconteurs officially raconteur out of Nashville, but the idea for the band gelled when Detroit friends Jack White (White Stripes) and Brendan Benson got together and wrote "Steady, As She Goes." Buzzed by that collaboration, they soon added Greenhornes' bassist Jack Lawrence and drummer Patrick Keeler and began disappearing into Benson's home studio at every available opportunity until they had their debut album, *Broken Boy Soldiers*. Based on the band's pedigree and radio's enthusiasm for the "Steady, As She Goes" single, the album entered the UK charts at #2 and the US charts at #7.

Though the band's second album, *Consolers of the Lonely*, and the single "Salute Your Solution" were announced only a week before their simultaneous release — depriving reviewers of their usual advance listen — the album's success paralleled that of its predecessor.

In the Australian market, the Raconteurs are known as the Saboteurs, as a Queensland band already holds the name Raconteurs.

It Was My Evil Twin

The Vagrants
Melbourne, Australia
The Vagrants got their name from a life on the road, playing festivals and clubs in Australia, New Zealand, Germany, Holland, Denmark, Scotland, England, Spain, Switzerland, Norway, Sweden, the US and Canada.

The Outlaws
London, UK
This instrumental group was formed by producer Joe Meek in 1960 as the backing band for the Mike Berry recording *Set Me Free*.

The Prowlers
Montreal, Quebec, Canada
An Oi! band formed in 1998, the Prowlers pay tribute to Montreal bands such as the Discords and Drunken Skinheads.

Robbers on High Street
New York City, New York, USA
Their name came from a lyric in an early discarded composition. Albums: *Tree City* and *Grand Animals*.

The Grifters
Memphis, Tennessee, USA
The band formed in the late 1980s as A Band Called Bud. After a minor lineup change in 1990, they renamed themselves the Grifters, after the novel by Jim Thompson.

Grand Theft Canoe
Winnipeg, Manitoba, Canada
Art-rock featuring drummer Sean Allum of Duotang.

BMX Bandits
Glasgow, Scotland
Formed in 1986 out of the ashes of the Pretty Flowers, BMX Bandits also shared members with Teenage Fanclub and the Soup Dragons. The band takes its name from the title of a 1983 Australian film. Kurt Cobain claimed on a New York radio show that if he could be in any other band it would be BMX Bandits.

Professor Murder
New York City, New York, USA
They released their debut EP, *Professor Murder Rides the Subway*, in 2006. In comedy sketches on the HBO TV series *Mr. Show*, Professor Murder is involved in the East Coast ventriloquists' feud with the West Coast ventriloquists, mimicking the regional divide in the world of rap music.

Slayer
Huntington Park, California, USA
Their 1986 release, *Reign in Blood*, has been called "the heaviest album of all time." Often credited as one of the "Big Four" thrash-metal bands, along with Metallica, Anthrax and Megadeth.

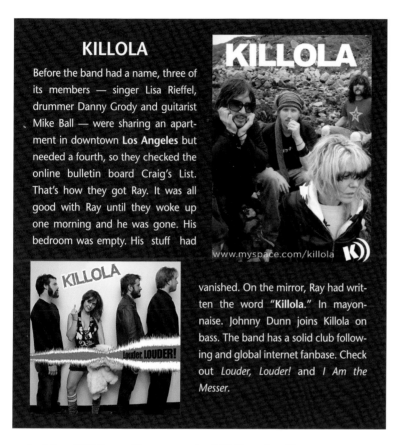

KILLOLA

Before the band had a name, three of its members — singer Lisa Rieffel, drummer Danny Grody and guitarist Mike Ball — were sharing an apartment in downtown **Los Angeles** but needed a fourth, so they checked the online bulletin board Craig's List. That's how they got Ray. It was all good with Ray until they woke up one morning and he was gone. His bedroom was empty. His stuff had

www.myspace.com/killola

vanished. On the mirror, Ray had written the word **"Killola."** In mayonnaise. Johnny Dunn joins Killola on bass. The band has a solid club following and global internet fanbase. Check out *Louder, Louder!* and *I Am the Messer.*

...And You Will Know Us by the Trail of Dead
Austin, Texas, USA

According to the band's website, their name is taken from an ancient Mayan ritual chant. However, this may be an in-joke. The chief creative elements of the band are Jason Reece and Conrad Keely. The two switch between drumming and lead vocals and guitar, both on their records and during their shows. The band is often simply called Trail of Dead.

Die Cheerleader Die
Baltimore, Maryland, USA

Die Cheerleader Die was formed in the winter of 1999. Album: *Down with the Pom Poms, Up with the Skirts.*

Kill Cheerleadër
Toronto, Ontario, Canada

Nikki Sixx of Mötley Crüe called them the "best new band" in his online journal. Lemmy from Motörhead declared Kill Cheerleadër the "greatest rock 'n' roll band since Guns N'Roses."

Kill Hannah
Chicago, Illinois, USA

The band is named after singer-songwriter Mat Devine's ex-girlfriend. Devine was singing and playing guitar in a band called In a Jar UK. After the fallout with Hannah, Devine printed up "Kill Hannah" stickers to place on In a Jar UK records.

NAMES STILL AVAILABLE

Counting Infractions

Loan Shark
Feeding Frenzy

Pickpocket Pinch

The Mink Stole

Counterfeit
Air Miles

Melany's Felony

The Whackjob
Hitpersons

Mascots
Who Murder

Homicidal
Bridal Party

Rob the Verb

Stabbing
Chestward

213

ANGRY JOHNNY & THE KILLBILLIES

Bloodgrass music from "Killville" (Easthampton), Massachusetts. Do visit the Killville Historical Museum of the Strange. Angry Johnny has released numerous solo and band recordings. Albums include *Putting the Voodoo on Monroe, Hankenstein, Where's Your Jesus Now?* and *Killville Tales*. The Killbillies include Sal Vega on drums, Jimmy Ratfink on bass and Goatis T. Ovenrude on mandolin, banjo and guitar.

The Killers
Las Vegas, Nevada, USA
Brandon Flowers decided not to relocate to Los Angeles with his previous band, Blush Response. He met David Keuning by responding to a newspaper ad. The name "The Killers" appears on the bass drum of a band in a New Order video for their song "Crystal."

The Kills
UK/US
Singer Alison "VV" Mosshart was in the Florida band Discount, and Jamie "Hotel" Hince was in the British rock bands Scarfo and Blyth Power. The duo met when Mosshart heard Hince practicing in the hotel room above hers. First recorded as VV & Hotel.

Raging Pimps of Doom
Thompsonville, Illinois, USA
Young guys playing ska and pop-punk like raging pimps. Highly compelling. Adding "of Doom" to your name is always a good idea.

Pimps Delite
Stockholm, Sweden
An 8-piece band that pimps a chocolate cake recipe on their MySpace page.

The Stabs
Melbourne, Australia
Self-description: "Think of an angrier, fuzzier Mudhoney and you'll be in close proximity."

Rough Trade
Toronto, Ontario, Canada
The band began in 1968, when Carole Pope and Kevan Staples began performing as "O." In 1970 they changed their name to the Bullwhip Brothers. In 1975 the band expanded and became Rough Trade. Their first album, *Avoid Freud*, stirred controversy with its lesbian-themed single "High School Confidential."

Hack

The Iranian electro-rock band Hack was started in Tehran in 2001 by singer-guitarist Moni Safikhani. The band's lyrics are derived from contemporary Iranian poet Mehradad Fallah's books *Becoming Crow Again* and *About Me*. The band's music has drawn comparisons to Depeche Mode. Synthesizers and production are by Shahram Sharbaf of the Iranian alternative band O-Hum.

Punishments

I Fought the Law and the Law Threw the Switch

The Police
London, UK

Founded by drummer Stewart Copeland, whose father worked for the CIA. Stewart named his band the Police before recruiting the other members. The band's bleached-blonde hair, a trademark, came about when they were asked to do a Wrigley's chewing gum commercial but had to appear as blondes. Short of cash, they complied.

Officer Jones & His Patrol Car Problems Diest, Belgium

The band has put the patrol car in the garage and turned in their badges, "but the gun's a keeper." Rise & Fall, Engine of Doom and Fallen helped them say goodbye.

Officer Flossie
Gainesville, Florida, USA

Frontman Donnie Marsh: "Officer Flossie is the name of a minor character in the children's book *Cars and Trucks and Things That Go* by Richard Scarry. I used to make my dad read it to me all the time when I was five."

Nicole Willis & the Soul Investigators
Finland

MOJO magazine made their debut album, *Keep Reachin' Up*, its Urban Album of the Month.

Female Bureau of Investigation
New York City, New York, USA

Started as an all-female horn band, now fronted by singer King Solomon.

Ben Harper & the Innocent Criminals

Ben Harper's grandparents ran the Folk Music Center and Museum in Claremont, California. While other teenage boys were into heavy metal, he was working out slide-guitar licks. Blues legend Taj Mahal took him on tour at age 20.

Harper's career is built on music with a message. His lyrics portray a strong social conscience, and he has been a vocal advocate for grassroots political action in recent US elections. Album titles such as *Fight for Your Mind*, *The Will to Live*, *Burn to Shine*, *Diamonds on the Inside*, *There Will Be Light* and, most recently, *Lifeline*, reflect equal parts struggle and hope.

Harper and his Innocent Criminals enjoy huge popularity in Europe, and the French edition of *Rolling Stone* named him Artist of the Year in 2003.

On the name of his band, Harper has said, "The Innocent Criminals is the name of my band. Innocent Criminal is the name of my publishing society...In the United States, you are presumed innocent before being declared guilty, but generally, if you are Black, you are not necessarily guilty, but you are certainly an innocent criminal — you are suspect."

Joan as Police Woman

Joan as Police Woman is Brooklyn-based Joan Wasser's band with bassist Rainy Orteca and drummer Parker Kindred. Wasser is an accomplished singer and multi-instrumentalist whose previous bands include the Dam Builders, Black Beetle and Those Bastard Souls. Full-length albums: *Real Life* and *To Survive*.

Tokyo Police Club is based in Newmarket, Ontario, Canada. The band broke big in Montreal and since 2005 has played Pop Montreal, Edgefest, Coachella, Lollapalooza, Bumbershoot and Glastonbury. Their name comes from a lyric in the first song on their *A Lesson in Crime* EP. However, in a Gothamist.com interview, they offered this explanation to fans: "A study was conducted to find out if a band's name can correlate to their success. And so a computer formula took all the results of the study – what words showed up most frequently in successful bands' names – and generated the ultimate fame-ensuring name: Tokyo Police Club. The second choice was Madonna Jackson Pac."

Interpol
New York City, New York, USA
Sources say they played an early gig at NYC's Luna Lounge as Cuddleworthy. A *Spin* magazine article suggested that the name Interpol came as a result of one of singer-guitarist Paul Banks' classmates chanting, "Paul, Paul, Interpol," pronouncing the name Paul as "Pol."

Receiving End of Sirens
Boston, Massachusetts, USA
Drummer Andrew Cook: "A bunch of police cars and ambulances went screaming by and the name popped in my head. Like, thinking about how people never really think what's 'on the receiving end of sirens,' because it's such a common thing just to hear the sirens…It can [also] be taken as the Greek mythology example with the Sirens that lure sailors in with their singing, so being on the receiving end of those sirens isn't a great thing. It works both ways."

The Perpetrators
Winnipeg, Manitoba, Canada
Often called "the Perps." Tagline: "Blues for people who hate blues." Sue Foley has called them her favorite band. Albums: *The Gas & the Clutch* and *Tow Truck*.

Warrant
Hollywood, California, USA
This glam-hair-metal group's 1989 debut album, *Dirty Rotten Filthy Stinking Rich*, went double platinum, as did the 1990 follow-up, *Cherry Pie*. For a trashy flashback, view that album's eponymous single on YouTube.

Under Suspicion, featuring the mighty Suicide Horns, is one of Minneapolis–St. Paul's premiere R&B bands. Powered by two female vocalists, as well as the voice and guitar of Paul Holland, the band has played clubs, concerts, festivals and opened for national touring bands. *Guilty* is their 1997 CD.

The Accüsed
Oak Harbor, Washington, USA
Comes with metal-approved umlauts. They play something called "crossover thrash."

Alibi for a Murder
Warendorf, Germany
"Alibi for a Murder stands for vigorous, brutal metalcore, characterized by riffs full of pressure combined with deadly sweet melodies."

Stockton, California's **Blameshifters** offer up their punk blast of political dissent on 2007's *Disenfranchised Anarchist*. Guitarist Mat Loman: "The Blameshifters were spawned out of irony…From citizens to politicians, guilty/responsible is the one thing no one will admit to being, yet it's something everyone is."

Five Star Prison Cell comes from Melbourne, Australia. (A country colonized by convicts should know a good prison cell when they hear one.) Their debut album, *The Complete First Season*, and subsequent tour won the band the MusicOz award for Best Metal/Hardcore Act in 2006. Their follow-up album is the recently released *Slaves of Virgo*.

Justice France
The electronic music duo of Gaspard Augé and Xavier de Rosnay. Their debut album was nominated for a Grammy and was on *Blender*'s "25 Best Albums of 2007" list.

As Your Attorney
Denver, Colorado, USA
Previously called Trial by Fire, "but we felt As Your Attorney was more original."

The High Court
Mount Holly, New Jersey, USA
It's all in the acronym: THC. As in the active ingredient in marijuana.

Secret Trial Five Vancouver,
British Columbia, Canada
All-female punk band fronted by Muslim — and openly lesbian — singer Sena Hussain. They take their name from a group of Canadian Muslims being held on suspicion of terrorism.

The Inmates
North London, UK
Formed in 1977. Robert Plant is said to have called the band's original singer, Bill Hurley, "the best British singer."

Jail Weddings
Los Angeles, California, USA
Ten members, including three lead singers. Sounds like: "A heated argument in a car parked on Lover's Leap, where everyone wins while the Shangri-Las and Flesheaters blare through blown speakers. The most embarrassing diary in the world somehow gets left behind at the scene of the crime. Coppers laugh and cry simultaneously...Narrated by Henry Miller, brought to you in part by Bubblicious."

The Prisonaires
Nashville, Tennessee, USA
Five African-American male inmates of the Tennessee State Penitentiary. The Prisonaires one and only hit was "Just Walkin' in the Rain." They were discovered by radio producer Joe Calloway, who heard them singing while preparing to broadcast from the prison.

Former Cell Mates
Sunderland, UK
Past and present members of Leatherface, the Golden Virgins, Los Coyote Men and the Mercury League.

NAMES
STILL AVAILABLE

The Shuns

By Lethal Inflection

An Executioner's Holiday

Shackledance

Firing Squad Rehearsal

Gas Chamber Choir

Penal Potluck

The Bruising Stones

The Rolling Heads

No-Neck Hangmen

Whipping Post Flayboys

Jailbreak Tardy Slip

Soft Cell Leeds, UK

Somewhat obsessed by cultural decay and hypocrisy, Soft Cell immortalized themselves with the single "Tainted Love" and their debut album, *Non-Stop Erotic Cabaret*. The name is thought to be a pun on the "soft sell" sales approach, with padded cell subplot.

Free London, UK

Formed in 1968 when a group of teenagers came together to jam at the Nag's Head pub in London. Fronted by singer Paul Rogers, the band joined the British blues explosion and hit it big with the single "All Right Now," off their 1970 album, *Fire and Water*. Rogers and drummer Simon Kirke went on to play with Bad Company. Bassist Andy Fraser eventually moved to California to write songs, including hits for Rod Stewart, Robert Palmer, Paul Young, Joe Cocker and others.

Alice in Chains

Seattle, Washington, USA

Singer Layne Staley formed a dress-in-drag speed-metal band called Alice N'Chainz following the breakup of his band Sleeze in 1986. The name carried over to a new band formed with guitarist Jerry Cantrell, with the spelling change to Alice in Chains.

Flogging Molly

Los Angeles, California, USA

Founded in 1997 by Dublin-born Dave King. Their name comes from Molly Malone's, the bar where they got their start. The band combines Celtic instruments such as fiddle, mandolin and accordion with electric guitar and rock drums, and they are regulars on the Vans Warped Tour.

California's **Doom Kounty Electric Chair**'s releases include *Cuban Healed Killers, Homicide, Stealing Defeat from the Jaws of Victory* and *A Boy Named Ho*. Singer-guitarist Ho: "I kinda made up my own geographical location, Doom Kounty...I wanted a name that was kinda roller-derby, part '50s motorcycle gang and maybe the name of a fucked-up country & western watering dive. So Doom Kounty Electric Chair was a logical choice. I think the name is pretty appropriate for the music we make."

Deathrow Bodine

Lexington, Kentucky, USA

Jethro Bodine Clampett was the name of the L'il Abner-like son on the 1960s TV series *The Beverley Hillbillies*.

The Hangmen UK/USA

The UK-based psychobilly Hangmen have recorded 7 albums, including *Last Train to Purgatory*, *Tested on Animals*, *Play Dead* and *Cacklefest!* The Los Angeles-based roots-rock Hangmen have also been around awhile. Their new 7-track EP, *In the City*, was produced by Social Distortion's Mike Ness.

Thin White Rope

Davis, California, USA

A William S. Burroughs description of human semen.

End of the Rope

Tampa, Florida, USA

A dangling deadpan pun on "end of the road." With the E in End usually printed backwards to make it scarier.

Slipknot

Des Moines, Iowa, USA

The name comes from a song title on their full-length demo, *Mate. Feed. Kill. Repeat.* Many lyrics and the album title itself come from the game *Werewolf: The Apocalypse*.

Rockpile UK

Leader Dave Edmunds' 1972 solo album, with the hit "I Hear You Knockin'," bore the title *Rockpile*. His tour band for that album took the name, as well. As a band in its own right, Rockpile existed from 1976–81, with Edmunds, bassist-singer Nick Lowe, drummer Terry Williams and guitarist-singer Billy Bremner. Edmunds and Lowe have enjoyed long careers as solo musicians, sidemen and producers. Williams played with Dire Straits from 1982-89. Bremner played on two albums by the Pretenders and produced and recorded with the Refreshments.

Building a
Better World

Excuse Me While I Scrape the Sky

Living for the City

Ever Upwards We Must Spruce

Building a Better World

Architecture in Helsinki

Architecture in Helsinki is based in the Melbourne suburb of Northcote, but founder Cameron Bird began his musical career in Albury, New South Wales, as part of a teenage band called the Pixel Mittens.

In 2000, while studying photography at art school, Bird regrouped fellow Pixel Mittens Sam Perry and Jamie Mildren as Architecture in Helsinki, adding James Cecil, Kellie Sutherland, Isobel Knowles, Tara Shackell and Gus Franklin. Inspired following an extended holiday in Portland, Oregon, Bird finished the bulk of the songs for the band's debut album, *Fingers Crossed*, in just six days. The songs marked a new direction — short, catchy pop songs.

It wasn't until the summer 2007 Flow Festival that Architecture in Helsinki appeared in Finland. Bird: "There were a few Finnish interviewers...I think they were quite perplexed. To us, the name means having to answer many questions about the name. The architecture in Melbourne has changed so much in the last year (let alone, the five years since the band was named) that I'm still not quite sure whether I like it or not. It's becoming quite the retro-futurist high-rise metropolis right now...."

Gardening, Not Architecture
Madison, Wisconsin, USA
Gardening, Not Architecture started in 2004 as a musical collaboration (in an upstairs apartment hallway) between singer-songwriter Sarah Saturday and producer Beau Sorenson. It is also the title of a song by the Drift off the album *Noumena*.

Rococo
London, UK
This prog-rock band was founded 1970. Disguised as a band called the Brats, they inadvertently became involved in the development of British punk. Rococo is an overly ornate or ornamental style popularized in 18th-century Europe.

Bauhaus
Northampton, UK
Formed in 1978, the band initially went by the name Bauhaus 1919, dropping the date within the year. With their dark, gloomy sound and image, Bauhaus are considered by many to be the first real goth band. According to founding member David J Haskins, they chose the name Bauhaus 1919 — a reference to the German Bauhaus art movement — because of its "stylistic implications and associations."

Life Without Buildings
Glasgow, Scotland
The band was assembled by Glasgow School of Art students in 1999 and named after a Japanese B-side. Album: *Any Other City*.

Excuse Me While I Scrape the Sky

Swaying Buildings
Brisbane, Australia
Swaying Buildings emerged in 2005 "after several years of 4-track recording, cassette tape albums and live gigging under various indie rock guises." The band paints a near-futuristic sound that blends together folk, pop and rock. In mid-2006 Swaying Buildings self-recorded and released its debut album, *Something in My Shoes*. International interest led to a club tour of Los Angeles and appearance at the International Pop Overthrow Festival.

The 13th Floor Elevators
Austin, Texas, USA
Founded in 1965, the 13th Floor Elevators shared stages with the Byrds, Janis Joplin and Quicksilver Messenger Service. The band found only limited commercial success before dissolving amid legal troubles and drug use.

Cold Chisel
Adelaide, Australia
The band was formed in 1973 and became a popular heavy metal act with working-class themes. They were inducted into the Australian Recording Industry Hall of Fame in 1993.

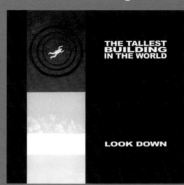

The Tallest Building in the World isn't in Dubai, it's in Seattle. Or it was until, according to their blog, guitarist Jared McSharry moved to Yakima to "pursue his dreams of financial success." McSharry's return is anticipated. Meanwhile, keyboardist Isaac Marion has been working on a solo project called Isaac Marion's Moon Colony. Tallest Building's recent album is *Look Down*.

Built to Spill
Boise, Idaho, USA

Former Treepeople leader Doug Martsch formed Built to Spill in 1992. On the band name, Martsch says, "It's about the way this world works. There are going to be disappointments and failures. We're designed to fail. We're very limited. But this isn't a horrible thing; it's more about the idea of what our potential is and how exaggerated we've become. I think we're built to try to be bigger than ourselves."

Nine Inch Nails
Cleveland, Ohio, USA

In 1987 Trent Reznor played keyboards with a Cleveland band called the Exotic Birds. Then he left to work on his own material. In 1994 Reznor said that he coined the name Nine Inch Nails because it "abbreviated easily," rather than for any literal meaning. Other explanations have been rumored over the years, including that Reznor chose to reference Jesus' crucifixion with nine-inch spikes or *Nightmare on Elm Street* villain Freddy Krueger's "nine-inch fingernails."

Crowbar
Hamilton, Ontario, Canada

Having spent most of a year simply known as Ronnie Hawkins' backup band, they were fired in 1970, with Hawkins saying, "You guys are so crazy you could fuck up a crowbar in three seconds." So they stayed together as Crowbar. A New Orleans sludge-metal band of the same name started up in 1989.

Tool   Los Angeles, California, USA

The future members of Tool moved to Los Angeles in the 1980s. Paul D'Amour and Adam Jones wanted to enter the film industry, while Maynard James Keenan found employment remodeling pet stores, after having studied visual arts in Michigan. Danny Carey was the drummer for Green Jellÿ, Carole King and Pigmy Love Circus. Keenan has said, "Tool is exactly what it sounds like: It's a big dick. It's a wrench. We are...your tool; use us as a catalyst in your process of finding out whatever it is you need to find out, or whatever it is you're trying to achieve."

NAMES
STILL AVAILABLE

Architecture
in Omaha

The Wobbly Floors

Prefab Grout

The Screw Clamps

Surreal Estate
Agents

Building with Jell-O

My
Semi-Detached Life

Ominous Bungalow

Hell's Walk-Up

The Nodding
Subcontractors

Really Big House

The Black Windows

Incredible Steel Erectors

Stockholm, Sweden

"Sweden's latest rock sensation, the hard-hitting trio known as the Incredible Steel Erectors! Check out our debut EP, *Bull Muzika*, 27 minutes of indescribable excitement, jam-packed with special surprise action for your listening pleasure! The Incredible Steel Erectors, well rehearsed in cool rock poses and rude gestures, are sure to be the next big thing coming from Sweden!"

The Concretes Stockholm, Sweden

Formed in 1995, they gradually acquired new members until they became an eight-piece band. One of their songs, "Say Something New," has been featured in a number of TV advertisements for US discount retailer Target. "You Can't Hurry Love," also from their debut album, has been used in films. Lead singer Victoria Bergsman has since moved on to her solo project, Taken By Trees. Lisa Milberg now provides lead vocals for the band, both on stage and on the band's third album, *Hey Trouble*, released in 2007.

Pavement Stockton, California, USA

Pavement formed in 1989 as a studio project for Stephen Malkmus and Scott Kannberg. Malkmus: "[The name] was Scott's doing. I didn't think twice about the name. I figured we'd make one single, it'd be sold at obscure single auctions, and we'd disappear."

Brick Atlanta, Georgia, USA

Formed in 1972, Brick was big throughout the '70s. Their most popular single was 1976's "Dazz," which hit #3 on the US Pop charts and #1 on the R&B charts.

Metallica

Los Angeles, California, USA

Early in 1981, drummer Lars Ulrich's friend Ron Quintana was thinking up names for a metal fanzine. Quintana asked him his opinion on the names Metal Mania and Metallica. Ulrich convinced him to use Metal Mania and took Metallica for the name of his band. That band achieved substantial commercial success right from the start. Its self-titled 1991 album debuted at #1 on the *Billboard* 200. Metallica has since released 9 studio albums, 2 live albums, 2 EPs, 9 videos and 39 singles, with 100 million records sold worldwide. The band has won seven Grammy Awards and has had four albums peak at #1 on the *Billboard* 200. Since 2000 Metallica's album catalog sales have been second only to the Beatles'.

Birmingham, Alabama's **Liquid Brick** touts the tagline: "Six guys, total improv. You can't get more modern caveman than that." Founder Keith Goodwin: "I basically thought it was such a ridiculous name we would never have to run into another Liquid Brick. We named the band in '96, and since then we have found eight other Liquid Bricks. Crazy huh?" Songs: "The Virgin Morons" and "Please Don't Eat My Mother."

Arthur Loves Plastic

Silver Springs, Maryland, USA

The stage name of electronic artist Bev Stanton. Stanton has won over a dozen Wammies (Washington D.C. Area Music Awards) in the Electronica category. Her tracks have also appeared on soundtracks for *Access Hollywood*, *Extra: The Entertainment Magazine*, *America's Most Wanted*, *MTV's Undressed and Cribs, the Playboy TV's Sexy Girls Next Door, American Idol,* and *The Oprah Winfrey Show.* Stanton also plays bass in the Baltimore band the Window Shoppers and is an honorary Space Dot.

Moving Sidewalks

Houston, Texas, USA

Moving Sidewalks formed in 1967, with a guy called Bill Gibbons on guitar and vocals, Tom Moore on keyboards, Don Summeres on bass and Dan Mitchell on drums. The band's debut single, "99th Floor," written by Gibbons, was #1 on the Houston Top 40 charts for six weeks. Wand Records signed the Moving Sidewalks to their first major record deal, and they soon found themselves opening for such headliners as the Doors, the Animals, the Young Rascals, Joe Cocker, Stevie Wonder and others. In June 1968 the Sidewalks were asked to join the the the Texas leg of the Jimi Hendrix tour, along with the English group Soft Machine and Jimmy Vaughn's Chessmen. Hendrix stood stage right to listen to their set each night and later spoke on *The Tonight Show* about how impressed he was. Bill Gibbons is better known today as bearded Billy Gibbons of ZZ Top.

The quintet **Eat More Plastic** are from Koblenz, Germany, "and this is what they actually sound like: Blues meets punk mixed with some energetic chords and the rhythm section's mental stuff. Be prepared for tunes as sticky as melting plastic." Drummer Caspar Walbeck: "Eat More Plastic is the answer to all bollocks surrounding us. Plastic stands for assiduously produced rubbish, which is after us in any situation. So, just eat it by trusting in the power of digestion."

Living for the City

City & Colour
St. Catharines, Ontario, Canada
Began in 2004 as an acoustic side-project fronted by Dallas Green, rhythm guitarist and singer for Alexisonfire. Green felt uneasy about putting the album out under his own name, so he came up with City [i.e., Dallas] & Colour [i.e., Green].

Dappled Cities
Sydney, Australia
Originally called Periwinkle, the band came together in 1997 when 15-year-olds Dave Rennick and Hugh Boyce were joined by Alex Moore and English-born Tim Derricourt. Ned Cooke is now also a permanent member of the band. After various name changes, the guys settled on Dappled Cities Fly, chosen because it was such a bad band name that it made them laugh. They claim to have regretted it ever since. Their second album, *Granddance*, recorded in LA, features cover art with the band's name as Dappled Cities, minus the word Fly.

Sweden's **Suburbia** was formed in 2002 by singer-guitarist Magnus Sörensen and drummer Peter Lärk. Both had previously played in the cover band Samuel Twice. Suburbia's song "Easier to Dream" took second place in the international "Song of the Year" songwriting competition hosted by music channel VH1. The jury consisted of singer Norah Jones, producer Tim Palmer (U2 and HIM) and drummer-singer Sheila E (Prince). Album: *Songs for a Perfect Mixtape.*

The Residents
Shreveport, Louisiana, USA
Formed in 1969, the group sent a reel-to-reel tape to Hal Halverstadt at Warner Brothers in 1971, since he had worked with Captain Beefheart, one of the group's musical heroes. Halverstadt was not impressed with "The Warner Bros. Album," but because the band had not included a name in their return address, his rejection slip was simply addressed to "The Residents." The group embraced the name, first becoming Residents Unincorporated, then shortening it to the Residents. Their first performance as the Residents was at the Boarding House in San Francisco in 1971.

Sunny Day Real Estate
Seattle, Washington, USA
Ironic name for emo band. The core of Sunny Day Real Estate formed in 1992 and supposedly was called Thief, Steal Me a Peach, Flatland Spider and One Day I Stopped Breathing before finally becoming Sunny Day Real Estate. *Thief, Steal Me a Peach* and *Flatland Spider* became titles for EPs, and One Day I Stopped Breathing remains their official company name for publishing and copyright matters.

Lifehouse
Malibu, California, USA
Lifehouse's 2001 hit single, "Hanging by a Moment," from their major label debut, *No Name Face,* won a Billboard Music Award for Hot 100 Single of the Year, beating out Janet Jackson and Alicia Keys. Recent album: *Who We Are.*

223

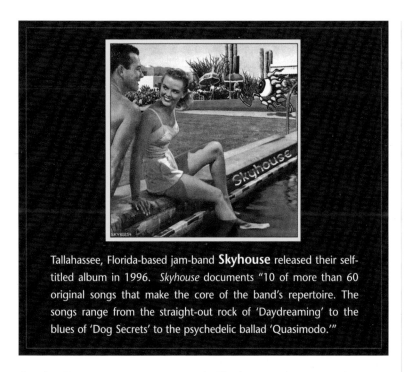

Tallahassee, Florida-based jam-band **Skyhouse** released their self-titled album in 1996. *Skyhouse* documents "10 of more than 60 original songs that make the core of the band's repertoire. The songs range from the straight-out rock of 'Daydreaming' to the blues of 'Dog Secrets' to the psychedelic ballad 'Quasimodo.'"

Greeley Estates
Phoenix, Arizona, USA

Formed in 2002 with a name taken from a road sign in Greeley, Colorado. "Um, it's just kind of random. It really has no meaning. None of us are from Colorado."

Junkhouse
Hamilton, Ontario, Canada

Consisting of singer-guitarist Tom Wilson, bassist Russ Wilson (no relation), guitarist Dan Achen and drummer Ray Farrugia, Junkhouse got its first exposure opening for Crash Vegas. In 1993 the band signed to Sony Records and released their debut album, *Strays*. In 1995 they released *Birthday Boy* and in 1997 their final album, *Fuzz*. Tom Wilson has also released two solo albums, *Planet Love* and *Dog Days*, and has collaborated in the Canadian supergroup Blackie & the Rodeo Kings.

Flophouse
Detroit, Michigan, USA

Formed in late 2004, Flophouse is a funk-rock band in a city known for it history of funk-rock bands. The band was handpicked from thousands of entries to perform at Eric Clapton's Crossroads Festival in Chicago in 2007.

Hawthorne Heights
Dayton, Ohio, USA

The post-hardcore-emo-screamo-pop quintet Hawthorne Heights came to-gether in 2001 as A Day in the Life. The collective went through a name change, numerous lineup changes and shifting music styles before settling on its "final" formation — only to have persistent legal troubles with their label, then the death of singer-screamer-guitarist Casey Calvert due to a medication mishap. Time to find a new neighborhood.

Crowded House
Melbourne, Australia

The famous Australian band led by New Zealander Neil Finn. It was during their Split Enz farewell tour, Enz with a Bang, that Neil Finn and Paul Hester decided to form a new band. The first incarnation, the Mullanes, formed in Melbourne in 1985. After landing a record contract with Capitol Records, the band moved to Los Angeles, where they were asked to come up with a more marketable name. Band members had been sharing a cramped apartment in West Hollywood during the recording process, so Crowded House it was. Australian fans refer to them as the Crowdies.

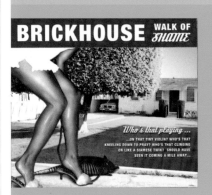

The foundation for **Brickhouse** was laid in Malmö, Sweden, around 1997 by singer-songwriter-guitarist Magnus Andersson. Joined by Björn G Stenberg and Uppsala Nya Tidning, Andersson combines his deep fondness for American blues and soul with a raw rock & roll performance style. Recent album: *Walk of Shame*.

Ever Upward We Must Spruce

Red House Painters
San Francisco, California, USA

Considered one of the founders of the slowcore movement, singer-song-writer Mark Kozelek used Red House Painters to convey his "very personal and emotional songs of despair, pain and suffering."

Inspiral Carpets
Oldham-Manchester, UK

Formed in 1986, the band took its name from a store outside Manchester. Albums: *dung 4* (cassette), *Life* (UK #2), *The Beast Inside* (UK #5), *Revenge of the Goldfish* (UK #17), *Devil Hopping* (UK #10).

Kitchens of Distinction
London, UK

The trio began rehearsing together in 1985. They took their name from a company specializing in kitchen and plumbing fixtures and home decor, which they saw advertised on the side of a bus. Their first single, "The Last Gasp Death Shuffle," was recorded on an 8-track in a Kennington basement but was named a Single of the Week in the *New Musical Express*. The band shortened their name to Kitchens O.D. when they signed to Fierce Panda Records, and their May '96 single, "Feel My Genie," was named *Melody Maker's* Single of the Week, but the Kitchens O.D. disbanded that summer.

The Spiral Starecase
Sacramento, California, USA

The Spiral Staircase is a 1945 psychological thriller based on Ethel Lina White's novel *Some Must Watch*. The Spiral *Stare*case are best known for their single "More Today Than Yesterday." The group evolved from the Fydallions, formed in 1964 for an Air Force talent contest. Columbia later signed the band but insisted they change their name. "They loved our work, but they hated the name, and they didn't like the way we dressed. This was in the late '60s, when all the musicians were wearing long hair. We looked very square!"

The Modernettes
Vancouver, British Columbia, Canada

Formed around 1980, the trio consisted of ex-Active Dog guitarist John "Buck Cherry" Armstrong, bassist Mary Jo Kopechne and drummer John "Jughead" McAdams, all of whom sang. But Armstrong eventually became uncomfortable playing shows as the Modernettes: "That band name was a joke to begin with, just as 'Buck Cherry' was a joke name. We were all on welfare and they'd kick you off welfare if you used your real name. When that LA band buckcherry came out in the late '90s, it was great because they had to pay me a whole bunch of money...The only smart thing I've ever done in my entire musical career was that I didn't get a showbiz lawyer; I got a trademark-and-copyright lawyer.

I said, look, I've got a body of work here that spans a number of years, I've got a book, the book's been optioned as a film...and I smiled when I saw buckcherry was on Dreamworks — brand-new, big label with lots of money to spend. The first thing the lawyer said when he took a look at the material we supplied them with was, 'Is this a problem that money can solve?' So I got a really nice payout in American dollars...and my lawyer earned every penny I paid him by saying, 'Don't sell them the name, *license* it to them...So I can't print Buck Cherry as all lower-case, one word, and I can't call the band Buck Cherry, but I personally am Buck Cherry and have been for much longer than they've been around."

225

Furniture
London, UK

Furniture was founded in London in 1981. Their album titles tell their story. EP *The Boom Was On* leads to record contract. String of singles become the LP *The Lovemongers*. Album *The Wrong People:* new label goes into liquidation but album is picked up by ZTT label (who abruptly delete it). A three-year court battle leads to Arista Records and 1989's *Food, Sex and Paranoia*.

The Doors
Los Angeles, California, USA

Formed in 1965 by vocalist Jim Morrison, keyboardist Ray Manzarek, drummer John Densmore, and guitarist Robby Krieger. The band took their name from Aldous Huxley's 1954 book *The Doors of Perception*. Huxley had taken the title from a line in a William Blake poem.

Red Walls & Black Curtains
Helsinki, Finland

The room is making this female-fronted duo very sad. The cellos played by friends aren't helping.

The Curtain Society
Southbridge, Massachusetts, USA

Formed in 1988, the band has released four albums, numerous EPs and singles, and backed poet-musician Jim Carroll (as the Catholic Boys) and Shana Morrison (Van's daughter).

Little Green Chairs
Athens, Georgia, USA

Best Jam Band at the 2006 Flagpole Magazine Music Awards.

Washington, DC's **Land of Malls** was formed in 1995. Songwriter David Walls-Kaufman: "Land of Malls came about, in name and song concept, from the five-member band's refusal to produce an album that musically resembles the modern shopping mall. A mall is laid out to suck in shoppers through the 'anchor stores,' and the rest ride the coattails. On an album, the hit, the single, is the 'anchor store,' and the rest of the album is often drek." One reviewer called their album *Suburban & Gomorrah* "the Beatles White Album dragged through Austin, Texas."

Silverchair Newcastle, Australia

Formed as the Innocent Criminals in 1992. They changed their just prior to releasing their first single. The name Silverchair evolved from a misspelling of "Sliver Chair," combining the Nirvana song title "Sliver" and the You Am I song title "Berlin Chair."

The Ottomen
St. Louis, Missouri, USA

Began recording demos in their dorms at the Kansas City Art Institute in 1996. The name was derived from the Dead Milkmen song "I Tripped Over the Ottoman" on *Metaphysical Graffiti*.

3 Doors Down
Escatawpa, Mississippi, USA

The trio of Brad Arnold (vocals, drums), Matt Roberts (guitar) and Todd Harrell (bass) formed in 1994. During a trip to Foley, Alabama, they were walking through the town when they saw a sign with some words missing, so that it read "Doors Down." It seemed like a good name, but was missing an element. Since they were a trio, they added the "3" to create 3 Doors Down. The band signed to Universal Records after the success of their song "Kryptonite."

We've Got the Power

Electricity

Gas

Steam

Nuclear

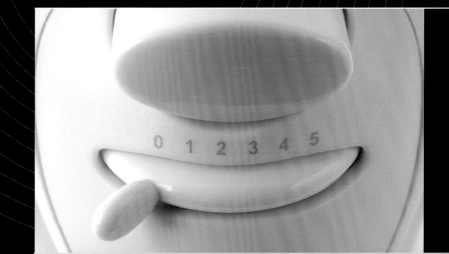

0 1 2 3 4 5

We've Got the Power

Power Station

Following completion of Duran Duran's third album, *Seven and the Ragged Tiger*, in 1984, band members wandered off into two different side-projects. One was Arcadia, the other was Power Station.

Power Station was started by bassist John Taylor and guitarist Andy Taylor to provide backing for model-turned-singer Bebe Buell, who wanted to cover the T. Rex song "Bang a Gong." The Taylors enlisted former Chic drummer Tony Thompson and bassist-producer Bernard Edwards.

The idea expanded to an album project for which Taylor, Taylor and Thompson would provide backing for a different singer on each track. They approached Mick Jagger, Billy Idol, Mick Ronson and others, including suave soul singer Robert Palmer, whose track was to be "Communication." But when Palmer heard about the "Bang a Gong" demo, he asked to try it, as well.

The result: They decided to record the entire album with Palmer, under the name Power Station, after New York City's Power Station recording studio where this all took place.

Released in 1985, the album reached # 6 in the US and #12 in the UK. Despite their success, the band moved on to other projects.

Tower of Power
Oakland, California, USA

In the mid-60s, saxophonist Emilio Castillo, still a teenager, moved from Detroit to Fremont, California, where he started a band called the Gotham City Crime Fighters. During 1968, Castillo moved to Oakland, put together a band with a full horn section, and began performing original funk-soul material in the Bay area as Tower of Power. The Tower of Power horns have also appeared on recordings by Little Feat, Santana, Elton John, John Lee Hooker, Jefferson Starship, Huey Lewis & the News, Lyle Lovett, Poison, Phish, Aerosmith and many other artists.

Powerman 5000
Boston, Massachusetts, USA

The Powerman Duathlon ("World's Most Formidable Duathlon") sometimes includes 5000-meter running events. Powerman 5000 was formed in 1991 by frontman Spider One (Michael Cummings), the younger brother of Rob Zombie (Robert Cummings). The band's powered-up sound has landed them on lots of game soundtracks.

Blyth Power   Harrogate, UK
Formed in late 1983 by singer-drummer Joseph Porter, formerly of Zounds and the Mob. Named after a steam engine. Porter is a trainspotter, and the band hosts an annual music and cricket festival. The decommissioned Blyth Power Station served as the location for *Alien 3*.

Rise Electric
Toronto, Ontario, Canada

Rise Electric is fronted by Lukas Rossi, the winner of the TV reality show *Rock Star: Supernova*. Other members include bassist Jay Cianfrini (Jaww) and former members of Pulse Ultra, drummer Maxx Zinno and guitarist Dominic Cifarelli.

Breakerbox
Buffalo, New York, USA

Formed in late 2005, Breakerbox is Christina Reilly (vocals, bass) Joe Pinnavaia (guitar) and Scott Calandra (drums).

The Jolt
Glasgow, Scotland

Formed in 1976, the Jolt moved to London, signed with Polydor, opened for bands such as the Jam, the Stranglers and Generation X, and were precursors to the mod revival, which erupted around 1979, the year the band split up.

AC/DC   Sydney, Australia
Formed in 1973 by guitarist brothers Angus and Malcolm Young, who got the idea for their band's name after seeing "AC/DC" on the back of their sister's sewing machine. AC/DC stands for alternating current/direct current. An AC/DC device can use either type of power. The brothers liked the reference to electrical power. Many Australian fans refer to their band as "Acca Dacca."

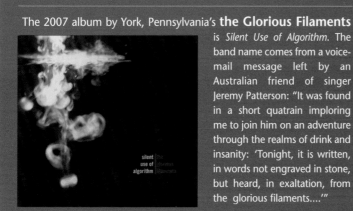

The 2007 album by York, Pennsylvania's **the Glorious Filaments** is *Silent Use of Algorithm*. The band name comes from a voice-mail message left by an Australian friend of singer Jeremy Patterson: "It was found in a short quatrain imploring me to join him on an adventure through the realms of drink and insanity: 'Tonight, it is written, in words not engraved in stone, but heard, in exaltation, from the glorious filaments....'"

60 Cycle Hum
Chattanooga, Tennessee, USA
Formed in 2004 and still struggling with drummer issues. A 60-cycle hum, or power line hum, can be produced by amplifiers and loudspeakers and is often the bane of musicians onstage.

Rheostatics
Toronto, Ontario, Canada
A rheostat is an electrical component that permits control of resistance in an electrical circuit, for dimming lights, varying motor speed, etc. Guitarist Dave Bidini and bassist Tim Veslely formed the band in 1980 and chose the name Rheostatics while in a high-school chemistry class. Bidini recently ended an epic solo tour and published the book *Around the World in 57 1/2 Gigs.*

Magnolia Electric Co.
Chicago, Ohio, USA
In March 2003, while on tour with his band Songs: Ohia, Jason Molina announced that he would rename the band Magnolia Electric Co. The Magnolia Electric Power Association is an electric power cooperative based in McComb, Mississippi.

Bowery Electric
Manhattan, New York, USA
The name of a bar at the corner of Bowery and 2nd Street in Manhattan's East Village. The Manhattan-based duo Bowery Electric emerged in the mid-90s, using electronic music, hip-hop beats, samples and live bass, drums and guitar.

Pacific Gas & Electric
Los Angeles, California, USA
In 1967 guitarist Tom Marshall and bassist Brent Block formed a band named Pacific Gas & Electric Blues Band, later shortened. "Are You Ready" became their first mainstream hit, reaching #14 in the summer of 1970. There really is a Pacific Gas & Electric Company. It was founded in 1905 and is headquartered in San Francisco.

Five Man Electrical Band
Ottawa, Ontario, Canada
The group originally recorded and toured as the Staccatos. *Five Man Electrical Band* was the title of their second album, in 1969, and they subsequently took it as their band name.

NAMES STILL AVAILABLE

Torquing Heads

The Atom Splitters

Diesel Zappa

Ohmnivores

100 Watt Headshop

Photovoltaic Voltaire

The Gasholes

More Batteries Bruce

30 Billion Barrels

Evernuclear

Crude Oil Countdown

Still Windmills

229

AMAZED BY LIGHTBULBS (ABL) formed in 2000 when Brian Michalski and Mark Gartner started the project as an acoustic duo, taking their originally penned songs on the coffee-shop circuit near their home base in Lake County, Ohio. A few years later Kevin Burker joined on drums and Angela Gartner on bass, and the band went electric.

Rolling Blackouts
Lomita, California, USA
They were in *Alternative Press*'s "100 Bands You Need to Know" in 2004. They then won the *Los Angeles Times* Best Live Band of 2005 award. *Amplifier* called their music a "halcyon pop puree of soul punk, garage and hard rock that heroically hurdles between retro and futuristic." Debut album: *Black Is Beautiful*.

Midnight Oil
Sydney, Australia
They began in the early '70s as Farm. Later, fronted by towering, shaved-headed singer Peter Garrett, Midnight Oil took a vocal stance on environmental concerns and aboriginal rights, and their international breakthrough album, 1987's *Diesel and Dust*, featured the openly political singles "Beds Are Burning," "The Dead Heart," "Put Down That Weapon" and "Dreamworld."

Coal Chamber
Los Angeles, California, USA
Formed in 1994 when singer-songwriter Dez Fafara and guitarist Miguel Rascón met through a classified ad. They made a band name by each choosing a word. Rascón chose *Coal*, Dez chose *Chamber*.

Steampacket London, UK
Formed by Long John Baldry after the breakup of his previous group the Hoochie Coochie Men. It included singer Rod Stewart, singer Julie Driscoll, organist Brian Auger and guitarist Vic Briggs.

Atomic 7
Toronto, Ontario, Canada
Nitrogen? (See Periodic Table.) Here's a rough Brian Connelly twang-guitar lineage: Buick McKane to Good Guys to Crash Kills Five to Shadowy Men on a Shadowy Planet to Heatseekers to Phono-Comb to Atomic 7 (and Ancient Chinese Secret, and Neko Case & Her Boyfriends).

Steam
New York City, New York, USA
The 1969 #1 hit "Na Na Hey Hey Kiss Him Goodbye" was created by studio musicians and attributed to a nonexistent band named Steam. Writer-producer Paul Leka quickly assembled a band to send out on tour. Then another. Meanwhile, Paul Leka and the studio musicians recorded one album and two additional singles.

Fall Out Boy Chicago, Illinois, USA
The band remained nameless for their first two shows, but at the end of the second show, they asked for audience suggestions. One audience member yelled, "Fallout Boy!" Fallout Boy is a Robin-like comic-book superhero sidekick created by Matt Groening for his TV series *The Simpsons*. Radioactive Man is Fallout Boy's Batman. Bart and Milhouse are big fans.

Nuclear Power Pants
Baltimore, Maryland, USA
IndyWeek.com: "Nuclear Power Pants is an electrospazz spectacle with a revolving cast of players, though its primary incarnation ties brothers Benjamin and Robert O'Brien together in a two-headed monster outfit as they sing. The rest of the band performs dressed as creatures of the single-headed, day-glo shark variety."

The Magnetic Fields
Boston, Massachusetts, USA
The band began in 1990 as Stephin Merritt's studio project, under the name Buffalo Rome, with him playing all instruments. With the help of Claudia Gonson, who had played in Merritt's band the Zinnias during high school, a live band, the Magnetic Fields, was assembled.

Department of Transportation

Get Your Motor Running

Parts & Pile-Ups

Trains & Planes

Department of Transportation

Get Your Motor Running

The Cars

Singer-guitarist Ric Ocasek and singer-bassist Benjamin Orr met at a party in Columbus, Ohio, and performed together briefly before moving to Boston and adding keyboardist Greg Hawkes and guitarist Jas Goodkind to form the short-lived folk group Milkwood. Ocasek and Orr's next project was a club band, Richard & the Rabbits, while Hawkes did a stint with Orphan and then with Martin Mull & His Fabulous Furniture.

Ocasek and Orr found future Cars guitarist Elliot Easton when they joined Cap'n Swing. The guys soon managed to subsitute that band's swinging drummer for rock drummer David Robinson, who had been in Modern Lovers, DMZ and the Pop!

It was Robinson who contributed the name "the Cars." Ocasek: "It's so easy to spell; it doesn't have a 'z' on the end; it's real authentic. It's pop art, in a sense."

The Cars released six studio albums between 1978 and 1987 and had numerous Top 40 singles and videos in the MTV '80s. Since the band's breakup in 1988, Ocasek has maintained a solo career. Easton and Hawkes have appeared with Todd Rundgren and others on occasion as the New Cars, to perform Cars tunes and material by Rundgren.

Car Full of Midgets
Kimberly, Wisconsin, USA
Pre-van-owning, ska-playing midgets.

Delorean Grey
London, Kentucky, USA
From the famous Oscar Wilde novel *The Picture of Dorian Gray* and the infamously failed automobile the DeLorean, named for creator John DeLorean.

The Lambrettas
Brighton, UK
A late '70s mod-revival band named for a make of Italian scooters preferred by the original Mods.

Booker T & the MGs
Memphis, Tennessee, USA
Organist Booker T. Jones played the lead role in this band of ace studio musicians for the famous Stax/Volt record label. Some say MG stands for Memphis Group, but former Stax musician-producer Chips Moman claims they were named after his sports car.

Chevy Metal
Topanga, California, USA
More Chevy than heavy metal. They play "music that a meth dealer from 1973 would have listened to."

Founded in 2004, the Atlanta, Georgia, instrumental-rock band **Sorry No Ferrari** consists of guitarist Brett Kelly, bassist Drew Mobley, guitarist Chad Shivers and drummer Dave Ragsdale. EPs: *Oh Snap* and *The Get Down Syndrome*. The Ferrari sports car company was created in 1947 by Enzo Ferrari.

Mitch Ryder
& the Detroit Wheels
Detroit, Michigan, USA

Mitch Ryder's gravelly soul-styled vocals landed him a job as a backup singer in an African-American group called the Peps while still a teen. He founded his first group, the Tempests, in high school. But it was while fronting Billy Lee & the Rivieras that he met writer-producer Bob Crewe. Crewe renamed the band Mitch Ryder & the Detroit Wheels and recorded several of the band's early hits, including the classic "Devil with a Blue Dress On."

The Impalas
Brooklyn, New York, USA

A racially integrated '50s doo-wop group with lead singer Joe "Speedo" Frasier.

The Camaros
Washington, DC, USA

Named for the Chevrolet Camaro. Students from Eastern High School and Elliott Junior High School started an R&B group by this name in 1966. A more recently established rockabilly band called the Camaros works out of NYC, fronted by Louisiana singer Jen Jones.

Camaro Rouge
Chicago, Illinois, USA

Camaro meets Khmer Rouge in a dual female-fronted rock trio. The Khmer Rouge, a succession of ruling Communist governments in Cambodia in the 1970s, killed over a million of its own people through work camps, starvation and execution for dissidence.

Silversun Pickups are named for a liquor and convenience store near the junction of Sunset and Silver Lake Boulevards in Los Angeles. The band has opened for and/or toured with Wolfmother, OK Go, Snow Patrol, Kaiser Chiefs, Foo Fighters and others. Their first full-length album is *Carnavas*.

Bang Camaro
Boston, Massachusetts, USA

"…all about the good times that were shunted aside and put away as 'adulthood' beckoned."

Camarojuana
Eliot, Maine, USA

They claim to have created the Mullet Bomb: a shot of Jagermeister dropped in a half-pint of Pabst Blue Ribbon.

The Fastbacks
Seattle, Washington, USA

Formed in 1979 and having somewhere between 12 and 20 drummers. More than Spinal Tap.

NAMES
STILL AVAILABLE

Buicks in Jerkwater

Punchbuggy
Punchback

No Spare
Road Glare

Porsche Dorks

The Slow
Traffic Lights

Used Car Czars

Smart Car
Dim Driver

Trainspotter's
Daughters

Shinjuku Station
Jukes

The Blimps

Norman Lear Jets

The Runway Rosary

The Hell Caminos
Honolulu, Hawaii, USA

Hawaiian psychobillies. The Chevrolet El Camino, Spanish for "the road" and manufactured from 1959 to 1960 and 1964 to 1987, was essentially a Chevelle with a low-slung pickup bed extending from behind the front seats to the rear bumper. In an episode of the TV show *Monster Garage*, a stock El Camino was "pimped" into a Hell-Camino.

The Deuce Coupes California, USA

A working vehicle for writer-producer Gary Usher, who sought to combine instrumental surf music with '60s hot-rod culture. Deuce coupes were 1932 Ford coupes, easily modified into signature hot rods. They lasted longer on the west coast due to the warm climate and therefore absence of rust-advancing road salt.

The GTOs
Los Angeles, California, USA

In this case, GTO stands for Girls Together Outrageously, a group comprised of seven groupies/artists/nannies connected to the Zappas. The women initially called themselves the Laurel Canyon Ballet Club, changing their name to the GTOs on Frank's advice. Their act was a mix of theater, dance, singing and conversation. The Pontiac GTO was manufactured between 1964 and 1974 in the US and considered among the first "muscle cars."

Delta 88 Michigan, USA

Moody, Tom Waitsian, Nick Drakean tunes. And a powerful Oldsmobile.

The Detroit Cobras, Rachel Nagy and Mary Ramirez, really are from Detroit. They have released four full-length albums, the most recent of which is *Tied & True*. Nagy and Ramirez have employed a variety of sidemen to deliver their message since 1995. Summer 2008 saw them touring in support of X.

Monroe Mustang
Austin, Texas, USA

The band's recent album, *The Imaginary Band, Regretfully Declines*, is a digital-only release produced in their home studio. A Monroe Mustang is a Ford Mustang customized with non-stock Monroe auto parts.

Mustangs & Madras
Longmont, Colorado, USA

In the S.E. Hinton novel *The Outsiders*, the character Ponyboy Curtis dismisses a group of people as "white trash in Mustangs and madras shirts."

Galaxie 500
Cambridge, Massachusetts, USA

A slacker band that has been described as "the greatest band of all time to pass out to." Named after a friend's car.

The Fabulous Thunderbirds
Austin, Texas, USA

The title of the band's 1979 debut album, *Girls Go Wild*, foreshadowed the current wave of drunken, caught-on-Handicam randiness. The band's music is deeply rooted in the blues and has featured some of the hottest guitarists this side of John Mayall's bands. The first round of Ford Thunderbirds were produced from 1955–97. The reintroduced retro-look Thunderbird was an attempt to inject some old-time fabulousness into Ford's lineup.

God Drives a Galaxy
Austin, Texas, USA

Austin Chronicle on their third album: "*Pale Blue Dot* is the closest thing to divine inspiration Austin has seen in a while."

The Edsels Campbell, Ohio, USA

Named after one of the biggest automobile duds of all time, this doo-wop band had success with "Rama Lama Ding Dong" and a few other singles. They originally called themselves the Essos, after the oil company.

The Cadillac Kings London, UK

Six of the UK's most long-lasting blues-roots musicians.

Mink Deville
San Francisco, California, USA

Based around frontman Willie DeVille (Billy Borsay). "One of the guys said, 'How about Mink DeVille? There can't be anything cooler than a fur-lined Cadillac, can there?'"

Fleetwood Mac US/UK

Fleetwood, not from the Cadillac Fleetwood, but from drummer Mick Fleetwood, and Mac from bassist John McVie and keyboardist Christine McVie.

Gruntruck

Seattle, Washington, USA

Formed in 1989 from members of Skin Yard, the Accused and Napalm Beach. A regular tour opener for Alice in Chains in the mid-90s.

REO Speedwagon

Champaign, Illinois, USA

REO are the initials of Ransom Eli Olds, founder of the Oldsmobile car company. The REO Motor Car Company produced the REO Speed Wagon, a flatbed truck often outfitted as a fire truck. The band struggled to keep a lead singer but scored a US #1 album with *Hi Infidelity* in 1980.

Big Ass Truck

Memphis, Tennessee, USA

Members have played in or currently play in Vending Machine, the Lost Sounds, River City Tanlines, the Bloodthirsty Lovers and the Secret Service.

GARAGELAND

Australian *Rolling Stone* says **Garageland** (from Auckland, New Zealand) creates "melodies McCartney would kill for. Brilliant!" The name comes from a song on the Clash's debut album. Most of Garageland's recorded performances appear on Christchurch-based Flying Nun Records.

The Drive-By Truckers are based in Athens, Georgia. Founders Patterson Hood and Mike Cooley recorded the Truckers' first two albums, *Gangstabilly* and *Pizza Deliverance*, with help from studio musicians. The current band includes John Neff (guitar, pedal steel), Shonna Tucker (bass, vocals) and Brad Morgan (drums). Recent album: *Brighter Than Creation's Dark*.

Supergarage

Toronto, Ontario, Canada

Started in 1996, toured with the Headstones, Big Sugar, I Mother Earth, Barstool Prophets, Matthew Good, Soul Asylum and Green Day.

Camper Van Beethoven

Santa Cruz, California, USA

College radio hits include "Take the Skinheads Bowling." Ludwig Van Beethoven meets camper van.

Bran Van 3000

Montreal, Quebec, Canada

Debut album, *Glee*, went gold and won a 1998 Juno Award for Best Alternative Album.

Econoline Crush   Vancouver, British Columbia, Canada

The band took their name from Euxebe Auxtry's novel *Jeu de Fountaine*, in which econoline crush is a drug that gives the hopeless a sense of optimism. The Ford E-series van, the Econoline, has been produced since 1961.

Black Rebel Motorcycle Club

San Francisco, California, USA

Called the Elements until they discovered a band with the same name. The Black Rebel Motorcycle Club is the name of Marlon Brando's motorcycle gang in the 1953 film *The Wild One*.

Parts & Pile-Ups

The Accelerators
Raleigh, North Carolina, USA
Recent compilation CD: *Road Chill*.

Bachman-Turner Overdrive
Winnipeg, Manitoba, Canada
Band members saw a trucking magazine entitled *Overdrive* at a truckstop and thought it also described their music. The surnames belong to Randy Bachman (the Guess Who), brothers Tim and Robbie Bachman, and C.F. "Fred" Turner (recommended by Neil Young).

Flat Duo Jets
Chapel Hill, North Carolina, USA
Rockabilly trio led by Dexter Romweber. Ten albums exist, including 2008's *Two Headed Cow*.

Brakesbrakesbrakes
Brighton, UK
Known simply as Brakes. Song: "Porcupine or Pineapple." Recent album: *The Beatific Vision*.

The Rumble Strips
Tavistock, UK
Rumble strips are those bumpy lines on roads. *New Music Express* included the Rumble Strips in their September 2006 "Best New Bands" and June 2007 "Essential New Bands."

The Radiators
Sydney, Australia
The Radiators call themselves "Australia's hardest working rock band." They have been going strong for 30 years, 15 albums and over 4,000 performances.

The New Orleans Radiators
New Orleans, Louisiana, USA
Like their Australian counterparts, these guys have also been at it a long time, 30 years and 12 albums with the same lineup, playing a style of swamp-rock that they call "fish-head music."

The Wipers
Portland, Oregon, USA
Formed in 1977, they were among the first to play tightly structured songs using heavy distortion — in other words, grunge. Nirvana covered two songs off their debut album, *Is This Real?*

Autosalvage
New York City, New York, USA
According to guitarist-vocalist Tom Donaher, Frank Zappa chose their name in 1967. "Frank had a particular liking for our signature song, 'Auto Salvage'…with a different meaning implied than junkyard for cars."

Chrome
San Francisco, California, USA
Experimental sci-fi rock from the turn of the '80s.

Alcohol Funnycar
Seattle, Washington, USA
Albums: *Time to Make Donuts* and *Weasel*.

Jesus Chrysler Supercar
Tempe, Arizona, USA
Pretty cool DIY punk Americana. The name is a pun on the 1970 "rock opera" *Jesus Christ Superstar* by Tim Rice and Andrew Lloyd Webber.

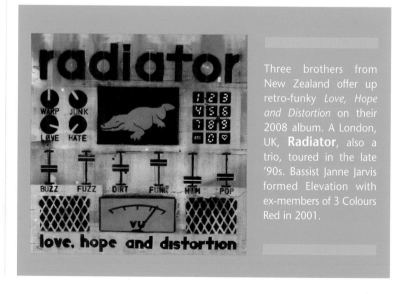

Three brothers from New Zealand offer up retro-funky *Love, Hope and Distortion* on their 2008 album. A London, UK, **Radiator**, also a trio, toured in the late '90s. Bassist Janne Jarvis formed Elevation with ex-members of 3 Colours Red in 2001.

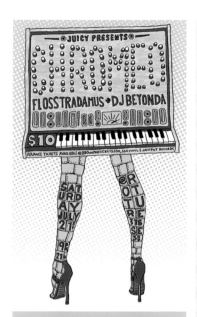

Patrick Gemayel (P-Thugg) and Dave Macklovitch (Dave 1) play Montreal electrofunk as **CHROMEO**. The Arab-Jewish duo have been best friends since childhood. Their songs have been used in video-game soundtracks and national ad campaigns. Albums: *She's in Control* and *Fancy Footwork*.

Demolition Doll Rods
Detroit, Michigan, USA

Danny, Margaret and Christine Doll Rod as half-naked glam-garage trio. "One memorable performance featured the band performing with only toy cartoon mouse heads covering their breasts, and only plastic wrap and semi-strategically placed slices of Swiss cheese covering their nether regions."

Box Car Racer
San Diego, California, USA

A side-project for Blink-182's Tom DeLonge and Travis Barker.

Hello Saferide Stockholm, Sweden
Fronted by songwriter and music journalist Annika Norlin. According to Norlin, the name Hello Saferide was "inspired by an intelligent bus driver in a drug-addicted small town — don't ask."

Dashboard Confessional
Boca Raton, Florida, USA

Perhaps to emulate those intimate parking confessions, the band makes use of quiet dynamics to connect with their audiences.

Ride Oxford, UK
The group considered the name Donkey, but called itself Ride after a piece of graphic design produced by band member Mark Gardener for a typography workshop. Bassist Andy Bell joined Oasis.

Swearing at Motorists
Dayton, Ohio, USA

The duo of singer-guitarist Dave Doughman and drummer Joseph Siwinski. Doughman has challenged the White Stripes to a "who can rock harder" contest.

The Crash
Turku, Finland

Started as Ladies & Gentlemen, became New Deal, then in 1997 the Crash. Nominated for Best Nordic Artist at the 2002 MTV Europe Awards.

Crash Test Dummies
Winnipeg, Manitoba, Canada

Started as Bad Brad Roberts & the St. James Rhythm Pigs. A med-school friend suggested the name Crash Test Dummies. They won the Canadian Juno Award as 1991 Group of the Year. Their second album, *God Shuffled His Feet*, sold more than 5.5 million copies worldwide.

Traffic Birmingham, UK
Drummer Jim Capaldi is generally credited with naming this legendary band, the idea having come to him while watching cars drive by. Traffic was inducted into the Rock and Roll Hall of Fame in 2004.

Eddie & the Backfires are based in Hannover, Germany, and record on the retro-rockabilly label Rhythm Bomb Records. They call their music "50s desperate rock'n'roll." *Cat Killer* is their 2006 album.

Swervedriver
Oxford, UK
Started as Shake Appeal. Hometown friends Ride passed Swervedriver's demo "Son of Mustang Ford" along to their record label.

Old Lady Drivers
New Jersey, USA
Started as Regurgitation. Record label: Earache.

Night Driving in Small Towns
Valdosta, Georgia, USA
Female-fronted alt-country band who sound exactly like their name.

Grand Theft Bus
Fredericton, New Brunswick, Canada
From the video-game *Grand Theft Auto*. Independent filmmaker Greg Hemmings made a mockumentary about the band entitled *Rubarbicon*.

TAXI TO THE OCEAN

Taxi to the Ocean began while its members were still students at the Lyceum in Baarn, Netherlands. With "sweet FA" to do in Baarn, they got together every Friday and Saturday nights to "play a bit of music, drink Coke and eat chocolate éclairs...Taxi to the Ocean was born." Now based in Utrecht, the band has three albums and countless club and festival gigs under their collective belt.

HERE COMES SUMMER
(THE CORINTHIAN/LEATHER EP)

Milwaukee, Wisconsin's **Trolley** released their *Here Comes Summer* EP in 1997. They have four CDs to date and appear regularly on the festival circuit. The band employs a '60s surf-pop sound and have toured with Reel Big Fish and New Found Glory.

Honeybus
London, UK
Honeybus...like honeywagon? UK #8 hit: "I Can't Let Maggie Go" (1968).

Superbus
France
Singer Jennifer Ayache stumbled across the word *superbus* in a Latin dictionary. It means proud or arrogant. The band won Best French Act at the 2005 MTV Europe Awards.

Death Cab for Cutie
Bellingham, Washington, USA
Singer-guitarist Ben Gibbard got the band's name from the title of a Bonzo Dog Doo-Dah Band song that was included in the Beatles' 1967 film, *Magical Mystery Tour* (the only non-Beatles composition). Death Cab's recent album *Narrow Stairs* reached #1 on the *Billboard* Top 200 chart.

TRAFFIC PROBLEMS: One Car Pile-Up (Scunthorpe, UK); **Three Car Pile-Up** (Philadelphia, USA); **Five Car Pile-Up** (Georgia, USA); **Seven Car Pile-Up** (Chandler, Arizona, USA). **Note: Cars only crash in odd numbers.**

Trains & Planes

Train

San Francisco, California, USA

Frontman Patrick Monahan started in a Zep cover band. Three of Train's four albums have reached the Top 10 in the *Billboard* 200, with sales of over 4 million copies.

Southern Pacific

Bay Area, California, USA

Early Doobie Brothers songs had a lot of train references. Southern Pacific members Keith Knudson and John McFee were former Doobie Brothers.

Grand Funk Railroad

Flint, Michigan, USA

A riff on Grand Trunk Railroad, a rail line that runs through Flint. The band does not play funk. Weird fact: Scorned by many critics and with little AM airplay, in 1971 the band sold out Shea Stadium in 72 hours, breaking an attendance record set by the Beatles.

Graham Central Station

San Francisco, California, USA

A pun on Grand Central Station, using the surname of bassist-singer Larry Graham (Sly & the Family Stone). This was a grand funk railroad station.

Ohio Express Ohio/New York, USA

Sir Timothy & the Royals from Mansfield, Ohio, connected with the NYC production team of Kasenetz and Katz (Super K Productions), who renamed them the Ohio Express and turned them into a backing band for singer-songwriter Joey Levine. A string of bubblegum hits included "Yummy Yummy Yummy" and "Chewy Chewy."

Brownsville Station

Ann Arbor, Michigan, USA

The "Smokin' in the Boys Room" guys. The character Lucky on the TV series *King of the Hill* declared Brownsville Station his favorite band.

The Leaving Trains

Los Angeles, California, USA

"The Leaving Trains were formed out of sheer boredom and suburban desperation in Los Angeles in the summer of 1980…."

Sopwith Camel

San Francisco, California, USA

Named for the British airplane used in World War I. Second album: *The Miraculous Hump Returns from the Moon.*

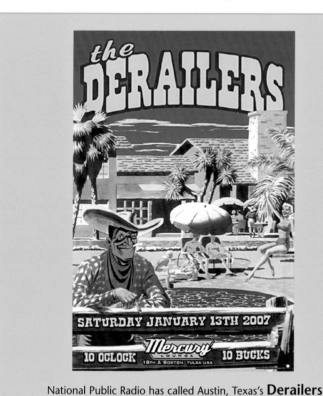

National Public Radio has called Austin, Texas's **Derailers** "hangdog honky-tonk at its best." Equal parts twang, jangle and harmony.

Chapel Hill, North Carolina's **STRATOCRUISER** recently released their new album, *Egg Shells. All Access Magazine* commented: "Long compared to the likes of Cheap Trick and Badfinger, Stratocruiser's sound could very well be the one that other bands get compared to from now on...." The Boeing 377 Stratocruiser was a long-range passenger aircraft introduced following WWII.

Led Zeppelin
London, UK

The dominant story behind the name is that bassist John Entwistle and drummer Keith Moon, both of the Who, mused about a group comprised of them and ex-Yardbirds guitarists Jeff Beck and Jimmy Page, deciding ultimately that such a combination would go down like a "lead zeppelin" commercially. Page picked up the name, half as a joke, and on the advice of manager Peter Grant, the *a* was dropped from Lead to avoid mispronunciation.

Aerosmith
Boston, Massachusetts, USA

The name was suggested by drummer Joey Kramer, who confessed to having doodled the word Aerosmith on his high-school notebooks after hearing Harry Nilsson's *Aerial Ballet* album. (Nilsson's grandparents had an aerial circus act.) It was a cool word. Also under consideration: The Hookers.

Jefferson Airplane
San Francisco, California, USA

"Blind Thomas Jefferson Airplane" was a made-up blues name, a la Blind Lemon Jefferson, concocted by Steve Talbot, a friend of guitarist Jorma Kaukonen.

Jet Melbourne, Australia

From the song "Jet" off the 1973 album *Band on the Run* by Wings. The band's break came when *New Musical Express* praised the single "Take It or Leave It" from their *Dirty Sweet* EP (named for the "Bang a Gong" lyric). Elektra Records soon offered Jet a contract and flew them to LA to record their debut album, *Get Born*. Next came the Rolling Stones' request that they join the Australian leg of their 2003 tour.

Sparklejet Fresno, California, USA

Sparkle Jet is guitar model manufactured by Gretsch Musical Instruments.

Mystery Jets
Eel Pie Island, Twickenham, UK

Two very good words put in the correct order.

747s Dublin, Ireland

Played their first show at Piazza del Gesu during a massive G8 protest.

Hellacopters Stockholm, Sweden

Formed in 1994, they received a Swedish Grammy for their debut album, *Supershitty to the Max!*, in 1996. The recently announced their dissolution with the release of their 7th album, *Head Off*.

The Missing Planes
Buffalo, New York, USA

A trio with female singer-guitarist Michelle Buono. Album: *Leaving the Scene*.

Black Box Diaries
Nottingham, UK

Flight data recorder. Three "really great good-looking guys" who just broke up.

Eve of Destruction

Anarchy Loves Chaos

Burn Baby Burn

Pollution & Plagues

Eve of Destruction

The Clash

The Clash consisted of singer-guitarist Joe Strummer, guitarist Mick Jones, bassist Paul Simonon and drummer Nicky "Topper" Headon. Formed in 1976, the Clash were a major UK success from the release of their first album. Their third, *London Calling*, brought international fame. Though it was released in the US in January 1980, *Rolling Stone* later declared *London Calling* the best album of the 1980s.

Simonon came up with the band's name: "It really came to my head when I start reading the newspapers, and a word that kept recurring was the word 'clash.' Other possibilities included the Weak Heartdrops and the Psychotic Negatives.

Joe Strummer's real name was John Graham Mellor. The stage name "Joe Strummer" came from time spent strumming the ukulele as a busker in the London Underground.

The Clash had their first gig, as supporting for the Sex Pistols, on July 4, 1976, (the bicentennial anniversary of the US).

They were inducted into the Rock and Roll Hall of Fame in January 2003.

The Alarm Rhyl, Wales

The Alarm started in the early '80s as a punkish acoustic-driven band called Seventeen, playing a final gig under the name Alarm Alarm. Thinking better of the doubled name in a time of Duran Duran and The The, they regrouped as the Alarm, went electric and took on a military-influenced look. The Alarm opened for U2 on that band's tour in support of the *War* album.

The Fray
Denver, Colorado, USA

Formed in 2002, the band chose their name from a suggestion bowl at the graduation party for Caleb Slade, younger brother of pianist-singer Isaac Slade.

The Ruiners
Detroit, Michigan, USA

Influences: "Evel Knievel, John Waters and Wayne Cochran, 'the White Knight of Soul.'" Songs: "Bee Stung Lips" and "More Tongue, Less Lip."

The Vandals
Huntington Beach, Virginia, USA

Formed in 1980, the Vandals liberally employ humor and irony to make their points. Albums include *When in Rome Do as the Vandals*, *Fear of a Punk Planet*, *Hitler Bad, Vandals Good*, *Internet Dating Superstuds* and *Hollywood Potato Chip*. Actor Keanu Reeves played bass for their 1993 New Year's Eve show.

Minneapolis-St. Paul band **the Alarmists** formed in 2005. They debuted with their 2006 EP, *A Detail of Soldiers*, which made the Top 10 of 2006 lists in both of the Twin Cities' major newspapers, as well as in the national alternative publication *The Onion*. The band subsequently took Best New Group and Artist of the Year honors at the Minnesota Music Awards. Their first full-length album is *The Ghost and the Hired Gun*.

The New Violators
Tronheim, Norway

Though only on the scene since 2006, this Scandinavian band's infectious '80s new-wave sound led Pitchforkmedia.com to say, "I will resort to begging: somebody, please, put out this band's record."

The Barbarians
Cape Cod, Massachusetts, USA

They attempted a barbaric look, and of course it helped that drummer Victor "Moulty" Moulton had lost part of one arm. Moulty played with a prosthetic limb ending in a hook that clamped onto his drumstick. He lost part of his left arm in an explosion at the age of 14. The song "Moulty" is a tongue-in-cheek tune chronicling the drummer's loss of appendage and subsequent misadventures.

Corrosion of Conformity
Raleigh, North Carolina, USA

Formed in 1982, this band chose a name that reflects its philosophy: "We really try hard to be true to what our hearts tell us to do. We do what we feel and we don't want to get caught up in any '90s-style production bullshit…So many bands are gonna laugh at themselves in ten years. We don't want that."

Infidels   Toronto, Ontario, Canada

In 1990 singer Molly Johnson reunited with her partner from Alta Moda, Norman Orenstein (guitarist, songwriter, producer). The band released a self-titled album in 1991. Johnson is now a jazz singer.

Devo   Akron, Ohio, USA

The name was developed by art students Gerald Casale and Bob Lewis. Devo refers to their theory of de-evolution, the idea that mankind is now regressing, "as evidenced by the dysfunction and herd mentality of American society." Around 1970, they met Mark Mothersbaugh, who showed them a pamphlet entitled "Jocko Homo Heavenbound," with its illustration of a winged devil labeled "D-EVOLUTION." With their love of costumes and biting satire, Devo became pioneers in music video, though they remain best known for their 1980 hit "Whip It."

Formed in Syracuse, New York, in 2006, **Ra Ra Riot!** in comprised of vocalist Wes Miles, bassist Mathieu Santos, guitarist Milo Bonacci, cellist Alexandra Lawn and violinist Rebecca Zeller. Spin.com called them "one of the best young bands we've heard in a really long time." They have opened for Art Brut, Editors, Bow Wow Wow and toured North America supporting Tokyo Police Club. Debut album: *The Rhumb Line*.

NAMES
STILL AVAILABLE

Out of Order

Bedlamp for Bedlam

Chaos Theory
Interns

Anarchist AmEx

1 Hour Terrorist

Megaton Soother

Plague of
His Own Making

Doom De Doom

Riot Wing Politicians

The MayHemis

Parsons of Arson

Asunder
Teakettle

Methods of Mayhem
Los Angeles, California, USA
Formed in 1999 by Mötley Crüe drummer Tommy Lee as a collaboration with rapper TiLo, with appearances by Fred Durst, the Crystal Method, Kid Rock, Snoop Dogg, Lil' Kim, George Clinton and Mix Master Mike. Lee has a large, ornate "Mayhem" tattoo across his stomach and reportedly "Methods of Mayhem" across his buttocks.

Quiet Riot
Los Angeles, California, USA
According to singer Kevin DuBrow, the name came from a conversation with Rick Parfitt of Status Quo, who, in his British accent, said he'd like to name a band "Quite Right."

Arsonists Get All the Girls
Santa Cruz, California, USA
Started in 2005 as a joke-between-friends band, developed as a death-metal-mathcore group with scary vocals. They've only been around since '05 but already list 9 former members, including a deceased bassist.

We Start Fires   Darlington, UK
Three firestarter women and a drummer named Ashley. *New Musical Express*: "Like one of the Deal sisters in a cosmic death-ray fight with Be Your Own Pet's Jemina."

High on Fire
Oakland, California, USA
Founded in 1998 by frontman Matt Pike, who previously played guitar for the stoner metal band Sleep.

ALEXISONFIRE

Formed in 2001, in St. Catharines, Ontario, Canada, the band describes their music as "the sound of two Catholic high-school girls in mid knife-fight. The name Alexisonfire was derived from Alexis Fire, the lactating-contortionist, stripper, porn actress-lobbyist and Moonlite Bunny Ranch worker who hopes one day to get her Ph.D. Side-projects: City & Colour, the Black Lungs, Bergenfield Four, Fucked Up.

Jason & the Scorchers
Nashville, Tennessee, USA
Led by singer-songwriter Jason Ringenberg, the Scorchers started in 1981 and helped opened the saloon doors for all brands of rock-with-boloties bands.

The Fiery Furnaces
Brooklyn, New York, USA
It sounded catchier than the Friedberger Furnaces or the Fiery Friedbergers. Primary members are brother and sister Matthew and Eleanor Friedberger.

244

Set Fire to Flames
Montreal, Quebec, Canada
A 13-member side-project of Godspeed You! Black Emperor, with eerie ambient sounds featured on their two recordings.

The Fireballs
Melbourne, Australia
The Fireballs formed in 1990 and have performed on support tours with KISS, 5,6,7,8's, surf king Dick Dale, the Supersuckers, Porno for Pyros, Midnight Oil and Primus. Between 1994-1997, they played up to 400 shows a year and "broke enough house attendance records to warrant their own Fire Department file [for over-capacity]."

Amusement Parks on Fire
Nottingham, UK
Formed in 2004 by Michael Feerick, who wrote all the songs and played all the instruments for their self-titled debut album. The band now writes and performs as a quintet.

Arcade Fire
Montreal, Quebec, Canada
Fronted by husband and wife Win Butler and Régine Chassagne, the band formed while Butler was attending Philips Exeter Academy in Exeter, New Hampshire. The name of the band refers to an actual fire that occurred in the Exeter Arcade.

Megadeth
Los Angeles, California, USA
Megadeth is, in theory, a unit of measurement equal to the death of one million people by nuclear explosion. Founder, frontman, guitarist and songwriter Dave Mustaine formed Megadeth after leaving Metallica in 1983.

BRUTAL TRUTH
is a New York City grindcore band formed in 1990 by ex-Anthrax, Nuclear Assault, and Stormtroopers of Death bassist Dan Lilker. The group disbanded in 1999, but reformed recently. Brutal Truth are pioneers of extreme metal and enjoyed particular success in Japan and Australia. Band members also play for Nuclear Assault, Venomous Concept, Damaged and Total Fucking Destruction

Napalm Death
Birmingham, UK
Formed by Nicholas Bullen and Miles Ratledge in 1982. "The early history of the band is one of constant member rotation: the group did not contain any original members by the time of the recording of the second side of their debut album *Scum* in 1987." Previous members of Napalm Death moved on

to form bands such as Carcass, Godflesh, Cathedral, Scorn, Jesu and Black Galaxy, and side-projects including Lull, Painkiller, Brujeria, Lock Up, Meathook Seed, Defecation, Teeth of Lions Rule the Divine and Venomous Concept.

Black Death
Cleveland, Ohio, USA
Formed in 1977, Black Death is thought to have been the earliest all-African-American metal band.

Anthrax
New York City, New York, USA
Anthrax is an acute disease in animals and humans created by bacterium transmitted via spores. It can be grown in a lab and used in biological warfare. Guitarists Scott Ian and Danny Lilker formed Anthrax in 1981. They found the band's name in a biology textbook and claim it sounded sufficiently evil. During the 2001 anthrax attacks in the US, the band's website provided factual information about the disease. In October that year, the band jokingly announced they were going to change their name to "something more friendly, like Basket Full of Puppies."

Thinking Plague
Denver, Colorado, USA
Thinking Plague was created by in 1982 by Mike Johnson and Bob Drake. According to Johnson, "The idea was to say something about that sort of existential condition of being unable to stop thinking, analyzing or otherwise intellectualizing…."

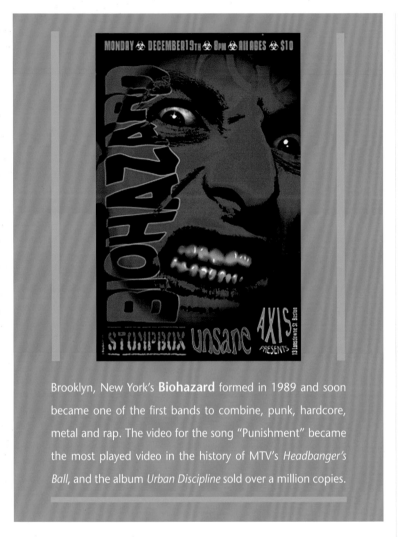

Brooklyn, New York's **Biohazard** formed in 1989 and soon became one of the first bands to combine, punk, hardcore, metal and rap. The video for the song "Punishment" became the most played video in the history of MTV's *Headbanger's Ball*, and the album *Urban Discipline* sold over a million copies.

Garbage
Madison, Wisconsin, USA

Formed in 1994, the band consists of Scottish-born Shirley Manson and Americans Duke Erikson, Steve Marker and Butch Vig. Manson had been a keyboardist and backup singer with Edinburgh's Goodbye Mr. Mackenzie, then briefly fronted side-project Angelfish. Erikson, Marker and Vig had done some rough recordings that someone said sounded like "garbage," the inspiration for their name. They saw Manson perform in an Angelfish video on MTV and asked her to be their lead singer.

Golden Smog
Minneapolis, Minnesota, USA

This loosely assembled group formed in 1989 as a reaction to the Twin Cities' hardcore scene and took their name from the Mel "the Velvet Fog" Tormé character parody "the Golden Smog" in the animated TV series *The Flintstones*. The band's lineup has at times included members of the Jayhawks, Wilco, Soul Asylum, the Honeydogs, Gear Daddies, Big Star, Son Volt and Run Westy Run.

The Walkin Talkin Toxins
Auburn Hills, Michigan, USA

Featuring past and present members of the Sillies, the Denizens, Red September and the Hypnotics. Self-description: "The Walkin' Talkin' Toxins' stage is littered with inflatable love-dolls and trampolines, a camouflage backdrop and life-size Tony Montana. The band rips through a version of the Velvet Underground classic "Heroin" when gas-masked guitarist Dick Monster breaks into his solo...a chain-saw solo....." Full-length album: *Apocalypse Au-Go-Go*.

Winds of Plague
Upland, California, USA

Originally named Bleak December, but changed their name to Winds of Plague in 2005, taking their name from lyrics in the Unearth's song "Endless."

Plaguesayer
Indianapolis, Indiana, USA

Massive-sounding grindcore band with guitar and string endorsement deals.

The Plague Monkeys
Dublin, Ireland

A plague monkey is an employee who comes to work sick and spreads his or her germs to fellow employees. The Plague Monkeys were fronted by singer Carol Keogh and multi-instrumentalist Donal O' Mahony, who are now Tychonaut (formerly Tycho Brahe, the name of a Danish astronomer from the late 1500s).

Introduction
to Religion

Gods, Faith,
Souls & Afterlives

Christianity, the Church,
Saints & Angels

Non-Christians, Heathens
& the Hellbound

Introduction to Religion

Gods, Faith, Souls & Afterlives

God Is My Co-Pilot

The band averages a show a week in New York City. They must have God as a co-pilot, given all the competition for gigs.

From MusicianGuide.com: "Under the leadership of the openly bisexual husband-and-wife duo of vocalist, clarinetist and keyboardist Sharon Topper and guitarist Craig Flanagin, God Is My Co-Pilot emerged as one of the most crucial voices in the underground music community of the 1990s. Along with a loose, revolving cast of downtown New York City players, Flanagin and Topper explored lyrical themes ranging from sexuality to radical politics to religious enlightenment, while their hard-to-define musical sound meshed no-wave noise, hardcore thrash, post-funk, avant-garde jazz, and even occasional touches of Middle Eastern chants, Finnish folk music, and Jewish music."

The band has been part of John Zorn's Radical Jewish Culture series and in 1994 released a collection of traditional Hebrew and Yiddish songs, *Mir Shlufn Nisht*,

The name originated as the title of Robert Lee Scott's autobiography. Scott was an American pilot with the Flying Tigers in Burma and China. His book was also made into a film with the same title.

Eyehategod
New Orleans, Louisiana, USA
Originally called Snuffleupagus on Acid. Snuffleupagus being a Sesame Street character. Lead singer Michael Williams was arrested for narcotics following Hurricane Katrina but subsequently kicked his heroin addiction.

God Lives Underwater
Perkiomenville, Pennsylvania, USA
Started by David Reilly and Jeff Turzo, and good enough to be produced by Rick Rubin and released on American Recordings subsidiary Onion. Turzo's previous band was GLU, which they used as an acronym to arrive at God Lives Underwater.

Godflesh   Birmingham, UK
Guitarist-vocalist Justin Broadrick: "The word God conjures something immense and inconceivable. The 'flesh' part is what affects you on a physical level. Our music is loud and destructive. Godflesh is the American Indian term for peyote, but that really is kind of a coincidence. It's a coincidence that suits me just fine, though.""

Waiting for God   Vancouver, British Columbia, Canada
The band claims to have borrowed the name from an episode of the TV series *Red Dwarf*. There was also a '90s BBC series with the exact title. And it seems like a short hop to Beckett's *Waiting for Godot*.

Santa Barbara, California's Chris O'Connor became **Primitive Radio Gods** when he departed his previous band, I-Rails, in 1991. That band had a song titled "Primitive Radio Gods." PRG's 1996 single "Standing Outside a Broken Phone Booth with Money in My Hand" received major airplay, and the album *Rocket* went gold in the US. O'Connor enlisted his former I-Rails members Jeff Sparks, Tim Lauterio and Luke McAuliffe for live shows, and they remained together to create the recent album *White Hot Peach*.

Godsmack
Lawrence, Massachusetts, USA
The band's name was taken from the Alice in Chains song "God Smack." The British term "gobsmacked" means to be utterly surprised by something.

Static of the Gods
Boston, Massachusetts, USA
Drummer Mike Latulippe encountered the phrase "Static of the Gods" while reading the Will Ferguson novel *Happiness*.

Amateur God

Ljubljana, Slovenia

Self-declaration: "Amateur God's name and concept offended some people…Not that I like to offend folks, but I am glad that I am causing reactions, a chance to get into colorful discussions, checking many points of view — humans' richness and at the same time menace." Recently toured Europe with Marilyn Manson.

Absurdeity

Hultsfred, Sweden

Band members have also played in G.O.D., Human Death, Matricide, Pornographical Harmony, Excessum, Wolverine, Mysterion and the Doomsday Cult.

By Divine Right

Toronto, Ontario, Canada

Formed by songwriter José Miguel Contreras in 1989 and including Leslie Feist and Brendan Canning (Broken Social Scene), and Rob Carlson and Scott Maynard (Rock Plaza Central).

Spirit

Los Angeles, California, USA

Led by guitarist Randy California (Randy Craig Wolfe), who played with Jimi Hendrix in Jimmy James & the Blue Flames in 1966. Originally called Spirits Rebellious, after the Khalil Gibran book *al-Arwah al-Mutamarrida* (*Spirits Rebellious*). Offered the spot before Jimi at Woodstock but turned it down.

Spiritualized

Rugby, UK

Formed by singer-guitarist Jason Pierce (aka J. Spaceman) after the breakup of Spacemen 3 in 1990.

The Devotions

Queens, New York, USA

This doo-wop group had a hit with the single "Rip Van Winkle" in the early '60s and still perform as an event band.

The Undisputed Truth

Detroit, Michigan, USA

Trademark painted faces and white afros. Had a #3 US hit with "Smiling Faces Sometimes" in 1971, recorded "Papa was a Rolling Stone" before the Temptations, and the lead singer on 1976's "You + Me = Love" was Chaka Khan's younger sister Taka Boom.

Blind Faith   Surrey, UK

Supergroup formed in 1969 with Ginger Baker, Eric Clapton, Steve Winwood and Ric Grech. The name is said to have been Clapton's take on performing with the new group.

Faith No More

San Francisco, California, USA

Started as Faith No Man in 1982. Original members included Mike "The Man" Morris. When the band decided to fire "The Man," they renamed themselves Faith No More. Courtney Love sang with the band in the early '80s.

True Believers

Austin, Texas, USA

Three-guitar assault from the '80s, with former members of the Nuns, the Zeros, the Lift and the Skunks.

Aphrodite's Child

Greece / France

Their last album, *666,* was based on the Book of Revelations. Keyboardist Vangelis Papathanassiou wrote the music for the films *Chariots of Fire* and *Blade Runner*.

NAMES
STILL AVAILABLE

Din of Odin

Scarfaith

God of Afterthoughts

The Deity Diet

Afterlife Curfew

B-League Believers

The Spirit Blisters

Collective Soul Bargaining Agreement

Godfellas

Tunnel, No Light

The AfterLavaLife

Mall Souls Day

Soul Asylum
Minneapolis, Minnesota, USA
Formed in 1984 from an earlier band called Loud Fast Rules. They played Clinton's inauguration in 1992. Members of Soul Asylum and the Replacements now play together in Golden Smog.

Soul Coughing
New York City, New York, USA
"'Soul Coughing' was the title of a really, really bad poem that [leader Mike] Doughty wrote about Neil Young throwing up in the back of a bus."

soulDecision
Vancouver, British Columbia, Canada
Boy band formed in 1994 as Indecision (they weren't really sure what style of music they played). They changed their name to soulDecision because there were already a few bands with the name Indecision.

Soul II Soul
London, UK
"We came up with the name Soul II Soul not just because of the music we played, but it also stood for Daddae and myself — two souls moving together."

The Soul Stirrers
Trinity, Texas, USA
Formed in 1926 by Roy Crain. First recorded in 1936 by Alan Lomax for the Library of Congress American Music Project. Inducted into the Rock and Roll Hall of Fame in 1989. At various times the group included Sam Cooke and Lou Rawls.

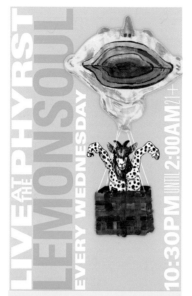

Lemonsoul was formed in the summer of 2003 and has developed a strong following in the State College, Pennsylvania, area by playing their own eclectic mix of material. The name Lemonsoul was created through attempts "to conjoin random words." Rejected: Creamtree and Snapplebird. Like so many band names, it wasn't meant to be permanent, but it stuck.

Soulfly Belo Horizonte, Brazil
Singer Max Cavalera formed band after his split from Sepultura in 1997. The name was chosen at a time when Cavalera was mourning the death of his stepson.

Collective Soul
Stockbridge, Georgia, USA
The name comes from Ayn Rand's *The Fountainhead*. Leader Ed Roland would like us to know they're "not preaching Ayn Rand, objectivism, egoism or anything."

Soulajar
Bakersfield, California, USA
Won a competition for bands with members who work at Starbucks (drummer Brian Boozer).

The Plimsouls
Los Angeles, California, USA
Evolved out of previous band, the Nerves. The word *plimsoul* comes from "Rock My Plimsoul," a traditional blues recorded by Jeff Beck and Rod Stewart in 1967. Which basically means "rock me to my soulful sneakers." Plimsolls are rubber-soled canvas shoes. First developed in Liverpool in the 1800s, they were informally referred to as "Plimsolls" because the colored band that joins the sole to the upper resembled the international load line on ocean freighters, a standard that British MP Samuel Plimsoll fought to establish. Not very rock and roll (or soul), but there you have it.

Neverending White Lights
Windsor, Ontario, Canada
Main guy Daniel Victor: "It just seemed like my lyrics are about having a soul and my soul being about all the energy that would continue to live on even after your body. If you die, and your body's here, your soul which was what gave you life would continue on into the next world; Almost like a neverending white light."

Sofamecca
Brisbane, Australia
Making the religious pilgrimage to the sofa. Assembled in 2002 to record the soundtrack for a short film entitled *Wilfred*. The band's singer, Jason Gann, also acted in the film.

Mecca Normal
Vancouver, British Columbia, Canada
The duo of Jean Smith (vocals) and David Lester (guitar) have recorded together for Kill Rock Stars since 1984 (13 albums). An early influence on Riot Grrrl music.

Heaven 17
Sheffield, UK
They took the name of a fictional band on a Top 10 list in chapter 4 of Anthony Burgess's *A Clockwork Orange*. Formed when Ian Craig Marsh and Martyn Ware split from Human League.

Nirvana
London, UK
A pre-Nirvana British Nirvana. The prog-rock duo of Alex Spyropoulos and Patrick Campbell-Lyons flourished in the late '60s early '70s. They were signed and produced by Island Records' Chris Blackwell. They reformed in the '80s, and in the '90s settled out of court on a lawsuit with some scruffy Seattle band. Both bands agreed to use the name.

Nirvana
Aberdeen, Washington, USA
Names under consideration: Skid Row, Pen Cap Chew, Bliss and Ted Ed Fred. They settled on Nirvana in early 1988 because Kurt Cobain "wanted a name that was kind of beautiful or nice and pretty instead of a mean, raunchy, punk-rock name like the Angry Samoans."

Fish Karma
Tuscon, Arizona, USA
Punk-rock satirist Terry Owen has worked with Jello Biafra. Albums include *Theory of Intelligent Design* and *Teddy in the Sky with Magnets*.

Karma to Burn
Morgantown, West Virginia, USA
They obviously aren't worried about karma. Songs: "(Waltz of the) Playboy Pallbearers," "Mt. Penetrator," and "Twin Sisters and a Half Bottle of Bourbon."

Karma 69
Henin-Beaumont, Nord-Pas-de-Calais, France (funk-reggae); Grosseto, Italy (rock); Querétaro, Mexico (alt-rock); Scarborough, Ontario, Canada (indie-rock).
Karma works on a credit system, with good or bad works transferred through chromosomes (loosely speaking). You need a score of 70 to be reincarnated as a human. Obviously, 69 is one short.

"Based in Philadelphia and Bucks County, Pennsylvania, **the Kharmacists** are the latest musical incarnation of four musicians who began playing together in the mid-1980s as the second generation of the Tough Luck Band. With inspirational roots in American blues, funk, swing, jazz, folk and classic rock, the result is an eclectic mix of original high-energy, syncopated, introspective and soulful songs. Unabashed and unapologetic, the Kharmacists seek to express musically their social views and personal emotions."

HIM

HIM formed in Helsinki, Finland, in 1991. The name is an acronym for His Infernal Majesty, a play on His Imperial Majesty as a title for Haile Selasse, which the band thought was funny at the time.

They have given many different explanations for their name in interviews.

HIM has toured under the name HIS and HER due to copyright issues over the name, but the Finnish HIM bought the rights from the Chicago post-rock band HiM and now uses it exclusively.

The band's logo, a "heartagram" (pentagram with two top points rounded to create a heart shape) is recognizable to fans worldwide.

Christianity, the Church, Saints & Angels

Black Leather Jesus
Houston, Texas, USA
Shock-rock and experimental noise, with S&M iconography.

The Jesus & Mary Chain
Glasgow, Scotland
Started as the Poppy Seeds. The band has said that the name was inspired by a cereal-box offer in which one could send away for a "Jesus and Mary chain."

Jesus Christ Superfly
Austin, Texas, USA
Jesus Christ Superstar meets *Superfly*. Side-project: Gravy Boat.

Jesus Jones   London, UK
They were on vacation in Spain and noticed all the (local) Jesuses and (UK tourist) Joneses.

MC 900 Ft. Jesus
Dallas, Texas, USA
The stage name of Mark Griffith. Disillusioned with the music biz, he got a pilot's licence, took a job as a bookstore clerk and currently DJs on weekends. The name came from Oklahoma televangelist Oral Roberts' claim of having seen a 900-foot Jesus in a vision.

Teenage Jesus & the Jerks
New York City, New York, USA
From 1976 to 1979 they played super-fast 30-second songs. Their career retrospective CD, *Everything*, is 18 minutes long.

Whoa! Man! Jesus!
Jamaica Plain, Massachusetts, USA
Song: "Jesus Was Not American."

Dropkick Me Jesus
Ontario, Canada
From the title of a Paul Craft song sung by Bobby Bare, "Dropkick Me Jesus, Through the Goalposts of Life."

Midget Jesus
Phoenix, Arizona, USA
Album: *What Would Midget Jesus Do?*

The Christians   Liverpool, UK
The surname of the three brothers in the band (Garry, Roger and Russell) and guitarist Henry Priestman's middle name.

Luxury Christ
Windsor, Ontario, Canada
Or Luxury Chrysler (in Canada's motor city)? Formed in 1988 by ex-Butthole Surfers Trevor Malcolm with percussionist Mark Sikich. Has since morphed into Citywide Vacuum.

Formed in 2000, Helsinki's **Superchrist** released their long-awaited debut album, *Colorgun*, in 2005. The record was praised highly in Finnish music publications, and the national newspaper, *Helsingin Sanomat*, gave the album 5 out of 5 stars. The band's follow-up album is 2007's *Surfing the Zeitchrist*.

Oakland's **Bean Bag Apostles** call themselves "new, hip, Beatlesque, smaller than Jesus!" They blend vocal and acoustic guitar harmonies into "a genre-bending ride through audio vistas. Hear a variety of acoustic-driven songs, inspired by the music they listened to growing up. NASA/CIA BBQ's, living room parties of the Seventies, and the pioneers of counter-culture reform movements…."

Christ on a Crutch
Seattle, Washington, USA
The name is from a blasphemous cursing expression.

Nervous Christians
Portland, Oregon, USA
Members also played in Wehrmacht, Bastard Children of the Roman Empire and Nixon Flat.

Impaled Nazarene
Helsinki, Finland
Meanwhile…this band "stopped wearing corpse paint in the mid-1990s due to it being too trendy." And at least one song on each album is to have the word "goat" in it ("Goat Sodomy," "Goat Vomit and Gas Masks," "Sadogoat," etc.).

Genesis
Godalming, Surrey, UK
Peter Gabriel and Tony Banks were students at Charterhouse School in Godalming. What became Genesis formed out of school bands Garden Wall and Anon. Songwriter-producer Jonathan King, a Charterhouse alumnus, discovered the band and named them Genesis. His first, dismissed suggestion was Gabriel's Angels.

Funky Blue Messiahs
Winter Park, Florida, USA
Albums: *The Further Adventures of Reverend PP Pettibones Traveling Tent Revival, Lost in Mississippi* and *Crawzilla*.

Disciples of Ed
Cloverdale, California, USA
Ed was Ed the Aardvark, a local character known for freaking kids out by eating ants.

Screaming Blue Messiahs
London, UK
They played several shows and recorded some early singles as Motor Boys Motor (the title of a Joe Strummer song) before settling on Screaming Blue Messiahs. Singer-guitarist Screaming Bill Carter was known for his wildly improvised lyrics and narrative rant. The rhythm section went on to form the Killer Bs.

Shotgun Messiah
Skövde, Sweden
This glam-hair band went by the names Kingpin & the Cools before moving to Hollywood in the mid-80s and changing their name to Shotgun Messiah (i.e., finding religion at gunpoint).

Apostle of Hustle
Toronto, Ontario, Canada
Broken Social Scene guitarist Andrew Whiteman spent two months in Havana in 2001, then returned to Toronto and formed a quartet to play Brazilian and Cuban folk songs and select covers. Recent album: *National Anthem of Nowhere*.

Levitikus
New York City, New York, USA
This Jewish-American band's founders met at Yeshiva in Florida. "Leviticus…is all about *Korbanos* (sacrifices)…a way of connecting us human beings in a physical world to a higher, non-physical power; namely God."

The Creation   Middlesex, UK
An English psychedelic group formed in 1966. Guitarist Eddie Phillips is said to have been the first to use a violin bow on a guitar on stage. Bassist John Dalton later joined the Kinks.

Adam & the Ark
Cumbernauld, UK
Self-declaration: "Adam & the Ark are in better bands called Eat Your Face Yes, Chemikal Lung and Physic."

All About Eve   Coventry, UK
Started as the Swarm in 1982. After the lineup change, they considered the names Electric Funeral and Red Red Wound, but All About Eve was chosen, after the 1950 Bette Davis movie.

Eve's Plum
New York City, New York, USA
Name derived from Eve Plumb, the name of the actress who played Jan Brady in *The Brady Bunch*.

Eve 6 Los Angeles, California, USA
Drummer Tony Fagenson was an *X-Files* fan. The episode "Eve" features genetically engineered "Eves," one of which, Eve #6, makes a remark about biting a guard's eyeball, which caused the drummer to commit Eve 6 to memory.

Blood of Cain
Chico, California, USA
Guitarist-vocalist Kirk Williams: "We read an essay in my 11th grade English class called 'Children of Cain' about the idea that the human race is the offspring of Cain, Cain being the first murderer. Children of Cain sounded too much like Children of Bodom, so we went with Blood of Cain."

The Ark Malmö, Sweden
"They made their own stage clothes with the help of [guitarist] Jepson's mother, who teaches in the art of sewing…At first their look was a bit hippie and glam-inspired, but soon they developed a new style which they called 'apocalyptic.'" A preacher's son, singer Ola Salo was convinced that the time of the apocalypse was upon us in 1991.

Sodom Gelsenkirchen, Germany
Formed by Tom "Angelripper" in an attempt to get out of having to work in coal mines.

Sodom & Gomorrah Liberation Front Denton, Texas, USA
Their song "Bludgeon" appears on the 1994 compilation *Welcome to Hell's Lobby*.

Judas Jump UK
Guitarist-keyboardist Andy Bown also played for Storyteller, Status Quo and with Peter Frampton in the Herd.

Judas Priest Birmingham, UK
From Bob Dylan's song "The Ballad of Frankie Lee and Judas Priest" off the *John Wesley Harding* album

Abraham's Meat Plow
West Virginia, USA
Began as Impending Doom but received a cease-and-desist order from another Impending Doom on the west coast. The band says the name Abraham's Meat Plow was taken from one of their early songs.

Revelation 21
Wilkes Barre, Pennsylvania, USA
"We adopt the name Revelation 21 — the Bible's description of God's ultimate destiny for the world — with the hope that those who worship and sing with us will experience a foretaste of that destiny."

Samson South East London, UK
Metal band formed by guitarist-vocalist Paul Samson in 1977. Famous for playing with future Iron Maiden singer "Bruce Bruce" (Bruce Dickinson) and drummer Thunderstick (Barry Graham), who played in a leather mask and surrounded by a steel cage.

Extra Virgin Mary is a vehicle for New York City singer deerfrance. She has performed live with David Bowie at Carnegie Hall, toured for two years with John Cale, and sung with Tom Verlaine. She formed Floor Kiss with Michael Paumgharden, a band deemed by the *New York Times* to be one of the best bands of the late '80's. She was also in the Blue Picts and the Lowriders, and in 2000 formed Extra Virgin Mary with Paul Chapin.

Casting Lots for Judah
Buffalo, New York, USA
From the biblical reference (in "Leviticus") to making decisions by throwing dice. Guitarist Tim Reardon studied at a seminary in Kentucky.

The hurtin' **Hillbilly Preachers** work the musical pulpit from Zagreb, Croatia (or Memphis circa 1950s). Their most recent album is Welcome to Confession, featuring "Brand New Fool," "Down the Drain" and "Leave the Bottle Open." Singer-strummer Don Karlos of Mississippi Queen is joined by veteran players Axel Praefcke (Cherry Casino & the Gamblers), Humpty Kirscht (Roundup Boys), Ike Stoye (Ike & the Carpers) and Don Pit (Mojo Stuff).

Nazareth Dunfermline, Scotland
Formed in December 1968, the band took its name from the opening line of the Band's song "The Weight": *I pulled into Nazareth / I was feelin' about half past dead.*

Pontius Copilot
Lexington, Kentucky, USA
Funny thing: A Pontius Copilot search on Google returned 666 page hits.

Future Bible Heroes
Boston, Massachusetts, USA
Side-project of Stephin Merritt (the Magnetic Fields, the Gothic Archies, the 6ths) and Chris Ewan (Figures on a Beach).

Whitechapel
Knoxville, Tennessee, USA
Named after the district in London, England, where Jack the Ripper killed his victims.

Lords of the New Church
London, UK
Before becoming Lords of the New Church, this punk supergroup played a one-off gig in 1980 as the Dead Damned Sham Band, referencing their previous bands, the Dead Boys, the Damned and Sham 69.

Amen Corner Cardiff, Wales, UK
Named after a 1954 play by James Baldwin. They had two late '60s hits in the UK: #1 with "(If Paradise Is) Half as Nice" and #6 with "Natural Sinner." Two members went on to form Judas Jump. Organist Blue Weaver played with the Bee Gees.

Metal Church
Aberdeen, Washington, USA
Metal Church started as Shrapnel and toured with Metallica. Metal enough?

Reverend Horton Heat (vocalist-guitarist Jim Heath) shares with the flock from Dallas: "There used to be this guy who ran this place in Deep Ellum, Texas, who used to call me Horton, and my last name is Heath. Anyway…right before the show, he goes, 'Your stage name should be Reverend Horton Heat! Your music is like gospel'…So I'm up there playing…people are saying, 'Yeah, Reverend!' What's really funny is that this guy gave up the bar business and actually became a preacher! Now he comes to our shows and says, 'Jim, you really should drop this whole Reverend thing.'"

Stone Temple Pilots
San Diego, California, USA
Began as Mighty Joe Young but were informed by a lawyer that Mighty Joe Young was the name of an existing blues musician. Based on fascination with the STP Motor Oil logo, they went for an STP name: Shirley Temple's Pussy. And when they had trouble booking gigs under that name, they became Stereo Temple Pirates and ultimately Stone Temple Pilots (though it would be fun to riff off the acronym STP with a new name for each gig).

Evangelicals
Norman, Oklahoma, USA
From press release: "Singer-guitarist Josh Jones leads the listener through tales of religion and revivalism, plus insanity, drugs, black-outs, zombies, good and evil, car crashes, love and a mental institution called Bellawood."

Manic Street Preachers
Blackwood, Wales, UK
Started as Betty Blue, after a Jean-Jacques Beineix film. While busking in Cardiff, singer James Dean Bradfield was told by a passerby that he looked like a "manic street preacher."

Deacon Blue
Glasgow, Scotland
"Deacon Blues" is a song off Steely Dan's 1977 album, *Aja*.

Ministry
Chicago, Illinois, USA
Formed in 1981 as a synth-pop band, then went heavier. The name was inspired by filmmaker Fritz Lang's 1944 classic, *The Ministry of Fear.*

The Proclaimers
Auchtermuchty, Scotland
Identical twins Craig and Charlie Reid were in a punk band called Eight-Eyes (both having been teased for wearing glasses). Regarding the name the Proclaimers: "It's a strong name, and it has certain gospel overtones to it, as well. Not that we set out to be a gospel band. We certainly didn't."

Smoking Popes
Chicago, Illinois, USA
Started as Speedstick in 1990. Became Smoking Popes in 1991. "Smoking" because they smoke excessively. "Popes" from the film *The Pope of Greenwich Village.*

Popemobile Perth, Australia
Short-lived band with Laura Macfarlane and Ben Butler. Macfarlane went on to form Ninety Nine in Melbourne.

Antique Seeking Nuns
Oxford, UK

"Cast Iron Bitch was an early favorite for a potential band name. That was until Nun Matt [Baber, keyboards] recalled his girlfriend's education at a convent school and [her] shocked midnight discovery of several highly respectable nuns heaving valuable religious artefacts into the back of a Ford Transit in order to...well, no one really knows what they were doing, but the mysterious Antique Seeking Nuns deserved to be honored anyway."

The Sisters of Mercy
Leeds, UK

Named after the Leonard Cohen song, but they are also a religious order.

The Holy Modal Rounders
New York City, New York, USA

Started in 1964 by Peter Stampfel and Steve Weber. Stampfel in the webzine *Perfect Sound Forever*: "First it was the Total Quintessence Stomach Pumpers. Then the Temporal Worth High Steppers...It kept changing names. Then it was the Total Modal Rounders. Then when we were stoned on pot, someone else, Steve Close maybe, said Holy Modal Rounders by mistake. We kept putting out different names and waited until someone started calling us that. When we got to Holy Modal Rounders, everyone decided by accumulation [sic] that we were the Holy Modal Rounders. That's the practical way to get named." Both men also played in the Fugs and the Clamtones. Stampfel formed the Unholy Modal Rounders and the Bottle Caps, as well. And Rounder Records is so named because of its affiliation with the band.

Atlanta's **Hot Young Priest** is a tight trio that "sonically embodies a constant struggle of give-and-take, where a stark melodious arrangement often erupts into snarling chaos at a moment's notice." Mary Byrne's vocals have been compared to those of Carol van Dijk and early P.J. Harvey. Byrne is joined by bassist Daniel Winn and drummer Chris Hansen. Their new record is *Fiendish Freaky Love*.

Leather Nun Gothenburg, Sweden
Named after an American underground comic book series *Tales from the Leather Nun*, which started in 1973 and featured the work of Robert Crumb, Manuel "Spain" Rodriguez, Dave Sheridan and Pat Ryan.

The Hostile Omish
Middlefield, Ohio, USA

Hey, seven albums since 1986 and the band wears Amish clothing for their live shows. From review in [Cleveland] *Scene*: "... much like the Dead Milkmen or the Vandals, [they] coin catchy choruses in songs such as 'Lizard Up My Butthole,' 'Who Put Sea Monkeys in Mom's Douche,' and 'Never Shake My Baby (My Fetus in a Jar)' that are screamed over punk rock guitar chords."

Horny Mormons
Sacramento, California, USA

Song "Red Neck Woman from Planet Mars" on the 1992 *Can of Pork* compilation.

Jehovah's Witness Protection Program
Ypsilanti, Michigan, USA

Guitar-vocals and drums duo. "JWPP loves to rock. We don't care what you think about rock and roll or 36-year-old boy-men who play it." Also the title of a book by Rich Kelly.

Jehovah's Shitlist
Minneapolis, Minnesota, USA

Band members: Johnny Heartless (guitar), Reverend Phil (vocals), Sister LeeAnn MacDougal (bass) and Pete Rex (drums). "The concept of Jehovah's Shitlist was initially created in the church basement of Our Lady of Perpetual Suffering, where Rev. Phil was an altar boy and Johnny was employed as a janitor. The two were drawn together by a deep love of smoking and sacramental wine. They initially started a two-man religious folk band but quickly discovered that Phil, only having a half-octave vocal range was going to be a strong deterrent."

All Saints London, UK
A band comprised of backing vocalists with ZTT recording studios near All Saints Road. Called themselves All Saints 1.9.7.5., after the street where they met and their year of birth. Later shortened to All Saints.

Altered Saints
Punto Fijo, Venezuela

Previous bands: Blasphemy, Slow Death, Hemera, Serpent Christ. A pun on Altered States.

Saint Alvia Cartel
Burlington, Ontario, Canada
Named after Ernest Alvia "Smokey" Smith, Canada"s last living recipient of the Victoria Cross for valor in WWII.

Saint Etienne Croydon, UK
Named for the French soccer team AS Saint-Étienne, European Cup runners-up in the '70s.

Saint Vitus California, USA
The doom-metal band started as Tyrant but changed their name to Saint Vitus, after the song "St. Vitus' Dance" by Black Sabbath. Saint Vitus Dance is a disease characterized by rapid jerking movements of the face, feet and hands.

St. Germain Paris, France
An acid jazz/ house project navigated by Ludovic Navarre, whose other projects go by the names Subsystem, Modus Vivendi and Deepside. Name from an historical figure: In the court of Louis XV, there was a character named Saint Germain who claimed to be several centuries old.

Armored Saint
Los Angeles, California, USA
Formed in 1982, the band went on hiatus in the '90s while singer John Bush sang with Anthrax, but reformed in 1999. Bassist Joey Vera has also played with Anthrax.

The Fair Saints
San Francisco, California, USA
As opposed to Unfair Saints? "The name Fair Saints came from a Breeder's lyric, after we found that the name Jackyl was taken."

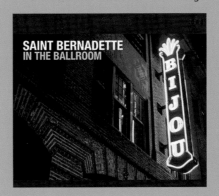

Though Bridgeport, Connecticut's **Saint Bernadette** plays music that seems born of '40s girl singers and epic '70s rock, songwriters Meredith DiMenna and Keith Saunders met through a hip-hop band and one of their first shows was an opening slot for Run-DMC. Saint Bernadette's first full-length album is *In the Ballroom*. *Fairfield Weekly* called them "a group that has matured like Uma Thurman — getting sleeker, sexier and ever more butt-kicking as time progresses."

Pale Saints Leeds, UK
Stared circa 1987, disbanded 1996. First EP: *Barging Into the Presence of God*. Spin-offs: Spoonfed Hybrid, the Terminals, ESP Summer, White Hotel and Rykarda Parasol.

Our Lady Peace
Toronto, Ontario, USA
First name: As If. Developed their sound through seminars with songwriter-producer Arnold Lanni, the owner of Arnyard Studios.

Comsat Angels Sheffield, UK
Named after the J.G. Ballard story "Comsat Angels." Comsat is short for communications satellite. The corporation Comsat threatened legal action, prompting the band to be called C.S. Angels in the US. Singer Steve Fellows went solo album. The rest of the band became Soup.

Black Angels Austin, Texas, USA
From the Velvet Underground's "Black Angel's Death Song."

Grievous Angels
Toronto, Ontario, Canada
Named after *Grievous Angel*, the second solo album by Gram Parsons, the band began as a collective of street buskers. One its members is now a federal Member of Parliament. Fiddler Peter Jellard also fronts Swamperella.

Blue Angel
New York City, New York, USA
Most famous for being Cyndi Lauper's band before she went solo. "Blue angel" is the slang expression for an ignited blast of human methane. Think frat party.

Morbid Angel
Tampa, Florida, USA
A death-metal band formed in 1983. They claim to have achieved "mainstream success" in 1992 when their video for "God of Emptiness" was used in an episode of *Beavis and Butthead.*

NAMES
STILL AVAILABLE

Faithbook Pals

Angels &
Tracheal Shunts

Java Church

Tight with Almighty

Church of the
Poisoned Mime

The Lazy Saviours

Pastor Pussycat

Collection Plate
Combo

Substitute Preacher

Our Lady Priest

The Bejesus
Brothers

100-Meter Moses

American Angel
Jersey City, New Jersey, USA
Formed in the '80s by vocalist Rocco Fury. Their website features an "American Angel of the Month," a sexy photo submitted by a fan.

Angel'in Heavy Syrup
Osaka, Japan
All-female retro-psychedelic band formed in 1990. The name? Guitarist Mine Nakao: "Canned fruit!" And the apostrophe is for kicks.

Angelic Upstarts South Shields, UK
An anti-fascist, skinhead Oi! band formed in 1977. The National Front used to come to their concerts to start fights.

Angels & Airwaves
San Diego, California, USA
Fronted by former Blink 182 and Box Car Racer guitarist Tom DeLonge, guitarist David Kennedy (Over My Dead Body, Box Car Racer), bassist Mat Wachter (30 Seconds to Mars) and drummer Atom Willard (Offspring, Rocket From the Crypt).

Angels in Anarchy
Sherbrooke, Quebec, Canada
"Angels in Anarchy's music made the eardrums of many snowmobile lovers vibrate at the Grand Prix de Valcourt 2005."

The Halo Benders
Olympia, Washington, USA
A '90s side-project of Beat Happening's Calvin Johnson with Doug Martsch of Built to Spill. Albums include *God Don't Make No Junk* and *Don't Touch My Bikini.*

Cool Blue Halo
Halifax, Nova Scotia, Canada
Album: *Kangaroo.* Guitarist-singer Barry Walsh now plays with Galore in Toronto.

Johnny Jones & the Suffering Halos Los Angeles, California, USA
"Singer-guitarist Johnny Jones was born the son of a Hellfire & Brimstone-preaching Baptist minister and a psychiatric-ward head nurse. At the age of 16, he left the church choir and his strict bible-belt home on a religious pursuit of Art, Sex, Drugs & Rock-n-Roll."

The Harptones
Manhattan, New York, USA
A doo-wop group who started in 1951 as the Skylarks. They added members and became the Harps, then changed their name to the Harptones to avoid conflict with Little David Baughn & the Harps. They have continued to tour successfully with original members and are considered an influential doo-wop group. They sang with Paul Simon on his 1983 album *Heart & Bones.*

The Miracles
Detroit, Michigan, USA
Started in 1955 as a doo-wop band called the Five Chimes, became the Matadors, then changed their name to the Miracles with the addition of a female singer. The band featured a guy named William Robinson, nicknamed "Smokey" because of his love of cowboy movies. Robinson was one of the early founders of Motown records, with Berry Gordy Jr., the Miracles manager. The band's "Shop Around" was the first Motown tune to reach #1 on the US R&B charts. After 1965 the band was billed as Smokey Robinson & the Miracles.

Non-Christians, Heathens, & the Hellbound

The Temptations
Detroit, Michigan, USA

Vocal groups the Primes and the Distants merged into the Elgins, but there was already a band called the Elgins. The Temptation was a suggestion from singer Otis Williams and Miracle Records employee Billy Mitchell. The *real* Temptations are considered to be the mid-60s lineup of Melvin Franklin, Eddie Kendricks, Otis Williams, Paul Williams and David Ruffin. But there are so many former members that in recent times, five groups called the Temptations were touring the US.

The Pagans
Cleveland, Ohio, USA

Designed to offend. Songs: "She's a Cadaver (and I Gotta Have Her)," "What's This Shit Called Love." Lead singer Mike Hudson wrote several books, including *Diary of a Punk*. Band memorabilia is included in the Rock and Roll Hall of Fame collection.

Sinphonic
Toronto, Ontario, Canada

Toronto is sin city. Sinphonic is fronted by George Westerholm, a writer on CBC news-hour comedy *This Hour Has 22 Minutes*. Westerholm has also performed with his brother Derek in the Creeping Nobodies.

Les Sinners
Montreal, Quebec, Canada

Started in 1967 after the break up of the Silver Spiders. Had some Canadian chart success with "Go Go Trudeau" in 1968.

Small Sins
Toronto, Ontario, Canada

Fronted by Thomas D'Arcy (the Carnations). Started a "Small Sins" blog on MySpace asking fans to send in a photo and confession of a small sin.

The Burning Effigies
Dublin, Ireland

"The themes in the lyrics range from suburban nervous breakdowns, to phone sex, to 19th-century revenge ballads."

Bad Religion

This Los Angeles punk band started in 1980 with Brett Gurewitz on guitar, Greg Graffin on vocals, Jay Ziskrout on drums and Jay Bentley on bass. Their MySpace page, 28 years later, states, "In a world ruled increasingly by superstition and intolerance, Bad Religion's rousing wall-of-sound punk seems about as necessary now as ever before. It is the impassioned sound of reason, anthems of a bittersweet idealism and a guarded hope set to propulsive guitars and charging drumbeats."

Despite the name of their band, Bad Religion members don't consider themselves antitheist. The band uses religion as a broad metaphor for anything that inhibits an individual's freedom to think or express themselves as they choose. Graffin is an atheist and co-author of the book *Is Belief in God Good, Bad or Irrelevant?* Gurewitz is an agnostic. Bentley has stated that he has a belief in God.

Graffin: "Faith plays an important role, but faith in people you don't know, faith in religious or political leaders or even people on stages...you shouldn't have faith in those people. You should listen to what they have to say and use it."

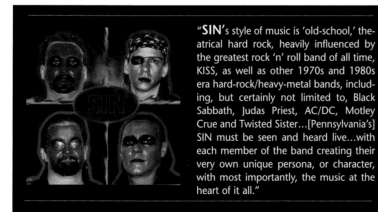

"**SIN**'s style of music is 'old-school,' theatrical hard rock, heavily influenced by the greatest rock 'n' roll band of all time, KISS, as well as other 1970s and 1980s era hard-rock/heavy-metal bands, including, but certainly not limited to, Black Sabbath, Judas Priest, AC/DC, Motley Crue and Twisted Sister...[Pennsylvania's] SIN must be seen and heard live...with each member of the band creating their very own unique persona, or character, with most importantly, the music at the heart of it all."

The Heathens Live from Los Angeles: "The music is about getting out and riding choppers...We're influenced by beards, dirty Levis, clean welds, coffin tanks, rigid frames, Frisco style, motorcycling's past and our California scene and out-of-state extended motorcycle brotherhood. We practice so our friends, who smash their fingers making brackets and suffer flash-burn after hours at the welder all day, have something cool to do at the end of the week." Their recent album: *Beach Blanket Beatdown*.

Toasted Heretic Galway, Ireland
Album: *Now in New Nostalgia Flavour*. Songs: "Love Theme from Yeats: The Movie" and "LSD Isn't What It Used to Be." Singer Julian Gough has written two novels, *Juno & Juliet* (2002) and *Jude: Level 1* (2007).

Agnostic Front
New York City, New York, USA
Among the first on the NYC hardcore front. Formed by ex-Eliminators guitarist Vinnie Stigma, who co-owns a tattoo parlor called New York Hardcore Tattoos with Murphy's Law singer Jimmy Gestapo.

The Searchers Liverpool, UK
Formed in 1959, the band took its name from the 1956 John Wayne western. Several '60s hit singles.

The Seekers
Melbourne Australia
The first Australian band to achieve commercial success in the US and UK. "I'll Never Find Another You," written by Dusty Springfield's brother Tom, was a #1 UK hit in 1963 and #4 in the US.

The Rationals
Ann Arbor, Michigan, USA
Lead guitarist Steve Carroll's brother suggested the mathematical term Rational Numbers.

The Fraternity of Man
Los Angeles, California, USA
Evolved out of the Factory in the late '60s. From liner notes: "Fraternity of Man is the band that forms the link between Frank Zappa & the Mothers, Lowell George & the Factory, Little Feat, and Captain Beefheart & His Magic Band."

The Fratellis Glasgow, UK
It means "brotherhood" in Italian. The band got their name from the family of bad guys in the 1985 film *The Goonies*.

The Brotherhood of Man
London, UK
Formed in 1969 by producer Tony Hiller. An early lineup featured Roger Greenaway, who co-wrote "I'd Like to Teach the World to Sing," and Tony Burrows who sang with Edison Lighthouse and as a studio singer on various 60s hit records. Lots of lineup changes and an ABBA-like approach to music, leading to their enduring popularity in the gay community.

Atheist Sarasota, Florida, USA
Founded in 1984 as Oblivion, became R.A.V.A.G.E. (Raging Atheists Vowing A Gory End), simplified themselves as Atheist in 1988. Members have also played with Neurotica, Pestilence and Cynic.

THE MENTORS

Where to enter the legend?! In 1976 the three friends attending Roosevelt High School in Seattle started to play primitive heavy metal with punk attitude and offensive lyrics. **The Mentors** were guitarist Sickie Wifebeater (Eric Carlson), bassist Heathen Scum (Steve Broy) and singer-drummer El Duce (Eldon Hoke). They wore black executioner hoods in concert, recorded an album, had the lyrics to their song "Anal Vapors" read aloud at the Parents' Music Resource Center Hearings (as evidence of sinful, corrupting compositions), and opened for the Revolting Cocks. El Duce (pictured here on the cover of the band's 2006 album) hit the media again in 1997 when he claimed that Courtney Love had offered him $10,000 to kill Kurt Cobain. This led him to appear on the *Jerry Springer Show*, where he made certain comments about underage groupies that led even his fellow guests, theatrical shock-rockers GWAR, to condemn him. That April, an inebriated Eldon "El Duce" Hoke was struck by a train while standing on the tracks near his home. R.I.P., El Duce. In his absence, Heathen Scum has stepped forward as lead vocalist, and Moosedick (Clark Johnson) has filled the vacant drummer's throne.

Nihilist Spasm Band

London, Ontario, Canada

Founded in 1965 and apparently still playing almost every Monday night ("audience welcome, but not necessary") at the Forest City Gallery. Most members have been artists, academics and librarians. The "Nihilist" came from the parody political organization the Nihilist Party of Canada. "Spasm Bands" were organized by poor African-Americans who of necessity constructed their own instruments.

Nihilistics

Long Island, New York, USA

Started in 1979 and played their last show at CBGBs along with the Dead Boys. A 1984 *Newsweek* article quoted their guitarist as saying, "I'd rather hear the worst, filthy truth than the most beautiful lie."

The Jews Brothers

Auckland, New Zealand

"The lineup is two Kiwis, two New Yorkers and a Londoner. Between them they play accordion, mandolin, banjo, double bass, guitar, soprano and tenor saxes, melodica and zydeco washboard."

Jewdriver Oakland, California, USA

Started out as G.I. Jew. The thought that started it all: "Wouldn't a Jewish skinhead band be a great idea?" Jewdriver is a pun on Skrewdriver, the name of a neo-Nazi skinhead band.

Kinky Friedman & the Texas Jewboys Medina, Texas, USA

Richard "Kinky" Friedman is a singer, former columnist, detective-fiction novelist and politician. His first band was King Arthur & the Carrots. Song: "They Ain't Makin' Jews Like Jesus Anymore."

"Filthy grooves. Freakish songforms. Unabashed virtuosity. Combining influences and studies in jazz, rock, classical and world musics, **Buddha's Belly** creates a unique form of entertainment: Crime Jazz. Rock fans headbang. Funk fanatics get down. And jazz enthusiasts are blown away by the mind-teasing, ear-pleasing experience of Buddha's Belly…Buddha's Belly has shared the stage with a wide array of bands, including Umphrey's McGee, the Virginia Coalition, ulu, and Rachael Yamagata. They've also headlined shows at Chicago's House of Blues, New York's Elbow Room and festivals across the Midwest."

The Angry Buddhists

Falkirk, Scotland

The Angry Buddhists were Arab Strap, but Aiden Moffat left and took the name for his new band, so the guys left standing nameless called themselves the Angry Buddhists, which was actually a name thought up by Aiden's brother Gavin, who had played in an earlier incarnation of the band. An Arab Strap is a sexual garment involving metal rings and leather straps.

Buddha Thunkit

Morgantown, West Virginia, USA

Members have since joined with Drain Babies to form Jonestown.

Lewd Buddha

Bronx, New York, USA

Hey, what's lewd now may not have been lewd 2,500 years ago. Debut album: *Soap & Tobasco*. Lewd Buddha has played with George Clinton. If anyone could stir the Buddha's freak, it would be GC.

Zen Bungalow

Winnipeg, Manitoba, Canada

Bassist Rod Slaughter formed the duo Duotang with Sean Allum (Bovine). Bovine and Zen Bungalow shared rehearsal space. Slaughter also plays in Novillero.

Bungalow Zen London, UK

Started out as Bungalow Zenn in 2002 but dropped the second "n" for their debut album *Holier than Thou*.

Zen Guerrilla

San Francisco, California, USA

Previous bands: Marcus Hook, the Gollywogs, Stone Groove and No Comment. Collaborated with Jello Biafra on the album *Positronic Raygun* (1998).

Monks of Doom

Santa Cruz, California, USA

Formed out of Camper Van Beethoven. Disbanded when guitarist-vocalist David Immerglück joined Counting Crows.

The High Llamas London, UK

Started in 1991. Took their name from a character played by Michael Nesmith on *The Monkees* TV show. In a skit called "The Monkey's Paw," the High Lama has to sleep it off. Also lama vs. llama.

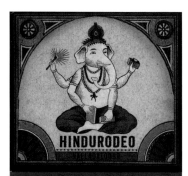

PopMatters.com reviewer Gary Glauber on the album *Nalladaloobr*: "**Hindurodeo** champions the disaffected card-carrying intellectual elite of power-pop, a moniker sadly no longer even remotely connected to the term 'popular.' These songs manage to tout this latest generation coming of age in the new millennium while at the same time poking fun at them. Songwriter, bassist, lead vocalist, and main creative force Joel Sayles does this in a convincing manner, his acerbic vitriol filtered through pleasant, well-crafted songs that sport melody, harmony, and infectious hooks."

Hindu Garage Sale
Milwaukee, Wisconsin, USA
This incarnation survived from 2003 to 2007. Several members also played in Batteries Not Included and the Freak Show.

Hindu Love Gods
Athens, Georgia, USA
A one-off side-project with Warren Zevon. R.E.M. (minus Michael Stipe) and backup singer Brian Cook, who were hanging out because they were recording Zevon's *Sentimental Hygiene* album.

The Hindi Guns
Portland, Oregon, USA
Fronted by Deedee Cheriel (Adickdid, the Teenangels). Guest appearances: Lemmy (Motorhead) and Henry Rollins (Black Flag). Band also included filmmaker Kurt Voss.

Cynic Guru Reykjavik, Iceland
Leader Roland Hartwell (violin) started the band in Los Angeles in the 1990s as Where's My Hair, changed the name to SkotLaPop then Cynic Guru. Hartwell accepted a job with the Icelandic Symphony Orchestra and reformed his band with new members in Reykjavik in 2001. First single, "Drugs," went #1 in Iceland.

Boogaloo Swamis
Boston, Massachusetts, USA
Formed by fiddler Mickey Bones in 1984. Bones also plays in Krewe De Roux, Mickey Bones & Jump Crew, Hot Tamale Brass Band, the Hubcaps, the Bones of Contention, Spitwhistle, and Sticky Chicken.

The Gandharvas
London, Ontario, Canada
Started in 1989 as the Droogs, then the London Droogs, became the Gandharvas in 1993. In Hindu mythology, the gandharva are male nature spirits, part human, part animal — "wild drinkers, sensual, ravishers of women."

Hoodoo Gurus Sydney, Australia
The Hoodoo Gurus' first performance was on a kids' TV program. A revised edition of the band scored some college radio hits and toured with the Bangles, who sing backing vocals on "What's My Scene." The Hoodoo Gurus were inducted into the Australian Recording Industry Association Hall of Fame in 2007.

The Mojos Liverpool, UK
A 1960s Merseybeat band originally called the Nomads, and later Stu James & the Mojos. Biggest hit: "Everything's Alright" at #9 UK in 1963.

Wall of Voodoo
Los Angeles, California, USA
Started by Stan Ridgway (keyboards, vocals) as a film-score business called ACME Soundtracks. The name arrived when drummer Joe Berardi jokingly referred to Ridgway's production techniques being "Wall of Voodoo" in comparison to Phil Spector's famous "Wall of Sound."

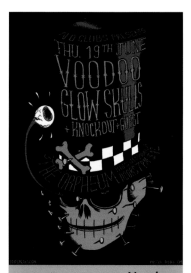

Riverside, California's **Voodoo Glow Skulls** include brothers Eddie, Frank and Jorge Casillas, with childhood friend Jerry O'Neill on drums. They often add a horn section for live shows and recordings. The name comes from "the little glow-in-the-dark skull that you get at Disney." The band sings in Spanish and English, sometimes recording the same song in alternate language versions, and sometimes perform in Mexican wrestling masks.

The Hex Dispensers
Austin, Texas, USA

Members previously in Blacktop, Feast of Snakes, Manikin, the Winks, Tractor Sex Fatality, This Damn Town and the Brotherhood of Electricity.

The Cult Bradford, UK

Formed by vocalist-songwriter Ian Astbury in 1981 as the Southern Death Cult, an anthropological reference to a certain 14th-century Native American tribe. Gradually became Death Cult, then just the Cult, with addition of Bill Duffy on guitars. Astbury has recorded with ex-Doors members as Riders on the Storm. Members past and present have played with Guns N'Roses, Porno for Pyros, Coloursound, Velvet Revolver, Holy Barbarians and the Sisters of Mercy.

The name **Hellzaboppers** is derived from the 1941 dance movie *Hellzapoppin'*. On New Year's Eve 2001, guitarist Cliff Quan and singer Dave Townley, both Los Angeles natives, decided to put together a top rockabilly band. That band now includes bassist Randy Stanton, drummer Lance Tamanaha and Japanese saxophonist Takao. Their full-length CD is *L'il Swamp Girl*.

Zodiac Mindwarp & the Love Reaction
London, UK

The creation of Mark Manning (aka Zodiac Mindwarp), editor of *Flexipop* magazine. Band members went by Kid Chaos, Slam Thunderhide, Evil Bastard, Trash D Garbage, Flash Bastard, Suzy X, Tex Diablo and Robbie Vom.

Adolf Satan
Boston, Massachusetts, USA

Their website notes that guitarist Josh Martin was released from prison and requests that we watch for updates.

Beta Satan Aarhus, Denmark

Self-declaration: "Elitist, prophetic, defiant psychic violence in a pop-coating from Denmark's self-appointed band of genius." Just imagine how good Alpha Satan will be!

Buck Satan & the 666 Shooters
El Paso, Texas, USA

A side-project for Ministry's Al Jourgenson in "Hell Paso." Meant to be an industrial-metal-country band.

Satan's Cheerleaders
Austin, Texas, USA

Performances feature psychobilly go-go dancers in "a Texas-style pep rally from Hell." Named after Graydon Clark's 1977 sexploitation flick, in which a high-school janitor must find a virgin for a coven of Satanists to sacrifice.

Devildriver
Santa Barbara, California, USA

Formed when singer Dez Fafara left Coal Chamber in 2002 to join the band formerly known as Area 51. With Fafara, they became Deathride, until they learned of a Deathride bike-racing team. Then came Devildriver.

Oslo's **Glucifer** hit the Norwegian music scene in 1994, determined to create a new golden age of Scandinavian rock. Their aggressive debut single, "God's Chosen Dealer," kicked off a career that saw them pack European clubs, appear with the likes of Motörhead and release five full-length albums, joining Hellecopters, Turbonegro and the Hives at the forefront of Norwegian rock. Their *Best of and Rarities 1994–2005* two-disc album was released in 2008.

Full Devil Jacket
Jackson, Tennessee, USA

A pun on Stanley Kubrick's 1987 film, *Full Metal Jacket*. The band met in a tattoo parlor owned by lead singer Josh Brown's brother. Started as the Voodoo Hippies.

NAMES
STILL AVAILABLE

Atheist
Breakfast Club

Dallas Tao Boys

The Zorroastrians

Demonic
High Colonic

Hell's
Checkout Line

Black Juju
Jujubes

Mine Says 665

Lucifer's
Septic Service

Virgil
the Virtuous Pagan

Beale Street
Beelzebubs

Leeches of the Styx

Suntan Satan

Plaid Tongued Devils started as an alt-country duo in Calgary, Alberta, Canada, in 1990, but by 1992 had grown to a quintet, playing a mix of country, klezmer, roma, ska, rock and jazz. Or *romaklezkarock*. "Think *Fiddler on the Roof* on steroids with Eddie Van Halen on violin and a guy with horns singing. Then dance!" The band has released five albums, completed four highly praised European tours, and created the hit play *Klezkavania*.

Electric Hellfire Club
Kenosha, Wisconsin, USA
Formed in 1991 by keyboardist-vocalist Thomas Thorn after his departure from My Life with the Thrill Kill Kult. Thorn was inspired by Britain's legendary 18th-century Hellfire Clubs, private dens of upper-class debauchery.

The Demonics
Santa Cruz, California, USA
"Tracks about cars, girls and Satan!" They perform in devil costumes, naked and/or in drag.

Dantalian's Chariot
Bournemouth, Dorset, UK
In demonology, Dantalian is the Great Duke of Hell. This late '60s psychedelic rock group evolved from Zoot Money's Big Roll Band. A young Andy Summers held he guitar chair for a while. They receive a 4 out of 5 on the Trip-O-Meter from Dr. Schluss' Garage of Psychedelic Obscurities website.

Richard Hell & the Voidoids
New York City, New York, USA
Richard Hell (vocals, bass) started music with the Neon Boys, who became Television, then went to the Heartbreakers (not Tom Petty's band) with ex-members of the New York Dolls before forming the Voidoids in 1976. Punk anthems "Blank Generation" and "Who Says It's Good to Be Alive?""

As Hell Retreats
Hendersonville, Tennessee, USA
"We are a five-piece metal/death-metal band who are using our music to spread the word of God."

Elevator to Hell
Moncton, New Brunswick, Canada
Lo-fi psychedelic rock. Spinoff from Eric's Trip lead man Rick White. Started in 1994 when Rick wrote a song called "Elevator to Hell." Dallas Good of the Sadies was added as a second guitarist in 1997.

Styx   Chicago, Illinois, USA
Started as the Tradewinds in 1961. When signed to Wooden Nickel Records in 1963, they chose the name Styx because it was the only name on the list that none of them hated.

Arts & Letters

The Same Old Song & Dance

Your Shutter Is Bugging Me

Sorry, I'm Booked

Arts & Letters

Culture Club

In 1981 George O'Dowd sang with Bow Wow Wow using the stage name Lieutenant Lush. The audience attention led him to adopt the name and persona Boy George and to start his own band with bassist Mikey Craig.

At one point Culture Club was to be In Praise of Lemmings or the Sex Gang Children. The name Culture Club had nothing to do with the cultured nature of its members, but was a reference to the different cultures in the group, including a bassist of Jamaican descent, a Jewish drummer, a straight Englishman on guitar and an Irish transvestite as singer.

Culture Club's first album, *Kissing to Be Clever*, was released in 1982. The first two singles fared only modestly, but the third, "Do You Really Want to Hurt Me?," went to #1 in the UK and eventually hit #1 in over a dozen other countries. Their second album, *Colour by Numbers*, had the singles "Church of the Poison Mind," "Karma Chameleon," "Miss Me Blind," "It's a Miracle" and "Victims."

When Culture Club won the 1984 Grammy Award for Best New Artist, Boy George gave his speech via satellite: "Thanks America, you've got taste, style, and you know a good drag queen when you see one."

Art Brut
Deptford-Bournemouth, UK
Debut album: *Bang Bang Rock & Roll* (2005). Named for French painter Jean Dubuffet's definition of art by prisoners, the mentally ill and other marginalized people; art made "without thought to imitation or presentation."

The Art of Noise   London, UK
Formed in 1983, the band hoped in part to pay homage to composer Claude Debussy and to the "Art of Noises" experiments of Italian futurist Luigi Russolo. Their 1999 album was entitled *The Seduction of Claude Debussy*.

Based in Portland Oregon, **Trash Art** creates thoughtful arrangements and layered harmonies, then presents them with honest art-rock energy. The band's first full-length album is *Little Broken Words*. Trash Art is Chris Robley (songwriter, vocals, guitars, keyboards), John Stewart (vocals, drums, percussion), Robert PeArt (guitars, keyboards, effects) and Steve Keeley, (vocals, bass, violin).

The Same Old Song & Dance

Electric Light Orchestra
Birmingham, UK
In the late 1960s, Roy Wood of the Move had the idea to form a band that would use strings, horns and woodwinds to give rock music a classical sound, "picking up where the Beatles left off." Jeff Lynne, then frontman for the Idle Race, was excited by the concept. Wood added cellos to Lynne's "10538 Overture," and it became the first Electric Light Orchestra song and a UK Top 10 hit. The group's name is an intentional pun on the use of electric instruments with a "light" orchestra.

Orchestral Manoeuvres in the Dark
The Wirral, Cheshire, UK
Andy McCluskey and Paul Humphreys were in several Wirral Peninsula bands as teenagers, including Pegasus, Hitlerz Underpantz, and in 1978 an ambitious 7-piece band called the Id. Eventually, the two gave in to their love of synths and electronic new wave, becoming Orchestral Manoeuvres in the Dark, or simply OMD.

THE POLYPHONIC SPREE was formed in Dallas, Texas, in 2000, by Tim DeLaughter (ex-Tripping Daisy), with a 10-member choir and more than a dozen musicians to perform "choral symphonic rock."

The Neon Philharmonic
Nashville, Tennessee, USA
Formed in 1967 by songwriter-keyboardist Tupper Saussy and singer Don Gant. Album: *The Moth Confesses*. Saussy's previous work includes *A Swinger's Guide to Mary Poppins*.

Love Unlimited Orchestra
San Pedro, California, USA
A 40-piece orchestra formed in 1972 by the immortal Barry White to spread the love over countless lush tracks.

Pukka Orchestra
Toronto, Ontario, Canada
A new-wave band formed in 1979. The band's name was donated unknowingly by a relative of guitarist Tony Duggan-Smith, who felt that Tony should forget rock bands and find paid work with a "pukka orchestra," *pukka* being Hindi for "proper."

Haunting Oboe Music
Austin, Texas, USA
Or Oboe Hunting Music? Curious. Kinda good. No oboes, of course.

The Asylum Choir
Tulsa, Oklahoma, USA
The Asylum Choir was the duo of songwriter-pianist Leon Russell and guitarist Marc Benno, recorded in Russell's studio in the late '60s.

The Choir Practice
Vancouver, British Columbia, Canada
A large collective of West Coast band members and solo artists who assemble to drink wine and perform non-choral music in a choral style.

Spandau Ballet
London, UK
Formed in 1976 as the Cut, later becoming the Makers. Singer Gary Kemp and guitarist Steve Norman had both attended Dame Alice Owen's School, so ballet may have been a natural reference. However, the two claimed the name Spandau Ballet was a reference to Nazi war criminals dancing at the end of the rope when hanged at Spandau Prison.

NAMES
STILL AVAILABLE

Finnegan's
Wake-Up Call

Zwan Lake

Fully Loaded
Baryshnikovs

Call of the Wild Thing

Faceless
Expressionists

Snoop Don Quixote

A Choir of
Watercolorists

Orchestral
Manoeuvres in Aisle 6

The Missing Reel

Time of the Cezannes

The Indexers

Catcher in the Tequila

The Bolshoi
Bath, UK
Well, the singer-guitarist and the drummer were in the punk band Moskow and....

Asphalt Ballet
San Diego, California, USA
A term used to describe a motorcyclist who, in a crash situation, skids along the highway at high speed. Album: *Blood on the Highway*.

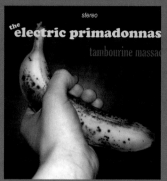

THE ELECTRIC PRIMADONNAS are a modern garage-rock trio from Oklahoma City. "The name was the only way to explain our style and personality." They have written, recorded, produced and released two full-length indie albums, *Tambourine Massacre* and *Subconscious Overdrive*. Members consist of Brian Pierce on drums, Chance Pickett on bass and vocals, and Chris Anderson on guitar, vocals and keys. "Chance has been in the band since November '06. We had two bass players before him but one got hit in the head with a softball."

Formed in 1977 in Syracuse, New York, **the Flashcubes** combine timeless British Invasion melodies with the energy of punk and new wave. In 2002 the band celebrated their 25th anniversary with a tour of Japan and the release of *Brilliant*.

Aztec Camera Glasgow, UK
Acoustic-guitar indie-pop from Roddie Frame and a rotating crew of collaborating musicians. The two words "sounded right," with the "Camera" coming from the B-side title of the first single by Liverpool's the Teardrop Explodes.

Your Shutter Is Bugging Me

The Stills
Montreal, Quebec, Canada
The name was chosen for them by a friend, "a small star of the New Ethiopian Cinema in the late 1980s," who died young. The friend was a fan of 1950s American film noir.

Focus Netherlands
Guitarist Jan Akkerman: "The name Focus provides an insight into the musical intentions within the band." It also got them more airplay in 1971 because DJs got to say, "That's 'Hocus Pocus' by Focus."

Cinema Strange
Los Angeles, California, USA
They are cinematic...and strange: a "cacophonous blend of American death-rock and European post-punk ."

Dirty Projectors
Brooklyn, New York, USA
Music by Dave Longstreth and friends. Album: *Graceful Fallen Mango*.

Toronto-based guitarist, singer, songwriter, creative force Joel Gibb leads his **Hidden Cameras** through live performances that have been known to include go-go dancers, strippers, guest musicians, videos, and projected lyrics for audience participation.

Sorry I'm Booked

Modern English
Colchester, UK
They were modern. They were English. They were the Lepers. Well, before they added drums and keyboards and became Modern English. Probably best remembered for 1982's "I Melt With You," which has been used in several commercials and films.

Saga
Oakville, Ontario, Canada
A saga is a long story of heroic achievement. Band members played in the Pockets, then in Fludd, before settling in as Saga. Their 1978 debut album did only modestly well in Canada but sold over 30,000 copies in Germany as an import. It also took off in Puerto Rico. Further investigation revealed that a local stereo store was using part of the single "Humble Stance" in its radio ads.

Bad English
Los Angeles, California, USA
Formed in 1988, Bad English reunited keyboardist Jonathan Cain with singer John Waite and bassist Ricky Phillips, former band mates in the Babys. The band got its name from a game of pool. Waite missed a shot, and Cain ragged him about the bad "English" he put on the ball. Bad English was *not* chosen because the Babys had failed to use the correct plural spelling.

The Crime Novels
Minneapolis, Minnesota, USA
"Melding '70s soul with film noir imagery and raw rock and roll." And dark suits and ties, all gangster-like.

The Divine Comedy
Ireland
The epic poem *The Divine Comedy* was written by Dante Alighieri between 1308 and his death in 1321. Many of leader Neil Hannon's songs have literary references, as well. Their first album was *Fanfare for the Comic Muse*. Eight albums later, their most recent album is *Victory for the Comic Muse*.

This Birmingham, UK, band was initially known as Pilot but discovered the name had already been used by a '70s Scottish group, so they became the Pride. They then changed drummers and became Snowfield. It wasn't until the end of 2004, when the group signed to Kitchenware Records, that they decided to become **Editors**.

Dewey Decibel System
Denver, Colorado, USA
Named for the Dewey Decimal System of library cataloging and for band leader Dewey Paul Moffitt, whose day-job is audio engineer at Denver's Pepsi Center.

Copyright
Vancouver, British Columbia, Canada
Formed by ex-members of Slow. The band spelled its name as the symbol ©, but pronounced it "Circle C." They released the first © album in 1991 and, for some reason, it sold poorly. They also tried the names Flour, Mo, and Christian Thor Valdson's Freeze-Dried Dog.

Milton & the Devil's Party
Philadelphia, Pennsylvania, USA
Derived from a passage in William Blake's *The Marriage of Heaven and Hell* in which Blake calls poet John Milton "a true Poet and of the Devil's party without knowing it."

Uriah Heep
London, UK
It was the 100th anniversary of Dickens' death in 1970 when the name of *David Copperfield* villain Uriah Heep was suggested as a band name by producer Gerry Bron.

Alice in Thunderland
Bridlington, UK
Alice's Adventures in Wonderland is that wildly inventive, much morally scrutinized tale written by the Reverend Charles Lutwidge Dodgson (Lewis Carroll) and published in 1865.

Malice in Wonderland
Bergen, Norway

Alice's Adventures in Wonderland has been published in 125 languages and never been out of print. This book will likely run a close second.

Frumious Bandersnatch
San Francisco, California, USA

Frumious Bandersnatch was a psychedelic band active from 1967-69. The Bandersnatch is a fictional creature in Lewis Carroll's poems "Jabberwocky" and "The Hunting of the Snark," as well as in *Through the Looking Glass*, the sequel to *Alice's Adventures in Wonderland*. In "Jabberwocky" the hero is told to "Beware the Jubjub bird and shun the frumious Bandersnatch."

Phantom Tollbooth
New York City, New York, USA

Post-punk band founded in 1984. *The Phantom Tollbooth* is a 1961 children's novel by Norton Juster and illustrator Jules Feiffer.

Veruca Salt Chicago, Illinois, USA
A rough-edged girl-band with a couple of backup rhythm guys. Toured with Hole. Released *American Thighs*. Veruca Salt is the selfish girl who wants a trained squirrel and ends up down the garbage chute in Roald Dahl's 1964 book *Charlie and the Chocolate Factory*. And in the films.

A Handful of Dust
New Zealand

Free-noise band with guitar, violin and drummer. A novel by Evelyn Waugh published in 1934. Waugh took the title from a line in a 1922 T.S. Eliot poem entitled "The Waste Land."

Montreal, Quebec's **Tricky Woo** was nominated for Best Alternative Album at the 2000 Juno Awards. Tricky Woo is the name of a wealthy woman's pampered lapdog in James Herriot's *All Creatures Great and Small*.

Steppenwolf
Los Angeles, California, USA

Der Steppenwolf was Hermann Hesse's 10th novel. It has lone wolves and despair; good for art. Steppenwolf began life in Toronto as the Sparrows, and then s-less as the Sparrow. Producer Gabriel Mekler suggested the name change from the Sparrow to Steppenwolf, noting the Hesse novel. Hippies dug Hesse. And Johnny Kay looked over his sunglasses and said, "Whatever gets your motor running."

The Triffids Perth, Australia
Inducted into the Australian Recording Industry Hall of Fame in 2008. *Day of the Triffids* is sci-fi author John Wyndham's 1951 novel. It became the basis for a BBC radio series and TV serial, as well as a feature film.

Fahrenheit 451 Essex, UK
Punk trio. Recent album: *The Digerati*. A 1953 novel by sci-fi author Ray Bradbury. The title's reference is to the temperature at which paper is said to combust, 451 degrees Fahrenheit.

Hot Water Music
Gainesville, Florida, USA

Hardcore band with double vocals. The title of a 1983 collection of stories by Charles Bukowski. Of course Bukowski's title references Handel's *Water Music*.

Kiss Me Deadly
Montreal, Quebec, Canada

Kiss Me Deadly is Mickey Spillane's 1952 novel, the 6th featuring private investigator Mike Hammer. It was also the 1955 film noir drama based on the novel, and the 1981 album by Billy Idol's Generation X, their last.

Duran Duran
Birmingham, UK

In the 1968 Roger Vadim film *Barbarella*, Milo O'Shea plays the role of Dr. Durand-Durand. (Jane Fonda plays Barbarella. Keith Richards 1967–79 squeeze, Anita Pallenberg, is in it, too.) Anyway, Nick Rhodes and John Taylor were watching the film, heard "Duran Duran" and thought, *Cool name*.

Virginia Wolf
Worsley-Manchester, UK

Late '80s band with Jason Bonham on drums for their two albums. Virginia Woolff was an English novelist and essayist.

Jack Kerouac Knapsack Band
Toronto, Ontario, Canada

Album: *She Said Boom*. Jack Kerouac was a Beat generation novelist and poet.

Bands Are People Too

- Writers, Artists & Musicians

- Stars of Stage & Screen

- Leaders, True or False?

- Dead People in Encyclopedias

- A Rogue's Gallery

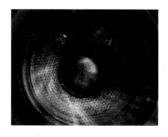

Bands Are People Too

Gogol Bordello

Originally named Hütz & the Béla Bartóks (their madly animated leader is Eugene Hütz), but, says Hütz, "nobody knows who the hell Béla Bartók is in the United States." The multilingual Gypsy punk band derives its current name from Ukrainian writer Nikolai Gogol and the more gentlemanly name for a brothel. Hütz has remarked that Gogol smuggled Ukrainian culture into Russia, and likewise Gogol Bordello will sneak Gypsy culture into English-speaking society.

Band members (8 or so musicians and dancers) live in New York City and first became known for their wild stage shows in clubs on the city's lower east side in 1999. While Gogol's drummer is from Florida, the rest of the band have recent roots in the Ukraine, Russia, Israel, China, Ecuador and other far-flung musical worlds.

Albums: *Voi-La Intruder* (1999), *Multi Kontra Culti vs. Irony* (2002), *Gypsy Punks: Underdog World Strike* (2005) and the critically acclaimed *Super Taranta!* (2007), which *Filter* magazine said "cements further the untouchable status of Gogol Bordello." National Public Radio's *All Songs Considered* declared them "the greatest live band in New York."

Garrison Killer
Madison, Wisconsin, USA

From the name of *A Prairie Home Companion* writer-host Garrison Keillor. The band offers "the Punk Rock Home Companion."

H.P. Lovecraft
Chicago, Illinois, USA

Late '60s psychedelic band named after American fantasy-horror writer H.P. (Howard Phillips) Lovecraft.

Dali's Car   UK
A short-lived (1984) band formed from the ashes of Bauhaus and Japan, and named for a track from the album *Trout Mask Replica* by Captain Beefheart & His Magic Band.

The Dandy Warhols
Portland, Oregon, USA

From the name of pop artist Andy Warhol.

Dead Man Ray   Berchem, Belgium
Man Ray (Emmanuel Radnitzky) was a major contributor to Dadaist and Surrealist movements through his avant-garde photography and painting.

Gocart Mozart
Winona, Minnesota, USA

From the lyrics of Manfred Mann's "Blinded by the Light": *And Go-cart Mozart was checkin' out the weather to see if it was safe outside....*

The Rembrandts
Los Angeles, California, USA

Here is the reason you never hear the rest of Rembrandt's name: it's Rembrandt Harmenszoon van Rijn. He is considered one of the most important painters in European art history. The Rembrandts are two pop songwriters known as the authors of the theme from *Friends*.

Van Gogh's Ear
Minneapolis, Minnesota, USA

A Minnesota surf band! Over 30 different diagnoses have been made regarding Vincent Van Gogh's mental illness. On Christmas Eve 1888 he cut off his left earlobe during "some sort of seizure."

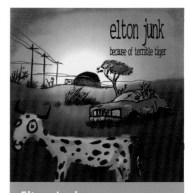

Elton Junk is an inventive art-rock band from Chianti, Italy, featuring Andrea Tabacco on vocals and guitar, Alessandro Pace on bass and Marco Bianciardi on drums and percussion. Their *Because of Terrible Tiger* CD was released in 2007.

Picastro Toronto, Ontario, Canada
Folk-rock with cello. Why not.
Picasso/Castro. Cuban Cubism.

Bram Tchaikovsky Lincolnshire, UK
The name of the band and stage
name of its lead singer. Peter
Bramhall kept his Bram and nicked
the surname of Russian composer
Pytor Iiyich Tchaikovsky.

The Dead Kenny Gs
Seattle, Washington, USA
A spin on the Dead Kennedys, with
smooth jazz saxophonist (Seattle
native) Kenny G as the victim.

Gringo Star Atlanta, Georgia, USA
Tip of the hat to Ringo Starr.

Ringo Deathstarr
Austin, Texas, USA
Combining a drumming Beatle with the
"Death Star" space station from *Star
Wars* to produce big-reverb shoegaze.

Founded by childhood friends Bob
Place and Brandon Pittman, with the
recent addition of Jeff Snider on
drums. Atlanta's **Swank Sinatra**
released their debut album, *John
Merrick Was a Handsome Man*, in
2007. (John Merrick being "the
Elephant Man.") CreativeLoafing.com
says, "Swank Sinatra is neither
swanky nor Sinatra, but they're damn
good on stage."

Bastard Sons of Johnny Cash
Austin, Texas, USA
Former punker Mark Stuart had a
dream about the name. "The new
name was a joke, sort of. And yet,
soon enough, it wasn't a joke anymore. Soon enough, it was a band,
and soon enough, it was enough of a
band that Johnny Cash himself gave
them his personal seal of approval,
and Johnny Cash's own legitimate son
helped produce their first album."

**The Fat Chick
from Wilson Phillips**
Chico, California, USA
A reference to Carnie Wilson. Two of
Beach Boy Brian Wilson's daughters
made up the Wilson component of
early '90s pop trio Wilson Phillips.
Standing just 5'3", Carnie is said to
have reached 300 lbs. before having
a webcast gastric bypass. After dropping from size 28 to size 6, she posed
in *Playboy*.

Trashcan Sinatras
Irvine, Scotland
Name came in 1986 when someone
mentioned Frank Sinatra while bash-
ing on trashcan lids as part of a school
music exercise.

Neil Diamond Phillips
Chicago, Illinois, USA
Combining singer Neil Diamond with
actor Lou Diamond Phillips. "MySpace's
Most Popular Neil Diamond Tribute
Band."

Jon Cougar Concentration Camp
San Diego, California, USA
This mid-90s punk band lifts their
name from Rock and Roll Hall of
Famer John Cougar Mellencamp.

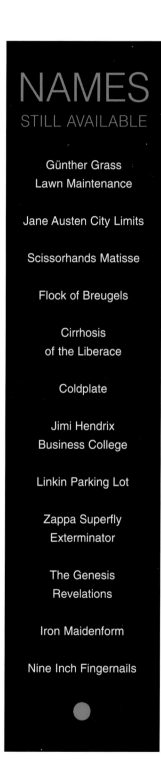

NAMES
STILL AVAILABLE

Günther Grass
Lawn Maintenance

Jane Austen City Limits

Scissorhands Matisse

Flock of Breugels

Cirrhosis
of the Liberace

Coldplate

Jimi Hendrix
Business College

Linkin Parking Lot

Zappa Superfly
Exterminator

The Genesis
Revelations

Iron Maidenform

Nine Inch Fingernails

The Shemps

The Shemps were an early '80s Seattle cover band whose members included Chris Cornell (on drums!), Hiro Yamamoto (bass), Kim Thayil (guitar) – basically the seeds of Soundgarden.

The Shemps were named for one of the original Three Stooges, Shemp Howard (Samuel Horwitz). The story goes that Sam's mother's Lithuanian Jewish accent rendered his given name as "Shemp." Shemp left show business for several years and was replaced by brother Jerome ("Curly"). But Curly suffered a stroke while filming *Half-Wits Holiday* and was unable to continue working. Shemp returned to the Stooges in 1947, coincidentally the year James Newell Osterberg Jr. (aka Iggy) was born.

A New York City band named the Shemps has a new album that invites you to *Spazz Out with the Shemps*. "We use expletives and make you dance like someone grabbed ya by the family jewels."

Stars of Stage & Screen

The Lost Valentinos
Sydney, Australia
Described by the *New Musical Express* as "a skittering shitstorm of punk fury, disco beats and psychedelic excursions…"; whereas, silent-film star Rudolph Valentino was a 1920s sex symbol whose death at age 31, following complications from surgery for a perforated ulcer, caused female fans around the world to mourn.

Bogart! Calgary, Alberta, Canada
Album: *In a Post-Oil World*. Song: "Taste the Pavement." In 1999 the American Film Institute named Humphrey Bogart the Greatest Male Star of All Time.

The Brandos
New York City, New York, USA
Trying to be as rough and ready as their namesake, Marlon Brando, Jr.

Marilyn Manson
Canton, Ohio, USA
Name shortened from Marilyn Manson & the Spooky Kids. Lead singer Brian Hugh Warner takes his stage name from actress Marilyn Monroe and murderer Charles Manson.

The Gena Rowlands Band
Los Angeles, California, USA
The Gena Rowlands Band "plays songs about b-movie starlets, x-movie starlets, ex-movie starlets…people born in the wrong skin, blonde strangers, convenience stores, bad parties…." American actress Gena Rowlands has twice been nominated for an Academy Award and has won a Golden Globe and three Emmies.

Kinski Seattle, Washington, USA
Klaus Kinski was an intense, deep-eyed German actor who performed in over 130 films, most notably five collaborations with director Werner Herzog. Father of actress Nastassja Kinski.

Don Knotts Overdrive
California, USA
Headset was formerly Don Knotts Overdrive. Don Knotts was the comedic actor who played deputy Barney Fife on the TV series *The Andy Griffith Show* and landlord Ralph Furley on *Three's Company*.

Doris Daze
Portland, Oregon, USA
All-American girl Doris Day appeared in some 40 films and recorded nearly 45 albums.

Hornets Attack Victor Mature
Hollywood, USA
The name Hornets Attack Victor Mature stems from a headline that ran in LA in the early '80s after the film star was attacked by wasps while playing golf. Pranksters created reports of Hornets Attack Victor Mature concerts, and in the mid-80s REM is said to have used the name for surprise gigs in small venues. For one such gig REM was booked into Athens, Georgia's Uptown Lounge as Hornets Attack Victor Mature, claiming to sound like "a combination of Jerry Lee Lewis and Joy Division."

Sandy Duncan's Eye
Los Angeles, California, USA
Hyper-perky Sandy Duncan lost sight in her left eye due to a tumor that damaged the optic nerve. She does not have a glass eye, as is often rumored.

The Voluptuous Horror of Karen Black

New York City, New York, USA

From the Whitney Biennial 2008 online bulletin: "Kembra Pfahler is the woman behind the Voluptuous Horror of Karen Black, a theatrical rock group that links a hideous monster aesthetic to a dark, hysterical feminine arche-type. Named in honor of cult horror film heroine Karen Black, Pfahler's band performs heavy-bottomed punk-metal songs amid elaborate hand-constructed sets where she engages an animalistic, fetishistic practice of acting out transgressive physical feats."

The Hefners

Lawrence, Kansas, USA

In hopes of one day visiting the Playboy mansion, each band member adopted Hefner as his surname. So far, no invitation.

The Travoltas hail from the Netherlands but play punchy power-pop in English with summery Beach Boys-like harmonies. Founded in 1990, they have toured Europe, the United States and Japan. Travolta-wise, they are perhaps more *Grease*-era than, say, *Battlefield Earth*, but with a hint of *Pulp Fiction*-al aggression in the guitar work.

Jodie Foster's Army (JFA)

Arizona and
Southern California, USA

A skate-punk band formed in 1981. The name refers to John Hinckley Jr.'s obsession with Jodie Foster and his subsequent attempt to assassinate President Ronald Reagan in order to get her attention.

Kathleen Turner Overdrive

Atlanta, Georgia, USA and Toronto, Ontario, Canada and US Army 4th Infantry Division, Iraq

It *is* a funny name, but 3 bands?! Sultry '80s actor Kathleen Turner replaces Randy Bachman and Fred Turner of Bachman-Turner Overdrive. You ain't seen nothing yet.

Mel Gibson & the Pants

Minneapolis, Minnesota, USA

Their alternate website is totallygross-nationalproduct.com.

Sharon Stoned   Germany

Supported 1996 Lemonheads tour of Europe. Named for American film seductress Sharon Stone.

Samuel Jackson Five

Oslo, Norway

Experimental instrumental band named for actor Samuel L. Jackson. No one named Jackson, only 4 mem-bers, none of African ancestry, none have (yet) battled a plane full of snakes.

The Al Roker Death Cult Wind Ensemble

Denver, Colorado, USA

Albert Lincoln "Al" Roker, Jr. is a long-time weather anchor on NBC's *Today Show*.

NAMES
STILL AVAILABLE

The Tuesday Welders

Discount Tom Cruises

George Harrison
Ford Dealers

The Denzel Washingtones

Keira Knightley
in White Satin

The Ryan Seacrest
Whitening Experience

Panic at
the Streep Club!

Generic Brandos

Minnie Driver Go-Karts

FondaHonda

Michael Caine Mutiny

Geena Davis's Inseam

The Dead Kennedys

In 1978 San Francisco, guitarist "East Bay Ray" Pepperell posted ads for musicians to form a punk band in 1978. In response, he got Jello Biafra on vocals, Klaus Flouride on bass and a guy calling himself 6025 on drums. Political from the start, Biafra took his name to juxtapose a mass-marketed American food product known for its entertainment value and a burgeoning nation state plagued by mass starvation. 6025 lost his drum job to Ted (real name Bruce Slesinger) the following year.

The name Dead Kennedys had enormous shock value, alluding as it did to the assassinations of John and Robert Kennedy in the 1960s, but it was meant as a comment on "the end of the American Dream," according to Biafra, not as a celebration of violence and anarchy.

Albums: *Fresh Fruit for Rotting Vegetables*; *In God We Trust, Inc.*; *Plastic Surgery Disasters*; *Frankenchrist*; and *Bedtime for Democracy*. While everything about the Dead Kennedys courted controversy – album art, song titles, lyrics, performance style – most of it was acerbically aimed at right-wing political policy and left-wing intellectual elitism.

Leaders, True or False?

Louis XIV
San Diego, California, USA
New album: *Slick Dogs and Ponies*. Louis XIV was the King of France for 72 years starting in 1654, a longer reign than any other monarch in history.

Boxing Gandhis
Los Angeles, California, USA
Putting some punch in nonviolent protest. "The more colors, the more accurate the picture" is still this multi-race, multi-gender band's philosophy."

Bullwinkel Gandhi
North Carolina, USA
We are led by a pacificist cartoon moose. Members of Stratocruiser, Clone Farm and the Dickens.

ABE LINCOLN STORY founder Steve Moramarco: "It was just one of those names that was on a drunken list of band name ideas, but I liked the idea that an 'Abe Lincoln Story' is also literally a tall tale." The Los Angeles-based ten-piece band sounds like "Louis Prima backing Booker T and the MGs." Pictured here is their 1996 album, *Dance Party*. Their most recent album is *The Kings of Soul Punk Swing*.

Propagandhi
Portage la Prairie, Manitoba, Canada
Vegan progressive-thrash band against imperialism, facism, capitalism, religion, racism, homophobia, human rights abuses, and so on. Website illustration depicts a slaughterhouse.

Octagandhi
South Bend, Indiana, USA
Their album *Backyard Sprouts* features a street intersection with an octagonal Stop sign bearing the image of Gandhi.

The Presidents of the United States of America
Seattle, Washington, USA
Because the name Queen was already taken.

Thomas Jefferson Slave Apartments
Columbus, Ohio, USA
Yes, America's 3rd president, the author of the phrase "that all men are created equal," owned slaves, maybe 200 or so, most of them inherited from his father and father-in-law.

Franz Ferdinand
Glasgow, Scotland
The assassination of Archduke Franz Ferdinand of Austria in Sarajevo in 1914 precipitated World War I. Glasgow's Franz Ferdinand was formed by musicians who had played together in Yummy Fur, 10p Invaders, Embryo and the Karelia. A discussion of a racehorse named the Archduke led to a digression about the Archduke Franz Ferdinand. "I don't want to over-intellectualize the name thing," singer-guitarist Alex Kapranos has said.

Cleveland's Calvin Coolidge on their 2006 album: "On its way to diminutive masterpiece of irresponsible postmodernism, **Calvin Coolidge**'s latest release, *Calvinism 3.0*, follows formula: drumkit, bass, guitar, vox, and a rotating cast of thirteen percussion samples...." Clean-shaven, small-government Republican Calvin Coolidge became the 30th president of the United States in 1924. He is said to have embodied the spirit and hopes of America's middle class.

The Churchills
Tel-Aviv and New York City
The Israeli Churchills played from 1965 to 1973. From a fanzine interview at Ugly-Things.com: " At one point we were 'Churchill's Hermits,' you know, as in Herman's Hermits." The NYC Churchills have played with OK Go, Yellowcard, They Might Be Giants and were on an episode of *Spin City*.

The Dick Nixons
Donaldsonville, Louisiana, USA
Songs about their beloved President Richard Milhouse "I Am Not a Crook" Nixon.

The G. Gordon Liddys
Oshawa, Ontario, Canada
Canadian Indie Band Database, 1998: "The seminal 1970s punk icons are back and better than ever with the release of their new concept album *Space Brains from Outer Space*, a story of Vikings, public transit, and dangerous things to do with your hands." Press release, February 1999:"Herbert R. Duffleworm, member of Canadian indie band the G. Gordon Liddys announced yesterday his plan to take a short nap." G. Gordon Liddy engineered the break-in at Democratic headquarters for President Nixon in what became known as the Watergate scandal.

Reagan Youth
Queens, New York, USA
A play on the infamous Hitler Youth of pre-war Nazi Germany. Reagan Youth performed regularly at CBGB during the '80s. Both of leader Dave Rubinstein's parents were Holocaust survivors.

From their website: "In addition to being sexy, **Dirty Lenin** is one of the 5 smartest bands in the world. Last February they defeated Radiohead in a game of Trivial Pursuit. The co-ed foursome resides in New York City. They have no children." Their *2% Faster* EP was released in 2006. Quirky, witty, party alterna-pop. Oh, the name: Dirty Lenin...dirty linen. Vladimir Lenin led the October Revolution and in 1922 became the first leader of the Russian Soviet Socialist Republic (back in the USSR).

NAMES STILL AVAILABLE

Ribbing Ramses II

Trotsky Horse

Groover Cleveland

Chairman Mao & the La-Z-Boy Rebellion

Ho Chi Minh Trail Mix

Thatcher's Iron Handbag

One Ayatullah Toomeini

Clinton Cigar Shop

Texas Cheney Saw Massacre

Kim Jong-il Scarlett

277

Cocteau Twins

The Cocteau Twins are a trio. They formed in Grangemouth, Scotland, in 1979 and were named by friends in the Glasgow band Johnny & the Self-Abusers, who themselves became Simple Minds (as a result of all the self-abuse). The Self-Abusers had a song entitled "The Cocteau Twins," which was eventually retitled "No Cure" and released on the Simple Minds album *Life in a Day*. This song makes no reference to Cocteau or twins and has the refrain "There is no cure," so "No Cure" was probably a better song title than "The Cocteau Twins," which freed it up as a band name. Pause for breath.

Jean Cocteau was a French intellectual — novelist, playwright, poet, filmmaker — and he wasn't a twin. I'm not sure if twins ran in his family.

To connect this back to the Self-Abuser: Cocteau claimed to be able to reach orgasm through the powers of his imagination, without touching his fiddly bits.

They've recorded nine albums and enjoyed chart success in the UK and elsewhere. Vocalist Elizabeth Fraser provided the vocals "Lament for Gandalf" in the film *Lord of the Rings: The Fellowship of the Ring.*

Dead People in Encyclopedias

Socrates (Drank the Conium)
Athens, Greece
Big-sound blues trio. Socrates (ca. 469–399 BC), father of ethics and also irony, was accused of corrupting the minds of Athens' youth and sentenced to death by drinking a potion derived from conium, or hemlock.

Full Throttle Aristotle
Brighton, UK
Somebody sign these lads. Seriously. Great sound. Great name. Aristotle was Plato's student and Alex the Great's teacher and was the first guy really into systematic logic.

Alexander the Great
Bloomington, Indiana, USA
Alexander the Great has played the Spazzatorium Galleria in Greenville, North Carolina. The ancient Greek guy was *Megas Alexandros* (I hear a Mel Brooks joke) and between 336 and 323 BC he was undefeated in battle, conquered the world (at least as much of it as was known to the ancient Greeks), and married two foreign princesses. All this by age 32.

The Maccabees Brighton, UK
They claim to have opened a Bible and picked a name at random. Earlier Maccabees established Jewish independence in Israel from 164 to 63 BC.

Tang Dynasty Beijing, China
Often referred to as the first heavy metal band in China, Tang Dynasty sold over 2 million copies of their debut album in 1992. In Chinese history, the Tang dynasty existed from 619 to 907 (with a brief interruption). It was a golden age of poetry, and the band employs such lyric poetry in its music. During this dynasty, China grew to an estimated 80 million people. The big thing, though, is that they figured out how to use hydraulics to power air-conditioning fans.

Joan of Arc Chicago, Illinois, USA
Red Yellow Blue got together after their first show, burned themselves at the stake, and changed their name to Joan of Arc. They've recorded 12 albums since 1997.

Jethro Tull Blackpool, UK
Quirky, inventive rock with flute. Named (by a history buff on their booking agent's staff) for 18th-century English agricultural pioneer Jethro Tull, inventor of the seed drill and author of *The New Horse-Houghing Husbandry*.

Paul Revere & the Raiders
Boise, Idaho, USA
Lots of late '60s pop hits. Mr. Revere was born Paul Revere Dick, with given names commemorating the American Revolution patriot who is said to have made "the midnight ride" from Boston to Lexington to warn Samuel Adams and John Hancock of movement by the British Army.

Quoting Napoleon
Portland, Oregon, USA
Napoleon is said to have said: "An army marches on its stomach"; "A picture is worth a thousand words"; "England is a nation of shopkeepers." A bunch of stuff. But he said it in French.

THE EDISONS are a Tampa, Florida-based pop quartet with a jangly vintage '60s-'70s sound. Rickenbacker guitars and harmonized vocals. Thomas Alva Edison invented a number of things and perfected many others but is best known for having developed a long-lasting lightbulb that was able to be mass produced and a system of centralized power-generating stations. He was the youngest of seven children.

Combustible Edison
Providence, Rhode Island, USA
Members of the rock band Christmas explore their loungier side as Combustible Edison, with debut album *I, Swinger*. Combustible Edison is a pun on New York power company Consolidated Edison.

Edison Lighthouse London, UK
The name is a play on Eddystone Lighthouse, off Cornwall, but also a nod to the Edison Memorial Tower in Edison, New Jersey, and the idea of lighting up the world.

Gang of Four Leeds, UK
The thinking person's punk band? Their name refers to political theorists Foucault, Barthes, Lacan and Lévis-Strauss. Not to be confused with China's Gang of Four: the widow of Mao Zedong and three of her closest allies, arrested in 1976 and blamed for the negative aspects of the Cultural Revolution.

The Jean-Paul Sartre Experience
New Zealand
A pun on the Jimi Hendrix Experience. A lawsuit by Sartre's estates turned them into the JPS Experience. Sartre was an important French existentialist philosopher who wrote, among many things, *Being and Nothingness*.

Tesla Sacramento, California, USA
In 1984 they were City Kidd. Their manager pointed out that it wasn't a good name. Tesla was more mysteriously electric. Nikola Tesla discovered and invented a whack of principles and things electrical, including wireless communication.

Now That's Contemporary is the 2003 album from Boise, Idaho's **EINSTEIN'S ITCH**. John Warfel writes, "Einstein's Itch was brought together in the spring of 2000. Each member came from other bands (that they had been kicked out of) with a desire to write original music. This music mixed unusual harmony and exploring rhythm with a love for the latest seasonal colors." Einstein's itch is that niggling urge to create something genius.

NAMES
STILL AVAILABLE

Hissy Fit Spinoza

The Thomas Crapper Experience

Hiphopocrates

Pythagore US

Rorschach's Soup Stain

Darwin's Finger Eleven

B.F. Skinner Daycare

Erik the Sparkling Rosé

Orange Julius Caesar

The Starstruck Galileos

Hammurabi Williams

Catherine the Great Pony Club

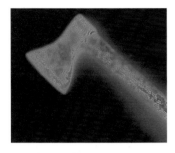

Molly Hatchet

Jacksonville, Florida-based vintage southern rock. The band is named for a 17th-century southern prostitute who allegedly decapitated and/or chopped up her clients.

The band formed in 1975 with Danny Joe Brown on vocals, Bruce Crump on drums, Banner Thomas on bass, and Dave Hlubek, Steve Holland, and Duane Roland on guitar. Their eponymous debut album, released in 1978, went platinum in the US, and its successor, *Flirtin' with Disaster*, went double platinum.

The three-guitar lineup gave the band a sound that appealed to fans of groups such as fellow Jacksonvillians Lynyrd Skynyrd, and through the end of the '70s they played upward of 250 gigs a year, touring with acts such as Aerosmith, REO Speedwagon and Bob Seger.

To date, the band has recorded 12 studio albums and an additional 12 live or compilation albums. Despite numerous changes in personnel, Molly Hatchet marches on — and even sails on, having been booked on Lynyrd Skynrd's "Simple Man Cruise" for 2009, with Skynyrd, the Marshall Tucker Band, Cigar Store Indians, and others.

A Rogue's Gallery

Attila the Stockbroker
East Sussex, UK
The "band" and the alias of poet-singer John Baine (who also fronts the punk band Barnstormer). Named for Attila the Hun, aka "Scourge of God."

Marquis de Sade
Rennes, France
Turn-of-the-80s post-punk, new-wave band sometimes referred to as "the French Joy Division." Through his lifestyle and writings (the latter mostly completed while in prison or insane asylums), Donatien Alphonse François de Sade, the scandalous Marquis de Sade, an aristocrat by birth, embraced sexual pleasure (and pain) devoid of social mores and religious morality. It is from his name that the term "sadism" is derived.

The James Gang
Cleveland, Ohio, USA
Known as the band that Joe Walsh played in back in the late '60s. A lot of musicians played in the James Gang, among them Glen Schwartz (Pacific Gas & Electric), Domenic Troiano (Guess Who) and Tommy Bolin (Zephyr, Deep Purple). The James Gang and the James-Younger Gang, which included brothers Jesse and Frank James, robbed an untold number of banks, trains and stagecoaches in seven states between 1866 and 1882.

Pretty Boy Floyd
Hollywood, California, USA
Named by producer Kim Fowley. Best known for *Leather Boyz with Electric Toyz* (1989).

Jack Ripper
Phoenix, Arizona, USA
Hard-rock band with a young kid named "Jack Ripper" playing Sabbath-worthy licks. Jack the Ripper is one of history's most famous killers. More than 200 books have been written about his life and crimes in late 19th century.

Dillinger Escape Plan
Morris Plains, New Jersey, USA
Pioneers of mathcore-style rock, which adds abrupt tempo changes and polyrhythms to hardcore rock. Depression-era bank robber John Dillinger used such tactics as pretending to be an alarm salesman and faking the use of a bank as a film set to extract hundreds of thousands of dollars from Midwest banks. Having escaped prison previously, he was placed in the "escape-proof" Indiana jail known as Crown Point. He escaped and drove off in the sheriff's new Ford.

Albert Fish   Lisbon, Portugal
Straight-ahead punk-rock. Their first demo tape was entitled *We Don't Eat Children for Breakfast*. I feel better. The real Albert Fish was an American pedophile, serial killer and, by his own accounts, a cannibal. He was executed via the electric chair in 1934.

Hitler Stole My Potato
Coventry, Rhode Island, USA
Mid-90s high-school band who released one album: *Don't Play with Your Food*. They look forward to a reunion gig.

Elvis Hitler
Detroit, Michigan, USA

A psychobilly band named after the stage persona of leader-singer Jim "Elvis Hitler" Leedy. The band played various venues in Detroit and Chicago between 1986 and 1992, and released three albums: *Disgraceland*, *Hellbilly* and *Supersadomasochisticexpialidocious*.

Mussolini Headkick
Belgium/ UK

Their 1989 album, *Themes for Violent Retribution,* contains such uplifting tracks as "Your God Is Dead" and features a naked body draped across a swastika.

Zodiac Killers
San Francisco, California, USA

This pop-punk quartet produced four albums, the most recent, 2005's *Radiation Beach*. In the late '60s a serial murderer calling himself the Zodiac Killer took the lives of five people in northern California. He claimed to have taken the lives of 37, but positive links could not be made. He was never captured.

Ed Gein's Car
New York City, New York, USA

This irony-drenched '80s punk band from New York City takes its name from American serial killer Ed Gein. Police became suspicious of Gein after discovering that he had exhumed corpses from local graveyards. Upon searching his house, they found human skulls mounted on his bedposts, flesh-upholstered chairs and clothing made from human skin, skull-top soup bowls, a collection of shrunken heads, and still grislier items.

Chicago's **LEE HARVEY OSWALD BAND** "is a pack of wild dogs begging at your table for sexual scraps and demanding the quick extinction of your dull affairs." Albums include: *A Taste of Prison* (1994) and *Blastronaut* (1996). But other info places them as active since the late '70s. I think it's a conspiracy. Lee Harvey Oswald was found guilty of having assassinated President John Fitzgerald Kennedy on November 22, 1963.

NAMES STILL AVAILABLE

Ripperjack Cheese

Slobo Dan

Pinochet's Wooden Nose

Gambino Barbershop

Stalin Grad School

Colin Ferguson Car Pool

Mugabegabba Hey

The Klaus Barbies

Belle Gunness & the Basement Boys

Steve & Idi Amin

Kamp Schicklgruber

Timothy McVeigh Fireworks Stand

281

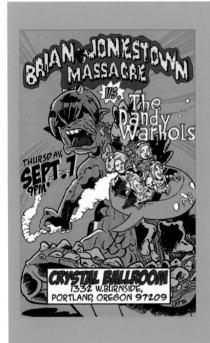

The Brian Jonestown Massacre
SAN FRANCISCO, CALIFORNIA, USA

Combining the name Brian Jones, co-guitarist in the original Rolling Stones lineup, with the Jonestown massacre perpetrated by cult-leader Jim Jones. Charismatic leader Jim Jones founded Jonestown in Guyana in 1977 with more than 900 of his followers. Convinced that the settlement was soon to be attacked by US troops, on November 18, 1978, he instructed his followers to commit "revolutionary suicide" by drinking a cyanide-laced, grape-flavored drink.

Ted Bundy's Night Watchmen
Worcestershire, UK

What else but death-metal. I'm not even going to tell you the title of their EP. Yikes. Ted Bundy was another American serial killer. He murdered dozens of young women across the US between 1974 and 1978. He eventually confessed to 30 murders, though he may have lost count.

Somewhat Ted Bundy
Lancashire, UK

A short-lived band.

Manson Youth
Kreuzberg, Germany

The band that became Jingo de Lunch. EP *Death Dance*.

Jim Jones & the Kool Aid Kids
Kalamazoo, Michigan, USA

With their 1986 album, *Trust Me*.

Dahmers Icebox
Parts Unknown, USA

No. 2 on RollingStone.com's "Most Gruesome Band Names." Dahmer murdered 17 men and boys between 1978 and 1991. During the summer of 1991, he was murdering approximately one person a week. These murders often involved necrophilia and cannibalism.

Wayne Gacy Trio
Portland, Oregon, USA

They play "murder rock" and on their website welcome "those who love murder, serial killers and crime scenes in the making." John Wayne Gacy Jr. was convicted and executed for the murder of 33 boys and young men between 1972 and '78. He was often referred to as the "Killer Clown" because he used to dress in his "Pogo the Clown" suit and entertain the kiddies at the many block parties he threw. He made the *Guinness Book of World Records* by receiving 21 consecutive life sentences and 12 death sentences for his crimes.

Kevorkian Death Cycle
Long Beach, California, USA

Formerly known as the Grid, the guys renamed their band after pathologist and euthanasia advocate Jack Kevorkian, who claims to have assisted over 100 patients in terminating their own lives. Kevorkian is a fellow musician. He plays flute and released a jazz album, *Very Still Life*, in 1997.

The New Husseins
Perth, Australia

Formed for a punk gig in 2003, the New Husseins are all veterans of the Perth punk scene, with former members of No Wonder, the Kuillotines, MUTT, Runt and Zombie Porn. The band excels at manically picked eighth-note basslines. In 2004 an Iraqi tribunal charged Saddam Hussein with crimes against residents of Dujail in 1982, following a failed assassination attempt against him. Specific charges included the murder of 148 people, torture of women and children, and the illegal arrest of 399 others. On November 5, 2006, Saddam Hussein was found guilty of crimes against humanity and sentenced to death by hanging. Saddam's half brother, Barzan Ibrahim, was convicted of similar charges as well. Fortunately, the New Husseins can only be charged with aggressive barre chords and the odd offensive lyric.

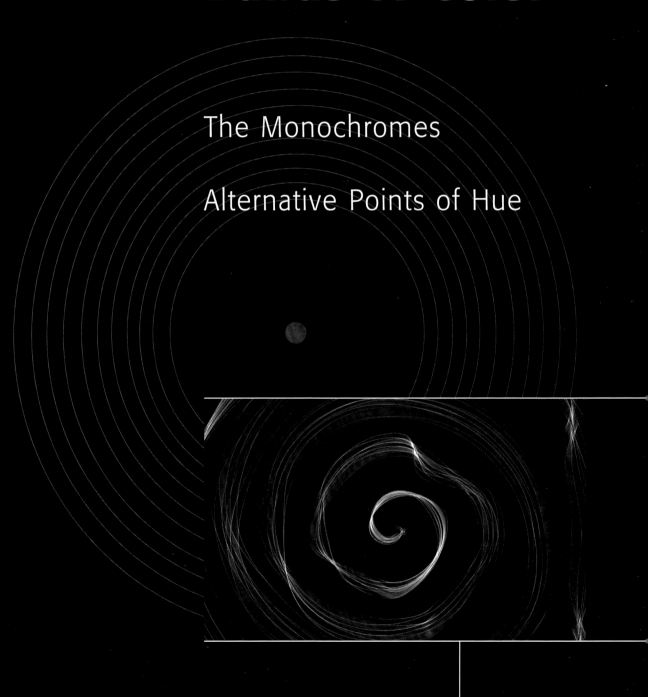

Bands of Color

The Monochromes

Alternative Points of Hue

Bands of Color

Living Colour

Guitarist Vernon Reid was British-born but a long-time New York resident, and he assembled a number of NYC bands under the name Living Colour between 1983 and 1986.

In 1986 he put together a focused rock band with bassist Muzz Skillings, drummer Will Calhoun and vocalist Corey Glover. Calhoun and Skillings comprised a tight, versatile rhythm section, and Glover was a singer capable of delivering both soul and rage.

The band soon had regular gigs at CBGBs and other NYC clubs. Mick Jagger became a fan and hired Reid and Calhoun to play on his 1987 solo album, *Primitive Cool*. With a nudge from Jagger, Living Colour landed a deal with Epic and released their debut album, *Vivid*. It rose to #6 on the *Billboard* 200 and the video for "Cult of Personality" received heavy rotation on MTV.

The band's second album, *Time's Up*, won a Grammy for Best Hard Rock Album but signalled an eclecticism that would prove difficult to market. *Stain* was released in 1993 and made it to #26 in the US, but band members' failure to agree on a common musical path brought breakup in January 1995.

The Colourfield Manchester, UK
Formed in 1984 when former Specials and Fun Boy Three frontman Terry Hall joined forces with ex-Swinging Cats Toby Lyons and Karl Shale. Lyons now works in the color field as a university tutor of graphic design.

Colourbox London, UK
This electronic band struggled along from 1982-1987 before finally having a hit with "Pump Up the Volume."

Pennsylvania-raised guitarist-singer-songwriter Fred Mascherino currently calls New Jersey home base. Mascherino started his the Color Fred project while still leading his band Breaking Pangaea. It was put on hold when he joined Taking Back Sunday as guitarist and backup singer in 2003. In 2007 he left that band to devote his full attention to **the Color Fred**. The result is a debut album, *Bend to Break*, that hit #8 on the *Billboard* Heatseekers chart.

Brighter Side of Darkness
Chicago, Illinois, USA
Heavy name for a group whose lead singer was 12. Song: "Love Jones" (1972).

The Brilliant Corners Bristol, UK
Took their name from a 1957 album by jazz legend Thelonious Monk.

The Pastels Glasgow, Scotland
Since 1982, with a few lineup changes. They now operate their own label, Geographic Music.

The Swirlies
Boston, Massachusetts, USA
Formed in 1990 to bring colorful swirls of guitar noise and tantrums to the world.

Alive in Wild Paint
Phoenix, Arizona, USA
Debut album: *Ceilings*. Introspective guitar and piano rock.

Color Me Badd
Oklahoma City, Oklahoma, USA
Formed in 1987 and discovered by Kool & the Gang's Robert Bell in 1990. "I Wanna Sex You Up" made the *New Jack City* soundtrack and hit #1 in the UK.

Black Liverpool, UK
Colin Vearncombe released his first single as Black in 1982. He has recorded more or less steadily since then. In 1993 he formed the label Nero Schwartz, the two words meaning black in Italian and German, respectively.

ORANGE GOBLIN/SOLACE
WED. MAY 11TH THE UNDERWORLD LONDON

London's heavy-metal cult heroes **Orange Goblin** formed in 1995 under the name Our Haunted Kingdom, adopting their current name the following year. Singer-guitarist Ben Ward: "Back in the '70s, all the big bands had a color in their name — Black Sabbath, Pink Floyd, Deep Purple — and we like orange. At the time, we were into *Lord of the Rings*, hence the interest in goblins."

Black Flag

Hermosa Beach, California, USA

The name was suggested by songwriter-guitarist Greg Ginn's brother, artist Raymond Pettibon, who also designed the band's logo. Pettibon: "If a white flag means surrender, a black flag represents anarchy." An anarchist symbol, an insecticide and a nod to Black Sabbath, one of Ginn's favorite bands.

Average White Band

Dundee, Scotland

Scottish funk and soul since 1971. Definitely white, but not average. Their 1974 album, *AWB* (with the W in the cover art curvaceously outlining a woman's derriere), reached #1 in the US.

Barely White

Orange, Massachusetts, USA

A fairly serious rock band with a joke name derived from that of disco godfather Barry White.

The White Stripes

Detroit, Michigan, USA

Jack and Meg, from their married surname, White, which they like to alternate with red, which makes stripes. They woke us all up with just two instruments.

Opaque Buff

Helsinki, Finland

Self-description: "The glammest band in Finland." Have a look.

Blue Cheer

San Francisco, California, USA

Named for a type of LSD. Or after a laundry detergent, as per the title of their 1969 album, *New! Improved! Blue Cheer*.

Blue Rodeo

Toronto, Ontario, Canada

The kings of Canadian country-rock with 10 platinum albums and 7 Juno Awards.

NAMES STILL AVAILABLE

Color People

All Green

Deep Eggplant

Wild Blue Yawn

Rise of the Ochre

Magenta Force OMG

A Nation
of Vermillions

The Taupe Cubicles

Azure
Turning Left

School Bus
Redcard

The Purplenauts

Buff

285

Shocking Blue
The Hague, Netherlands
A big #1 hit with "Venus" in 1970, which was covered and taken to #1 (again) by Bananarama in 1981, used in several films and the basis for a Schick razor campaign.

Green Day
East Bay, California, USA
You've heard of them. Green Day refers to taking the day off school to roll and smoke greenery.

Rhymes with Orange
Lake County, Illinois, USA
Sounds like: "If Rush was a punk band."

Simply Red Manchester, UK
"Simply Red" is said to refer to singer Mick Hucknall's hair and football team (Manchester United).

The Red Chord
Revere, Massachusetts, USA
Deathcore. The Red Chord refers to a slit throat, from Austrian composer Alban Berg's opera *Wozzeck*.

The Red Krayola
Houston, Texas, USA
Psychedelic band formed by university art students in 1966. Note: Avoid cheap joke about Crayolas in Texas university art programs.

Red Rider Toronto, Ontario, Canada
Formed in 1979 and led by singer-guitarist Tom Cochrane. Red Ryder was a Dell Comics cowboy hero created by Stephen Slesinger and illustrated by Fred Harman between 1939 and 1957.

IllScarlett
Mississauga, Ontario, Canada
Fashioned from the name of a local street, Will Scarlett Drive.

A Block of Yellow

London, Ontario, musicians Anthony Nastasi, Alex Whalley, Dan Thomas and Paul Everest were in need of a new name after Foxy Fox disbanded. Suggestions included Banana Socks and Magic Laps. Where **A Block of Yellow** (ABOY) came from is unclear, though Whalley has an interesting story about a talking yellow block in his basement. The band's two albums are *Grow Up or Grow Out* and *Do I Do*.

Grow Up or Grow Out

A Block of Yellow

The Pinker Tones
Barcelona, Spain
Mister Furia, Professor Manso and DJ Niño play electronica with English, French, Spanish and German lyrics. They have appeared in over 40 countries. Founded in 1850, the famous US-based Pinkerton National Detective Agency (the Pinkertons) is now a division of Swedish security company Securitas AB.

Pink Floyd Cambridge, UK
Guitarist-singer Syd Barrett came up with the name the Pink Floyd Sound from credits on a Blind Boy Fuller album for blues musicians Pink Anderson and Floyd Council. It was soon shortened to *The* Pink Floyd and later simply Pink Floyd. Some earlier incarnations were Sigma 6, the Meggadeaths, the Architectural Abdabs, the Screaming Abdabs, and the Tea Set.

The Legendary Pink Dots
London, UK
Thought to refer to the unexplained pink dots on certain keys of their recording piano.

Maroon 5
Los Angeles, California, USA
Started as Kara's Flowers, but make a big fuss about not saying where the name Maroon 5 came from.

Deep Purple Hertfordshire, UK
"Deep Purple," a 1930s piano composition by Peter DeRose, was guitarist Ritchie Blackmore's grandmother's favorite song.

Yello Switzerland
Electronica duo known for their '80s singles "The Race" and "Oh Yeah."

Yellow Magic Orchestra
Tokyo, Japan
Electropop group formed in 1978. They appeared on the US dance program *Soul Train* in November 1980.

Yellowcard
Jacksonville, Florida, USA
Their name comes from the soccer penalty. First album: *Midget Tossing* (1997). Recent album: *Live from Las Vegas at the Palms* (2008).

I Need My Space

I Need My Space

Bill Haley & His Comets

The band started as Bill Haley & the Saddlemen in Pennsylvania around 1950, performing country songs with a bluesier feel. Haley's career took its first turn toward rock with his cover of "Rocket 88" and then "Rock the Joint." The Saddlemen name suddenly seemed incongruous, and a friend of Haley's, noting the common mispronunciation of Halley's Comet, suggested the name Haley's Comets.

With their new name, the band scored a national hit in 1953 with "Crazy Man, Crazy," the first nationally televised rock tune.

The Bill Haley & His Comets classic "Rock Around the Clock" fared modestly when it was released in 1954, but soared up the charts in summer of 1955 after appearing in the soundtrack to *Blackboard Jungle*. It rose to #1 and stayed there for eight weeks. In 1956 the band starred in two full-length films, *Rock Around the Clock* and *Don't Knock the Rock*.

Alas, Haley & His Comets popularity began to fade with the appearance of more charismatic, sexually charged performers such as Little Richard, Elvis Presley and the Beatles.

This Space for Rent

Øresund Space Collective
Copenhagen, Denmark
Formed in 2004, the collective consists of Danish, Swedish and American musicians who create "free-form improvised space-rock." Øresund (literally "the Sound") is the strait that separates the Danish island of Zealand from the southern Swedish province of Skåne.

Apple Not Asteroid
Chino Hills, California, USA
The name refers to the band's Christian belief that life started in the Garden of Eden, not as a long-term result of the Big Bang. Songs: "Killing One Bird with Two Stones," "Big Numbers Without Commas."

Fuzzy Comets
Pittsburgh, Pennsylvania, USA
This female-fronted band held a weekly Girls' Night Out gig at a club called Rosebud, where they invited other female performers, as well as hairdressers, cosmeticians and massage practitioners. The cloud of material around the nucleus of a comet is called the *coma*.

Fishing for Comets
Dallas, Texas, USA
A pun on the expression "fishing for compliments." This impossibly upbeat, acoustic-driven band is led by singer Camille Cortinas.

Cosmic Psychos
Melbourne, Australia
Wikipedia entry, 2006: "Known for their hard-drinking behavior and vulgar lyrics, the Cosmic Psychos are one of the defining bands of the yob rock genre, a movement that celebrates the Australian male lifestyle." Recent album: *Dung Australia*.

Comets on Fire was founded in Santa Cruz, California, in 1999 by singer-guitarist Ethan Miller and bassist Ben Flashman. They have released four albums – *Comets on Fire*, *Field Recordings from the Sun*, *Blue Cathedral*, *Avatar* – and toured as an opening act for Sonic Youth, Dinosaur Jr. and Mudhoney.

London's **Slaves to Gravity** formed in 2006 from the remains of The*Ga*Ga*s. The band's first two singles debuted in the UK Top 10 with strong video support, and their debut album, *Scatter the Crow*, was released to favorable reviews in Spring 2008.

Cosmic Slop Tucson, Arizona, USA
Based on "the guitar of Jimi, the driving rhythms of James Brown, combined with the funky freakiness of Sly & the Family Stone and Funkadelic." In Tucson.

Galactic
New Orleans, Louisiana, USA
Originally formed in 1994 as Galactic Prophylactic. The recent album by this funk-fusion band, *From the Corner to the Block*, includes guest MCs.

Galactic Cowboys
Houston, Texas, USA
Formed in 1989 by former members of the Awful Truth. The band has released six albums and appeared in the 1994 film *Airheads* as a band called Sons of Thunder.

Love Outside Andromeda
Melbourne, Australia
Formed in 2000 as Andromeda, but took their love outside Andromeda to avoid confusion with the Swedish Andromeda.

Starving for Gravity
Grand Forks, North Dakota, USA
Starving for gravity in Grand Forks, the band recently moved to Orange County, California.

Gravity Kills
St. Louis, Missouri, USA
Their single "Guilty" reached #24 on the *Billboard* Modern Rock chart, and their music has been featured on soundtracks for games such as *Mortal Kombat* and *Test-Drive Off-Road*, and the film *Se7en*.

Maids of Gravity
Los Angeles, California, USA
Formed in 1994 by ex-Medicine singer-guitarist Ed Ruscha and named after a band he saw in a dream. Who makes more of a mess than gravity? Someone's got to clean it up.

The Quark Alliance
Atlanta, Georgia, USA
The latest ensemble assembled by Col. Bruce Hampton, ret. (Gustav Berglund III), the eccentric musical leader who brought us the Hampton Grease Band, the Last Bronze Age, Aquarium Rescue Unit, the Fiji Mariners and the Codetalkers. Album: *Give Thanks to Chank*.

Dorks in Space
Tempe, Arizona, USA
"Three unhip science dorks" who got together in 2001. Their 2004 album: *Free Range Astromeat*.

NAMES
STILL AVAILABLE

The Spacesavers

Seething Stars

What's the Antimatter

Puny Universe

The Gamma
RayBans

Gravitational
Tractor Pull

Supermassive
Supercluster

Doubter Space

The Meatier Meteors

Lipstick
Cosmologists

Light Years After

Slingshot
Orbit Pop

Swallow the Sun
Jyväskylä, Finland
"Melodic death-metal." Formed by former members of Plutonium Orange and Funeris Nocturnum. Debut album: *The Morning Never Came*.

The Sun Sawed in 1/2
St. Louis, Missouri, USA
Albums: *The Happiness and Other Short Stories*, *Hot Feet for Monkey God*, *Fizzy Lift*, *Bewilderbeest*.

Sunn O)))
Los Angeles, California, USA
Pronounced *Sun*. But they are not sunny. The dark drone-metal duo consists of Stephen O'Malley (Burning Witch) and Greg Anderson (Goatsnake). The name and accompanying markings are taken from the logo of the Sunn Musical Equipment Company, which was started by Kingsmen ("Louie, Louie") bassist Norm Sundholm and his brother Conrad in a effort to supply the former with the first stadium-worthy bass amp.

Frozen Sun Denmark
Death-metal band formed in 1992. Members went on to play in Angel Accelerator Death, Infernal Torment and Panzerchrist.

Kings of the Sun
Sydney, Australia
Formed in 1986 following the breakup of the Young Lions. The band toured with Joe Satriani, KISS and Guns N'Roses. At the Sydney Entertainment Centre, irked by Axl Rose, singer Jeffrey Hoad dropped his pants and bad-mouthed G N'R. Their next album: *Full Frontal Attack*.

The all-male trio **Space Bikini** is based in Farnborough, Hampshire, UK. Their recent EP is entitled *Breaking Me*. The name is inspired by "the attire of a certain space princess whilst she is prisoner to an evil gangster." Princess Leia Organa Solo of Alderaan (aka Carrie Fisher, 1983) ?

Solar Lodge Stockholm, Sweden
After the title of a song by Coil.

Behind the Sun Israel
Heavy rock from the Holy Land.

Dorks in Space
Tempe, Arizona, USA
"Three unhip science dorks" who got together in 2001. Their 2004 album: *Free Range Astromeat*.

The Radio Galaxy
New York/New Jersey, USA
Formed in 2004, the Radio Galaxy is comprised of Virginia Kamenitzer (vocals), Dave DeRiso (drums), Tim Dempsey (guitar, vocals), Ryan Headley (guitar, mandolin) and Randy Artiglere (bass). Their recent EP: *Don't Forget to Listen*. Radio wave emissions move through space with the release of substantial energy, such as during the death of stars.

The Space Heaters
Detroit, Michigan, USA
Four post-punk survivors from bands such as the Denizens, the Ramrods, the Boners, the Almighty Lumberjacks of Death, the Hysteric Narcotics and the Waffle Hoppers. Recent album: *Warming Up*.

Stars Montreal, Quebec, Canada
Several of the band's songs have appeared on the soundtracks to the TV series *The O.C.* and *Degrassi: The Next Generation*. Recent album: *In Our Bedroom After the War*.

Small Stars Reno/Austin, USA
Two thirds of Fastball, and friends. NPR Best of 2007: "*Tijuana Dreams* is both unique and 100 percent fun from the first spin. Though their stage show may owe a lot to The Tubes, The Small Stars' members pilfer primarily from old Paul McCartney, Joe Ely and Big Star records to charming effect."

Billy Starfire & the Orbit Boys
Chicago, Illinois, USA
Influences include Brian Eno, "The Bob Newhart Show theme" and Ice Cube. Albums: *Crazy Monkey* and *Androgynaut*.

Beard of Stars
Columbus, Ohio, USA
"We Play Fun-Time Worship Music!" Lo-fi for Jesus.

Turn Off the Stars
Toronto, Ontario, Canada
From a song by jazz pianist Bill Evans. They've opened for Switchfoot and the Tea Party. Named a Best Bet at 2008's NXNE Festival. *AllMusicGuide*: "a gem of modern rock."

Trembling Blue Stars
London, UK

Mid-90s jangly, introspective (trembling blue?) band formed by Robert Wratten (the Field Mice, Northern Picture Library) and Beth Arzy (Aberdeen).

Behind the Stars
Illinois, USA

"Behind the Stars has incorporated the noise of today's broadband world into a modern alternative sound for the iPod generation." Astronomers look behind the stars with infra-red telescopes. Neil Young looks through the "blue, blue windows behind the stars" in the song "Helpless."

Deathstars Stockholm, Sweden
Built primarily from members of the heavy-metal band Swordmaster. Recent album: *Deathglam*. A space station and super-weapon in the *Star Wars* films.

Star Death & the White Dwarfs
Oklahoma City, Oklahoma, USA

The band creates "genre-bending sound that might occur if King Crimson and Coldplay got stoned and had sex with each other." A white dwarf is a small, dense star. Think mass of our sun but the size of Earth.

Diamond Star Halo
Seattle, Washington, USA

From a lyric in the T. Rex hit "Bang a Gong (Get It On)." Apparently Seattle has seen two bands named Diamond Star Halo.

Low Stars
Los Angeles, California, USA

Acoustic guitars and harmony vocals, low-key stars.

Star Assassin Big Star
Memphis, Tennessee, USA

Founded in 1971. When your debut album is *#1 Record*, certain assumptions may be made about the choice of the band name Big Star. However, Big Star was named after a Memphis supermarket.

Blinker the Star
Pembroke, Ontario, Canada

Started by Jon Zadorozny, the band released four albums. Zadorozny's deal with Dreamworks and his work on Hole's *Celebrity Skin* gave him enough money to fulfill his dream of buying a house and building a recording studio in his hometown.

Planes Mistaken for Stars started in Peoria, Illinois, then moved to Denver en masse with 13 friends. The band's name does not suggest its musical style. Unless the planes are armed with nuclear warheads. Members now play in Hawks & Doves, Ghost Buffalo and Git Some.

Drive By Star
Seattle, Washington, USA

Short-lived project of Rafe Pearlman and Jonathon Plum. Pearlman's vocal style combines rock with "mellismatic middle-eastern singing styles associated with orthodox Judaism."

The Wooden Stars
Ottawa, Ontario, Canada

Their collaboration with singer Julie Doiron won a Juno Award for Best Alternative Album. Recent album: *People Are Different*. Guitarist Mike Feuerstack also fronts Snailhouse.

The Velcro Stars
Murfreesboro, Tennessee, USA

Recent album: *Hiroshima's Revenge*. The drummer is currently spending more time with How I Became the Bomb.

Star Assassin
Melbourne, Australia

Killing stars or starring at kills. Their "Hey Kid" single launch was held at Melbourne's Ding Dong Lounge.

The Stargazers London, UK
Founded in 1949 by Cliff Adams, and loosely based on Bill Haley & His Comets, the Stargazers were voted Most Popular Vocal Group five years straight by the *New Musical Express*. They also backed such performers as Frank Sinatra, Peggy Lee and Petula Clark.

Andromeda:
Australia (hard rock); Bergen, Norway (prog-rock); Skåne, Sweden (prog-rock); UK (prog-rock); Berkel-Enschot, Holland (doom); Guatemala (prog-metal); Lima, Peru (heavy metal); San Martin, Argentina (hard rock).

Love and Rockets

The UK band Love and Rockets evolved out of Bauhaus in 1985, minus singer Peter Murphy. Singer-guitarist Daniel Ash and drummer Kevin Haskins had also played together in Tones on Tail, Ash's side project during Bauhaus.

The band is named after the Fantagraphics comic-book series *Love and Rockets* by Los Bros Hernandez (Jaime, Gilbert and sometimes Mario). Gilbert later wrote a book of comic stories set around the time of the LA Riots and entitled *Love and Rockets X*. In the stories, several bands are named Love and Rockets. Whether this was mutual promotion or writer's revenge, you can decide.

Love and Rockets had a huge hit with the single "So Alive" and released seven albums between 1985 and 1999. Their 1989 self-titled album reached #14 on the US Album charts.

The band went on hiatus in 1999 but reformed in 2007 to play tribute song ("Cast a Long Shadow") at a Joe Strummer tribute concert to raise money for his Foundation for New Music. That experience led to further bookings in 2008.

I Wanted to Be a Spaceman

NASA
Sweden

This synth-pop group had their first Swedish Top 10 hit with "Paula" in 1985. Their US label, Columbia, asked the band to change its name following the explosion of space shuttle *Challenger* in 1986.

Black NASA
Long Branch, New Jersey, USA

In a documentary examining the theory that the US moon landing was a hoax created on a Hollywood set, the narrator makes reference to NASA as "Black NASA." The band is a side-project for members from Atomic Bitchwax.

All Systems Go!
Montreal, Quebec, Canada

A standard NASA pre-launch expression. This Canadian punk band is comprised of members from Big Drill Car, the Doughboys and the Carnations. The name is being used simultaneously by about a half dozen other bands.

Building a Better Spaceship
Los Angeles, California, USA

A twist on the expression "building a better mousetrap," in reference to the Ralph Waldo Emerson quote, "Build a better mousetrap and the world will beat a path to your door." BBS has shared the stage with Lifehouse, the Killers, Hot Hot Heat, Hard Fi, Hoobastank, Avenged Sevenfold and others.

Max Q   Houston, USA
and Melbourne, Australia

Formed in early 1987 by Robert L. Gibson, George Nelson and Brewster Shaw. Max Q members are all Houston-based NASA astronauts. Gibson named the band after the engineering term for maximum dynamic pressure from the atmosphere during liftoff. The name was also chosen by the late INXS frontman Michael Hutchence for his side-project with producer Ollie Olsen, whom Hutchence met on the film set for *Dogs in Space*. Max Q was the name of Olsen's "deaf, insane Queensland blue heeler."

Bring Us Meat is the full-length debut album by Denver's **Thank God for Astronauts**: singer-guitarist Kent Phillips, guitarist Al Riach, bassist Steve Jones and drummer Chad Peterson. The band's name came from Phillips's great-grandmother in Oklahoma, who when saying Sunday grace would add, "Thank God for Jesus, the Kennedys, freedom...and Astronauts."

Xybor & the Cosmonauts

is the alter-, cyber-ego of Ottawa, Ontario, Canada, multi-media artist and multi-instru-mentalist Terry Atkinson, who calls his work "an eclectic blend of rock, jazz, blues and pop, laced with hope, cynicism and social commentary." The name Xybor came about during a des-perate attempt to find a Hotmail account name that wasn't already taken.

Astronaut Tang
St. Louis, Missouri, USA

Tang was invented by General Foods in 1957 but gained popularity in 1965 when NASA began using it on its Gemini flights.

Astronauts of Inner Space
Turgovia, Switzerland

Formed in 2007 by three high-school friends. The name comes from the title of an avant-garde Beat reader edited by William S. Burroughs and Jeff Berner in 1966.

The Buzzaldrins   Manchester, UK

Astronaut Buzz Aldrin was the second man on the moon. "Buzz" was a child-hood nickname created as a result of his baby sister mispronouncing "brother" as "buzzer." He made it his legal first name in 1988.

Space Negros
Boston, Massachusetts, USA

Founder Erik Lindgren also created the record label Arf! Arf! Lindgren's other bands include Birdsongs of the Mesozoic and the Moving Parts.

Space Boyz   Jyväskylä, Finland

The previous incarnation of the band now called Lost Madison.

Space Cadet   Denton, Texas, USA

"One night our drummer threw a bro-ken stick across the stage, and the stick hit our guitar player in the neck! I looked over at him, and there it was, just protruding out of his neck. It was the strangest thing. He pulled the stick out and blood starting spurting all over the place…I finished the night with an acoustic set."

Space Cadet Steve
Cambridge, UK

Ska punks who changed their name to Offbeat Contingency in 2007.

Spaceman Bill
& the Groovy Gravy
Springfield, Missouri, USA

"Spaceman" Bill Lee was a left-handed pitcher for the Boston Red Sox (1969-78) and the Montreal Expos (1979-82). He ran for president of the US on the Canadian Rhinoceros Party ticket in 1988.

Spacemen 3
Rugby, Midlands, UK

Founded in 1982 by Jason Pierce and Peter "Sonic Boom" Kember. Sub-sequent projects have included Spirtualized, Spectrum, the Darkside and collaborations with Yo La Tengo, My Bloody Valentine and others.

NAMES
STILL AVAILABLE

Deep Space
Philosophers

The Shuttle Puppets

The Astronewbs

Starship Demo Derby

MC Massive Thrust

Zero-G
Twist-Top Mishaps

Phssst Oxygen Leaks

Commander Chunky
& His Lost Lunch Liftoff

Theory of a NASA
Summer Student

Capsule Detachment
Nostalgia

Moon Unit's
2001 Odyssey

Acrophobic Astronaut

NEW ANCIENT ASTRONAUTS

According to singer-guitarist Kasey Elkington, this Denver-based band started out as a loose project called Ancient Astronauts, but the bassist joked, "Let's call it *New* Ancient Astronauts." The name lay dormant, scrawled on a cassette tape, for a few years. When they started new band in 2000, they came up with pages and pages of ridiculous names. Then, in the spring of 2001, Elkington spoke with Mermen guitarist Jim Thomas after a Mermen gig in Malibu. "He asked the name of my band, and before I could think, I said, 'New Ancient Astronauts.' Back in Denver, I told the story to the band, and they decided we should use it, especially since Jim Thomas thought it was our name."

Commander Cody & His Lost Planet Airmen
San Francisco, California, USA
Began in Ann Arbor, Michigan, in 1967. Pianist-songwriter Commander Cody was born George Frayne IV. His band takes its name from a 1951 Fred C. Brannon serial about "a scientist who dons a jet-pack to pursue a madman."

Man or Astro-Man?
Auburn, Alabama, USA
Space-age surf-rock revival.

Astroboy
Colonia del Sacramento, Uruguay
Astro Boy is a Japanese cartoon character created by Osamu Tezuka in 1952. The series is often credited with being the first to use the kind of animation now called anime.

Huge Spacebird
Seattle, Washington, USA
Guitarist Mark Hoyt, bassist Jeff Taylor and drummer Peter Lansdowne have also played together in Stumpy Joe, the Purdins, and Sister Psychic.

Red Rocket
Sweden
Albums: *Voyager* and *The Moray Eels Eat the Space Needle*.

Rocket Dog
Sydney, Australia
A quartet started in 2003 that shares its name with a dog adoption society in San Francisco and a shoe company.

Apollosdown
Guelph, Ontario, Canada
Younger, crunchier Dave Matthews-style jamband tunes. Apollosdown guitarist Ferg and drummer Brain are identical twins.

Rocket Queen
Japan
Named after the Guns N'Roses song from *Appetite for Destruction*.

Rocket Science
Melbourne, Australia
Shortly before the release of their third album, *Eternal Holiday*, singer Roman Tucker fell into a coma for around two weeks. He's back now.

The Rocket Summer
Colleyville, Texas, USA
Named for writer Ray Bradbury's story "Rocket Summer," from *The Martian Chronicles*.

The Effects of Eating Too Much Television is **Rocket Park**'s 2000 follow-up to their debut album, *Teenage Folklore*. Based in St. Louis, Missouri, the eclectic quartet has opened for national headliners such as the Fixx, Saigon Kick, the Strokes and the Marshall Tucker Band.

Jefferson Starship
San Francisco, California, USA
Evolved from Jefferson Airplane. An early edition was called Paul Kantner– Jefferson Starship and featured David Crosby, Graham Nash, Grace Slick and members of the Grateful Dead. When Kantner left in 1984, the band became simply Starship to avoid any legal action.

Starship Parking
Waverly, Iowa, USA
Leader Evan Campbell (guitar, vocals): "I thought of the name Starship Parking while I was sitting at my computer doing absolutely nothing…I just thought it would look cool if a starship parked in, like…a Wal-Mart parking lot or something."

Sloop Jon Spaceranger
Detroit, Michigan
A pun on the Beach Boys' song "Sloop John B," the 7th track on *Pet Sounds*. But the origins of that song go back to at least 1917 and Richard Le Gallienne's novel *Pieces of Eight*, in which the narrator starts a "quaint Nassau ditty": *Come on the sloop John B / My grandfather and me…*

Sigue Sigue Sputnik London, UK
Led by ex-Generation X bassist Tony James. The name, which means "burn, burn, satellite," is said to be the name of a Moscow street gang. The band's single "Love Missile F1-11" reached #3 in the UK in 1986 and was used on the soundtrack to *Ferris Bueller's Day Off*.

Space Junkie
Destin Harbor, Florida, USA
Began in 1997 as 90 Proof, became Space Monkey, then Space Junkie.

The Ballroom Rockets

Rhythm Bomb recording artists the Ballroom Rockets fire off 20 authentic rockabilly tracks on their album *Atomic!* Based in Essen, Germany, the trio, brothers Fabian and Christoph Rosmaity and René Lieutenant, sound like they were raised in the Sun Records studio in the 1950s. Their new record is *Ready… If You're Willin'*.

Space Monkey
London, UK
This mid-80s group was led by Paul Goodchild and included Wham!'s backup band and former members of Bow Wow Wow.

Space Raiders
Middlesborough, UK
Their name was inspired by a UK snack food with an alien on the package front and mini-comics on the back.

Books About UFOs
Salt Lake City, Utah, USA
Slogan: "Keep it stupid…keep it loud." The name is from the Hüsker Dü song "Books About UFOs" on the 1985 album *New Day Rising*.

UFOFU
Dallas, Texas, USA
Started in New York in 1993 but moved to Dallas so their 14-year-old drummer could finish high school there. Brothers Brendon (bass) and Ben Curtis (drums) also played in Tripping Daisy, Captain Audio and the Secret Machines.

Simply Saucer
Hamilton, Ontario, USA
The name refers to Syd Barrett-era Pink Floyd's *Saucerful of Secrets* album. The Simply Saucer album *Cyborgs Revisited* was released in 1989, a decade after the band broke up. Songs: "Dance the Mutation" and "Here Come the Cyborgs."

295

Alien Ant Farm

This Riverside, California, band formed in the mid-90s and called their 1999 debut album *Greatest Hits*. It won the Best Independent Album at the Los Angeles Music Awards. Their supercharged 2001 cover of Michael Jackson's "Smooth Criminal" hit the Top 10 in the UK, and Australia and on the US Modern Rock charts. Their second album went platinum in the US with steady radio play and support from friends Papa Roach.

According to original guitarist Terry Corso, the band's name came about when "I was day-dreaming at my dull desk job with my feet up, and I thought to myself, 'Wouldn't it be cool if the human species were placed on earth and cultivated by alien intelligence?' Maybe the aliens added us to an atmosphere that was suitable for us, and they've been watching us develop and colonize, kind of like what a kid does with an ant farm, where the aliens are the kids and humans are the ants."

Alien Invaders

Rock & Roll has long associated itself with the alien, probably because of their status as the ultimate outsiders and their mysterious, potentially dangerous powers.

Overlords of the UFO
Southwest USA

Devotee and performer of Indian spiritual music Sat Kartar combined forces with trance-house producers to form this short-lived techno group. It is also the title of a stunningly bad 1976 documentary that professes to reveal "the origin of the alien intelligences who are the overlords of the UFO." Albert Walker, on agonybooth.com, writes: "And since we're at it, let's also find out about the slumlords of the UFO, shall we? Or maybe we can also look into who are the lords of the dance of the UFO?" Funny guy.

Alien Vampires
Rome, London and Hell

Creators of the hardcore techno CDs *No One Gets Out of Here Alive*, *Evil Generation*, and *Nuns Are Pregnant*, and a truly offensive T-shirt suggesting how the nuns got that way.

Electric Blue Peggy Sue
& the Revolutionions from Mars
Oulu, Finland

There is no Electric Blue Peggy Sue. The head Martian here is Ray Katz, whose voice, according to trouserpress.com reviewer Andrea Enthal, "sounds like he drinks Drano for breakfast and washes it down with lighter fluid, tossing in the lighter for good measure." Their debut CD, 1987's *You Say You Want a Revolutionion*.

Hideous Sun Demons
Los Angeles, California, USA

This trio of studio musicians toured as David Lee Roth's band before going solo…er, trio. The name comes from *The Hideous Sun Demon*, a 1959 sci-fi flick in which an atomic scientist is exposed to radiation and subsequently changes into a homicidal lizardman when exposed to sunlight.

ALIEN OVERKILL: The world is full of Aliens. Or bands named Alien. Hotspots: Cherbourg, France (hard rock); UK (heavy metal); Gothenburg, Sweden (melodic rock); Turnov, Czech Republic (heavy metal); Christchurch, New Zealand (alternative metal); New York City, USA (glam); Caibarién, Cuba (heavy metal).

Space Cretins
SEATTLE, WASHINGTON, USA

Guitarist and vocalist Paul Diamond Blow says he was inspired by a chance encounter with William Shatner in a Hong Kong karaoke bar, where Shatner convinced him to start a "super-cyber" rock band. Hailing from "Jet City," the Space Cretins play "big, loud, stupid buzzsaw rock" with lyrics that "speak of jet-riding in the stratosphere, androids…and partying in the electric skies." Self-described as a "cross between Ziggy Stardust [space] and the Ramones [cretins]," Blow and bandmates Danger Dayne, Bam Bam and Markass "Starkiss" Karkass released their debut CD, *Rocket Roll*, in 2005. Its cover features illustration by famed underground-comic artist Wes Crum, colored by Paul Baresh. The alien character above first appeared in Crum's *Anal Intruders from Uranus.*

Winged Space Beast
Sydney, Australia

To rehearse for a one-off reunion gig at Sydney's Homebake Festival in 2001, the Hoodoo Gurus played a series of performances around town as Winged Space Beast. No strangers to spacey matters, the Gurus 1985 hit album was titled *Mars Needs Guitars!*

Alien Mindbenders Finland

Zak McKracken & the Alien Mindbenders was a Lucasfilm adventure game originally released for the Commodore 64 and later adapted to Atari and Amiga.

The Heretiks Aliens from Space
Castres-Toulouse, France

Gothic industrial punk metal that some aliens may find heretical.

Cowboys & Aliens
Bruges, Belgium

A pun on Cowboys and Indians. Their first full-length CD was titled *A Trip to Stonehenge.* UFO "scholars" have suggested that Stonehenge was either built by aliens or built as a place to worship our alien ancestors and/or creators. A graphic novel by this title depicts a battle between Arizona cowboys and Apaches interrupted by the crash of an alien spaceship. Native people and cowboys join forces to thwart the alien takeover of the Old West. Now a DreamWorks production.

aLIEN cOWBOYS
New York City-San Francisco, USA

Neither space-rock alien nor Travis-picking country, but two New Yorkers and two Bay-area players with five incredibly tight instrumental rock CDs and a new album of rootsy vocal tunes.

297

Raygun Cowboys
Edmonton, Alberta, Canada

Rockabilly from Canada's cowboy province. It would appear that the bassist might have been the one to block the raygun's rays. His acoustic bass is now covered in a thick layer of bumble-bee-striped fur that could only be fashionable on another planet.

Naked Raygun
Chicago, Illinois, USA

Fully Dressed Raygun and Scantily Clad Raygun watch out, post-punkers Naked Raygun are back with a DVD/CD *What Poor Gods We Do Make.* Their 1980–1992 anthology has the catchy title *Huge Bigness.*

Death Ray Café
Dunedin, New Zealand

This late-80s New Zealand band featured vocalist-guitarist David Pine, formerly of Sneaky Feelings. That name comes from the title of a 1977 Elvis Costello song. A number of weird inventors claimed to have invented "death-ray" weapons in the 1920s and '30s, including Nikola Tesla, though none were able to publicly demonstrate their capabilities.

The Raygun Girls
Queens, New York, USA

Three guys, one girl, heavy-metal guitars, no raygun, but they do record on KillZone Records.

Disarmed Universe
Bolívar, Venezuela

The peace-filled idea behind this band name may account for their choice of music genre: something called "melodic metal."

Alien Headshot Disaster
Persenbeug-Gottsdorf, Austria

Not sure if we're talking about messy green-goo splatter wounds or the photogenic deficiencies of most alien life-forms. Whatever it is, it sounds angry.

Alien Showgirls   California, USA
Sounds like "New York Dolls meet Pussycat Dolls meet Marilyn Manson."

Alien Agent   Eugene, Oregon, USA
CD title: *Diamonds Are for Breakfast.* Alien agents have been rumored to be among us for decades, perhaps most creatively depicted in the *Men in Black* films. The 2007 Canadian film *Alien Agent* bore the tagline "Only one man stands in the way of an alien invasion…and he's not even human!"

Alien Sex Cult
San Francisco, California, USA

According to their press kit, Alien Sex Cult is "frequently at the top of the Japanese Pop category on mp3.com." The name came to Cult leader Chris Bertram while working at a college cable TV station and experimenting with electronic music.

ALIEN'S CAB • Even aliens have to get around. These guys from Drummondville-Trois-Rivieres, Quebec, Canada, are willing to drive themselves where they need to go. Alien's Cab is now in its third incarnation since the mid-90s, playing "the best punk rock with all the energy" and brushing off my suggestion that they were having fun with the Alien's Cab/Alien Scab pun when they named their band.

Alien Crime Syndicate
Seattle, Oregon, USA

"Stratospheric big rock … sharing the bill with rock & roll pipe bombs like Weezer, Sugar Ray, American Hi-Fi, Girls Against Boys, Everclear…."

UFO

BRITISH BAND UFO began their metal-edged blues and extended-jam collaboration in 1969 under the name Hocus Pocus, but soon became UFO in tribute to the London music club where they were discovered by a record executive, and perhaps to overtly chart their "space rock" course.

The band's first two albums were popular in Japan and Germany but turned few heads in the US and UK. A who's who of early metal guitarists came and went from the band as it continued to tour. By the mid-70s, UFO had developed a tougher metal sound and finally found its home audience.

There have been numerous departures and reunions over the past three decades, but the wobbling saucer of hard-edged British rock tours America in 2008 with three of its original members.

Alien Sex Fiend Cardiff, Wales
This electronic goth-rock band's first major performance was in 1982 at the Batcave club in London. The following year, they released the album *Who's Been Sleeping in My Brain?* A good primer on alien sex is the book *Alien Sex: 19 Tales by the Masters of Science Fiction and Dark Fantasy.*

Alien Porno Midgets UK
Their Discogs.com profile calls them "Small men with big heads in a space-craft making mutant Hawaiian music… Just why the hell they are so obsessed with Hawaii is unknown." Their 2001 mini-CD *The High Altitude Porno Waikiki Beach Alien Midgets* features such tunes as "Pagan Porno Love Thong Song" and "Blue Hawaiian UFO Farewell."

Not an introductory course on learning Alien from Coburg, Bayern, Germany. According to founding **Alien101** band member Christian Bögle, "There once in my youth was a time when I felt pretty alone…ALIEN. The number 101 came from an old car which I had to work with to bring older people's meals. It was the most worn-out car I ever drove and shortly later got wrecked, so I had to use that number."

Moody Alien Poland
Is Moody Alien moody because he was assigned to Poland instead of Miami's South Beach district or because he can create only drum'n'bass techno tracks?

Alien Nation
Netherlands, Germany and Canada
Turning alienation into Alien Nation is a natural for rock rebels. The film by this name, starring James Caan, Mandy Patinkin and Terence Stamp, won the 1988 Saturn Award for Best Science Fiction Film.

Alien Hand Syndrome
Melbourne, Australia
There really is a medical condition by this name. It's the feeling that your hand is controlled by a force outside of your control. It can occur after a stroke, a brain infection or brain surgery. There is no known treatment for it. Also known as Anarchic Hand or Dr. Strangelove Syndrome.

Sacred Alien Manchester, UK
According to metal-archives.com, "the Mancunian Glam Rock band have parted company with their drummer Daz because he 'didn't fit the part.' In a statement the band say that he was increasingly against the band's image, and while they were donning stockings and make-up, he was looking more like a 'lost roadie.'" The Internet Sacred Texts Archive lists numerous books of importance to the alien faithful, including 1950s classics such as *The Flying Saucers Are Real, Other Tongues–Other Flesh* and *We Met the Space People.* The aliens extol the benefits of vegetarianism, educational TV programming and banning nuclear testing.

NAMES
STILL AVAILABLE

Alien Versus Creditor

Überwookie
Space Stylists

The UFOff-ers

Six-Pack
Abductor Aliens

I'll Have the Crab Nebula

Giant Reptiles
with PhDs in Astrophysics

My Favorite Martian
Mother-in-Law

Plutonian Pizza Pilots

Lesbian Thespians
from the Planet Crouton

The Man Ray Rayguns

Beam-Me-Up Bovine
Organ Inspectors

Fair-Trade Venusians

Ozone Hole-in-One
Alien Golfers

We Are XkZ!3!YxL Jr.

Backseat Aliens

299

The Boss Martians
Seattle, Washington, USA

Won Coolest Song of the Year on Little Steven's International Underground Garage radio show. Iggy Pop sings on their new tune "Mars Is for Martians." Other Boss Martian classics include "Bad Ass '71 Dodge Super Bee," Chihuahua del Diablo" and "Coffin and a Six Pack."

Martian Puppits
Yuba City, California, USA

Not nearly as worrisome as their heat ray. However, their assault on correct spelling has paralyzed several primary school English teachers.

Martian Heat Ray
In H.G. Wells' *The War of the Worlds*, the heat ray carried by mechanical "fighters" was the Martian invaders' primary weapon. This London, UK, band is comprised of Ricky Lee Earl, Jimmy Cliftlands, Boris Furlong and the now absent Pirate Jim. Boasting two Track of the Day awards from Garageband.com, the band would like to "share our shizzle with the world (or at least 6 other people)... We don't make songs for money or any reason other than we like to. If you like our shizzle, please let us know, as we need that kind of encouragement at the moment."

Martians See Red
Atlanta, Georgia, USA

From a rock-is-life.com interview: "The band name actually comes from a neurology book called *Phantoms of the Brain* by V.S. Ramochandran. There is a chapter in the book entitled 'Martians See Red,' which deals mainly with people's ability to perceive and understand things around them. It really has nothing at all to do with people from space." That said, the soil on Mars is rich in iron oxide, which causes it to appear a rusty red. Whether or not Martians, if they existed, would perceive the color red as we perceive it is a whole other matter.

Igloo Martian
La Crosse, Wisconsin, USA

This Wisconsin-based Martian's experiments with keyboards and "circuit bent toys" have kept him alone in his igloo except for an appearance at Bent Fest 2007. With an average winter temperature of -81F/-63C, Mars is certainly cold enough for igloo living, but you'll need to bring your own snowmaker.

Beatniks from Mars
New York City, New York, USA

"We are a combination of the Sex Pistols and the Marx brothers." George Alec Effinger's story "Mars Needs Beatniks" appeared in *Isaac Asimov's Mars*.

Nazis from Mars Netherlands
This band's astralanarchy.com homepage states "We Come in Peace." Hmmm. Right. And didn't Hitler promise nonaggression against the Netherlands, then invade on May 10, 1940, and control the entire country five days later.

Bloodsucking Zombies from Outer Space • Austria • They play something called "Horrorbilly." There's a longer story about Transylvania and extraterrestrial space pirates in the 1880s on their website. Their CD *Monster Mutant Boogie* will delight bloodsucking alien zombie fans everywhere.

Alien Christ
Sydney, Australia

Guitarist-keyboardist Matthew Bright previously played in Distant Locust and drummer Stu Olsen played in Box of the Jesuit. The boys like their Christian references.

Invaders From Sears
Darien, Connecticut, USA

A side-project for Elisa Flynn and Bobby Bunny from BunnyBrains. Neither the Sears department chain's employees nor its patrons have been scientifically proven to be alien invaders from another planet.

Flying Saucer Attack Bristol, UK
Some question as to whether these experimental rockers may have taken their name, consciously or otherwise, from the Rezillos' 1978 album *Can't Stand the Rezillos*, which opens with the track "Flying Saucer Attack."

The Cleaners From Venus
London, UK

One of the originators of London's punk-new wave cassette underground, Martin Newell joined forces with Lawrence Elliot as the Cleaners from Venus. According to Ritchie Unterberger in an online interview with Newell, the Cleaners from Venus considered themselves anti-capitalist anarchists, and as such the pair hoped to swap their cassettes for produce and dry goods. "I think somebody did actually send us some tea bags. But that's as far as it got. Then we realized that if we couldn't swap tea bags for stamps, we couldn't mail the stuff out."

Legion of Green Men
Toronto, Ontario, Canada

Lexifer in Twilight and Rew B Dew B and friends, electronic pioneers "Givin' it the GRONK since 1991." New CD: *BAQONTRAQ*.

Funky Green Dogs
From Outer Space
Miami, Florida, USA

An alias for the popular Latin-sound house duo Murk. The guys are in demand at dance clubs worldwide, including Ibiza's celebrated endless-party venue, Space.

Spacehog Leeds, UK

Four Brits find each other in crowded NYC circa 1994, start a band and release a debut album entitled *Resident Alien*, which goes gold and gets them on MTV. By the late '90s, they're touring with Pearl Jam. Spacehog called it quits in 2002. Bassist-singer Royston Langdon married actress Liv Tyler the following year (but they split in 2008).

Based in Fletcher, North Carolina, **Alien Music Club** is a multi-instrumental, multitrack solo project for the highly inventive Jonathan Pearlman. Pearlman is a fan of all things extraterrestrial. Guest musicians who appear on each CD become lifetime members of the prestigious Alien Music Club. Aliens love their music, especially tunes with titles like "Velcro Nose Job," "Summer Hepatitis Party," "Little Green Pimp" and "Satan's in Her Pelvis."

The Spiders from Mars
London, UK

David Bowie has said that this band name came to him while writing the song "Ziggy Stardust." The Spiders from Mars were a hot glam-rock trio consisting of Mick Ronson (guitar, piano, vocals), Trevor Bolder (bass) and Mick Woodmansey (drums). Bowie's concept album *The Rise and Fall of Ziggy Stardust and the Spiders from Mars* has appeared on numerous Top 100 of All Time lists. These Spiders have no proven connection to the spider-web-like patterns discovered in Mars's south polar region a few years ago.

Big Fat Pet Clams
From Outer Space
Lakewood, New Jersey, USA

Rich Gelbstein and Gary Applegate travel together through 15 years and a dozen or more bands to become the CBGB-approved Big Fat Pet Clams from Outer Space.

Alien Soup
East Northport, New York, USA

Soup that asks the musical question "Is It Now Yet?"

Alien Corn
Des Moines, Iowa, USA

"Their CD, *In the Middle of Everywhere*...is an hour of well-crafted original songs in their own distinctive style that they call Confusion." W. Somerset Maugham's short story "Alien Corn" was first published in 1931.

Vermin From Venus
Las Vegas, Nevada, USA

The well-illustrated, hard-rocking Dirk Vermin operates Pussykat Tattoo Parlor in Vegas, where he performs with his band, the Vermin. In the '80s his band was Vermin From Venus. Apparently, he had to renounce his home planet to obtain American citizenship.

My Cat Is an Alien
Torino, Italy

Brothers Maurizio and Roberto Opallo are abstract-improvisational musicians and painters. According to *Stylus* magazine, "Their obsession with space and science fiction and alien life is boundless." No mention of the cat or which brother owns it.

The Androids

This Melbourne band was formed by guitarist Tim Henwood and drummer Marty Grech, who became friends while playing clubs with local bands throughout their teens.

The Androids got notice with their single "Do It With Madonna," from their debut album. It became a Top 10 hit in Australia, Top 20 in the UK, and the memorable video featured drag queens dressed as Madonna, Britney, Pink, Christina and Kylie.

After two years of touring, the band settled in to work on their second album, but scrapped the process when it started to sound self-indulgent. A new deal with Sony/BMG brought the band back together to record *Outta Ya Mind*, featuring the single "Whole Lotta Love."

Henwood: "I was playing guitar with Rogue Traders, who had that huge hit, 'Voodoo Child.' I was explaining to James Ash how Hendrix had a song with that title, and he had no idea! He's such an avid dance music fan that he'd never heard the Hendrix song. I thought that was so hilarious, so I decided I'd write a song with the title of another well-known rock anthem."

Does Your Robot Bite?

The Android Sisters USA

From the harmony trio the Andrews Sisters and the work of sci-fi author Philip K. Dick. This '80s band roboticized female voices and layered on the synths and electronic beats on songs such as "Electronic Sheep" and "SSS-X Minus One."

Android Lust

New York City, New York, USA

Formed in 1996 as a recording project for Bangladesh-born Shikhee. For live performances, she is joined by three additional vocalist-musicians.

Robot Love Story Chicago, USA

Tour blog, July 21, Peoria: "The beer started flowing. Our host, Kevin, lost his pants and walked around the rest of the night in his boxer briefs. He has the sickest tattoo of a burrito and a pizza holding hands under a rainbow that's raining sprinkles."

Brighton, UK's **Robot Ninja Dinosaur Bastards** invite us to enjoy such timeless tunes as "Cyberfreaks From the Planet Pukoid," "Slime Faced, Cut Throat, Cage Faced Weirdos," "Toxic Overload of Cybersonic Repugnant Vomit" and "Profit Margins!!!"

Attitude Robots

Baltimore, Maryland, USA

An on-hiatus band featuring Jason Willett (the Jaunties, Leprechaun Catering, the Pleasant Livers, Half Japanese, Louie Louise).

The Chocolate Robots

Toronto, Ontario, Canada

An admittedly lo-fi trio. Their 2007 album is entitled *Purr Quality*.

Cyborg Attack

Chemnitz/Liepzig, Germany

"Cyborg Attack have earned themselves an extremely faithful fanbase of EBM followers…even when the musical style was out of vogue on underground dance floors worldwide."

Killed By Robots

Wichita, Kansas, USA

"[Our] sound is emotional and a little chaotic…The songs have a certain flow, but can turn on themselves unexpectedly or, conversely, merge to create a powerful thunder."

Go Robot, Go!

Columbus, Ohio, USA

Album: *Wait Three Days…Then Attack!*

Les Robot

Edmonton, Alberta, Canada

The band and stage name of the man who won the North American Rock Guitar Competition in 2006.

Velveteen Robot

Los Angeles, California, USA

A pun on *The Velveteen Rabbit*, the title of Margery Williams' 1922 children's book.

Ex-Loma Lynda songwriters Sarah Ellquist and Dan White formed the **Robotanists** "in search of a more refined sound and a forum to deliver their gut-wrenching serenades." The Silverlake, California, duo often expands to a quartet (or larger) for live performances. *Filter Magazine Online*: "Ellquist's vocals keen through the din like Liz Frazier's (Cocteau Twins) angry baby sister — the result, nothing short of phenomenal."

Robot Juice Toronto, Ontario, USA
Previously called AOK, for guitarist-vocalist Kenta Aoki. The cough suppressant Robotussin (ROBOTussin) is referred to as robot juice when used in high dosages as a recreational drug.

Robot Lords of Tokyo
Columbus, Ohio, USA
Robot Lords of Tokyo: "Hardcore fans of groove-metal legends Clutch will recognize the name as a snippet from the lyrics to '10001110101,' a track off their 2005 classic *Robot Hive/Exodus..*"

Robots & Butterflies
South Florida, USA
Big and clunky, light and delicate, male and female vocals. Song: "White Teens in Tight Jeans"

hot like (A) robot
San Diego, California, USA
Frank Iero from My Chemical Romance called them his favorite up-and-coming band in the February 2007 issue of *Spin*.

Hotshotrobot
Halifax, Nova Scotia, Canada
It rhymes. EP: *Eat My Heart*. Song: "Kiss My Chernobyl."

Robot Whales
Brick, New Jersey, USA
Sounds like: "Slow and heavy." Label: Collapse Records.

Robotosaurus Adelaide, Australia
Robot + dinosaur = grindcore. Album: *Manhater*.

Robots in Disguise Liverpool, UK
The title of the English-language edition of the Japanese TV series *Transformers: CarRobot*. Also a line of Transformer toys in the US.

Robots in the Sky Cardiff, Wales
The original name of People in Planes. Also an Oklahoma-based jam band.

**Starvin Marvin
& the Paranoid Androids**
Ghent, Belgium
"Starvin" Marvin Siau and band. Marvin the Paranoid Android is a character in Douglas Adams' *Hitchhiker's Guide to the Universe* series.

The Robot Are Me
San Diego, California, USA
"Their critically acclaimed albums alternate between accessible pop and obscure musical art projects that tend to annoy or astonish."

NAMES
STILL AVAILABLE

My Android

Lloyd

Cyborgorgonzola

Fat Bottom
Robots

Robotomy

Way Wired
Man

Terminator®
Party Trick

Br'er Robot

Cyborg
Sabbath

Charged
and in Charge

Borg vs Björk

Hottentot
Robot

Planet X

Planet X evolved from the recording of ex-Dream Theater keyboardist Derek Sherinian's 1999 solo album, *Planet X*. Says Sherinian, "When I started Planet X, I had one goal: to start the sickest instrumental band in the world. I wanted to find musicians that played their instruments so fiercely, it would strike fear in the hearts of other musicians when they played."

The first three Planet X albums — *Universe*, *Live from Oz* and *MoonBabies*—feature Tony MacAlpine on guitar. MacAlpine received his formal training on piano and violin but is renowned in the guitar community as a formidable shredder. Fusion-master Allan Holdsworth and fellow guitarist Brett Garsed (from Sherinian's *Planet X* solo effort) took over guitar duties for 2007's *Quantum*.

Australian drummer Virgil Donati is perhaps one of the few rock drummers who could handle the multiple time changes in each song. Veteran drummer-producer Simon Phillips has said, "Planet X is a band that is playing the almost impossible." Bassists have included names such as Sheehan, Kennedy, LaRue, Fierabracci, Bynoe and recently Rufus Philpot.

Astronomer Percival Lowell began a search for Pluto in 1906, calling it Planet X.

A Planet of One's Own

The Mercury Seed
New York City, New York, USA
These guys seem to hover in the 4 out of 5 stars vicinity. New album: *Throwing Rocks at the Sun*. Singer-guitarist Volker Lemmer came up with the name. It "sounded good…felt kind of serious…and it wasn't shot down like the other 120 names."

Mountain of Venus
Fayetteville, Arkansas, USA
A *Relix* magazine "Band to Watch" fronted by Louisiana singer Tanya Shylock. In palmistry, the Mount of Venus is at the base of your thumb and a barometer of love. It is also another name for the *mons pubis*, a woman's pubic mound.

Venus Infers
Orange County, California, USA
New album tentatively titled *The Truth About Venus Infers*. The name is a pun of the Lou Reed-penned Velvet Underground song "Venus in Furs," the title for which was taken from the title of a novel by Leopold von Sacher-Masoch, the man from whom *masochism* derives its name.

Stealing Venus
Los Angeles, California, USA
Started out as an all-female band. Now two Venuses (Merritt and Mia), a Derek and a Joe. Novelist-poet Izola Forrester published an article entitled "Stealing Venus's Girdle" in the August 1909 edition of *The Scrap Book*.

Earth Crisis
Syracuse, New York, USA
Earth's crisis is the need to barbecue. Band members are straight-edge (no drugs or alcohol) metalcore vegans.

Manfred Mann's Earth Band
London, UK
Formed in 1971 by Manfred Mann following the breakup of the group Manfred Mann. The Earth Band band finally broke into the US market with the 1977 #1 single "Blinded by the Light," originally an acoustic song by Bruce Springsteen from 1973's *Greetings from Asbury Park, N.J.*

I Mother Earth
Toronto, Ontario, Canada
The name came from the acronym IME, standing for I Am Me, when the band decided they needed something better. Guitarist Jagori Tanna, a big Santana fan, arrived at I Mother Earth.

Rare Earth   Detroit, Michigan, USA
The first bunch of hit-making white guys signed to Motown. The band started in 1961 as the Sunliners but became Rare Earth in 1967. Their covers of the Temptations' "(I Know) I'm Losing You" and "Get Ready," and the song "I Just Want to Celebrate" were all Top 10 hits.

Earth to Nigel   Sydney, Australia
Nigel is Nigel Maher (guitar, vocals), brother of Dallas Maher (drums, vocals), joined by Clinton Maher (vocals, guitar).

30 Seconds to Mars
Los Angeles, California, USA
Formed by brothers Jared and Shannon Leto in 1998. The name comes from an article they read online in which a former Harvard professor disusses "the exponential growth of technology that relates to humans, saying that we are quite literally thirty seconds to Mars."

Omar Rodriguez-Lopez and Cedric Bixler-Zavala's creative partnership has lasted since 1993, through the bands At the Drive-In and De Facto, a move from El Paso to LA, and, since 2001, in the **Mars Volta**, a band *Rolling Stone* called the "Best Prog-Rock Band." Bixler-Zavala has said that the word "Mars" was chosen because of their love of science fiction, and "Volta" from a book in which film director Federico Fellini used the word to describe a change of scene (*volta* means time in Italian).

Mars Needs Women
New Jersey, USA
Started by guitarist-singer Shawn Mars (Shawn McCabe). Mars also sang lead vocals briefly in Skid Row and Ozone Monday. In the 1967 B-movie *Mars Needs Women*, a genetic mishap leaves Mars without females. They travel to Earth to pick up chicks.

The Jupiter Deluxe
New York City, New York, USA
Big, big rock, but not at all gassy.

Jupiter in January
St. Paul, Minnesota, USA
Piano rock of the Coldplay-ish kind. Jupiter has no seasons, as seasons are related to a planet's axis, and Jupiter has only a 3-degree tilt.

Jupiter Child
Clinton Township, Michigan, USA
"Jupiter's Child" is a song off Steppenwolf's 1969 album, *At Your Birthday Party*.

Saturn's Flea Collar
Santa Rosa, California, USA
A side-project for two Victim's Family members and the vocalist from Squat Thrust. Songs: "Sugar Frosted Loopholes," "Frolic with the Hunchbacks."

Uranus & the Five Moons
Middletown, Connecticut, USA
Early '60s frat-house cover band with roots at Wesleyan University.

Neptune Crush
St. Louis, Missouri, USA
Formed in 1999. Opened for Billy Corgan and Marilyn Manson. Became Salisbury.

Neptune's Buffalo
San Francisco, California, USA
They were going for a tie-dyed '60s name.

Pluto Auckland, New Zealand
Their song "Long White Cross" was Single of the Year at the NZ Music Awards in 2006, the same year Pluto was declared no longer a planet.

Phantom Planet
Los Angeles, California, USA
Their song "California" is the theme song for the TV series *The O.C.* The name comes from the 1961 B-movie *The Phantom Planet*.

NAMES
STILL AVAILABLE

Swallowing Mercury

Rhymes with Venus

Worms Rule Earth

Mars Needs Cable

Jupiter's Unsightly Red Spot

Hydrogen Breathing Hula Vixens of Saturn

Uranus Down

Neptune (Not Neptunes)

Don't Pluto Me

Planet of the Crepes

The Pump-Up Planets

Parking Side of the Moon

305

Florida-based **Planet 13** was formed in 2002 by Lance Benedict and Ray Zarate. Benedict came up with the band name one night when negative experiences kept replaying in his mind. "My head became a virtual planet of previous misfortunes. Hence, Planet 13." *One Way Ticket* was released in 2005. Recent album: *Third from the Right*.

The Other Planets
New Orleans, Louisiana, USA
Eccentric horn-funk with titles such as "Happy Time at the Mall" and "Walking Porno Zombies Part 2." Recent album: *Holiday for Vacationers!*

Chunky Planet   Cork, Ireland
Carl Plover and Linda Carroll. *Irish Times*: "Cork's most likely candidates for better things."

Rubber Planet
Denver, Colorado, USA
Power-pop songs that "won't stop bouncing off the walls of your head." Rubber Planet Company Limited is based in Thailand.

Green Milk from the Planet Orange
Tokyo, Japan
"Know progressive rock is not dead."

Planet P Project
USA / Germany
A collaboration between ex-Rainbow keyboardist Tony Carey and German producer Peter Hauke.

Shadowy Men on a Shadowy Planet
Toronto, Ontario, Canada
Formed in 1984 by Brian Connelly (guitar), Don Pyle (drums) and Reid Diamond (bass). Their most recognizable track is "Having an Average Weekend," the theme song for *The Kids in the Hall*. They won a 1992 Juno Award for Best Instrumental Album, *Dim the Light, Chill the Ham*. Spin-offs: Atomic 7 and Phono-Comb.

Planet of Women   London, UK
Three blonde women. Tagline: "AC/DC meets the Supremes."

The Planet Smashers
Montreal, Quebec, Canada
Ska band formed in 1994. The name came about as a result of singer-guitarist Matt Collyer overhearing someone at a party say that they liked the idea of "cruising all over the galaxy crushing planets." Recent album: *Unstoppable*.

The Moonbabies   Malmö, Sweden
The duo of Carina Johansson and Ola Frick. According to Frick, the name comes from the lyrics to a song entitled "Luna." There is also a Planet X album entitled *MoonBabies*.

The Moonglows
Cleveland, Ohio, USA
Founded in 1951, this doo-wop group was inducted into the Rock & Roll Hall of Fame in 2000. As with many groups, battles have raged over which former members have the right to tour under the name. The 1958 edition, Harvey Fuqua & the New Moonglows, featured a lead vocalist named Marvin Gaye.

Moonshake   London, UK
"Moonshake" is a song off the German band Can's 1973 album, *Future Days*.

Moonsorrow   Finland
They call their music "epic Pagan metal," as differentiated from "Viking metal." The name is from the Celtic Frost song "Sorrows of the Moon." ∎

Hillbilly Moon Explosion
Zurich-based Hillbilly Moon Explosion is a '50s revival group comprised of bassist-vocalist Oliver Baroni, rhythm guitarist-vocalist Emanuela Hutter, guitarist Duncan James and drummer Luke Weyermann. The name comes from Baroni's former band, the Hillbilly Headhunters, and Hutter's previous project, MD Moon. Album: *All Grown Up*.

Placed & Misplaced

You Are Here

We Are Not Here

Placed and Misplaced

Boston

The band had one of the fastest-selling debut albums in history, the 1976 self-titled *Boston*, and it consisted largely of tapes recorded in songwriter, keyboardist, guitarist and MIT graduate Tom Scholz's basement on his homemade 12-track, with some drums added by Jim Masdea and lead vocals provided by Brad Delp.

Of course, that was 30-plus years ago, and a lot of murky water passed under the bridge in the interim. Guitarist Barry Goudreau remembers Scholz joining *his* band, Mother's Milk, after answering an ad — though he agrees that they did rehearse in Scholz's home studio for ages and submit several unsuccessful demos to labels before recording the album that Scholz tweaked to perfection.

Or Epic made Scholz and Delp re-record the album in professional studios with studio musicians. (Reportedly, only Scholz and Delp were signed to Epic.)

Only the people in that basement really know for certain if Scholz made Boston from scratch or if Mother's Milk morphed into Boston. But there is no doubt that the songs on those basement tapes were potent enough to make the *Boston* album go 17 times platinum.

You Are Here

Polar for the Masses Norway
"We are three very different kinds of people. We found that the only thing we've ever had in common was a car...the old Polar by Volvo. Every one of us had this car, in different times, and we thought that this was a sign! Heavier and bigger than the others, a simple design that will be forever out of time." Album: *Let Me Be Here*.

Blue Swede Stockholm, Sweden
Originally called Blåblus (Blue Denim Shirt). Their biggest hit was a 1974 cover of the B. J. Thomas song "Hooked on a Feeling."

The Liverpool Scene
Liverpool, UK
Satire and sitars and poems. The band included Adrian Henri, Andy Roberts, Mike Evans, Mike Hart, Percy Jones and Brian Dodson. "It grew out of the success of *The Incredible New Liverpool Scene*, a CBS LP featuring Henri and McGough reading their work, with accompaniment by the guitarist [Andy] Roberts."

Abandon Kansas
Wichita, Kansas, USA
Album: *You Build a Wall, I'll Build a Ladder*.

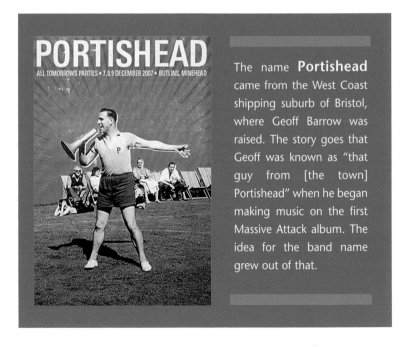

The name **Portishead** came from the West Coast shipping suburb of Bristol, where Geoff Barrow was raised. The story goes that Geoff was known as "that guy from [the town] Portishead" when he began making music on the first Massive Attack album. The idea for the band name grew out of that.

Iowa City's own **IOWA BEEF EXPERIENCE** formed in fall of 1986 and opened for Suburban Death Trip at a club called Gabe's the following January. There were lineup changes involving singers and drummers over the band's 7-year life, but the married core of the band, guitarist Chris and bassist Simone Rinehart, remained constant. The first Iowa Beef Experience recording was a cassette entitled *At Least It Ain't Nebraska*. Their two LPs are *Cool Ass Gravy Train* and *Personalien*.

The Merseybeats Liverpool, UK
The Mersey beat was named for the river Mersey, which runs through Liverpool. The Merseybeats played the Cavern Club with the Beatles, Gerry & the Pacemakers and others. They started as the Mavericks and briefly became the Pacifics before deciding on the Merseybeats, a name in tune with their place and time.

Better Outside Kansas
Lexington-Nicholasville, Kentucky, USA
They started in a band called Marshall Branch but were all kicked out of that band. So they started Better Outside Kansas. "Most of the original inspiration came from the whole band dispute, including discontinued songs like 'At Least I Didn't Lose Your Keys' and 'Drugs Can Replace Friends.'"

Georgia Satellites Atlanta, Georgia
Best known for their 1986 Top 5 single "Keep Your Hands to Yourself," which went to #2 on the *Billboard* Singles chart.

Kansas Topeka, Kansas, USA
From the state's capital city. They added a violinist and changed their name to White Clover in 1971, then thought better of it.

The Kentucky Headhunters
Edmonton, Kentucky, USA
They started out informally as the Itchy Brothers. The Kentucky Headhunters became known through their regular performances on the *Chitlin' Show*, on radio WLOC in Munfordville, Kentucky. Their first album was 1989's *Pickin' on Nashville*.

Brooklyn Funk Essentials
Brooklyn, New York, USA
A jazz, funk and hip-hop collective of musicians and poets.

Ohio Players Dayton, Ohio, USA
Back in 1959, they were the Ohio Untouchables. By 1967 they were the Ohio Players. And by the mid-70s they were one of the top funk bands in America.

NAMES
STILL AVAILABLE

The Boise Boys

Yeah Yeah Yemen

Sheffield Steal

Bolivia New-Tone Juans

Wollongong

Pines for Sweden

Portsmouth Chip Shop Daredevils

Blooming Mongolia

The Fijis

Rancho Cucamonga

Yellowknife

The Brussels Walloon

309

Ozark Mountain Daredevils
Springfield, Missouri, USA
Previous names include Rhythm of Joy, Burlap Socks, Buffalo Chips and the Emergency Band. Singer Steve Cash came up with the name Cosmic Corncob & His Amazing Ozark Mountain Daredevils, which was embraced by the band but later whittled down to size.

Appalachian Death Ride
Athens, Ohio, USA
The band was "formed as a way to kill time."

Chicago   Chicago, Illinois, USA
Started as Chicago Transit Authority. According to *Billboard* chart statistics, Chicago is second only to the Beach Boys as the most successful American pop band of all time.

Chilliwack   Vancouver, British Columbia, Canada
Began in 1964 as the Classics, became the Collectors in 1966, ended up as Chilliwack, which in the Salish native language means "going back up." Chilliwack is also the name of a city east of Vancouver.

Burning Down Centralia
Allentown, Pennsylvania, USA
Originally formed as Honest Mistake, then they fixed the mistake by changing their lineup, style and name. The historic Centralia Fire started in an abandoned coal mine more than 45 years ago. The flames on the surface were successfully extinguished, but the coal continued to burn underground. There is enough coal in the 8-mile vein to feed the fire for up to 250 years.

tourist
the relevance of motion

Vancouver, British Columbia's **Tourist** began with singer Blaine Braun and bassist Mark Radloff. Adding guitarist-singer Greg Whitbeck and drummer Bob Wagner, the band recorded some tracks and, without ever having played a live gig together, won the 2004 Radio CFOX "Seeds" contest, joining former winners Nickleback, Default and Matthew Good. They were soon opening for bands such as the Offspring, Billy Talent and Finger Eleven, and working toward the release of their debut album, *The Relevance of Motion*.

We Are Not Here

New Atlantic
Southport, Merseyside, UK
After this early '90s rave band appeared on *Top of the Pops*, *The Sun* held a competition "to find New Atlantic a singer."

Arctic   Vancouver, British Columbia, Canada
Guitarist Marcus Martin spent his childhood in Canada's isolated Northwest Territories. Arctic is "sometimes a solo project, sometimes a full band, never exactly the same from one show to the next."

Arctic Summer
Pennsylvania, USA
A four-piece band of "Enginerds" from Penn State University. They say they dislike their name but can't think of an alternative. Even if global warming causes the Arctic summer sea ice to melt, Pennsylvania will still not in be in the Arctic.

iForward, Russia!   Leeds, UK
Until 2006, the band only named tracks with numbers. And they occasionally typeset their name in Faux Cyrillic. They say the name sounds powerful, as if it is being shouted, and that it is a recognizable logo.

The Russian Futurists
Toronto, Ontario, Canada
Albums: *Let's Get Ready to Crumble* and *Me Myself & Rye: An Introduction To The Russian Futurists*

Zoviet*France
Newcastle, UK
Also known as :$OVIET:FRANCE:, Soviet France, :zoviet-france: but usually written as :zoviet*france.

Siberia
New York City, New York, USA
"Siberia gained notoriety as a solid band playing regularly at NY's Mercury Lounge, CBGB's, CB's Gallery, Wetlands and the Rodeo Bar."

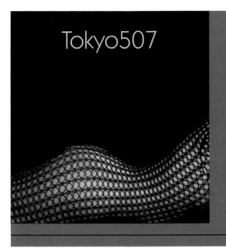

Tokyo507

Mark Southern is based in Sydney, Australia, and long-time collaborator Hayden Turner is in London, UK, when not traveling. Together they are **Tokyo507**, a dance-lounge-beat duo with a taste for groove guitar. Some of the vocals for their new album were recorded in Tokyo and Rome.

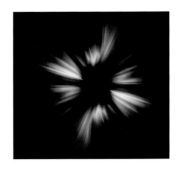

Asia

The original Asia formed in 1981 by Yes guitarist Steve Howe, King Crimson bassist John Wetton, drummer Carl Palmer of Emerson, Lake & Palmer, and roving keyboardist Geoff Downes.

Despite the players' backgrounds in the esoteric progressive-rock genre, their output as Asia was almost radio-friendly. Critics were disappointed, but they drew a broader audience immediately. The band's first album spent nine weeks at #1 in the US and sold over 4 million copies – 10 million worldwide.

The name Asia has always been rumored to have been a suggestion by manager Brian Lane. Perhaps playing off their name, the band recorded studio albums with one-word titles beginning with A: *Asia, Alpha, Astra, Aqua, Aria, Arena, Aura….*

There have been many lineup changes over the years and the usual bouts of animosity. As of 2008, there are two groups using the Asia name, one a reunion of the original lineup, the other featuring members from later incarnations.

The Trans-Siberian Orchestra
New York City, New York, USA
A rock orchestra founded by Paul O'Neill, Robert Kinkel and Jon Oliva in 1996. The name is inspired by the Trans-Siberian Railway in Russia, which Kinkel says connects many cultures otherwise isolated, much like music.

China Crisis
Kirkby, UK
Formed in 1979 in Kirkby, near Liverpool. Their 1985 album, *Flaunt the Imperfection*, rose to #9 on the UK Album chart.

Mission of Burma
Boston, Massachussetts, USA
Formed in 1979, they took their name from a "Mission of Burma" plaque a member saw on a New York City diplomatic building. He thought the phrase had a "sort of murky and disturbing" quality.

Japan
London, UK
Formed in 1974: "From rather humble glam-rock beginnings into stylish synth-pop (and beyond)."

Art in Manila
Omaha, Nebraska, USA
Orenda Fink, ex-Azure Ray, decided to form a new band called Art Belle, named for Art Bell, who created a late-night radio talk show that explored the paranormal and alleged conspiracies. But after Bell was personally threatened, he moved to the Philippines. To avoid stirring up paranoid radio listeners (or litigation), the band changed its name to Art in Manila.

Indochine   Paris, France
Very successful in France and other parts of continental Europe in the '80s.

Hanoi Rocks
Helsinki, Finland
One story has it that guitarist Andy McCoy was watching a documentary about a drug factory in Vietnam and screamed, "Hanoi Rocks!"

Saigon Kick
Miami, Florida, USA
Hard rockers Saigon Kick formed in Miami in 1988 but had their biggest following in Asia.

Towers of Hanoi
Gainesville, Florida, USA

The Appalachian Drinking League broke up, and the Towers of Hanoi were formed. The Towers of Hanoi (also known as the Towers of Benares) is a mathematical puzzle game.

Angry Samoans
Van Nuys, California, USA

This "savagely satirical" punk band began in 1978 as a Dictators cover band. After considering names such as the Egyptians and the Eigen Vectors (one member later became a math prof), they settled on the Angry Samoans.

Madras
Los Angeles, California, USA

"Radio friendly, but only for cool radio stations." Madras is the colonial name for Chennai, the capital of Tamil Nadu state and India's fourth largest city.

Garaj Mahal
San Francisco, California USA

Indian music, rock and funk, all with jazz elements. The band asked fans to suggest names in a contest on the internet. Out of over 800 entries, they chose Garaj Mahal. They liked the spiritual sound of the name. The Taj Mahal became a UNESCO World Heritage Site in 1983.

Timbuk 3 Madison, Wisconsin, and Austin, Texas, USA

"What comes after Timbuk 2?" The husband-and-wife duo, Pat and Barbara K. MacDonald, first performed live backed only by a large boombox. Best known for their Top 20 single "The Future's So Bright, I Gotta Wear Shades." Timbuktu is a city in the West African nation of Mali.

Belarus Wiltshire, UK

"Belarus are purveyors of stunning, melody-driven, often epic songs… their music reflects both the pastoral Englishness of their surroundings and the inevitability of modern technology. Lyrics form everyday stories of strained relationships and broken promises." On the other hand, Belarus is a land-locked country in Eastern Europe. Since 1996, Belarus has been negotiating with Russia to unify into a single state called the Union of Russia and Belarus.

The Well Hungarians
St Louis/Nashville, USA

Country southern rock. *New Music Weekly*'s 2006 Best Country Group of the Year.

A Sunny Day in Glasgow
Philadelphia, Pennsylvania, USA

Began as a collaboration between Ben Daniels and Ever Nalens. Both had spent several years in the UK. The band name came from Nalens, who had been living in Glasgow.

Birds of Wales
Toronto, Ontario, Canada

Birds of Wales is an alt-folk-country quartet. Frontman-founder Morgan Ross is of Welsh descent. "I've always had a thing for birds. I grew up with a cockatoo."

Amsterdam Liverpool, UK

Ian Prowse's group appeared on a compilation album, *Mersey Boys and Liverpool Girls*, alongside Paul McCartney and other Liverpool greats.

Berlin
Los Angeles, California, USA

"Take My Breath Away," from the *Top Gun* soundtrack.

I'm From Barcelona
Jönköping, Sweden

There were 29 participants in the group's debut EP, in part because of Sweden's generous labor laws. Part-time singer-songwriter Emanuel Lundgren invited friends to help him make an EP. When they were done, they took their band name from the incompetent waiter, Manuel, on *Fawlty Towers*: "I'm from Barcelona."

Spanish for Hitchhiking
Northampton, Massachusetts, USA

Spanish slang for hitchhike: *viajar a dedo.*

Basque Brooklyn, New York, USA

The duo of bassist Brandt and singer Maryasque. The Basques are an ethnic group who inhabit parts of north-central Spain and southwestern France. But if you put the *B* from Brandt together with the *asque* from Maryasque, you get Basque.

Portugal. The Man
Wasilla, Alaska, USA

With former members of Anatomy of a Ghost. The original band name was Portugal. The Man and the Approaching AIRballoons. Guitarist-vocalist John Gourley: "A country is a group of people. With Portugal, it just ended up being the first country that came to mind. The band's name is Portugal. The period is stating that, and The Man states that it's just one person." But they're a trio.

When in Rome
Manchester, UK

When in Rome had a US Top 20 hit with "The Promise" in 1988. "When in Rome" comes from the expression "When in Rome, do as the Romans do."

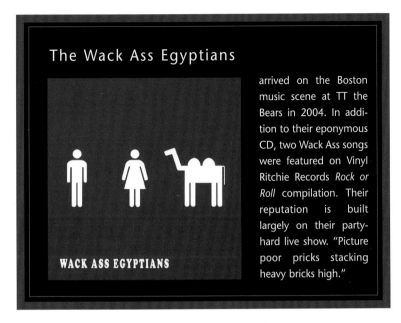

The Wack Ass Egyptians

WACK ASS EGYPTIANS

arrived on the Boston music scene at TT the Bears in 2004. In addition to their eponymous CD, two Wack Ass songs were featured on Vinyl Ritchie Records *Rock or Roll* compilation. Their reputation is built largely on their party-hard live show. "Picture poor pricks stacking heavy bricks high."

Je Suis France
Athens, Georgia, USA
A friend used to shout "Je suis France" over and over before taking French exams. Band members enjoy the way audiences shout out the name and get it wrong. "Some of the best: Juice de France, Jesus France, and *Je Suispants.*"

The Rivieras
South Bend, Indiana, USA
The Rivieras recorded "California Sun" in Chicago, not California, as many radio listeners assumed. The Buick Riviera that the band posed next to for the cover of the album had Illinois plates. That kind of Riviera.

Eyeless in Gaza
Nuneaton, Warwickshire, UK
The post-punk duo of Martyn Bates and Peter Becker. The name is the title of a 1936 novel by Aldous Huxley. Huxley's title comes from a phrase in John Milton's *Samson Agonistes*.

The Gaza Strippers
Chicago, Illinois, USA
Former Didjits and Supersuckers guitarist Rick Sims led the Gaza Strippers, a glammed-up punk quartet active in the late '90s. The Gaza Strip is a coastal strip of land along the Mediterranean Sea, about 25 miles long and between 4 and 7.5 miles wide (an area of about 360 km^2), over which a lot of blood has been shed.

Bedouin Soundclash
Kingston, Ontario, Canada
The name comes from the title of a 1996 dub record by Israeli DJ Badawi, reflecting the band's global influences.

The Afghan Whigs
Cincinnati, Ohio, USA
A soul-influenced American rock band named after a Florida-based white Muslim biker gang from the '60s who were into love, not war.

NAMES
STILL AVAILABLE

Boomtown

Arararat

Seoulfly

Marrakech 22

The Hague

Wolverhampton

Making Plans for Niger

Wahoo, Nebraska

The Price of Madagascar

Copehhagen Dazs

Frankie Goes to Moose Jaw

Romania. The Mad Lettuce

Queen Latvia

313

Beirut
Albuquerque, New Mexico, USA
After dropping out of high school, Zach Condon claims to have traveled through Europe at the age of 16, "in the process becoming exposed to the Balkan folk and gypsy music that's at the heart of [the album] *Gulag Orkestar.*"

Fearless Iranians From Hell
San Antonia, Texas, USA
Thrash. "The music of the dispossessed suburban child."

Brazilian Girls
New York City, New York, USA
Brazilian Girls are three men and one woman, who sings in no less than five different languages. Despite their name, no one in the band is Brazilian.

The Whole Bolivian Army
Seattle, Washington, USA
The name is a reference to the final scene in *Butch Cassidy and the Sundance Kid*, when the two American outlaws are surrounded by what seems like the entire armed forces of Bolivia.

Shot Down in Ecuador, Jr.
New Orleans, Louisiana, USA
The name comes from a conversation between Rhoda and a salesclerk in the 1973 *Mary Tyler Moore Show* episode "Angels in the Snow."

Alaska Zürich, Switzerland
A Swiss ska-reggae band: "Alaska are nine young musicians with tie and shirt, rich brass & wind arrangements, bubbling organ sounds and sweeping offbeats, combined to a highly dancing mixture 'à la Ska.'"

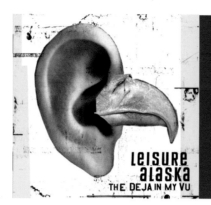

The three guitarists who eventually founded **Leisure Alaska** met for the first time on the rooftop of a shopping center when they took part in the same rappelling course. They moved to Copenhagen, found a bass player, a drummer, and a producer. Their first single, "Hey There Mr.," hit the Danish video chart at #1. Their debut album: *The Deja in My Vu.*

alaska!
San Francisco, California, USA
"The name alaska! has nothing to do with the state. Rather, it's about the state of mind. It is always written in lowercase letters and the exclamation point is always included." Must be hanging with moe. and Portugal. The Man.

Arizona
New York City, New York, USA
"The music sounds like sweetly sleeping faeries nestled in the dewy grass of a magical land while dark, sharp, drooling creatures lurk nearby."

The Dakotas Manchester, UK
The Dakotas formed in 1960, with the name suggested by a local promoter who wanted the band to dress up as American Indians.

Proof of Utah
Champaign, Illinois, USA
"Proof of Utah has no Utah connection at all. The name's just a phrase co-founder Louie Simon overheard in a conversation."

Girls in Hawaii Belgium
Neo-psychedelic pop and alternative rock from six guys. Not girls, and not in Hawaii.

Oklahoma Trio
Sweden
"The story of Oklahoma Trio begins in February 2004 in a snowy and cold Jönköping, Sweden, where Ida and Henrik started messing around with a guitar and a dusty recording device."

Texas Glasgow, Scotland
The band cultivates an American-influenced sound and took their name from the film *Paris, Texas*, with its score by Ry Cooder, whose slide guitar playing heavily influenced lead guitarist Ally McErlaine. Singer and rhythm guitarist Sharleen Spiteri sings with no discernible Scottish accent.

Texas Is the Reason
New York City, New York, USA
The name is from a Misfits song called "Bullet": *Texas is the reason that the President's dead....*

Lone Star Cardiff, Wales, UK
Originally called Iona, Lone Star was formed in 1975 by Paul 'Tonka' Chapman.

Awesome Sounds Like Austin
Olive Branch, Mississippi, USA
Acoustic electronica from Charlie, Austin and Chris.

Calexico had its origins in Southern California in 1990 when Joey Burns met up with John Convertino, who was playing drums in Giant Sand. Burns joined the band on upright bass. Giant Sand moved to Tucson, Arizona, where John and Joey formed the Friends of Dean Martin (later the Friends of Dean Martinez). In 1996 Burns and Convertino formed Calexico, named for the border town of Calexico, California, and influenced by traditional sounds of Mexico and the southwestern US.

The Bay City Rollers
Edinburgh, Scotland
They picked a band name by pointing at random to a spot on a map of the US: Bay City, Michigan.

The Midway State
Toronto, Ontario, Canada
"The Midway State comes at you from out of nowhere. The band's nakedly emotional, piano-driven rock songs bear no clear connection to any current sound or scene." Album: *Holes in Canada*.

The Bronx
Los Angeles California, USA
"The Bronx isn't your atypical alt-metal group inspired by nasty '70s punk. They are in a sense, but..."

Elk City
New York City, New York, USA
Band member Ray Ketchum: "It's a tiny town in West Virginia near where I grew up. We liked the rural-meets-urban thing. And it has a ring to it."

Memphis
Vancouver, British Columbia, Canada
Torquil Campbell and Chris Dumont (from North Carolina). Memphis was also once the name of Aretha Franklin's backup band.

Orlando
London, UK
Named after the Virginia Woolf novel, not the city in Florida.

Tulsa
Boston, Massachusetts, USA

"Tulsa took its name from a book of photographs by Larry Clark. His pictures seem to be largely about a group of people he grew up with who had a hard time maintaining their curiosity for life. That's the intent of Tulsa's songs, lyrically and musically, staying hungry for life, upholding that curiosity."

Frankie Goes to Hollywood
Liverpool, UK

Said to have taken their name from a *New Yorker* magazine article with the headline "Frankie Goes to Hollywood" and a picture of Frank Sinatra. Their debut single "Relax" was banned by the BBC, so of course it became one of the Top 10 bestselling UK singles of all time.

Glasvegas
Glasgow, Scotland

Glasgow and Las Vegas = Glasvegas. Lisa Marie Presley once invited them for drinks while in Edinburgh, and then invited them to record material with her.

I Am the World Trade Center
Athens, Georgia, USA

Musician Daniel Geller and singer Amy Dykes decided on the name in 1999 while living in New York City. They liked it as a metaphor for their personal and professional relationships. After September 11, 2001, they took some heat and played for a while under the name "I Am the World...," but soon went back to their original name.

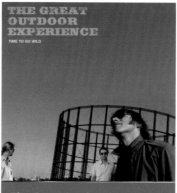

The Great Outdoor Experience was formed in London in 2001. Singer-guitarist Phil Ram has spent three decades playing with top musicians in Britain and the US, including Randy California's Spirit. In the '80s, Ram joined punk group the Vibrators, leading to the release of *Disco in Moscow*. His new band, the Great Outdoor Experience, features Adam Bickerton on bass and Adam Jones on drums. Their recent album is *Time to Go Wild*.

Diamond Head   Stourbridge, UK
Formed in 1976 by schoolfriends Brian Tatler and Duncan Scott, with Tatler playing on a cheap fuzz guitar and Scott on biscuit tins. The name Diamond Head came from a Phil Manzanera album that Tatler had a poster of in his room. Diamond Head is a famous volcanic crater on the Hawaiian island of O'ahu.

A Day in Attica
Lawrence, Kansas, USA

The Attica Correctional Facility is a maximum-security prison located in Attica, New York. In 1971 a prison riot resulted in 39 deaths. In the film *Dog Day Afternoon*, Al Pacino's character yells, "Attica! Attica!" to recall the people killed in the riot. A Day in Attica fans do the chant at concerts.

The Ivy League   UK
They had two Top 10 UK singles in 1965, thanks to their three-part harmonies, which were first heard as background vocals on the Who's "I Can't Explain." In 1967 they changed their name to the Flower Pot Men. In the US, Ivy League is the name applied to eight universities: Brown, Columbia, Cornell, Dartmouth, Harvard, Pennsylvania, Princeton and Yale.

Canada
Ann Arbor, Michigan, USA

It takes less than an hour to drive from Ann Arbor, Michigan, to Canada. Seven-piece chamber folk-pop band formed in 2004. Debut album: *This Cursed House*.

The Young Canadians
Vancouver, British Columbia, Canada

Originally the Vancouver hardcore band the K-Tels, but the K-Tel corporation made certain legal assertions, and they became the Young Canadians. In keeping with the misplaced-names theme: "Hawaii" is their Canadian punk anthem.

of Montreal
Athens, Georgia, USA

Singer-guitarist Kevin Barnes was inspired to form the group in the wake of a broken romance with a woman from Montreal. The band has released nine studio albums, the most recent being *Skeletal Lamping*. Title highlights include *Satanic Panic in the Attic* and *Hissing Fauna, Are You the Destroyer?*

The Best of the
& Bands

The Best of the & Bands

Skavoovie & the Epitones

Archie Bell & the Drells

Snowbud & the Flower People

Country Joe & the Fish

Gefilte Joe & the Fish

Bella & the Bottom Feeders

Captain Jeffrey & the Chumbuckets

Doug & the Slugs

Kid Congo & the Pink Monkey Birds

Michael Kearns & the Lonely Mammals

Sparky Parks & the Aardvarks

Cat Mother & the All-Night Newsboys

Echo & the Bunnymen

Captain Rat & the Blind Rivets

Candye Kane & the Swinging Armadillos

Mr. Quintron & the Flossy Unicorn

Sam the Sham & the Pharaohs

Zookie & the Potentates

Col. Bruce Hampton & the Aquarium Rescue Unit

Mink Wilde & the Gentlemen Callers

Veronica Lipgloss & the Evil Eyes

Wink & the Mansuits

Haphash & the Coloured Coat

Angel Jones & the Fall in Loves

Disco Tex & the Sex-O-Lettes

Labretta Suede & the Motel Six

Heloise & the Savoir Faire

Grace Potter & the Nocturnals

Steve E. Nix & the Cute Lepers

Brian Bonz & the Dot Hongs

Me First & the Gimme Gimmes

The Good, the Bad & the Queen

Lyin' Bitch & the Restraining Orders

Peter & the Test Tube Babies

Skiptowne & the Greyhounds

Lars Frederiksen & the Bastards

Nick Cave & the Bad Seeds

Matty B. & the Dirty Pickles

Johnny Cohen & the New Age Nazis

Coco Bongo & the Bonfire Ranch of Love

Special Ed & the Shortbus

True Fax & the Insaniacs

Norman Bates & the Showerheads

Cannibal & the Headhunters

Hedwig & the Angry Inch

Ted Leo & the Pharmacists

Doctor Ed & the Flushots

King Black Acid & the Womb Star Orchestra

Dr. Teeth & the Electric Mayhem

Mandy Jane & the Jaws of Life

Binky Griptite & the Dee-Kays

Dizzy Pumpkin & the Slivers

Dr. Castrato & the Measles

Goonmat & the Mumblers

Omar & the Howlers

Siouxsie & the Banshees

The Eye the Ear & the Arm

Starvin' Marvin & the Paranoid Androids

Lothar & the Hand People

Healthy Collins & the End of Trans Fats Band

Joe Lean & the Jing Jang Jong

Vivian Sims & the Space Hammer Encounter

Electric Blue Peggy Sue

& the Revolutionions From Mars

Commander Cody & the Lost Planet Airmen

Margot & the Nuclear So and Sos

Mr. Fusion & the Flux Capacitor

Flash Cadillac & the Continental Kids

LSD & the Search for God

Chubby Nuthin' & the Bone

Molly & the Ringwalds

Iggy Pop & the Stooges

Joe Strummer & the Mescaleros

LSD & the Search for God

Kid Creole & the Coconuts

Vic Vacume & the Attachments

Big Brother & the Holding Company

Sleazy Earl Ray & the Two Drink Minimum

Honest Bob & the Factory to Dealer

Rev. Angus Strychn

& the Paralyzing Doses of Fun

Shane Macgowan & the Popes

Binky Tunny & the Farmland Chokehold

A1AJake & the Half Conched Band

Johnny Jones & the Suffering Halos

Sweet Jesus & the Sacred Hearts

Teenage Jesus & the Jerks

Richard Hell & the Voidoids

Dr. Hellno & the Yessmen

Buck Satan & the 666 Shooters

Milton & the Devil's Party

Ricardo & the Dogmanauts

Davis & the Band of Hopeless

? & the Mysterians

Rex Stiff & the Kinky Morticians

Jerry & the Final Thoughts

Acknowledgments

I love the look of this book. And the look of this book is due entirely to graphic artist Gillian Stead. I can't thank her enough for her inspired vision, quirky ideas and instinctive ways of coping tastefully with Lime Spiders, Primitive Radio Gods, Electric Primadonnas and Radioactive Chicken Heads. Well, maybe I can thank her enough. We're married. I'll put this big new IOU at the top of the pile and see what happens.

Big thanks to my pal Simon Rogers, researcher, archivist and musician (Dog, Claire, Big Wet Love Cannon, Mohammad Chang, Wednesday Smith & the Distractions, Monkey Chow), for his incredible help (actually very *credible* help) with a lot of the research for this book and for his ongoing belief in the project.

Thanks to the many graphic and visual artists whose work appears in these pages, particularly those poster artists who contributed multiple images, including Willem Kolvoort, Groningen, the Netherlands; Tim Huesken, ShinyBlueRobot, Victoria, British Columbia, Canada; Joe Whyte and John Harris, Beyond the Pale, Melbourne, Australia; Scrojo, San Diego, California; and Billy Perkins, Cult of the Penhead, Austin, Texas.

Thanks to the many, many musicians who contributed information, CDs and morale-boosting emails at all hours of day and night, especially Johnny Dunn from Killola, Los Angeles; Jay Taylor from Bone-Box, Manchester; Oli Darley from Mad Staring Eyes, London; and Oskari Martimo from Knucklebone Oscar, Helsinki.

The artwork was always meant to be DIY indie CD covers and posters, but a few small record companies deserve gratitude for their assistance: Dennis Polowski, Meat Puppets Management; Ralph Braband at Rhythm Bomb Records, London/Berlin; John Graham, Two Sheds Music, Atlanta, Georgia; and Geoff Westen, Disturbing Music, Sherman Oaks, California.

Thanks to my friend and editorial comrade Kathy Fraser for her research in the "Placed & Misplaced" section, as well as her valuable proofreading skills. And to both Kathy and her husband Cam for years of shared music and music talk.

Thanks to Boston Mills Press publisher John Denison for his friendship, support, enthusiasm and all those offers to "do anything" to help.

Thanks to Lionel Koffler at Firefly Books for embracing *The Band Name Book* in its rough-idea stage, and to production manager Jacqueline Hope Raynor for adjusting scheduling and printing arrangements instead of flaying my flesh over deadline extensions.

Thanks to Marin Hudson for her help with the "Horror Chiller Monster Thriller" list, including riskily contacting death-metal singers after midnight; to Tess Hudson for her parade of band name suggestions, including Static Artichokes, Goatsmilk Wallpaper and Mandarin Doorknobs (stick with the piano lessons, Tess, the band name won't be a problem); and Walker Hudson for his bemused daily visits to read over my shoulder (and the suggestion that the suffix "of Doom" always improves a band name).

And finally, thanks to my friend, musical co-conspirator and bandmate Steve Bolton, with whom I've been playing music twice a week for over a decade. Rock, soul, funk or jazz — it don't mean a thing if it ain't got a band with a cool name.

Image Credits

All images in this book are used courtesy of their respective copyright holders for illustration and promotional purposes and may not be reproduced in any form without written consent of the original copyright holder(s).

9 **Tobi Kai & the Strays** cover art courtesy Tobi Kai and Jeff Bradley, copyright 2006 Tobi Kai & the Strays. www.myspace.com/tobikaiandthestrays

13 **The Shreep** cover art courtesy Alex Wise, copyright 2002 Alex Wise/the Shreep. www.cdbaby.com/cd/theshreep, www.alexwise.com

14 **Ergot Derivative** cover art by Darryl Avlward, Copyright 1993 the Ergot Derivative.

16 **Lousy House Pets** letters photographed and assembled by Jim St. James. Copyright 2008 Lousy House Pets. www.myspace.com/lousyhousepets

17 **Cat House Dogs** *That Was Now* cover photo by emmanouel V., layout & design by Randy James; *Five Licks* photo by Marja Flick-Buijs, illustration & design by Randy James; band promo photo by Randy James, layout and design by Randy James. All copyright Cat House Dogs 2008. www.cathousedogs.com

18 **Fluffy the Pitbull** cover art by Richard Pearman. Copyright 2004 Richard Pearman and Nicole Chaplain-Pearman. www.gabardineswine.com, www.pixelpalaces.com

19 **Hard Chihuahuas** *Back to Burbank* cover art courtesy of the Hard Chihuahuas, copyright 2003. cdbaby.com/cd/hardchihuahuas

20 **Switchblade Kittens** art and design by Tanja Richter. Copyright Switchblade Kittens 1999. www.switchbladekittens.com

21 **Catsplash** cover art by Jessica Novales (www.jessicanovales.com). Catsplash logo by Andy Marfia and Neil Klemz. Copyright 2006 Catsplash. www.catsplash.com, www.myspace.com/catsplash

Pimp the Cat cover photography and graphics by Sunrise Winburn, (www.sunrisealexiswinburn.com). Additional CD graphics by Sean Akers, (www.seanakers.com). Copyright 2006 Pimp the Cat and Kool Aid Records. www.pimpthecat.com, www.myspace.com/pimpthecat

22 **Hudson & the Hoodoo Cats** cover illustration by Kerry Awn. Design by Cindy Boeger. Copyright 1994 Hudson & the Hoo Doo Cats and BJAM Records. www.hudsonandthehoodoocats.com

SophistiCats & the SophisiKittens cover art by Mitch O'Connell (www.mitchoconnell.com). Copyright 2007 the SophistiCats & SophisiKittens and Mitch O'Connell. www.thesophisticats.com, www.myspace.com/thesophisticats

23 **Mountain Goats** press photo by Mark Van S. (www.markvans.com). Copyright 2008 the Mountain Goats and Mark Van S. www.mountain-goats.com

24 **A Sheep at the Wheel** cover art copyright 2008 A Sheep at the Wheel. www.asheepatthe wheel.com, www.myspace.com/asheepatthewheel

25 **Radioactive Chicken Heads** cover art by B.C. Sterrett. Copyright B.C. Sterrett and Radioactive Chicken Heads 2005. www.bcsterrett.com, www.myspace.com/chickenheads

26 **Kung Pao Chickens** cover art by Annie Wilkens. Copyright 2007 Kung Pao Chickens. www.myspace.com/thekungpaochickens

Amazing Rhythm Chickens cover art by Dande Evans, based on a stick-figure drawing by Neil Kingsley. Copyright Amazing Rhythm Chickens 1998. www.cdbaby.com/cd/rhythmchickens, www.neilkingsley.com

27 **Slippery Chickens** cover design by the Slippery Chickens. Cover photo by Dian Lofton. Copyright 2003 the Slippery Chickens. www.slippery chickens.com

28 **Duckmandu** press photo copyright 2008 Duckmandu/Aaron Seeman. www.duckman du.com, www.myspace.com/duckmandu

Honey Pig cover photo and art courtesy Debi Derryberry and Honey Pig, copyright 2001. www.cdbaby.com/cd/honeypig3, www.garageband.com/artist/honeypig

29 **The Pigs** cover art by Geoff Westen, Oz Studios, copyright 2006. www.ozstudios.com, www.disturbingmusic.com

30 **Radiant Pig** cover art E. Liz Downing, design by PFAD, copyright 2002. www.cdbaby.com/cd/radiantpig

31 **Technology Versus the Horse** cover art by Megan Kelly; inked, colorized and formatted by Rafe Heltsley; inspired by Jack Kirby art for *The Avengers* #17. Copyright 2008 Technology Versus the Horse. www.myspace.com/technologyvshorse

32 **Technicolour Stallion** poster courtesy of the band. Copyright 2008 Technicolour Stallion. www.myspace.com/technicolourstallion

33 **Used Cows** cover art by Numata, design by Ritchie, logo by Reed Rowe. Copyright Used Cows 2006. www.cdbaby.com/cd/usedcows

34 **Blood Drained Cows** cover photo by Kamala Gould, CD design by Mindy Palinkas. Used courtesy of Gregg Turner. Copyright 2008 Gregg Turner and the Blood Drained Cows. www.blooddrainedcows.com

35 **Disguised as Birds** art by Brian Kriederman, additional photography by Rob Nero. Copyright 2007 Brian Kriederman and Disguised by Birds. www.disguisedasbirds.com, www.myspace.com/disguisedasbirds

36 **Woodpecker** CD release party poster courtesy Josh Steinbauer. Copyright 2008 Woodpecker Music. www.woodpeckermusic.com, www.myspace.com/woodpeckermusic

37 **Suicidal Birds** posters used courtesy of Chay & Jessie, the Suicidal Birds. www.suicidalbirds.com, www.myspace.com/suicidalbirds

38 **Kid Congo & the Pink Monkey Birds** poster by Benjamin Bader (www.BenjaminMBader.com and www.NeoElegance.com). Copyright 2006 Benjamin Bader. www.kidcongopowers.com, www.myspace.com/kidcongoandthepink monkeybirds

39 **Fishtank Ensemble** cover art courtesy Douglas Smolens. Copyright 2005 Fishtank Ensemble. www.fishtankensemble.com, www.myspace.com/fishtankensemble

40 **Moofish** cover photo by Michael Jeans, design by Chris and Rhonda Johnson. Copyright 1999 Moofish/Chris and Rhonda Johnson. www.myspace.com/moofishnz

41 **Ultra Dolphins** poster by R. Kabaltan. Copyright 2003 Ultra Dolphins/R. Kabaltan. www.ultradolphins.org, www.myspace.com/ultradolphins

42 **Yucca Spiders** cover photo by Antje Seeger, design by Val Herdam. Copyright 2003 the Yucca Spiders. www.the-yucca-spiders.de, www.myspace.com/yuccaspiders

43 **Ticks** press photo by Robert Klein, used courtesy Sue LaVallee/the Ticks. Copyright 2008 the Ticks. www.myspace.com/theticksrock, www.theticks.com

44 **Anthill** press photo courtesy Anthill. Copyright 2008 Anthill (Canada). www.anthill.ca

45 **Termites** poster by Dave Tinkham (www.datapanikdesign.com). Copyright 2005 Dave Tinkham. www.myspace.com/terminaltermites

46 **Critters Buggin** poster by Mark S. Brinn for Nightlight Lounge, Bellingham, Washington. Copyright Mark S. Brinn/Nightlight Lounge. www.nightlightlounge.com, www.crittersbuggin.com, www.myspace.com/crittersbuggin

47 **Lushy/Bug Nasties** poster by Rod Filbrandt (www.chowderheadbazoo.typepad.com). Copyright 2008 Rod Filbrandt. www.myspace.com/lushymusic, www.myspace.com/thebugnasties

48 **Bee Zoo** cover art and design by Rick Ruthman. Copyright 1997 Rob Kudyba and Rick Ruthman. www.beezoo.com, www.myspace.com/rkudyba

48 **Bee Stings** cover-art press image courtesy Council Pop Records. Copyright 2008 Bee Stings. www.beestings.co.uk, www.myspace.com/beestingsmusic

50 **Grasshoppers** cover photo by Hubie Frowein, design by Jesse Sanchez, used by permission of Marco Joachim. Copyright 1996 the Grasshoppers. www.myspace.com/grasshoppersband

51 **Locust** poster by Jermaine Rogers (www.jermainerogers.com) for Mary Jane's. Courtesy Mary Jane's Greater Heights Club, Houston. Copyright 2007 Mary Jane's/The Locust/Jermaine Rogers. www.thelocust.com, www.myspace.com/thelocust

52 **Jack Rabbit & the Pubic Hares** cover art by Fred Negro, layout by Greg Hunt. Copyright Ian Bland 2007. www.jackrabbit.com.au

53 **White Rabbits** promo photo by Lucy Hamblin (www.lucyhamblin.com). Copyright White Rabbits, 2008. www.whiterabbitsmusic.com, www.myspace.com/whiterabbits

54 **Ultrabunny** illustration by Miwa Yagi. Copyright 2005 Miwa Yagi, Ultrabunny and Equation Records. www.ultrabunny.com, www.myspace.com/ultrabunny

55 **Bunnybrains** painting by Jack Ziegler. Copyright 1995 Jack Ziegler, BunnyBrains and Matador Records. www.ultrabunny.com, www.myspace.com/bunnybrains

56 **Monkeyfrog** cover art by Jonathan McEnroe. Courtesy Marc Twynholm. Copyright 2006 Monkeyfrog. www.monkeyfrog.co.uk, www.myspace.com/monkeyfrogtheband

57 **Monkey on the Bed** cover art by Larry Goode and design by Steve Fryer. Copyright 2000 Monkey on the Bed. www.monkeyonthe bed.com, www.cdbaby.com/cd/motb

58 **Wheat Monkeys** poster by Kipling West (www.foureyedbat.com) for Broken City, Calgary, Alberta (www.brokencity.ca). Copyright 2007 Kipling West/Broken City/Wheatmonkeys. www.wheatmonkeys.com, www.myspace.com/wheatmonkeys

Ape Foot Groove cover art: Monkey Man by John Gifford, Ape Foot Groove logo by John Proulx, design and layout by Synergen. Copyright 1998 Ape Foot Groove. www.myspace.com/apefootgroove

59 **Dust Rhinos** press photo copyright 2008 the Dust Rhinos. www.dustrhinos.com, www.myspace.com/dustrhino

60 **Wombats** poster by Willem Kolvoort (www.willemkolvoort.nl, www.myspace.com/willemkolvoort). Copyright 2008 Willem Kolvoort. www.vera-groningen.nl, www.thewombatsuk.co.uk, www.myspace.com/thewombatsuk

61 **Tigerbombs** press photo Tiikerikuva. Copyright Tigerbombs 2005. www.myspace.com/tigerbombs, www.tigerbombs.com

62 **Mighty Roars** cover art by Lara Granqvist. Press photo by Kate Garner. Copyright 2008 the Mighty Roars. www.themightyroars.com, www.myspace.com/themightyroars

63 **Japanther** cover art by Ian Vanek and UFO907. www.Japanther.com, www.myspace.com/ japanther, www.tapesrecords.com/japanther

64 **Peanutbutter Wolf** poster by Ryan S. Fleming/Field of Gravity. Copyright 2006 Ryan S. Fleming. www.myspace.com/fieldofgravity, www.myspace.com/pbwolf, www.stonesthrow.com

Fleet Foxes poster by Julia Green (www.myspace.com/jboob) for Kilby Court (www.kilbycourt.com), Salt Lake City, Utah. Copyright 2008 Julia Green/Kilby Court/ Fleet Foxes. www.myspace.com/fleetfoxes

65 **Gangly Moose** posters by Jamie Smith. Courtesy of Kliff Hopson. Copyright 2008 Gangly Moose. www.ganglymoose.com, www.myspace.com/ ganglymoose

66 **Vampire Mooose** press photo copyright 2008 Vampire Mooose. www.vampiremooose.com, www.rottenrecords.com

67 **Deerfoot** cover design by Dean Faulkner. Copyright 2006 Deerfoot. www.ilovedeerfoot.com, www.myspace.com/ilovedeerfoot

68 **Exploding White Mice** poster by Willem Kolvoort (www.willemkolvoort.nl, www.myspace.com/willemkolvoort). Copyright 2008 Willem Kolvoort. www.vera-groningen.nl, www.myspace.com/explodingwhitemice

69 **Anacondas** cover illustration by Claudia Hek. Copyright 2005 the Anacondas. www.anacondas.nl, www.myspace.com/theanacondas

71 **Luxurious Python** cover art cover art by Michael Bales. Copyright 2008 Mark Zayas. www.myspace.com/luxuriouspython

Emerald Lizards promo logo by Andy Link. Copyright 2006 the Emerald Lizards. www.emeraldlizards.com, www.myspace.com/theemeraldlizards

72 **Trip Lizard** cover art and design by Diana Bogus (www.thebogusart.com). Copyright 2004 Trip Lizard. www.cdbaby.com/cd/triplizard, www.myspace.com/doubledshouse

73 **Amphibious Jones** cover art by Neil Devoogd. Copyright 2007 Amphibious Jones. www.myspace.com/amphibiousjones

74 **Tadpoles** cover art: Far Out cover concept and design by Ann Manca, M. Design, 1996; *Use with Headphones* cover concept and design by Ann Manca, M. Design, photo Laura Kanter, 2001; *Know Your Ghosts* cover concept and design by Ann Manca, M. Design, illustration by Adam Boyette, 1997; He Fell Into the Sky cover concept and design by Ann Manca, M. Design, photos by T.L. Palumbo and Alexandra Kress. Copyright 1993. www.tadpoles.com, www.myspace.com/tad-polesmusic

75 **Killer Crocs of Uganda** cover art by Elektra Rose (www.elektrarose.com). Courtesy Scott Lambie. Copyright 2007 Killer Crocs of Uganda. www.myspace.com/killercrocsofuganda

79 **Porcupine Tree** press photo copyright 2007 Porcupine Tree. www.myspace.com/porcupinetree, www.porcupinetree.com

80 **Carbon Leaf** Indian Summer promotional image from Vanguard Records (www.vanguard records.com). Copyright 2004 Vanguard Records/Carbon Leaf. www.carbonleaf.com, www.myspace.com/carbonleaf

Maple State poster by Cameron Steward. Copyright Cameron Steward 2007. www.twoduck disco.co.uk, www.myspace.com/themaplestate, www.themaplestate.co.uk

81 **Morningwood** album press photo courtesy Capitol Records. Copyright 2006 Capital Records. www.morningwoodrocks.com, www.myspace.com/morningwood

82 **Trimmed Hedges** cover art by Brian David. Copyright 2007 the Trimmed Hedges. www.trimmedhedges.com, www.myspace.com/thetrimmedhedges

83 **Vines** poster by Lindsey Kuhn (www.swamp co.com). Copyright 2003 Lindsey Kuhn/Swamp. www.thevines.com, www.myspace.com/thevines

84 **Flower Kings** press photo copyright 2008 the Flower Kings. www.flowerkings.se, www.myspace.com/cosmiclodge

85 **Sonic Orchid** press photo copyright 2008 Orchid Entertainment. www.sonicorchid.com, www.myspace.com/sonicorchid

86 **Supergrass** album promo for Diamond Hoo Ha copyright 2008 Parlophone/Supergrass. Photo by Scarlett Page. www.supergrass.com, www.myspace.com/supergrass

89 **Pancake Fair** cover "Desert Scene" photo by Jack Delano, courtesy of the Library of Congress prints and photographs division. Complete cover artwork copyright Mike C. Webb 2004 (www.geocities.com/mikefresno).

90 **Toast** cover artwork copyright Toast 2004. www.toastmusic.net

91 **Electric Marmalade** cover art and design by Pre-Press Graphics, courtesy Robin Reda. Copyright 2006 Zebra Valance Records. www.theelectricmarmalade.com

92 **Wicked Relish** cover art by Brian and Mark Ferrero. Copyright 2005 Wicked Relish. www. wickedrelish.com, www.myspace.com/wickedrelish

93 **Astroburger** cover art copyright 1994 Geir Stadheim/Astroburger. Astroburger press photo copyright 2007 Geir Stadheim/Astroburger. www.myspace.com/astroburgerr

94 **Loudmouth Soup** poster by Matt Ferres for the Faversham, Leeds, UK. Copyright 2006 Matt Ferres/the Faversham. www.ferres.co.uk, www.the-faversham.com, www.loudmouthsoup.co.uk, www.myspace.com/loudmouthsoupuk

95 **Power Salad** cover art courtesy Chris Mezzolesta. Copyright 2006 Chris Mezzolesta/Power Salad. www.powersalad.com

96 **Fruit** press photo by Mark Van S. Copyright 2007 Fruit/Mark Van S (www.markvans.com). www.fruitmusic.com.au

97 **Cherries** cover art copyright 1998 the Cherries/ Badman Recording Co. www.badmanrecordingco.com, www.cdbaby.com/cd/cherries

98 **Deep Banana Blackout** cover art courtesy James "Fuzz" San Giovanni and Deep Banana Blackout. Copyright 2000, 2001 Deep Banana Blackout. www.myspace.com/deepbananablackout, www.deepbananablackout.com

100 **Strawberry Switchblade** press photo by Peter McArthur. Copyright 1984 Strawberry Switchblade/Peter McArthur. www.strawberryswitchblade.net

101 **Grapefruit** *Dorkabilly Stew* cover art copyright 1996 by Bill Given.

103 **Super Pineapples** cover art courtesy Julian Faras and the Super Pineapples. Copyright 2004 the Super Pineapples. www.myspace.com/thesuperpineapples

Pineapples from the Dawn of Time poster art and press photo copyright 1987 Pineapples from the Dawn of Time. www.myspace.com/thepineapplesfromthedawnoftime

104 **Meat Puppets** cover art by Curt Kirkwood. Copyright 1995 Curt Kirkwood/Meat Puppets. www.meatpuppets.com, www.myspace.com/themeatpuppets

105 **Greasy Beats** cover design by Tim Johnston. Copyright 2006 the Greasy Beats. www.myspace.com/thegreasybeats, www.cdbaby.com/cd/greasybeats

106 **2 Beans & a Grape** cover graphics by M.R. 80% (www.bytemestudios.com). Copyright 2005 2 Beans & a Grape. www.myspace.com/2beansandagrape, www.2beansandagrape.com

107 **Parsnip Revolt** logo by Michael J. Toth, courtesy Jake Williams. Copyright 2007 the Parsnip Revolt. www.theparsniprevolt.com, www.myspace.com/theparsniprevolt

108 **Fruitcake-Superbeing** cover designs by Chris Brown (both), Marci Fermier (*Developmental Texas How Now*). Copyright 2001, 2006 Fruitcake-Superbeing. www.fruitcake-superbeing.com, www.myspace.com/fruitcakesuperbeing

109 **Imaginary Cookies** cover art courtesy Scott Paris. Copyright 2006 Still Not Impressed Music. www.cdbaby.com/cd/imaginarycookies, www.myspace.com/theimaginarycookies, www.myspace.com/scottparis, www.scottparisonline.com

110 **24 Hour Church of Beer** cover art by Cory Harrison. Copyright 2006 24 Hour Church of Beer. www.myspace.com/24hourchurchofbeer

112 **Mad Staring Eyes** cover art courtesy Oli Darley. Copyright 2008 Mad Staring Eyes/Retina Records. www.myspace.com/madstaringeyes, www.themadstaringeyes.com

113 **Flatfoot Shakers** cover art contact info: Crawfish@rock-a-tiki. Copyright 2007 Rhythm Bomb Records. www.rhythmbomb.com, www.geocities.com/flatfootshaker, www.myspace.com/flatfootshakers

114 **Fallopian** album photograph by Larry Hirshowitz. Copyright 2006 Fallopian/Avebury Reccords. www.myspace.com/fallopian, www.aveburyrecords.com/fallopian

115 **Pleasures of Merely Circulating** cover art courtesy the Pleasures of Merely Circulating, copyright 2007. www.thepleasuresofmerelycirculating.com, www.myspace.com/thepleasuresofmerelycirculating

116 **Bad Veins** press photo courtesy Bad Veins/ Across the Universe Management, copyright 2007. www.badveins.net, www.myspace.com/badveins

117 **A-Bones** poster by Patrick Broderick (www.rotodesign.com). Copyright 2008 Patrick Broderick/Rotodesign. www.myspace.com/theabones, www.nortonrecords.com

Bone-Box poster by Nick Rhodes (www.switchopen.com). Copyright 2006 Nick Rhodes/Switchopen. www.myspace.com/jaytaylor, www.bone-box.com

118 **Knucklebone Oscar** cover by Jukka Mikander and press photo by A.J. Savolainen for Bluelight Records. Copyright 2007 Bluelight Records/ Knucklebone Oscar. www.knuckleboneoscar.com, www.myspace.com/knuckleboneoscar

Head of Femur poster by Ben Swift (www.nonoart.com) for Duffy's Tavern, Lincoln, Nebraska (www.duffysrocks.dainto.org). Copyright 2006 Ben Swift. www.headoffemur.net, www.myspace.com/headoffemur

121 **Star of Tragedy** poster by Hendrickson for Sisters, Oklahoma City, Oklahoma. Copyright 2004 Hendrickson. www.myspace.com/staroftragedy

122 **The Faded** cover photo by Joseph Corsentino. Copyright 2007 the Faded. www.thefaded.com, www.myspace.com/thefaded

Failed Teachers press photo copyright 2008 Failed Teachers. www.failedteachers.ch, www.myspace.com/failedteachers

124 **How to Win at Life** cover art copyright 2001 How to Win at Life. www.myspace.com/htwal, www.cdbaby.com/cd/howtowin

125 **Wonder Stuff** poster by Scrojo (www.scrojo.com) for Belly Up, Solana Beach, California (www.bellyup.com). Copyright 2005 Scrojo. www.thewonderstuff.co.uk, www.myspace.com/the_wonder_stuff

126 **Bright Men of Learning** poster by Chris Kahlich for the Proletariat, Houston Texas (www.myspace.com/proletizzle). Copyright 2006 Chris Kahlich/Proletariat. www.weare bright.com, www.myspace.com/brightmen

126 **Superfantastics** poster by Mike Holmes (Halifax, Nova Scotia). Copyright 2008 Mike Holmes. www.myspace.com/thesuperfantastics, www.thesuperfantastics.com

128 **Soccermom** image courtesy of Helen Nishimura & Matty. Copyright 2008 Soccermom. www.soccermomband.com, www.myspace.com/soccermom

129 **The Relatives** cover design by Dennis LeBlanc, photo by Jerri LeBlanc. Copyright 1999 the Relatives. www.myspace.com/therelativespop,

130 **Subteens** cover art copyright 2003 the Subteens/Memphis Records. www.memphis-recordsonline.com, www.cdbaby.com/cd/subteens

131 **Someday Tricycle** cover art courtesy Joe MacKenzie. Copyright 2007 Someday Tricycle. www.somedaytricycle.com, www.cdbaby.com/cd/somedaytricycle

132 **My Twin Sister Lulu** cover design by Adscape Art, photo by Gone Fishing Productions, courtesy Paddy McIvor and Lulu. Copyright 2006 L.I.P. Service Records/Paddy McIvor. www.lulufanclub.com, www.myspace.com/mytwinsisterlulu

133 **Turpentine Brothers** poster by Mike Sniper (www.myspace.com/sniperflyers) for Quai De Brumes, Montreal, Quebec (www.myspace.com/quaidesbrumes). Copyright 2006 Mike Sniper. www.myspace.com/turpentinebrothers

134 **Teenage Girls** cover art copyright 1998 Parody for Pedophiles Music. www.myspace.com/teenagegirls, www.teenagestyle.com

135 **Amateur Boyfriend** cover art copyright 2003 ButterMilk Records. www.buttermilkstudios.com, www.cdbaby.com/cd/amateurboyfriend

136 **Sonic Youth** poster by Ken Taylor, Beyond the Pale (www.beyondthepale.com.au). Copyright 2006 Ken Taylor/Beyond the Pale. www.sonicyouth.com, www.myspace.com/sonicyouth

Penfifteen Club cover art courtesy Luke Tierney. Copyright 2006 Penfifteen Club. www.thepenfifteenclub.com, www.myspace.com/thepenfifteenclub

138 **Small Change Romeos** cover photo Roland Guehennec, design Erin Gallup. Copyright 2004 Small Change Romeos/Milk Jug Records. www.myspace.com/smallchangeromeos, www.smallchangeromeos.com

139 **Dyslexic Love** cover art by Tim Bertulli. Copyright Tim Bertulli 2005. www.dyslexiclove.com

140 **Kisschasy** poster for Bones & Skin Tour copyright 2008 Nova, Channel V and MySpace. www.kisschasy.com, www.myspace.com/kisschasy

141 **Love & Mathematics** poster by J. MacDonald, bolo design. Copyright J. MacDonald/Aaargh Records. www.AaarghRecords.com, www.myspace.com/loveandmathematics

142 **Dropkick Murphys** poster by Joe Whyte, Beyond the Pale (www.beyondthepale.com.au). Copyright 2004 Joe Whyte/Beyond the Pale. www.joewhyte.com.au, www.dropkickmurphys.com, www.myspace.com/dropkickmurphys

143 **Melvins** poster by Justin Hampton (www.justin hampton.com). Copyright 2004 Justin Hampton. www.myspace.com/themelvins, www.themelvins.net (fansite)

144 **Donnas** poster by Joe Whyte, Beyond the Pale (www.beyondthepale.com.au). Copyright 2006 Joe Whyte/Beyond the Pale. www.joewhyte.com.au, www.thedonnas.com, www.myspace.com/thedonnas

146 **50 Cent Headrush** cover concept by Heaven Krawczyk, photographs Scott Legato. Copyright 50 Cent Headrush/Evil Beaver Music 2006. www.myspace.com/50centheadrush,

147 **Floydian Slip** cover design by Olaf Kirsten. Cover and press photo copyright 2001 Floydian Slip. www.floydianslipmusic.com

148 **Hate in the Box** poster courtesy QXT's/Hate in the Box. Copyright 2008 QXT/Hate in the Box. www.hateinthebox.com, www.myspace.com/hateinthebox

149 **Serotonin** cover art and design by Bob Paltrow. Copyright 2001 Serotonin.

150 **Widespread Panic** poster by Billy Perkins (www.cultofpenhead.com). Copyright 2008 Billy Perkins. www.widespreadpanic.com, www.myspace.com/widespreadpanic

151 **Paranoid Visions** art by Boz for Paranoid Visions. Copyright Paranoid Visions 2007. www.paranoid visions.com, www.myspace.com/paranoid visions

152 **Mad Men** cover art by Randy Richter. Copyright 2007 Rhythm Bomb Records. www.myspace.com/ rockinestmadmen, www.rhythmbomb.com

154 **Fastball** poster by Scrojo (www.scrojo.com) for Belly Up, Solana Beach, California (www.bellyup.com). Copyright 2003 Scrojo. www.fastballtheband.com, www.myspace.com/ fastballtheband

156 **Pavlov's Woody** cover art courtesy Don Simpson. Copyright 2007 Pavlov's Woody/Neat Guy Records. www.myspace.com/pavlovswoody

157 **Poets & Pornstars** press photo copyright 2008 Poets & Pornstars. www.myspace.com/poets pornstars, www.poetsandpornstars.com

159 **Bossa Nova Beatniks** *Danger Bongo Crossing* cover photo by Tom Gould. Copyright 1999 Tom Gould/Bossa Nova Beatniks. www.myspace.com/bossanovabeatniks

161 **Nerd Parade** cover art courtesy Randy Garcia. Copyright 2007 HeadphoneTreats Records. www.myspace.com/thenerdparade, www.thenerdparade.com

162 **Exceptional Gentlemen** cover art by Sue Breen. Copyright 2007 the Exceptional Gentlemen. www.myspace.com/theexceptionalgentlemen

164 **Anorexics** cover art by Jane Simmons. Copyright 2005 Jane Simmons/the Anorexics. www.cdbaby.com/cd/anorexics

165 **Ultrababyfat** cover design by Jeff Sheinkopf. Copyright 2006 Ultrababyfat. www.ultrababyfat.com, www.myspace.com/ultrababyfat

166 **Cry Ugly** cover art by Marty. Copyright 2005 Cry Ugly. www.cryugly.com, www.cdbaby.com/cd/cryugly Tubby cover design by Allen Hujsak. Tubby character illustration by Howard Weliver. Copyright 2002 Tubby. www.myspace.com/tubbyfunk

167 **Supaphat** cover art Erik Jon Mickelsen (www.brandnewmedia.tv). Logo by Chris Atagi. Copyright 2005 Supaphat. www.myspace.com/supaphat

Secret Aging Men cover art by Rick Meyer. Copyright 2007 Rick Meyer/Secret Aging Men. www.myspace.com/secretagingmen, www.secretagingmen.com

169 **Brunettes** poster by Jack Dylan (www.jackdylan.ca). Copyright 2005 Jack Dylan/the Brunettes. www.lilchiefrecords.com/ brunettes, www.myspace.com/thebrunettes

170 **Big Fuzz** cover art by Dante Grimm. Courtesy Fuzz. Copyright 2004 Big Fuzz. www.deep bananablackout.com, www.homegrownmusic.net

172 **Dog Fashion Disco** press photo for *Adultery* copyright 2006 Dog Fashion Disco. www.myspace.com/dogfashiondisco.

173 **Mannequin Makeout** poster copyright 2007 Club 156, University of Colorado. www.myspace.com/club156space, www.myspace.com/mannequinmakeout

174 **Skivies** cover art courtesy DJ Von Feldt. Copyright 2007 the Skivies. www.myspace.com/ theskivies, www.theskivies.com

175 **Modern Skirts** poster by Daisy Winfrey for the Bottletree, Birmingham, Alabama (www.thebottle tree.com). Copyright 2007 Daisy Winfrey/the Bottletree. www.modernskirts.com, www.myspace.com/modernskirts

176 **Dr. Pants** cover design and art by David Broyles and Terry Pham. Copyright 2006 Little Weasel Records. www.doctorpants.com, www.myspace.com/drpants5

178 **Fashion Failures** poster by Ryan Jackson, Thunderhouse Design, for Houlihan's, East Providence, Rhode Island. Copyright 2006 Ryan Jackson/Houlihan's. www.myspace.com/fashionfailures

180 **Pinups** cover image copyright 1994 the Pinups/ Poptown Music Co. www.poptownrecords.com, www.myspace.com/pinupsnyc

181 **Girl on Top** cover art by Phil Amoakohene (www.philsphantasy.com), courtesy Karen DeBiasse. Copyright 2004 Girl on Top. www.myspace.com/girlontopboston, www.girlontop.com

182 **Impure Thoughts** cover design by Andy Leuenberger. Copyright 2006 Impure Thoughts/ Cannery Row Records. www.cannery rowrecords.com, www.impurethoughts.net

183 **Seatsniffers** cover design courtesy Sonic Rendezvous Records. Copyright 2005 Sonic Rendezvous Records. www.sonicrendezvous.com, www.myspace.com/theseatsniffers, www.seatsniffers.be

183 **Lovewhip** cover art courtesy Jim Countryman. Copyright 2004 Lovewhip/Squirrelygirl Music. www.lovewhip.net, www.myspace.com/lovewhip

184 **Welcome to Nashville** guitar pick by Gill Stead.

44 Double D cover art by Enos Presley. Copyright 2000 Enos Presley/Panty Raid Records. www.myspace.com/44doubled, www.cdbaby.com/cd/44doubled

185 **Snatches of Pink** cover design by the Splinter Group, photo by Mr. Rank, courtesy Michael Rank. Copyright 2007 Snatches of Pink. www.myspace.com/snatchesofpink, www.snatchesofpink.com

186 **Pickled Dick** poster by Black Dave (www.myspace.com/blackdaveart). Copyright 2007 Black Dave. www.pickleddick.co.uk, www.myspace.com/miketv

187 **Foxycock** cover art by Douglas Smolens. Copyright 2005 Douglas Smolens/Foxycock. www.foxycock.com, www.cdbaby.com/cd/foxycock

188 **Tremendous Fucking** press photo copyright 2006 Higher Step Records. Design by Zero Echo Media. www.higherstep.com, www.tremendousfucking.com, www.tremfu.com, www.myspace.com/tremendousfucking

189 **Does It Offend You, Yeah?** press photo copyright 2008 Does It Offend You, Yeah? www.myspace.com/doesitoffendyou, www.doesitoffendyou.com

190 **Machine Gun Fellatio** press photo copyright 2008 Machine Gun Fellatio. www.myspace.com/machinegunfellatio

Butchies poster by Ryan August (www.ryanaugust.com), illustration by Sarah Wooten. Copyright 2004 Ryan August. www.myspace.com/thebutchies

192 **Vampire Lezbos** art and logo by the Vampire Lezbos. Copyright 2008 Vampire Lezbos. www.myspace.com/vampirelezbos

193 **Mutants** cover art courtesy Green Cookie Records. Copyright 2002 the Mutants/Green Cookie Records. www.colorcookies.moonfruit.com, www.myspace.com/greencookierecords, www.koti.mbnet.fi/mutants, www.myspace.com/themutants

194 **Devastator** cover art by Denis Gualtieri (www.squartato.blogspot.com). Copyright 2002 Devastator. www.devastator.it, www.myspace.com/devastatorcrew

195 **Big Head Todd & the Monsters** poster by Billy Perkins (www.cultofpenhead.com). Copyright 2008 Billy Perkins. www.bigheadtodd.com, www.myspace.com/bhtm

Electric Frankenstein poster by Tim Huesken (www.shinybluerobot.com). Copyright 2005 Tim Huesken. www.electricfrankenstein.com, www.myspace.com/electricfrankenstein

196 **Chainsaw Curtis & the Creepers** cover art courtesy Curtis Rodeheaver. Copyright 2009 C. Rodeheaver. www.geocities.com/chainsawcurtis, www.myspace.com/chainsawcurtisandthecreepers

198 **Funeral Diner** press photo copyright 2008 Funeral Diner. www.myspace.com/funeraldiner, www.funeraldiner.com

199 **Teenage Casket Company** cover art by Daz, Danger Creative, courtesy Jamie Delerict. Copyright 2006 Trash Pit Records. www.trashpitmagazine.co.uk, www.myspace.com/teenagecasketcompany, www.teenagecasketcompany.com

200 **Deadguy** T-shirts photo by B. Shelley. Copyright 1998 B. Shelley. myspace.com/deadguylives (fansite)

201 **Molten Lava Death Massage** cover art by Adrian Dexter, design by Ben Gagnon. Copyright 2006 Molten Lava Death Massage. www.myspace.com/moltenlavadeathmassage

202 **Rocket from the Crypt** poster by Joe Whyte, Beyond the Pale www.beyondthepale.com.au). Copyright 2002 Joe Whyte/Beyond the Pale. www.joewhyte.com.au, www.rftc.com, www.myspace.com/rocketfromthecrypt1

203 **Nick Noxious & the Necrophiliacs** cover art by Glenn Chadbourne. Copyright 2004 Glenn Chadburne. www.lincoln.midcoast.com/ ~jpfisher/Nick_Noxious.html, shocklines.stores.yahoo.net/glenchad.html

204 **Zombie Ghost Train** poster by Thom Self (www.myspace.com/astudiodesign). Copyright 2007 Thom Self/A Studio. www.myspace.com/zombieghosttrain, www.zombieghosttrain.com

206 **Weapon Shop** cover art by Bruno Alves. Copyright 2006 Bruno Alves/Weapon Shop. www.myspace.com/weaponshop, www.cdbaby.com/cd/weaponshop

207 **Cocked'N'Loaded** cover art by Dan Mayzee (www.mayzeeworks.com). Copyright 2007 Cocked'N'Loaded and Dan Mayzee. www.myspace.com/cockednloaded

208 **Popgun** cover art by Catherine Haanes Design (Oslo) courtesy Egil Stemkens and Catherine Haanes. Copyright 2006 Stack Records/Popgun. www.myspace.com/popguninfo, www.popgun.no/home.php

209 **Dirtbombs** poster by Martin Infanger (www.jollys.ch). Copyright 2003 Martin Infanger. www.myspace.com/thedirtbombs

Hollowpoint cover concept and design by Tony Pirrello. Copyright 2007 Hollowpoint. www.myspace.com/hollowpointtheband, www.hollowpointband.us

210 **Slow Poisoner** cover art by Andrew Goldfarb. Copyright 2005 Andrew Goldfarb/the Slow Poisoner. www.myspace.com/slowpoisoner, www.theslowpoisoner.com

210 **Slink Moss Explosion** cover art courtesy Slink Moss Explosion. Copyright Slink Moss Explosion/ Rattlesnake Records. www.myspace.com/ slinkmossexplosion, www.slinkmoss.com

213 **Killola** cover art and promo poster courtesy Johnny Dunn and Killola. Copyright 2006 Killola. www.killola.com, www.myspace.com/killola

214 **Angry Johnny & the Killbillies** cover art by Angry Johnny. Copyright 2008 Angry Johnny. www.getangry.com, www.myspace.com/ angryjohnnyandthekillbillies

Hack cover design by Zartosht Soltani (www.Zmandesign.com). Copyright 2006 Hack/Bamahang Productions. www.bamahang-pro-ductions.com, www.cdbaby.com/cd/hack, www.hackroom.net

215 **Joan as Police Woman** cover art courtesy Tom Rose, Reveal Records. Copyright 2008 Reveal Records. www.reveal-records.com, www.navigator records.co.uk, www.joanaspolicewoman.com, www.myspace.com/joanaspolicewoman

216 **Tokyo Police Club** poster by Tim Huesken (www.shinybluerobot.com). Copyright 2006 Tim Huesken. www.tokyopoliceclub.com, www.myspace.com/tokyopoliceclub

Under Suspicion cover art, layout and logo by Kii Arins. Copyrith 1997 Blanko d Soul Records. www.cdbaby.com/cd/undersuspicion

Blameshifters cover art courtesy Mat Loman. Copyright 2007 the Blameshifters. www.myspace.com/theblameshifters, www.freewebs.com/theblameshifters

217 **Five Star Prison Cell** cover art courtesy Adam Glynn. Copyright 2005 Five Star Prison Cell. www.fivestarprisoncell.com, www.myspace.com/fivestarprisoncell

218 **Doom Kounty Electric Chair** cover art courtesy HO. Copyright 1999 Doom Kounty Electric Chair/Persuasion Records. www.doomkountyelec tricchair.com, www.myspace.com/aboynamedho

221 **Tallest Building in the World** cover art by Isaac Marion. Copyright 2005 Tallest Building in the World. www.thetallestbuildingintheworld.com, www.myspace.com/tallestbuildingintheworld

222 **Liquid Brick** cover art courtesy Keith Goodwin and Liquid Brick. Copyright 2008 Liquid Brick. www.myspace.com/liquidbrick

223 **Eat More Plastic** art by Caspar Walbeck. Copyright 2007 Eat More Plastic. www.eatmore plastic.de/, www.myspace.com/eatmoreplastic

Suburbia cover photo by Joachim Nywall, design by Ulrik Hedin and Magnus Sirensen. Copyright 2006 Suburbia. www.suburbia.nu, www.myspace.com/suburbia

224 **Skyhouse** cover design by George Johnson. Copyright 1996 Skyhouse/Last Chance Records. www.myspace.com/skyhouse, www.cdbaby.com/cd/skyhouse

Brickhouse cover design by Malin Helgesson. Copyright 2006 Brickhouse. www.cdbaby.com/ cd/brickhouse, www.brickhouse.nu

226 **Land of Malls** cover design by Deirdre Cohalan (www.thundersites.com), photo by Shannon Cohalan, courtesy Davis Walls-Kaufman. Copyright 2000 Land of Malls. www.myspace.com/landofmalls, www.cdbaby.com/cd/landofmalls

229 **Glorious Filaments** cover photography by Dave DeHart and Jeremy Patterson, layout by the Glorious Filaments and Nicole Nagine. Copyright 2007 the Glorious Filaments. www.myspace.com/thegloriousfilaments

230 **Atomic 7** poster by Tim Huesken (www.shiny bluerobot.com). Copyright 2005 Tim Huesken. www.shadowy.brainiac.ca/a7-members.htm (fansite), www.atomic7brandladiesshoes.com

232 **Sorry No Ferrari** poster by A.o.k. Copyright 2006 Adam Ocean King/Sorry No Ferrari/Alaska Records. www.myspace.com/alaskarecordsatl, www.myspace.com/sorrynoferrari,

233 **Silversun Pickups** poster by Scrojo (www.scrojo.com) for Belly Up, Solana Beach, California (www.bellyup.com). Copyright 2006 Scrojo. www.silversunpickups.com, www.myspace.com/silversunpickups

234 **Detroit Cobras** poster by Chuck Loose for the Culture Room, Fort Lauderdale, Florida (www.cultureroom.net). Copyright 2005 Chuck Loose/Culture Room. www.detroitcobras.org, www.myspace.com/detroitcobrasband

235 **Garageland** cover design by Garageland. Copyright 2003 Garageland/Flying Nun Records. www.flyingnun.co.nz, www.myspace.com/ garagelandnz

Driveby Truckers poster by Jeff Lamm for Paradiso, Amsterdam (www.paradiso.nl). Copyright 2008 Jeff Lamm/Paradiso. www.drivebytruckers.com, www.myspace.com/drivebytruckers

236 **Radiator** cover art by Sam Trenwith. Copyright 2007 Sam Trenwith/Radiator. www.myspace.com/radiatornz, www.radiatorband.co.nz

237 **Chromeo** poster by Austin Sellers (www.austin madethis.com) for Rotture, Portland, Oregon (www.rotture.com). Copyright 2007 Austin Sellers/Rotture. www.myspace.com/chromeo, www.chromeo.net

Eddy & the Backfires cover art courtesy Rhythm Bomb Records. Copyright 2006 Rhythm Bomb Records. www.rhythmbomb.com, www.eddyandthebackfires.de

238 **Taxi to the Ocean** cover art by Steve Keene (www.stevekeene.com), courtesy Jacco at MANA Music, the Netherlands. Copyright 2005 Taxi to the Ocean/MANA Music. www.munichrecords.com, www.taxitotheocean.nl, www.myspace.com/taxi-totheocean

Trolley cover design Mandy Gries. Copyright 1997 Easter Records. www.myspace.com/easterrecords, www.myspace.com/trolley1

286 **A Block of Yellow** cover art for *Grow Up or Grow Out* by Jen Wilson (www.originalorange.net). Cover art for the *Do I Do* by Eugenia Zaharieva. Copyright 2006 and 2008 A Block of Yellow (ABOY). www.ablockofyellow.info, www.myspace.com/ablockofyellow

288 **Comets on Fire** poster by Matthew Terich (www.designmedicine.com). Copyright 2006 Matthew Terich. www.cometsonfire.com, www.myspace.com/cometsonfirerockinblues

289 **Slaves to Gravity** cover art courtesy Ronnie Gleeson. Copyright 2008 Slaves to Gravity. www.myspace.com/slavestogravityofficial

290 **Space Bikini** cover art copyright Space Bikini 2007. www.myspace.com/spacebikini, www.spacebikini.co.uk

291 **Planes Mistaken for Stars** poster by Phil Babcock, Phil Babcock Design (www.philbabcock.com). Copyright 2007 Phil Babcock. www.myspace.com/pmfs

292 **Thank God for Astronauts** cover photos by TGFA. Copyright 2007 Thank God for Astronauts/Needlepoint Records. www.thankgodforastronauts.com, www.myspace.com/thankgodforastronauts

293 **Xybor & the Cosmonauts** cover art by Terry Atkinson (www.xybornaut.com). Copyright 2007 Terry Atkinson. ww.myspace.com/xybor

294 **New Ancient Astronauts** image courtesy Kasey Elkington. Copyright 2007 New Ancient Astronauts. www.myspace.com/newancientastronauts, www.cdbaby.com/cd/newancientastro2,

Rocket Park cover art Jennifer Gibas. Copyright 2000 Rocket Park. www.cdbaby.com/cd/rocketpark2

295 **Ballroom Rockets** cover art by Fabian Rosmaity with photos by Thomas Willemsen. Copyright 2006 Ballroom Rockets. www.ballroomrockets.com, www.rhythmbomb.com

297 **Space Cretins** cover art by Wes Crum, colored by Paul Baresh. Copyright 2005 Paul Blow and Killing Pig Records. paulblow.tripod.com/spacecretins www.myspace.com/spacecretins

298 **Alien's Cab** cover art by martb (Martin Bussieres, www.martb.com). Copyright 2007 martb and Alien's Cab. www.alienscab.com, www.myspace.com/alienscab

299 **Alien101** poster by Christian Bîgle (www.myspace. com/chrismartkillerartworx). Copyright 2007 Christian Bîgle/Alien101. www.myspace.com/alien101

300 **Martian Heat Ray** cover art by Ricky Lee Earl. Copyright 2008 Martian Heat Ray. www.myspace.com/martianheatray

Bloodsucking Zombies from Outer Space cover art by Dead Gein. Copyright 2008 Bloodsucking Zombies from Outer Space. www.zombies.at, www.myspace.com/bloodsuckingzombiesfromouterspace

301 **Alien Music Club** artwork by Michael McGlothlen. Copyright 2008 Alien Music Club. www.alienmusicclub.com, www.myspace.com/alienmusicclub

302 **Robot Ninja Dinosaur Bastards** cover art courtesy Gordon Hannam. Copyright 2008 Robot Ninja Dinosaur Bastards. www.myspace.com/robotninjadinosaurbastards

303 **Robotanists** cover art courtesy Sarah Ellquist. Copyright 2008 the Robotanists. www.myspace..com/robotanists, www.robotanists.com

305 **Mars Volta** poster poster by Ken Taylor, Beyond the Pale (www.beyondthepale.com.au). Copyright 2006 Ken Taylor/Beyond the Pale. www.themarsvolta.co.uk, www.myspace.com/themarsvolta

306 **Planet 13** cover art by Michael Briscoe, creative concept by Karen Benedict. Copyright 2005 Planet 13. www.planetthirteen.com

Hillbilly Moon Explosion cover art courtesy Oliver Baroni, copyright 2007 Hillbilly Moon Explosion. www.myspace.com/hillbillymoonexplosion

308 **Portishead** poster by Marc Bessant(www.myspace. com/marcbessant) for Butlins, Minehead, UK. Copyright 2007 Marc Bessant. www.portishead. co.uk, www.myspace.com/PORTISHEADALBUM3

309 **Iowa Beef Experience** cover art copyright 1988 by Iowa Beef Experience. www.thesecrethistory.org/index.php/Iowa_Beef_Experience

310 **Tourist** cover art press image copyright 2005 Tourist. www.myspace.com/touristband, www.touristband.com

311 **Tokyo** 507 cover art copyright 2008 Tokyo507. www.myspace.com/tokyo507

313 **Wack Ass Egyptians** cover art copyright 2005 Wack Ass Egyptians. www.myspace.com/wackassegyptians

314 **Leisure Alaska** cover art by Lykke Sandal. Copyright Leisure Alaska 2005. www.leisurealaska.com, www.myspace.com/leisurealaska

315 **Calexico** poster by Daymon Greulich, (www.beyondthepale.com.au). Copyright 2007 Daymon Greulich /Beyond the Pale. www.casadecalexico.com, www.myspace.com/casadecalexico

316 **The Great Outdoor Experience** cover photo and design by Ryan Art (www.ryanart.com), courtesy Phil Ram. Copyright 2005 the Great Outdoor Experience. www.thegreatoutdoorexperience.com

318 **Psycho Nanny & the Baby Shakers** poster by Ross Radiation (www.weirdgalaxy.com). Copyright 2006 Ross Tesoriero/Triangle Sideshow Alley. www.myspace.com/triangleland , www.myspace.com/psychonanny

319 **Ruby Dee & the Snakehandlers** poster by Thom Self (www.astudiodesign.com). Copyright 2007 Thom Self/A Studio. www.rubydeemusic.com, www.myspace.com/rubydeeandthesnakehandlers

Mel Gibson & the Pants poster by John Grider, Broken Crow (www.brokencrow.com). Copyright 2007 Broken Crow. www.myspace.com/melgibsonandthepants, www.totallygrossnationalproduct.com

Bibliography

Bogdanov, Vladimir, Chris Woodstra and Stephen Thomas Erlewine, eds. *All Music Guide to Rock*, 3rd ed. Ann Arbor, Michigan: Backbeat Books, 2002

Buckley, Peter, ed. *The Rough Guide to Rock*, 3rd ed. London: Rough Guides, 2003.

Cross, Alan. *20th Century Rock and Roll: Alternative Rock*. Collector's Guide Publishing, 2000.

Dodd, Philip. *The Book of Rock: From the 1950s to Today*. New York: Thunder's Mouth Press, 2005.

Dolgins, Adam. *Rock Names*, 3rd ed. Secaucus, New Jersey: Carol Publishing Group, 1998.

George-Warren, Holly. *Punk 365*. New York: Abrams, 2007.

George-Warren, Holly, and Patricia Romanowski, eds. *Rolling Stone Encyclopedia of Rock & Roll: Revised and Updated for the 21st Century*. New York: Fireside, 2001.

Graff, Gary, and Daniel Durchholz. *Music Hound ROCK: The Essential Album Guide*. Farmington Hills, Michigan: Visible Ink Press, 1999.

Larkin, Colin. *The Virgin Encyclopedia of R&B and Soul*. London: Virgin Books, 1998.

Larkin, Colin. *The Virgin Encyclopedia of Sixties Music*. London: Virgin Books, 1997.

Larkin, Colin. *The Virgin Encyclopedia of Seventies Music*. London: Virgin Books, 1997.

Larkin, Colin. *The Virgin Encyclopedia of Eighties Music*. London: Virgin Books, 1997.

Larkin, Colin. *The Virgin Encyclopedia of Nineties Music*. London: Virgin Books, 2000.

Luckman, Michael. *Alien Rock: The Rock 'n' Roll Extraterrestrial Connection*. MTV Books, 2005.

Mathieson, Craig. *Hi Fi Days: The Future of Australian Rock*. Allen & Unwin Ltd., 1997.

Patterson, Gary R. *Take a Walk on the Dark Side: Rock and Roll Myths, Legends, and Curses.* New York: Fireside, 2004.

Rolling Stone Cover to Cover: The First 40 Years. New York: Bondi Digital Publishing, 2007.

Rosen, Craig. *The Billboard Book of Number One Albums*. New York: Watson-Guptill, 1996.

Sherry, James, and Neil Aldis. *Heavy Metal Thunder*. San Francisco: Chronicle Books, 2006.

Whitburn, Joel. *The Billboard Book of Top 40 Hits*. New York: Watson-Guptill, 1996.

Wilson, Dave. *Rock Formations*. Tegaron, Wales: Cidermill Books, 2004.

Primary Print Magazines

Alternative Press
Filter
Guitar Player
Magnet
Paste
Q
Rolling Stone
Spin
Under the Radar
Wonka Vision

Primary Websites

www.80s.com
www.allmusic.com
www.altpress.com
www.amiright.com
www.amo.org.au
www.answers.com
www.archive.org
www.avclub.com
www.aversion.com
www.bandminuslabel.com
www.bebo.com
www.bestofbands.com
www.boingboing.net
www.buttermilkstudios.com
www.canoe.ca/IndieBands
www.caughtinthecrossfire.com
www.cdbaby.com
www.channel4.com
www.chrisblackburn.com
www.dailyllama.com
www.dailyvault.com
www.dcrockclub.com
www.decoymusic.com
www.dustedmagazine.com
www.everything2.com
www.filter-mag.com
www.freewebs.com/punkpolls
www.garageband.com
www.ibiblio.org
www.imeem.com
www.independent.co.uk
www.indiemusicstop.com
www.indizoo.com
www.last.fm/music
www.library.thinkquest.org
www.listology.com
www.magnetmagazine.com
www.makingtime.co.uk
www.metropolis.co.jp
www.myspace.com
www.nme.com
www.pastemagazine.com
www.pitchforkmedia.com
www.plugawards.com
www.punkhistorycanada.ca
www.punkmagazine.com
www.q4music.com
www.record-labels-companies-guide.com
www.rock-is-life.com
www.rockhall.com
www.rollingstone.com
www.salon.com
www.skratchmagazine.com
www.spin.com
www.songfacts.com
www.sonicrendezvous.com
www.stereogum.com
www.store.itsaboutmusic.com
www.straightdope.com
www.thechickenfishspeaks.com
www.theonlythingiknow forsure.wordpress.com
www.theramblingman.com
www.thrasherswheat.org
www.trouserpress.com
www.umusic.ca
www.undertheradarmag.com
www.virb.com
www.voxonline.com
www.wikipedia.org

Index